THE
COMBAT DIARIES

TRUE STORIES FROM THE FRONTLINES OF WORLD WAR II

MIKE GUARDIA

Published by Magnum Books
PO Box 1661
Maple Grove, MN 55311

www.mikeguardia.com

ISBN-13: 979-8-9854285-5-1

For Mom, Dad, Marie and Melanie,
and to the memory of Joan Wipf Nassiri (1954–2022)

Also by Mike Guardia:

American Guerrilla
Shadow Commander
Hal Moore: A Soldier Once…and Always
The Fires of Babylon
Skybreak
Days of Fury
Danger Forward

Co-authored with LTG Harold G. Moore:

Hal Moore on Leadership: Winning When Outgunned and Outmanned

CONTENTS

ACKNOWLEDGEMENTS

I am indebted to several individuals who helped make this project a reality. First, I give special thanks to Colonel (ret) Don Patton of the *Minnesota World War II Roundtable*—a historical society dedicated to preserving the history of World War II and the oral histories of its veterans. Colonel Patton arranged my meetings with two of the veterans who appear in this volume: Marty Romano and Denzel Alexander. I am also indebted to Dr. Thomas Saylor, PhD; Mr. Al Zdon; and Mr. Ray Merriam, all of whom graciously granted me access to the oral histories and veteran stories they've collected over the years. Special thanks are also reserved for the Pacific War Museum and the Library of Congress. Without the collective help of these individuals and organizations, this book may never have been written.

INTRODUCTION

World War II was the most destructive conflict in human history. At its peak, the US military drew some 16 million men into its ranks to defeat the Axis Powers. They came from nearly every walk of life—farmers, tradesmen, teachers, lawyers, professional athletes, and even Hollywood celebrities. But whether they came from the wheat fields of Kansas, the streets of New York, or the backlots of Tinseltown, these everyday heroes answered the call of duty when their country needed them. They were ordinary men who accomplished extraordinary things. Today, we call them the "Greatest Generation."

The Combat Diaries is a collection of true stories from veterans who served on the frontlines during World War II. Their stories include:

- A young sailor aboard PT-306, who ferried British Commandos and Allied spies onto mainland Europe.
- A young fighter pilot who remains one of the few Americans to fly a British Spitfire into combat.
- A Navy combat diver ("frogman") who swam at night among the Japanese-held islands, defusing underwater mines, and setting demolitions to assist the Marines' amphibious assaults...

…and many more.

Members of the Greatest Generation are leaving us at the rate of several hundred per day. Indeed, the youngest cohort of World War II veterans are now in their nineties. *The Combat Diaries* is a testament to their enduring legacy.

1

OMAHA RED

WILLIAM C. SMITH: THE FIRST MAN ASHORE ON OMAHA BEACH, RED SECTOR

June 6, 1944. Lieutenant William C. Smith, a young artillery officer and forward observer (FO), steeled himself for the coming invasion. Allied forces were preparing to launch Operation Overlord—a coordinated amphibious/airborne assault into Northern France. "There have been a lot of books written about D-Day," he said.

But Bill had a unique perspective.

"You see, I was the first American on Omaha Red Beach on D-Day…about two hours before the invasion."

On the morning of June 6, there were only two ways for an FO to get to Omaha Beach: (1) Aboard the tactical dinghies, alongside Navy frogmen who would swim ashore hours before the invasion to disarm enemy mines and anti-ship barriers, or (2) aboard the landing craft with the first wave of troops, where they would suffer a 90% casualty rate.

Either way, the odds didn't seem to be in his favor.

In fact, on his first day in the Army, a senior officer told him: "If the Army loses a box of ammunition, there'll be trouble; but second lieutenants are expendable." Moreover, the life expectancy of an FO in the European Theater was less than ten months. "A forward observer's job was simple," Bill said, "just get close enough to the enemy to tell what type of toothpaste they use, and tell the artillery unit exactly where to aim their guns."

A few nights before D-Day, Allied commanders decided to send their forward observers onto the beach with the frogmen, two hours before the invasion. As Bill and his comrades sailed across the English Channel, the admiral in charge told him: "Find yourself a nice spot where you can keep an eye on the Germans."

Easier said than done.

The beaches of Normandy didn't provide much in the way of "hiding spots." Thus, if Bill could see the enemy, then the enemy could likely see him.

"And I would be the only target on the beach, for two hours," he added.

As Bill descended into the rubber raft, the admiral's parting words were clear: "Whatever happens, take good care of that radio. We can replace you, but the radio is important."

It was pitch black during the pre-dawn hours of the Allied invasion— no moon or ambient starlight. "No exterior lights were permitted on the ships for security," said Bill. As he made his way down the rope ladder, he saw that his designated "rubber boat" was more akin to "an oversized truck inner tube with a thin rubber bottom" powered by a cheap electric fan that someone had converted into a motor. Still, this half-baked rubber contrivance was "seaworthy" in the sense that it could float.

Bill settled into the raft alongside three Navy frogmen, detaching from the ship and sailing forward into the moonless night. "I checked to make sure I had my sidearm and extra clips." But then it occurred to him:

"What good is a pistol going to do against all those Germans with all that heavy firepower?"

Still, a Colt .45 was better than nothing. And this wasn't his first invasion, either. Bill had survived the invasions of Sicily and North Africa; and he had already surpassed his 10-month combat life expectancy.

Bill graduated from Ohio State University in 1937 at the tender age of twenty. While still in college, he had started his own insurance business. However, he couldn't *legally* sell insurance until he reached the age of 21. Undeterred, he simply hired a handful of legal-age adults to make his sales until he met the age requirement. A product of Ohio State's Army ROTC program, Bill took a commission in the Army Reserve while devoting his full-time energy to the insurance business. And when Bill was called to active duty in 1940, his father happily ran the agency in his stead. Bill received orders to the 1st Infantry Division on the eve of their initial deployment in 1942. Now, two years later, he was at the cutting edge of what General Eisenhower called the "Great Crusade."

Two days earlier, Bill had seen the invasion fleet in the daylight hours of June 4. "We had been told that 6,000 ships would be involved in the operation, including over 1,200 warships." Now, in the predawn

Lieutenant William C. Smith, US Army.

hours of June 6, he hoped that the invasion fleet was up to the task.

"In studying the aerial photographs," he said, "I had picked out a spot on the rightmost part of our sector." Based on the contours of the terrain, that farthest-right edge seemed to offer the best concealment. "While there were tank traps along most of the beach, this area seemed to be a swimming hole," said Bill. "If any Germans came down to take a dip, my trusty .45 would come in handy. Somehow, with all those

Allied ships in the [English Channel], I doubted if anyone would take the risk."

As the rubber raft churned and sallied towards the beach, its helmsman kept their bearings by way of a small phosphorescent compass. The journey seemed like hours. But when Bill glanced at his watch, he was stunned to see that his rough ride across the English Channel had lasted barely thirty minutes.

Suddenly, their raft turned hard left.

"Ok, the raft is parallel to the wire," whispered the helmsman. "Our bow is pointed in the direction you should find the opening. Good luck."

With that, Bill hoisted his legs over the side, bringing every ounce of his 120-pound frame knee-deep into the frigid waters. He pushed himself away from the raft, wading towards his designated redoubt—the place where, hopefully, he could keep a steady eye on the Germans... and escape detection.

"At that moment, I felt totally alone."

Of course, there were several thousand Germans waiting just beyond the beach.

Wading through the shallows, Bill weaved his way around the obstacles set by the *Wehrmacht*. First were the steel tridents, lined with explosives. "I knew that there would not be anti-personnel mines there because the Germans had to leave room to repair any damage done by the sea." Next came the anti-tank ditch, and its attendant anti-tank wall—a solid concrete barrier that would be troublesome for armored and infantry forces alike. "As I felt hard sand underfoot," he said, "I knew I was out of the water." But he had to get to the softer sand, so he wouldn't get caught in an undertow when the tide came in.

As he looked for his rockbound hiding spot, Bill felt another change in the grainy texture beneath his feet. "It was no longer the sand, but dirt and stone of the service road that ran around the beach. The map I had studied...showed that the road was underwater except at low tide. I crossed the road, and at long last felt the soft sand." He had made it to the beach proper.

After a few more moments of deliberate pace counting and night navigation, Bill found the rock formation that he intended to use for his observation post.

But this rock formation wasn't truly "rock."

The aerial photographs had failed to show that this "rock formation" was actually "an assortment of concrete blocks, piles of junk [and] excess cement." Undaunted, Bill tossed aside enough of the rubble to hide himself up to his shoulders. "I then used the loose rocks to cover all but my eyes, head, and hands." With the radio tucked under his chin, Bill laughed as he realized his newfound observation post made him look like a "turtle in his shell."

As he looked up, Bill could see a few lights from within the German bunkers.

That was odd, he thought to himself.

The Allied naval bombardment was supposed to have knocked out the enemy's power grid.

At daybreak, Bill recalled that the sky was so gray, he could hardly tell where the sea ended and the sky began. Through the gray luster of the morning haze, however, Bill discovered why the enemy's electrical grid was still intact.

The German defenses hadn't been touched.

"The bombing that had taken place before the invasion was supposed to destroy the Germans' ability to fend off the invasion" he said. "Either the bombing had missed the targets...or it had no effect whatsoever. I had the feeling that somewhere in France, there were a lot of dead cows"—victims of misplaced naval gunfire. The Germans, on the other hand, were "dry, well-fed, quite rested, and very well-protected in their concrete hotel." More to the point, these unharmed Germans would soon be directing their own gunfire onto the invasion fleet. "I realized in an instant," he said, "that unless I could call enough fire to silence the guns in those pillboxes, this part of the invasion would not succeed."

At about thirty minutes to H-Hour, Bill saw the first of the Germans' coastal batteries open fire on the Allied fleet. "I located the source of the fire as close as I could." The German battery, likely a group of 88s, fired a volley of ten rounds, all of which landed dangerously close to the destroyer USS *Emmons* and the battleship USS *Arkansas*. Keying his radio, Bill called out to the fleet.

"I registered my first target and gave the order to fire when ready."

The *Arkansas* answered with a volley of its own—twenty rounds of 12-inch naval gunfire, all of which promptly silenced the offending battery.

But when the first Allied shell impacted on the beach, the Germans fired up their searchlights, scanning the shore for anything that looked out of place. The Germans knew that if they were getting such accurate naval gunfire, there must have been an Allied spotter somewhere on the beach. Luckily, the beams of light never found Bill's hiding spot.

The first shot directed against the main German pillbox landed slightly left. "I adjusted [the firing coordinates] and ordered fire at will." A flurry of shells quickly descended into the pillbox, blowing its entire front into a medley of smoke and flames. "It looked like a horizontal volcano," Bill remembered. "That was one less gun the Germans had to kill our men. But there were so many more to hit."

That's when Bill noticed another gun emplacement; this one had been drilled into the side of a nearby cliff. He called for fire, but the incoming rounds fell a bit short. When he called for an adjustment, the shipboard battery liaison replied with:

"We see that target, and we'll get that son of a bitch closed up!"

A moment later, two streams of tracer rounds zoomed overhead, painting the gun emplacement for more follow-on fire. "In the next second," Bill said, "nearly half-a-dozen shells seemed to converge on a single spot"—the exact location of the offending gunfire. "The ground shook under me. A glorious flood of gravel, stone dust, gun parts, and chunks of medium, well-done German gunners fell down like a pouring rain."

But there was no time to celebrate. He had to register fire on the next target.

He soon spied another 88mm gun emplacement, which promptly disappeared under a hail of naval gunfire. "In scanning the area close to the bluff," he recalled, "I didn't see any of our DD tanks [amphibiously-modified Shermans]. I wasn't sure where they were, but I had to keep firing the guns that I had."

German mortar fire began to pepper the beach, but Bill could tell that this was feral, undirected fire. Indeed, the Germans were panicking. By now, they were hoping to land some "lucky punches" through volume of fire. But feral as it was, this incoming mortar fire was enough to disrupt the Allied landings because "our men and equipment occupied such a high percentage of the area."

Nevertheless, Bill kept calling for fire.

It was hard to get accurate counterbattery fire against the mortars because the German mortarmen were *behind* the crest of the bluff. Thus, Bill had to estimate the enemy's position based on the rounds' point of impact. Against these mortars, "I was shooting blind," he said.

As Allied troops began storming the beach, however, Bill realized he now had *two* problems. First, he had to make sure the Allied guns didn't fire on their own men. Second, "I had to be sure that the shots I called would not dump tons of concrete on our men" as they got to the bottom of the cliff.

After calling fire on another 88, Bill turned his attention towards a pillbox on a nearby cliff. He was ready to rain fire on the pillbox, but stopped himself as he saw a squad of Americans climbing ropes towards the top of that same cliff.

These climbing soldiers quickly neutralized the target.

"Another emplacement was just over the top of the bluff," he continued. "By this time our troops had reached the area but were unable to take the pillbox because of the firing coming out of it." Bill called for fire on the offending pillbox, but the naval shells hit just below the target. "I moved the shot up," he said, "but the second shell hit in almost the exact same spot." Luckily, a nearby destroyer, taking stock of the same enemy pillbox, opened fire with a volley of shells from its forward battery, obliterating the entire front end of the bluff. "That captain risked his men in support of our invasion," Bill recalled.

By this point, Bill was running on pure adrenaline. He had no idea how long he'd been on the beach, but he dared not look at his watch. In fact, he had taped over the watch's luminescent dial, lest it draw attention from a sharp-eyed enemy. All he knew was that he had been awake for the past 48 hours, and he was getting exhausted.

But this was no time to rest.

"I had to keep finding targets and destroying them."

That's when Bill noticed the German self-propelled guns firing from the edge of the bluff. "They would fire, then move back out of sight." Bill registered more gunfire in their direction; and although he knocked out a few of the mobile guns, he couldn't get *all* of them. Still, he kept calling for fire even after his voice had gone hoarse. "Again and again, the shots pummeled the fortresses on the shore," he said. "The enemy fire slowly but clearly dwindled down as the fire from the ships and our men on the beach took a toll on their defenses."

As the battle began to wane, a group of Army Rangers scaled to the top of the bluff and "captured the few remaining enemy still fighting."

After that, the enemy fire stopped.

"The only noises at that point were coming from the reinforcements and equipment coming on shore." Bill finally removed the tape from his watch, and glanced at the time.

"It was almost noon," he said.

He had been on the beach for eight hours.

He then had his first sustained look at the carnage along the shore. "It was indescribably horrible," he said. "There were thousands of bodies on the beach and in the water. I was sick to my stomach. I had done everything I could, but I still wasn't able to prevent the terrible slaughter of so many brave men." Closing his eyes, Bill let out a muffled prayer:

"God, please take care of these brave men that gave their lives to free this land. They deserve your personal attention. Amen."

Bill survived the incursion at Omaha Red, and he participated in many of the 1st Infantry Division's signature campaigns across Europe. In the years and decades following the war, however, Bill often sparred with a number of armchair historians and rear echelon commentators who doubted his claims of being the first man on Omaha Red. "After I gave a speech to a multi-service support committee in 2002," he said, "a [retired] general…came up and began to argue with me about how I got to the beach." The indignant general said: "I have seen the official records. You had to have gone in with the first wave of men and were not possibly on the beach before the invasion."

Bill was not impressed.

"General, what war were you in?"

"Korea."

"I thought so," said Bill. "You look far too young to have been in World War II. Besides I don't remember seeing you or any other high-ranking official at H-Hour -2."

"Well, no but…"

Realizing that Bill had just destroyed his argument, the general tried a different approach.

"I wanted to ask about the ships that you claim were used to fire on the German defenses. I can't see how a couple of 6 or 8-inch shells would destroy a cement pillbox so completely." Bill interjected: "As I said, the battleship USS *Arkansas* was there and used its 12-inch guns to hit the box." Bill punctuated the remark by saying there were several dead Germans who would disagree with the general's assessment.

And by now, the general's resilience was fading fast.

"I…wasn't sure," he stammered, "not sure…even 12-inch guns could do that much damage."

"General," said Bill, "I'm sure that the 88 in the pillbox had several shells standing by for rapid fire when it was hit by the multiple 12-inch shells. The entire box became concrete snowflakes drifting down like Christmas in June."

By now, the general knew he had been bested…and respectfully withdrew.

After the war, Bill remained in the Army Reserve for a number of years, and later became president of the Reserve Officers Association. Returning home to Ohio, he sold his insurance agency and joined the ER Kissinger Company—his father in-law's photo finishing business. He eventually became the company's general manager, and expanded its operations to encompass 82% of the photo finishing market in central Ohio. He later formed the inaugural Sales Marketing Department at Columbus Technical Institute, which became one of the most-respected marketing operations in the Midwest.

Even in retirement, Bill refused to stay idle. He became an active member in the VFW and participated in several events commemorating World War II and the Normandy landings.

He passed away on July 15, 2011 at the age of 93.

2

DARK VIOLENT SEAS

MARTY ROMANO & *PT-306*

The story of Marty Romano begins in the concrete jungles of Jersey City. Born on June 11, 1924, he was the fifth of seven children born to Gasparé and Margarita Romano—both of whom were Italian immigrants. As was typical in many Italian families, said Marty, "my mother was very hard and domineering; the matriarch of our family." Together, his parents ran a dry goods store in Jersey City—an established business serving the city's ever-growing population of Irish and Italian immigrants. And, as with many family-owned businesses, young Marty was expected to help run the store when he wasn't in school. "I would carry all the linens and the draperies," he said with a chuckle.

Marty's childhood was typical of most boys who grew up in the working-class neighborhoods of New Jersey. He enjoyed playing football and baseball, but the shortage of greenspace in Jersey City meant that he often found himself playing street hockey or stickball. During the summers, and after school, he and his brother would earn extra money by working on cars. "My brother and I polished cars and repaired dented fenders," he said. "I never worked in a garage, but I was able to take some cars apart. In fact, when I was dating my wife, Lorraine, I got up early one morning, took my Buick apart, and had it back together in time for my date that evening!" Aside from detailing the normal variety of Fords and Chevrolets, Marty remembered the fanciest cars he worked on were Packards. Indeed, Packards were considered the premiere luxury cars in America prior to World War II.

In many ways, Marty Romano was also a product of his time. His was the generation raised on the harrowing tales of the Great War, the decadence of the Roaring Twenties, and the economic hardships of the Great Depression. Although money was tight (as it was for most families during that era), the Romanos' dry goods store, and the five-unit apartment building they owned, kept the family solvent.

It was, however, a time when many Italian-Americans were either discriminated against, or looked upon with suspicion. To make matters worse, Italy itself had fallen into the orbit of fascism. Under the brutal reign of Benito Mussolini, Italy aligned itself with Nazi Germany, becoming a full partner in the newly-formed Axis Powers. Still, many Americans hoped that the saber-rattling of fascist dictators would run its course without their involvement.

But by the time Marty began his freshman year at Dickinson High School in 1937, the political climate in Europe was devolving further into chaos. Within the next two years, Adolf Hitler would annex Austria, invade Czechoslovakia, and make a public fool of British Prime Minister Neville Chamberlain, promising "peace" in exchange for territorial concessions. These illusions of peace were quickly shattered, however, on September 1, 1939 when Germany invaded Poland—the opening rounds of a yearlong blitzkrieg that would bury half of Europe.

But as Europe plunged itself into another war, Marty Romano busied himself with the normal variety of high school activities. Since his mother had forbidden him to play on the school's sports teams, he joined whatever school clubs were available. "My mother took my hockey stick and she had my father chop up my skates! So, any sport I played was hidden from her. She was stern but very protective." Marty remembers that when his father chopped the skates at Mom's insistence, he gave his son a look of resignation.

"Look, I have to live with her," he told Marty. "So, I gotta get rid of these skates."

These semi-idyllic routines were interrupted, however, on the afternoon of December 7, 1941. Marty was in the kitchen, having just returned from Sunday Mass, when the radio announcer broke in with the bulletin that Pearl Harbor had been bombed. Like most other Americans, Marty was stunned.

"What the hell does this mean?" he asked. "What are we going to do now?"

No one had expected a first strike against Hawaii, much less from the Japanese. To this point, nearly everyone had considered Japan's military to be an inferior force. Conventional wisdom said that the threat would come from Nazi Germany long before it came from the Japanese. The following day, the US declared war on the Empire of Japan.

The Crew of *PT-306*. Marty Romano is in the front row, second from right (kneeling).

Germany soon responded, however, by declaring war on the United States, thus forcing the US into a two-front conflict. Although Japan had initiated hostilities, the US adopted a "Europe First" policy—meaning that, while fighting on two fronts, Europe would be the priority. The reasoning behind this decision was that Germany could win the war without Japan, but Japan couldn't win the war without Germany.

Marty Romano, meanwhile, had graduated from Dickinson High School in 1941 and spent the next two years working as a machinist's apprentice, tooling subcomponents for firearms—skills that would serve him well when he joined the Navy in 1943. As a civilian machinist, he learned first-hand the excruciating precision that goes into manufacturing quality products. "I learned how to work within *1/10,000th* of an inch!" he exclaimed. Indeed, every subcomponent of the gun had to be measured within a specific tolerance, or the weapon wouldn't fire.

In the summer of 1943, Marty reported to the local induction center at the Newark Armory. Like many of his contemporaries, he had been drafted, but his work as a machinist had made him a prime candidate for the Navy. It was the branch of service that had an entire career field dedicated to his trade—the ubiquitous "Machinist's Mate" (MM). They would be trained as shipboard engineers, maintaining and troubleshooting the propulsion and auxiliary systems. Most of their time would be spent below deck, but their job was just as critical to maintaining the ship's warfighting functions. For without a steady crew of engineers, a ship would be literally "dead in the water."

Naturally, Mama Romano was none too thrilled that her son—the boy whom she had tried to shield from the perils of team sports—was going off to war. "I know she felt lousy that I had to go," he said. But Marty was proud to do his patriotic duty. On September 24, 1943, he was sworn into the United States Navy and reported to boot camp in Newport, Rhode Island.

All at once, Marty's new name was "Boot,"—the moniker given to all new sailors when they arrived for recruit training. After getting his inoculations and a standard-issue buzz haircut, he packed up his civilian attire, trading it for the normal variety of Naval uniforms. With little regard to size, or even proper fit, the Navy doled out these uniforms with the expectation that sailors would wear them to standard. The next issued item was his sleeping gear. In true naval fashion, they issued him a hammock with mattress, two mattress covers, two blankets, and a pillow. To store this ever-growing list of issued items, Marty and his new shipmates were each given a "Sea Bag"—the ubiquitous three-foot-long canvas duffle bag. As with everything else he received, Marty stenciled his name onto the side of the bag. His final gift that day was a copy of *The Bluejackets' Manual*—the so-called "Sailor's Bible." Its pages contained everything Marty needed to know about becoming a sailor.

Admittedly, boot camp was a culture shock. "I was out of shape," he said, "but they got me into shape in short order!" Indeed, every morning the drill instructors would take the recruits on endurance runs—steadily increasing the distance traveled every week. Aside from the exhaustive physical training, Marty also had to learn the basics of shipboard operations and damage control. Any ship could be a fickle mistress—and even the most innocuous things could throw her off balance, or cripple her ability to fight.

It was also during boot camp that Marty had his first exposure to the Patrol Torpedo boats. These "PT boats," as they were called, had become somewhat of a novelty within the Allied naval forces. By design, they were small and agile, relying on stealth and speed to launch torpedoes at enemy warships. PT boats typically had crews of 12-14 men, and carried four torpedoes as its primary armament. Marty first noticed the Patrol Torpedo boats during boot camp as they went sailing by, en route to the PT Center in nearby Melville, Rhode Island.

At first, Marty didn't know what to make of these newfangled PT boats.

"They're not big enough to be destroyers," he told himself.

Yet, they were too big to be gunboats.

But, whatever their classification, these boats carried guns, torpedoes, *and* they could engage the enemy at close range.

"So, yeah, I was impressed."

Upon completing boot camp, he volunteered for PT duty and arrived at Melville the following week from Newport.

As a newly-minted sailor and machinist's mate, Marty received the proverbial "crash course" on how to maintain the PT boat's massive engine suite: the triple-tandem Packard 3M-2500. Indeed, the same luxury automobile company whose cars Marty had polished in Jersey City was now manufacturing combat engines. Like other automotive giants of the day, Packard had converted its facilities to wartime production. Aside from producing PT boat engines, Packard also developed the V-1650, which powered the P-51 Mustang fighter.

The Packard engine would become Marty's "bread and butter" for the duration of the war. It was a twelve-cylinder, liquid-cooled powertrain capable of speeds in excess of 45 knots. Like most naval engines, however, the Packard 2500 series was a "gas hog." In fact, even at a cruising speed of 32 knots, the Packard consumed more than 200 gallons of fuel per hour. As such, the standard PT boat had to carry some 3,000 gallons of reserve fuel, just enough for the crew to make a 12-hour patrol.

"We also had to learn the silhouettes of the Japanese and German warships," he recalled. PT boats were expected to fight at night, and memorizing silhouettes was the surest way to guarantee that a sailor could recognize an enemy ship during low visibility. "We also had to recognize enemy aircraft," particularly the enemy's naval aviation assets. Although the PT boat wasn't optimized for anti-aircraft fire, its secondary .50 caliber machine guns could easily elevate and traverse to engage low-flying aircraft.

In the spring of 1944, Marty graduated from the PT Training Center and boarded the USS *Ranger* (the famed aircraft carrier) en route to Casablanca. That fabled city in North Africa had become one of the primary hubs for incoming Allied personnel. "By that time," he said, "the North African campaign was completed, Sicily was captured, Salerno was in Allied hands, and Anzio was in the mopping-up phase. That's when and where I came into this theater."

But although the Allies had gained control of North Africa (and most of Italy), the *Kriegsmarine* and *Regia Marina* were still running patrols throughout the Mediterranean. "When I got to North Africa, they horded us off the ship and into these 'Forty-and-Eight' railroad cars." These "Forty-and-Eights" were a common sight throughout Europe and North Africa. It was little more than a standard boxcar; and its name was a direct reference to its rated stowage capacity: forty men or eight horses. During both World Wars, the Allies had adapted the Forty-and-Eight as a troop transport. As expected, however, these troop-carrying boxcars lacked even the most basic amenities found aboard the standard passenger trains. Marty recalled that they were cramped, unsanitary, and poorly-ventilated.

"Cattle were treated better!" he laughed.

Throughout the first leg of the trip (on approach to Algiers), Marty enjoyed the occasional respite of climbing atop the boxcar for some fresh air. Indeed, a rooftop view of the North African landscape was better than sitting among the sweltering heat of 60-70 sailors packed into a 40-capacity railcar. Marty would have stayed atop the Forty-and-Eight for the remainder of the trip...had it not been for the swarm of locusts that greeted him outside of Algiers.

"There were thousands of them! And I don't know where they came from."

Perhaps the rail line went through their nesting ground, and the swarm had been vexed by the sudden appearance (and attendant noise) of a steam locomotive. But Marty, not wanting to endure another Old Testament plague, reluctantly settled back into the railcar.

"We were on that miserable cattle car for days," he said, "through Algiers, Oren, and Tunis." For food, Marty and his friends had nothing more than the standard "C" and "K" Rations. Because there were no bathrooms aboard the train, Marty recalled that: "We made a deal with the engineer." One blast of his whistle would indicate that a heavily-vegetated area was coming up; this would offer some degree of privacy for the sailors who had to relieve themselves. Two whistle blasts indicated that it was time to get back on board.

Arriving at the Replacement Depot in Tunis, Marty discovered that he'd been assigned to Motor Torpedo Squadron 15 (RON 15). At the time, RON 15 was stationed on La Maddalena, an island nestled among the narrow straits between Corsica and Sardinia. It was now May 1944, and the tide was turning in the Allies' favor. Over the past year, American forces had tightened their grip on the Mediterranean, and were slowly rolling back the tide of Japanese aggression in the Pacific. Meanwhile, these young torpedo boat squadrons were proving their mettle in both theaters of the war. In fact, the Japanese had begun calling them "devil boats" and the "mosquito fleet"—begrudgingly admiring the boldness and tenacity of American PT crews.

As it turned out, Marty's assignment to RON 15 was short-lived. In fact, he had barely set foot on La Maddalena when he was transferred to Motor Torpedo Squadron 22 (RON 22) in Bastia, Corsica.

"They needed a replacement engineman," he said. "I was it."

The new assignment put him aboard *PT-306*, nicknamed "The Fascinatin' Bitch." There were no pretenses of political correctness back then…and a ship's crew could choose any colorful nickname they wanted.

"Around this time, we invaded Elba, an island off the northwest coast of Italy. Both squadrons—RON 15 and RON 22—were involved in this operation." The invasion was carried out by the Free French Forces, supported by US and Royal Navy assets. "Before the invasion," Marty recalled, "I happened to be in the town square of Bastia, Corsica, and there was General De Gaulle—a tall, gaunt man rallying the crowd." Since the Fall of France in 1940, Charles De Gaulle had become the leader of the Free French Forces, an amalgamated resistance to the Vichy government run by Marshal Petain.

As May turned to June, Marty Romano completed the first of his 63 combat missions aboard *PT-306*. June 1944 was a watershed moment for the Allied cause. Operation Overlord (the invasion of Normandy), marked the beginning of the end for the Third Reich. However, the *Wehrmacht* still had a foothold on the Italian Peninsula, and they were prepared to defend every last inch of it. Reflecting on his first mission, Marty said: "I have to admit that an eerie feeling came over me when I saw the Italian coast for the first time. This was the land of my forefathers."

For the PT crews, their orders were simple: find, interdict, and destroy any Axis warships operating near the Italian coast or the Tuscan

Archipelago. However, they also had the curious mission of ferrying Allied spies to and from the Italian mainland. In fact, during his first few months aboard *PT-306*, it seemed that Marty and his shipmates were little more than a taxi service for the OSS and their Allied variety of field agents. These spies and saboteurs would often be dropped behind enemy lines, gathering intelligence on Axis troop movements before being picked up on the nighttime shore by a designated PT boat.

On any given day, Marty and his shipmates knew little of what was happening in the broader context of the war. Aside from the occasional news briefing, radio broadcast, or letter from home, the men of *PT-306* had limited information about the trajectory of the Allied campaign. During his night missions along the coast, however, Marty recalled seeing the muzzle flashes of the dueling tank and artillery positions along the mainland. The southern flashes, of course, were coming from the Allied ground troops. The northern gunfire, however, belonged to the fledgling German troops and the Mussolini loyalists. Yet, every night, Marty noticed that these dueling muzzle flashes were slowly migrating northward—indicating that the Allies were gaining ground against the enemy.

As an engineer, Marty split his time between the engine room and manning the guns on deck during his rotational watch duties. Indeed, every member of the PT crew had to be proficient in the use of defensive armaments, even if he wasn't a gunner's mate. Below deck, Marty and three other engineers kept a close eye on the Packard powertrains. "We would service the boat early in the afternoon," he said, "checking gas, oil, and getting her ready for mission." While underway, however, the engines were so loud that Marty and his fellow engineers had to communicate through written messages or lip-reading.

At a cruising speed of 32 knots, the engines were relatively easy to maintain. But even at lower speeds, the triple-tandem Packard engines were not immune to breakdowns or operational hiccups. For example, Marty recalled one mission where the skipper ordered "full reverse." Said Marty: "The engines were shifted out of the forward gear, right into reverse, but this sudden maneuver froze the engines! And there we were, dead in the water."

Soon, their sister PT boats (part of a three-ship formation) began pulling away, unaware that *306* was now immobilized.

"We then sprang into action."

Remembering that automobiles could be "push-started" (i.e., pushing the car fast enough and popping the clutch), they attempted a similar maneuver with the onboard Packard engines. "We got one engine running," he said, "and we had the Skipper rev the engine to maximum RPM." As *PT-306* lurched forward into the waves, "the second engine went off," said Marty, "so now we had two engines going, and we did the same thing with the third."

Temperamental engines aside, Marty's most memorable moment aboard *PT-306* was a near-brush with fratricide. "We took care of the night patrols, and during the daylight hours our aircraft would take over." One day at dawn, while coming back from a nighttime mission near Genoa, the skipper of *PT-306*, Lieutenant John Groweg, said:

"Well, let's make one more pass."

Likely, Groweg wanted to use the morning daylight to get a clearer look at the Italian coastline. But as *PT-306* ambled off the Genoese coast, Marty spied a plane overhead.

"Say, Skipper, take a look."

Groweg could tell by its markings that the plane was American.

"He's one of us," Groweg assured him. "He's all right."

But this American pilot had just identified *PT-306* as an enemy ship.

The *Kreigsmarine* and *Regia Marina* operated their own fleets of motor torpedo boats—respectively termed "E-boats" and "MAS boats." And, to a fatigued or untrained eye, these Axis torpedo craft could closely resemble an American PT boat.

"Sure enough," said Marty, "he opened fire, and I could see tracers coming straight out of the plane's wings."

Luckily, no one was killed by the friendly fire. But the strafing did cause considerable damage to another PT boat running the same mission alongside *306*. Sadly, that misplaced fire killed one sailor aboard the second PT.

"Hold your fire!" Groweg yelled. "He's one of us."

The pilot came around for another pass, but aborted the mission as soon as he realized the boats were American. "Somehow, he got the word," said Marty—but the crewmen of *PT-306* were alert and ready for action.

"How had the pilot mistaken us for an enemy ship?" Marty wondered.

"We had our radar on…our bow was painted. We were flying American pennants and the stern was painted the colors we were supposed to have." Yet, even with seemingly-ideal control measures, this incident demonstrated that no ship was immune to the ever-lurking danger of fratricide.

Shortly after the invasion of Elba, *PT-306* had a chance encounter with one of its Italian counterparts: *MAS 562*. On the night of June 29, 1944, while patrolling the northern coast of Elba, *PT-308* and *PT-309* encountered two MAS torpedo boats trying to infiltrate the harbor at Portoferraio. Both PTs opened fire at 800 yards, prompting the enemy vessels to run north, returning fire with their 20mm guns. *PT-308* and *309* gave chase for nearly ten miles until *MAS 562* began to fall back. As they closed in on the fledgling enemy boat, the PT crews noticed that *MAS 562* had caught fire. The Italian crew, in their panic, had jumped overboard, leaving *MAS 562* to its fate. The PT boats, meanwhile, recovered some fourteen surviving sailors from *MAS 562*, including the commander of the Italian MAS fleet at La Spezia. All fourteen sailors were ferried back to Corsica where they were turned over to the Master-at-Arms for prisoner processing and debriefing.

Following that mission, *PT-308* and *309* had reported *MAS 562* destroyed and sunk. Considering that the ship was badly burning when the PTs left the scene, it was logical to assume that *MAS 562* had succumbed to its wounds. The following morning, however, the Army Air Forces liaison officer approached RON 22, saying: "Hey, you guys put in a claim for this boat. It's still alive; and it's still out at sea." Indeed, aerial reconnaissance had confirmed that *MAS 562* was still burning off the coast of Elba, and it hadn't sunk.

Thus, RON 22 dispatched *PT-306* to recover the Italian torpedo boat, put out the fire, and tow it back to Elba. By the time *PT-306* arrived at the floating wreckage, however, "it had been stripped," Marty laughed. "You better believe it had been stripped!" Indeed, another MAS or PT crew had stripped *562* of most of its valuable hardware. Marty did, however, manage to secure two token souvenirs from *MAS 562*—a small mandolin and a brass warning placard for the ship's alarm system that read: "It is forbidden to use the alarm signal without plausible reason."

Still, Marty was fascinated by how the American PT boats differed from their MAS counterparts. For example, the Italian torpedo boats had two engines, whereas the American PTs had three. "The Italian boat had an auxiliary engine on the same shaft," Marty recalled. In fact, the layout and mechanical bearings of the MAS powerplant reminded him of the latter-day Ford Model T engines.

None of the PT crews ever learned why the MAS boats had been lingering off the shores of Portoferraio that night. However, it was possible that the Italian crews had gone there to evacuate the "high-

PT-306. Marty Romano is seated at the helm.

ranking German officers who had evaded capture by the occupying forces."

While wrangling enemy ships and patrolling the Italian coast, Marty and his shipmates also became adept at dodging enemy sea mines. "That was a crude thing the Germans and Italians would do," he said. "They knew where we were operating and, all of a sudden, we'd see these mines bobbing up and down in our path." Because they were highly visible, Marty shot many of these naval mines from a distance, using the onboard machine guns. He was hoping to see a forced detonation, but these mines would only detonate if they were hit in precisely the right place. Thus, Marty watched in disappointment as his bullet holes simply riddled the floating mines, allowing the sea water to trickle in, and sink from the resulting loss of buoyancy.

By August 1944, the Allies were preparing for Operation Dragoon— the invasion of Southern France. It had been nearly two months since the D-Day landings in Normandy, and the Allies were making steady progress across the battlefields of Northern France. "The invasion of Southern France and Northern France were scheduled [originally] for the same day, June 6," said Marty. "What happened was that there were just not enough ships to invade both the North and the South at the same time. So, Northern France got the priority…and that took most of the ships."

Before the invasion of Southern France, *PT-306* moved to Calvi, on the northwestern side of Corsica. *PT-306* had been assigned to ferry a unit of British Commandos to the beaches between St. Tropez and Cannes. "We were trained to put them in these rubber boats," he said—tactical rubber dinghies that would allow the Commandos to wade ashore undetected by the Axis defenders. After releasing the Commandos into their rubber rafts, *PT-306* would then take up its patrol station in the Ligurian Sea, ready to counter any enemy ships in the area.

With D-Day in Southern France set for August 15, 1944, *PT-306* departed Corsica late on the afternoon of the 14th. "We caught up with the invasion fleet between Corsica and Italy," he said. "And at 1:40 in the morning on August 15, we were at our landing site between St. Tropez and Cannes. Thankfully, the minesweepers had cleared a path… and we went in. We discharged 69 Commandos into those rubber boats. Meanwhile, four other PTs teamed up with three British gunboats and headed towards Genoa, simulating a big task force." This diversionary landing was orchestrated, in large part, by Lieutenant Commander Douglas Fairbanks—the Hollywood actor who joined the Navy and organized the famous "Beach Jumper" program (one of the Navy's first special warfare units).

Not talking above a whisper, Marty and his shipmates helped the Commandos into their rubber dinghies. As the Commandos floated away, Lieutenant Groweg steered *PT-306* back towards the Ligurian Sea. Unfortunately, none of the British Commandos made it to their inland destination. "I found out later that one of the Commandos tripped a land mine and alerted the Germans who opened fire, killing a few. Some returned to the drop-off point looking for us. Unfortunately, we were gone. The rest were taken prisoner."

For the next three days, *PT-306*, along with two other boats from RON 22, were assigned to guard an Allied communications ship anchored off the coast of San Remo. "There were a lot of generals and admirals aboard that ship," Marty recalled. "We had Admirals King and Davidson; General Divers, Wilson, Patch, and others." *PT-306*'s mission was to circle the ship on a 24-hour roving patrol and escort its personnel from ship to shore. "On one such trip," said Marty, "I recall coming up out of the engine room and I notice a guy dressed in khakis with a [Colt] .45 stuck in his hip pocket, one foot on a depth charger, reading a communique."

Curious, Marty asked one of his shipmates: "Who's he?"

"He's your boss," the shipmate replied. "That's Secretary of the Navy Forrestal."

James Forrestal would later become the inaugural Secretary of Defense in 1947.

On the second day of their guard mission, while tethered to the communications ship, the crew of *PT-306* was enjoying an afternoon lull in their daily operations. "Some of us were on deck," Marty recalled, "while others were below - relaxing, sleeping, playing cards, or writing letters when we heard an alarm aboard the ship and the call to General Quarters."

Trouble was on its way.

"Within seconds., I quickly jumped down into the engine room, started the engines, and reported to my battle station." As it turned out, a German reconnaissance plane had been detected several miles out, and the PT boats were taking defensive action. The Navy couldn't afford to lose a communications ship, especially one that carried so many flag officers. "We separated from the ship and laid down a smokescreen. By obscuring visibility from the air, the PT crews hoped to thwart the incoming recon mission. "By the time that reconnaissance plane showed up," said Marty, "the ship was engulfed in smoke"—completely invisible to the prying eyes of the *Luftwaffe*.

As their guard mission ended, *PT-306* was tasked to follow some Navy rowboat commandos into the harbor of Nice, France. *PT-306's* mission was to pick up maps for the heavy cruisers and battleships to coordinate their inland strikes. But *PT-306* had to follow the rowboat pilots into the harbor because they knew where the enemy sea mines had been laid. "You could see the mines as we passed."

"Events started to slow down for us after that operation," Marty recalled. Finding themselves with little to do, the crew of *PT-306* enjoyed the rare treat of sustained leisure time. Indeed, from the decks of their PT boat, Marty and his shipmates would dive into the Mediterranean for a leisurely swim. "We'd go swimming while the cruisers and battleships were lobbing shells overhead." As Allied ground forces moved farther inland, the naval task force continued pounding away at Axis positions in Italy and Southern France. All told, the naval gunfire was an interesting soundtrack to accompany the PT crew's swimming soiree.

"In September, we went back to Tunis, Africa for new engines, repairs, and mandatory shots for the bubonic plague,"—still a lingering health hazard in that part of the world. RON 22 then settled into its new base in Antibes, France. As the Allied ground forces moved farther up the European mainland, the naval bases moved accordingly. "We operated out of this base for the next two months, and then in November, we moved to Livorno, Italy. November and December were heavy duty. We went out on missions every night, foul or fair."

By this point in the war, however, German and Italian naval activity had fallen to near-negligible levels. As such, most of the latter-day patrols for *PT-306* passed without incident. But the hours of boredom were frequently punctuated by moments of heart-pounding terror. On one occasion, *PT-306* happened upon a French cruiser, southbound off the coast of Monte Carlo.

"We didn't know where the hell it was coming from," he said.

"And why was it coming through *here?*"

In the low visibility, Marty couldn't tell if the ship was friendly or enemy. But, manning his .50 caliber machine gun, he was ready to open fire if the ship failed to identify itself. *PT-306* challenged the cruiser, whereupon the French vessel rendered the appropriate "friendly" signal, indicating that she was an Allied ship.

The crewmen of *PT-306* breathed a heavy sigh of relief.

"That was pretty scary," Marty admitted. "The adrenaline was going."

Moreover, "I had a puny .50 caliber machine gun, compared to the 3-to 5-inch guns looking down at us!" Tacitly, Marty admitted that if the cruiser had been enemy, there was *nothing* his .50 cal could have done to stop the bigger ship or its gun batteries.

Marty also had several encounters with Italian dynamite boats. "What the Italians would do," he said, "was get a speed boat, load it up with dynamite, then try to ram us and blow us up." In their desperation, these die-hard Mussolini loyalists had created their own version of a *kamikaze* attack. The Italians' success rate, however, was far below that of their Japanese brethren. One night, while on watch, Marty spotted a silhouette that was typical of the Italian suicide boats.

"I see it! I see it!" he yelled to the skipper.

"Where?" asked the skipper.

Marty pointed to a spot on the horizon, where the breaking waves gave the telltale sign of an attack craft on approach. Calling the crew to General Quarters, Lieutenant Groweg gave them simple instructions:

"Where Marty's firing, you follow!"

Manning the twin .50 caliber guns, Marty Romano initiated the opening fusillade, his tracer rounds "painting" the target for his shipmates as they joined into the melee. Soon, every crew-served weapon aboard

PT-306 was firing in unison at the oncoming suicide boat.

Their efforts were not in vain.

For within less than 100 yards, the Italian suicide boat sank beneath the waves.

That December, Marty earned his eligibility for replacement, and was given a 33-day furlough back to the United States. During World War II, a PT sailor's eligibility for furlough was based on the number of missions he had served. After a certain number of missions, the Navy realized that a sailor would begin to suffer from "operational fatigue," thus losing their edge in the game of naval combat. After completing 63 missions, Marty Romano was tapped for rotation, along with two other shipmates from *PT-306*. "We were going back to Sardinia to pick up our replacements, and there they were." As *PT-306* underwent more repairs and maintenance, Marty handed off the engine room duties to his replacement. With orders authorizing his 33-day furlough back to the United States, Machinist's Mate 3d Class Marty Romano departed RON 22 on December 27, 1944.

By December 1944, the Allied offensive in Europe had stalled under the Germans' counterattack in the Ardennes Forest of France. History would call it the Battle of the Bulge. Soon, however, the Allied offensive was back on track; and by February 1945, the Allies had penetrated deep into the Fatherland.

Marty Romano, meanwhile, boarded a Navy supply ship back to the US. "There were three of us in the squadron that all went home together," he recalled—all of whom coincidentally lived in the greater New York City area. Landing at Norfolk on February 6, 1945, Marty and two fellow sailors, Gab Costello and Tony Sica, travelled up the East Coast to see their families. Marty recalled that seeing his mother, father, and siblings was the best homecoming present he could have wanted. As part of the celebration, his father opened a 50-gallon keg of homemade wine.

As it turned out, Marty's elder brother, Joseph, was serving in the Marshall Islands. And Mom Romano, now with multiple sons in the war, was elated to have young Marty back home, even if only for 33 days. After all, the country was still at war, and many sailors were being redeployed to the Pacific. Thus, it came as little surprise when, at the conclusion of his 33-day leave, Marty received orders to the Pacific theater.

It was now March 1945. Following the renewed Allied offensive on mainland Europe, it was clear that Nazi Germany was in its last throes. Meanwhile, in the Pacific, the enemy strongholds on Tarawa, Saipan, and Iwo Jima had collapsed under the fury of the "island hopping" campaign. That summer, the Japanese would fight their last losing battle on the island of Okinawa.

But for Marty Romano, the more pressing matter was simply *getting* to the Pacific theater. He had been ordered to report to PT Base 17 in the Philippines, whereupon he'd be assigned to any PT boat that needed a replacement. Departing from San Francisco aboard a troop carrier, he found the voyage to be an unusual affair. Onboard were several members of the WAVES (the US Navy Women's Reserve), all of whom were tightly-guarded by Marine Corps MPs. It was a slightly comical, albeit necessary, control measure: The skipper didn't want any romantic liaisons en route to the Philippines.

Mid-voyage, however, the captain suddenly vectored his ship onto a new course, deliberately sailing to cross the 180th Meridian (International Date Line) and the Equator at their point of intersection. According to naval traditions, such a maneuver would induct the ship's crew into an elite company of seafarers.

"Now, I did *not* think this was a good idea!"

The highest concentration of Japanese subs were in the Equatorial Pacific.

"All a Japanese sub captain had to do," said Marty, "was sit tight, and wait for our vain captain to come along, then nail it!"

After making its ceremonial crossing at the Equator and the Antemeridian, the troop carrier meandered around New Zealand, up through the northern coasts of Australia and New Guinea, before settling into Leyte Gulf. Allied forces had just invaded the Philippines, and were now in the "mopping up" phase of the Leyte Gulf naval battle. "We went to Base 17," said Marty, "that was in Samar"—the easternmost island province of the Philippines. "From there, I was waiting to be assigned to a boat."

After a few days, the personnel office told Marty that he'd be assigned to a new PT boat, sailing from the advance base on Borneo.

"Fine, I'm ready," he said.

When he got to Borneo, however, he was unwittingly placed upon the USS *Oyster Bay*—not a PT boat, but a "PT Boat Tender." In practice, the Tenders were floating logistical stations, responsible for carrying fuel and provisions to their designated PTs.

Still, the *Oyster Bay* had an illustrious combat history.

Marty Romano in his employee portrait for Edwards & Kelcey. As a civil engineer, Marty designed several prominent landmarks in Minnesota, including the Richard I. Bong Memorial Bridge.

"It was a converted destroyer," he said, whereas most Tenders were converted LSTs. "It had seen plenty of action—kamikaze attacks and all. Before I got there, they were involved in the Okinawa operation." But as a PT-rated engineer, Marty knew virtually nothing about the *Oyster Bay*'s propulsion system. Unlike the Packard-based powertrains aboard *PT-306*, the *Oyster Bay* was a double-shafted, diesel-powered vessel. Moreover, the ship's company already had a team of mechanics who were rated on the diesel powerplant; and they were doing a fine job of maintaining the *Oyster Bay*'s engine suite.

Thus, Marty had become an engineer with *no* engine to maintain.

The inopportune assignment, however, was short-lived. Days later, the US dropped its first atomic weapons over the Empire of Japan. Following the nuclear devastation of Hiroshima and Nagasaki, the Japanese government lost its will to fight.

Like many of his shipmates, Marty felt that the nuclear attacks ultimately saved more lives than they took. At the time, the *Oyster Bay* was being refitted for the invasion of Japan. And both sides were expecting a bloodbath. Some Japanese civilians were digging trenches along the beaches of Honshu, while others were being issued pitchforks to attack incoming paratroopers. But those fears never came to pass. For with the stroke of a pen, World War II finally ended on September 2, 1945.

Marty Romano was honorably discharged from the United States Navy on January 12, 1946. Under the terms of the newly-created "GI Bill," he enrolled at the Clarkson College of Technology (now Clarkson University) in New York. Inspired by watching the construction of the George Washington Bridge during his childhood, Marty enrolled in the Civil Engineering program, graduating with a Bachelor of Science degree in 1952. Meanwhile, as he approached his final semester in college, Marty married his longtime girlfriend, Lorraine, on September 15, 1951.

For the next 37 years, Marty was a proud employee of Edwards & Kelcey, a civil engineering and construction firm based in Morristown, New Jersey. A simple twist of fate, however, soon put Marty and his young family on the road to the American heartland. One morning, Edwards & Kelcey's Minneapolis office called in to the Morristown headquarters with a by-name request for "Marty Romano" - a top-flight structural engineer whom they needed for a series of projects in the Twin Cities. "They got a big job from the State of Minnesota," said Marty, "which included the Lowry Hill Tunnel." His by-name request had come via the office director at the Minneapolis branch, whom Marty had worked with on previous civil projects.

The Minnesota project was supposed to be a temporary assignment; but Marty, Lorraine, and their two daughters (Eileen and Joanne) soon made the North Star State their permanent home. Aside from the prominent Lowry Hill Tunnel, Marty went on to become the lead engineer for several high-profile infrastructure projects. Many of these structures have become prominent landmarks within the state of Minnesota. In addition to the Lowry Hill Tunnel, these projects included: the 11th Street South Bridge in Minneapolis; the Portland Avenue Tunnel in Minneapolis; and the Richard I. Bong Memorial Bridge connecting Duluth, Minnesota to Superior, Wisconsin. Marty retired from Edwards & Kelcey on December 29, 1989.

At this writing, Marty Romano is 97 years old, and still living an abundantly active life. He and Lorraine continue to reside in the Greater Minneapolis area.

3
BEHIND ENEMY LINES

KEN PORWOLL AND THE
BATAAN DEATH MARCH

The fires on Bataan burned with a primitive fury on the evening of April 9, 1942—illuminating the flags of surrender against the nighttime sky. Woefully outgunned, outnumbered, and ill-equipped, American-Philippine forces surrendered to the wrath of the Rising Sun. Some had escaped and eventually carried on as guerrillas. Most, however, like Sergeant Ken Porwoll, found themselves on the Bataan Death March.

Born on April 13, 1920 in St. Cloud, Minnesota, Ken Porwoll had no immediate draw to the military life. However, he joined the Minnesota National Guard in 1938 for reasons that had little to do with patriotism. "The National Guard sponsored a dance every New Year's, and it was the biggest social event of the winter," he said. "If you joined the Guard, you got a new uniform to wear to the dance." He saw the uniform as an opportunity to meet girls. "That was the incentive for three or four of us who signed up." Then, too, it was the middle of the Great Depression, and the extra monthly paycheck was a nice bonus.

Ken joined the National Guard as a tank crewman, assigned to the 34th Tank Company (later redesignated Company A, 194th Tank Battalion). At the time, the Minnesota Guard was on the verge of transitioning from the M2 Light Tank to the M3 Stuart. Both tanks, however, were thinly-armored, and neither had a particularly strong main gun. Still, Ken enjoyed learning how to operate the tanks, and he took readily to the life of a citizen-soldier. Even after World War II had officially started in Europe, Ken was certain that the war would never come to America. The Nazis were, after all, Europe's problem.

However, the 194th Tank Battalion was "federalized" in the fall of 1941—mustered into active service. A few weeks later, Ken and his comrades were on their way to Fort Lewis, Washington for additional training. In September of that year, the 194th received orders to the Philippine Islands. "All my life, I'd dreamed of going to the South Seas," he said. "Now, I'm going to get a free trip." He thought little of the war in Europe, and wasn't the least bit concerned about the Japanese. "Our only concern was getting our equipment clean. It was covered with that Marfak grease." His battalion arrived at Pier 7 in Manila Harbor on September 26, 1941—unloading 54 tanks for the convoy into Fort Stotsenberg in south-central Luzon.

An American Commonwealth since 1898, the Philippine Islands had enjoyed the full protection of the United States military. American forces in the Philippines fell under the jurisdiction of the United States Armed Forces—Far East (USAFFE). Commanded by an Army General, USAFFE encompassed all US military assets in the Philippine archipelago. This included American ground forces, the Far East Air Force, the Asiatic Fleet, and the semi-autonomous Philippine Army. USAFFE's mission was simple: continue providing combat-capable units for the Commonwealth's defense and assume responsibility for training the Philippine Army.

Despite these mission parameters, however, USAFFE remained in a deplorable state of combat readiness. In the midst of their isolationist fervor, Congress had straddled the US military with a draconian budget. As a result, USAFFE perennially subsisted on less than half of the money and equipment it needed for an adequate defense of the Philippines.

Upon arriving at Fort Stotsenberg, Ken discovered that there were no spare parts, no high-explosive tank ammunition, and minimal gasoline. To make matters worse, they had no extra ammunition for their M1 rifles. "When guards ended their watch, they'd pass their ammunition to the guy replacing them."

On the morning of December 8, 1941, Ken awoke to the news that Pearl Harbor had been bombed. That morning, "[our] tanks deployed around Clark Field," said Ken, moving into defensive positions against the incoming Japanese forces. "At about noon, we looked up, and saw a flight of planes coming over and said, 'Oh good, it's okay now because the Air Force is here'"—until those planes started dropping bombs. Ken said it was the first time in his military career that he felt truly helpless.

"What do you do?" he asked rhetorically.

From a tank, he couldn't shoot at the incoming bombs, and he couldn't traverse his main gun high enough to shoot down the incoming

Ken Porwoll as a POW. A member of the 194th Tank Battalion, Ken survived the Bataan Death March and a three-year internment at various POW camps.

planes. One hour later, Clark Field lay in ruins. "What wasn't blown up was on fire."

Company A was then ordered south into Muntinlupa to meet the anticipated Japanese landings. But when these landings came farther north, Ken's company had the unenviable task of turning northward to halt the enemy's advance—and the Japanese were already 30 miles inland. "When I came from Muntinlupa going north, we stopped at the Manila Hotel to get a drink, and the people in there were playing cards and having fun."

Ken could hardly believe it.

The Philippine Islands were under siege, and many of these Filipinos were carrying on as if nothing had happened. The cheerful Filipinos told Ken and his comrades: "Don't worry about it, boys. Uncle Sam will take care of these Japs. They'll never take Manila."

Ken wasn't so sure.

"You better get your walking shoes on," he told them. "And get out of town because they're coming and they'll be here." Yet these Filipinos paid no heed to his warning; such was their faith in the American military.

In the end, however, Company A was cut off, and had to make a hasty retreat. For a young tank sergeant like Ken Porwoll, the whole affair seemed like an exercise in futility. "All I can remember is running from one place to another with a tank," he said. Adding to the chaos was the growing blur between enemy and friendly lines. As the Japanese moved farther south, their positions became intermingled with the Allied defenders. For example, Sergeant Jim McComas, one of Ken's fellow tankers, inadvertently ran through a Japanese Command Post. During the ensuing chaos, a Japanese soldier tossed a thermite bomb onto the back of McComas' tank, "so that it burned a hole down through the armor and into the engine compartment; and got it so hot in the tank that some of the ammunition began to explode." The thermite fuse finally sank into the engine compartment, whereupon it disabled the tank. But miraculously, McComas survived.

Company A's retreat was cut short, however, when a group of nearby Filipinos heard the oncoming roar of American tanks and, mistaking them to be Japanese, blew up the local bridge in a panic. With no means of egress for their armored vehicles, Company A disabled and abandoned their tanks, rejoining the American lines on foot. To disable the tank, Ken said: "The only thing you could do was take the back plates off the guns, and throw them into the jungle someplace where they might not be found; and the guns become unusable."

When the remnants of Ken's battalion hobbled into Bataan, he was given command of another tank. Company A was then placed on coastal defense duty, firing on Japanese ships to prevent their landing. For a while, the American–Philippine forces were able to hold back the Japanese onslaught. But time was not on the Allies' side. The dwindling supplies and lack of reinforcements were beginning to take their toll. "As soon as we arrived [in Bataan], they put us on half rations," he said. "Then in February, they cut our rations again. They had armed guards on the chow wagons."

By now, disease was running rampant through the ranks.

Malaria began to claim more men than enemy gunfire. "They were out of Quinine, they were out of Atabrine, there was no mosquito netting," recalled Ken. "They didn't have anything." For the last two days of the battle, Ken survived on only one tin of sardines, which he shared with two of his friends. "We were so weak; it took three men to do one man's job."

Still, news of the Allied surrender came as a total surprise to him. "Runners came and told us we would be surrendered in the morning. They had us disable our tanks and disable our equipment."

Ken was incredulous; and some of his comrades refused to believe it.

"Well, I'm not going to surrender," they said.

They were determined to evade the Japanese and carry on the fight. But one of the officers said: "Well, if you don't surrender, that means you are deserting. You become a deserter and you will be court-martialed after the war." To some, however, a court-martial was better than becoming a POW. "And despite that threat, some of them still took off into the jungles," said Ken. Indeed, there was no legal basis to charge them for desertion as long as they continued fighting the enemy. In fact, many of these early American escapees—including Russell Volckmann, Robert Lapham, Wendell Fertig, and Charles Cushing—organized guerrilla movements against the Japanese. "My decision," said Ken, "was to stay with the group. What the group does, I will do."

The next day, April 10, the men of the 194th Tank Battalion assembled along a nearby road in the 100-degree heat. Before their departure, Ken recalled that one of the lieutenants opened the company treasury, dividing the money among the men. "And the cooks came with all the food they had left," he added, "dividing it out among the men and said: 'That's it. There is no more, guys.'" Awaiting the arrival of their conquerors, Ken didn't recall much anxiety among his comrades. Some seemed to think that the Japanese would treat them decently.

Those feelings would soon evaporate.

For when the first group of Japanese soldiers came through their area, Ken noticed that one of them was "real flushed…red in the face, as if he had a fever." The Japanese soldier collapsed, and his commanding officer, a Japanese lieutenant at the front of the column, quickly turned about, "unhitched his sword, and beat this man with the scabbard until the man got on his feet and walked off."

Ken was appalled.

If the Japanese did that to their own men, what would they do to the Americans?

When the Japanese got ahold of Ken and his fellow GIs, they took many of their personal belongings. "They picked our pockets. They took money, they took watches, they took rings. If a man had a ring they couldn't get off, they'd cut his finger off. If they found any item—a wallet, a comb—that had 'Japan' written on it, they killed the American on the spot. It meant you had taken it from a Japanese."

The Japanese then forced him to march some 65 miles to Camp O'Donnell. With 150 of his comrades, Ken made the grueling trek through the blazing heat with minimal food, water, and the constant threat of harassment from the Japanese. Some 12,000 Americans and 67,000 Filipinos were forced into this treacherous hike.

History would call it the Bataan Death March.

More than 7,000 would die along the way. "Anyone who lagged behind that first day was shot," said Ken. "After the first day, they just bayoneted you. They didn't think you were worth a bullet."

But for Ken Porwoll, the Death March was an intensely personal affair.

As National Guardsmen, most of the soldiers in Company A, 194th Tank Battalion were from the same hometown in Minnesota. It was a "very personal experience," he said, "in that I found myself walking with four other fellows that I had gone to high school with." They had played on the same football and basketball teams; they had competed for the same girls' affections; and they had grown up knowing each other's families. "You know almost everybody in the company," he added. In some ways, they drew strength from these bonds of familiarity—"and in another way," he said, "it's rather distressing too, when things get tough, and you have to make decisions as to who gets what…or who dies, who lives."

Ken hoped that he would never have to make that call. But his buddy, Jim McComas, who had survived the thermal charge aboard his tank during the invasion, came down with malaria on the second day of the Death March. Jim was a big, healthy man…and the fever didn't bother him at first. But when his fever devolved into a chill, he lost all control of his limbs. "So, we get one on either side of him," said Ken, "and helped drag him along the road." Ken and each of his friends took turns shouldering Jim. "We'd keep changing off about every hour or so until Jim said that we were going to have to drop him in the ditch because we won't make it if we have to carry him."

But Ken refused to leave his buddy.

"Let's keep trying a little while longer," he argued.

But Jim wouldn't have it.

"You've got to drop me in the ditch," he insisted.

By now, Jim knew that all the stragglers would be killed. "If you were beside the road when the column passed," Ken recalled, "the Japanese clean-up squad came by and killed you."

It was the horrible decision that Ken hoped he'd never have to make.

He and his friends knew they had to leave Jim behind.

"And I'm apologizing to him for our friendship coming to this kind of an end." But Jim McComas simply replied:

"Forget it, Ken. I'll just have to find another way."

With that, Jim crawled into the ditch, presumably leaving himself for dead. "We never spoke his name the rest of the walk. That was really tough."

For the next six days, Ken could hardly keep himself upright. The sweltering heat, humidity, and lack of nutrition were taking their toll. Moreover, he was astounded by the cruelty and barbarity of the Japanese Army. Some of the Japanese peeled the skin from their captives' feet, and forced them to walk through piles of salt. Other prisoners were deliberately run over by Japanese trucks racing at full speed. Yet, the most frightening stories were those of the Japanese eye gouging techniques: taking a rifle with a fixed bayonet, an enemy soldier would place the bayonet inside of a POW's bottom eyelid, and then let go of the rifle. Consequently, as the rifle fell to the ground, the bayonet would eject the prisoner's eye from his socket.

Aside from their astonishing cruelty, what angered Ken the most was the Japanese Army's casual, indiscriminate attitude towards its POWs. There was no rhyme or reason behind any of their methods. In fact, it seemed as though the Japanese were torturing Americans for their own amusement.

On the sixth day of the Death March, Ken found an opportunity. During a lull in the March, he spied a small pot cooking over a fire where a group of Japanese had bivouacked. Thinking that this abandoned pot might contain stew (or some other viable sustenance), he stealthily grabbed the pot and slipped back into the ranks of the Death March. After a few more paces down the road, he snuck a glance into the pot.

"I took off the lid and found that it was tea. That was a little disappointing."

Still, he happily shared it with the men around him. "We all had tea that afternoon." In his eight days on the Bataan Death March, Ken survived on nothing more than two handfuls of rice, two canteens of water, and a cup of tea.

The first stop on the Bataan Death March was the barbed-wire compound at San Fernando. "And the second morning I'm there…I look into the eyes of Jim McComas!"—the malaria-stricken GI whom they had presumed dead after he crawled into the roadside ditch.

Ken was ecstatic. "How did you get here?!"

"Well," said Jim, "when I went in the ditch and I looked up ahead, I saw a culvert, and I crawled into it and slept off the malaria attack. And the second day when another group of Americans came by, I crawled out and joined them."

Ken recalled that seeing Jim McComas, alive, helped restore some of his faith in God. He later confessed: "I was angry at God." In fact, he would often ask: "God, where are you; and what are you going to do about this?" On other occasions, particularly during the Death March, "I just hollered at Him," said Ken. But the second time he shouted at God, he heard a voice in the back of his head saying: "Ken, if you want to get to the end of this road, you have to walk it. So, you better focus on what your job is, and focus on walking. Stay attuned to what you have to do to get there." At the end of the Death March in San Fernando, Ken repented for his anger. "God, I'm sorry. You were there, weren't you? And you do care." But Ken admitted that, during the darkest days of his internment, he often vacillated between anger and gratitude—"every six months or so."

From San Fernando, Ken was among the many POWs crammed into the steel boxcars for the two-and-a-half-hour journey into Camp O'Donnell. "Men died of suffocation and from the heat…we were packed so tightly, there was no room to even fall down."

Camp O'Donnell itself was worse than the train ride.

Indeed, more than 400 Americans were dying every day at O'Donnell. "Burial details just went all day long. It never ended." To make matters worse, the camp was overcrowded and suffered from poor sanitation. "The water supply was one spigot that ran very slow," he said. "Too many people and not enough facility." The GIs who hoped that Camp O'Donnell would be a reprieve soon found otherwise. In fact, some of the prisoners who went to sleep that first night, didn't wake up in the morning. Some had died from malnourishment and exhaustion; some had died from their tropical diseases; while others simply committed suicide.

And the body count continued to rise.

As Ken recalled, many of his comrades were dying by the hour. Dysentery, malaria, beriberi, and a host of other diseases were running rampant through the camp. The "latrines" were nothing more than hastily-dug slit trenches, none of which were sanitized or had any type of drainage system. "And so, the flies moved in," he said—which inevitably carried fecal matter onto the prisoners' food. "And there were so many dying that there weren't enough [able-bodied] men to bury them, or to carry them to the burying grounds."

At one point, the Japanese began bribing POWs with extra rations of rice in exchange for burial duty. "They said whoever would work on the detail would get one and then two extra rations of rice," said Ken. Many of the POWs who accepted the deal, however, found that they simply couldn't bring themselves to bury their own comrades. When these POWs hesitated to throw their lifeless comrades into the mass graves, the Japanese simply threw the living POWs down into the graves as well…to be buried alongside their dead friends.

"The food was terrible," said Ken. POWs were normally given two rations of rice a day. But the Japanese deliberately overcooked it—"they boiled rice to a consistency of oatmeal…and they called it lugau." Getting water was also a hassle. A long queue of POWs formed by the water spigot every day; and the Japanese shut off the water at night. "So, you stood in line…because if you got out of line, you wouldn't get back into the same position you were in during the daytime."

After four weeks at Camp O'Donnell, Ken was unexpectedly transferred to Batangas—another prison camp where the POWs were placed on work details. "We were building a bridge over a gorge," he said. "In the beginning…I came down with yellow jaundice, and I was given the option of staying and doing light duty, or being sent back to O'Donnell." Without hesitation, Ken said: "I'll take the light duty." The piecemeal tradeoff for being at Batangas was that he received slightly better food and medical attention. "And my light duty was to carry water from a well that was about two and a half blocks away to the kitchen and the schoolyard where we were living."

For his lingering yellow jaundice, someone placed a one-pound bag of sugar by the well, with a note (written in English) that read: "Take three spoons each day. It will help with your yellow jaundice." Every few days, the one-pound bag of sugar would be replenished.

But who had left the bag there?

Ken never knew. "I never did see anybody. Or hear anybody."

Perhaps it was a sympathetic Filipino; or an altruistic Japanese soldier.

When he recovered from his yellow jaundice, however, he was thrust back into the realm of hard labor. Building that bridge, as he described it, was "really hard." Indeed, there were no automated tools—everything was done manually.

But, for what it was worth, this group of Japanese soldiers treated him better than the guards at O'Donnell. The Japanese officer-in-charge told his men that he would be the only one to administer punishment to a POW. "And so, they all understood that," said Ken. "And then he would give us the [same] rations that he gave his men, too."

Still, the Japanese were not gracious hosts.

Ken soon transferred to Cabanatuan, where he was given the mundane task of being a farm weeder. He stayed at Cabanatuan for three months before he was tapped for a work detail on the Japanese mainland. "I'm in this detail and I leave Cabanatuan," he remembered, "and I'm walking down the road and I need to take a leak." But as soon as he stepped out of line to relieve himself, he was attacked by two Japanese guards. With the butts of their rifles, they bashed Ken across the neck and the small of his back. "And I go tumbling in the ditch unconscious."

His handlers left him for dead. And Ken likely would have died by that roadside had it not been for the "cleanup squad" that came by a few minutes later—"a truck with American POWs on it picking up stragglers…they pick me up and throw me in the truck; and they take me to the railroad station." Once there, the Japanese loaded the POWs into boxcars for a short ride into Manila Bay. "Then, we get on a truck and I'm trucked to Pier Seven"—the very same dock where he had arrived with the 194th Tank Battalion months earlier. The Japanese intended to put this group of POWs on a ship to Japan, where they would likely take up hard labor in the mines or shipyards of Honshu or Hokkaido. But as he looked at the rusty old ship, he told himself:

"Ken, don't get on that ship. You'll die on that sucker."

Somehow, he was sure of that.

So, he crawled off behind some steel girders and went to sleep. When he awoke, the ship was gone and he was alone on the pier. Ken laid there until two Filipinos came passing by. He tried to convince them to provide food, or hide him temporarily. Normally, most Filipinos were happy to do so. But every war produces its own cadre of enemy collaborators—and this war was no different. Indeed, these two Filipinos came back a few minutes later with a pair of Japanese soldiers in tow. "I later learned," said Ken, "that they could get a hundred pesos for turning in an American."

The Japanese soldiers tried to make Ken walk, but given the condition of his health, he could barely stand. Frustrated, the Japanese tossed him onto a two-wheeled, horse-drawn carriage, and laid him across the reins, using Ken's body as a footrest as they took him to the POW camp in Bilibid. "They hammered on the gates until somebody opened them," he recalled, "and they have some conversation…then they leave…and take me to the execution chamber." They dragged him over to a cement block where an electric chair had once stood.

At first, Ken was certain that he was going to be killed.

But, as it turned out, he was just the newest resident of the prison's medical ward. It was the place where the Japanese sent POWs whom they considered terminally ill. As luck would have it, though, Ken met a familiar face in the crude medical ward—Jose Santos, a fellow trooper from the 194th Tank Battalion. Santos, however, was not a native Minnesotan. He had joined the 194th as a "replacement" when the battalion was at Fort Lewis. Santos helped nurse Ken back to health, slowly enabling the latter to regain his strength.

Ken was then sent back to Cabanatuan for three months, before he finally boarded a ship (Taga Maru) to Japan on September 20, 1943. The conditions onboard the ship, however, were no better than the POW camps. Describing the cargo holds: "They're so crowded, that you hardly have room for everybody to sit down at the same time. There were two [cargo] holds in this thing. Forward and the rear hold. The toilet was a washtub in the middle of the hold. There's no lid on it. And people that have diarrhea can't get to it anyway, because you have to walk on people to get there. And those that make an attempt, by the time they get there, they're all done. They don't need the tub anymore."

With the Taga Maru rocking back and forth along the waves, the prisoners' own fecal matter sloshed and sprayed around the cargo hold. "You end up living like rats in a sewer," he said, "awash in human feces." Every day, the Japanese lowered a single bucket of rice into the cargo hold, whereupon the ranking POW would have to ration out the contents to his fellow prisoners—"so that each man in that [cargo] hold got a dipper of rice." But, as Ken recalled, malnutrition was the least of their worries—looking at his fellow POWs, he could tell they were devolving into madness. "They're hungry. They're starved. They're crazy. They're out of their minds," he said.

Ken arrived in Japan in October 1943, where he would spend the next twenty-two months working in the Niigata coal mines. However, being a POW had taken a toll on his health; and he had trouble keeping pace in the coal yard. "I didn't know it then," he said, "but I had tuberculosis of the spine in three vertebrae. All I knew was that I was in a lot of pain."

All the while, he wondered how the war was going for the Allies.

He and his fellow POWs hadn't heard anything aside from the ever-present rumor mill, which changed from day to day.

Were the Allies winning?

Had the Americans recovered from Pearl Harbor?

What was happening in Europe?

He didn't know.

But, for now, his biggest concern was trying to stay alive.

He seemed to catch a break, however, when he noticed that one of his Japanese guards had a rosary…indicating that he was among Japan's Christian minority. Ken, a devout believer himself, also had a rosary; and he approached the Japanese guard hoping to find some common ground. At first, the guard hastily dismissed Ken, telling him to go away. The next day, however, Ken approached the guard a second time, showing his rosary.

Now, the guard seemed more receptive, but he told Ken to put away the rosary.

However, this chance encounter may have ultimately saved Ken's life. Indeed, the following day, Ken was run over by a minecart along the tunnel's inner track. He had been pushing his own minecart when it got stuck at a bend in the track—"and the cart behind me comes pushing, and slams into me; and my legs end up underneath it." Within moments, two Japanese handlers came running, separated the two minecarts, and "carefully take me out from underneath…and they examine me for broken bones." After determining that Ken had no injuries, his Japanese Christian friend reassigned him to an "easy job" working the coal chute levers.

"That's how I got through my one-and-a-half years in Japan," he said.

One day, in August 1945, the Japanese officers suddenly abandoned Ken's camp without warning. Apparently, there had been a massive bombing strike on the Japanese mainland.

No surprises here, Ken thought.

After all, the rumor mill had reported numerous fire bombings.

But this time something was different.

"Whatever this thing was," he said, "it was enough to send [these officers] off." A few days later, there came news of a second aerial attack, whereupon the Japanese noncommissioned officers (sergeants) vacated the camp, leaving only the privates to look after the POWs. With no direction from their commissioned or noncommissioned officers, the Japanese privates simply faded away.

Once Ken realized that all the Japanese sentries had abandoned their posts, he knew the war must have ended. The hungry POWs then raided the camp warehouse, drawing whatever food and provisions they could scavenge. "I think we fed ourselves for at least a week before the Air Corps found us and dropped supplies, clothing, and medicine." Soon thereafter, he discovered that the premature exodus of his Japanese handlers had been caused by the atomic bombs dropped on Hiroshima and Nagasaki.

"I still maintain that I was the only POW who was ever personally repatriated by his commander-in-chief." Indeed, Minnesota Governor Harold Stassen, came to Japan to coordinate the release of all Minnesota National Guardsmen held as POWs. "We were out of there [Niigata] two days after the Missouri docked." After his repatriation, Ken spent nearly a year in the hospital getting spinal fusions to treat his lingering tuberculosis.

Returning to civilian life, Ken married his wife Mary-Ellen in 1953, with whom he had nine children. Settling in St. Paul, Minnesota, he was a proud employee of Capitol Gears for nearly three decades. Inspired by his fellow veterans, Ken volunteered more than 5,000 hours at the Minneapolis VA Hospital; and volunteered countless additional hours to the Listening House of St. Paul. "People ask me all the time if I've forgiven the Japanese," he said during his later years. "I have. I really have. But I'll tell you, sometimes, I have to forgive them two or three times a month because it still recycles."

Ken Porwoll passed away on Veterans Day 2013, at the age of 93.

4

DAWN LIKE THUNDER

ED WENTZLAFF,
PEARL HARBOR SURVIVOR

O f the 335 men who survived the sinking of the USS *Arizona*, less than a handful were still living by the early 2000s. One of the last remaining survivors was Ed Wentzlaff, who by the age of 92, had already made arrangements to be buried with his comrades in Pearl Harbor. "My ashes will be interred on the *Arizona*," he said. "It only makes sense. I was on board for three years before she was sunk. That's where all my friends are."

Born in 1917, Ed was the third of nine children born to a saloon-operating family. Despite the Prohibition, Ed's family generated most of their income from selling illegal alcohol. And, as expected, the Wentzlaff family had numerous close calls with the federal Prohibition agents. "I remember saving my dad one time," he recalled. "I just happened to be out collecting for my paper route, when I saw this new big car coming into town. It had three guys in it."

But the car itself looked out of place, as did its occupants.

Typically, only federal agents conducted themselves in such a manner. "I raced home on my bike and told my dad, 'They're coming.' They were able to hide everything they had behind the bar before the agents got there."

After graduating from high school in 1935, Ed went to work for the Great Northern Railroad in Walker, Minnesota. Even during the midst of the Great Depression, Ed recalled: "I never had any trouble finding jobs because I always worked hard. I always believed in giving them their dollars' worth. The best job I had in those days was picking corn for $6.00 a day. That was big money in the 1930s." Indeed it was. When adjusted for inflation, his daily wages had the purchasing power of nearly $125 in today's money.

Ed worked a variety of farm and labor jobs throughout the Depression, but it was tough getting ahead. "I got disgusted about always being poor," he admitted. "A friend of mine had joined the Navy earlier that year, and then another friend joined up. For some reason, I decided I would too."

For a young man growing up in the Great Depression, the Navy seemed like a good way to make a living. Sailors got free uniforms, free meals, endless opportunities for travel, and the chance to learn a technical trade that could carry over into the private sector.

Ed Wentzlaff enlisted in the United States Navy on December 8, 1937. He completed boot camp at Great Lakes Naval Training Station in Chicago; then it was off to the Naval Ordnance School in San Diego, learning about the common variety of naval weapons. Ed was fascinated by the concept of torpedoes, and requested duty aboard a submarine. "But, of course, this was the Navy," he said, "and they sent me to a battleship."

That battleship was the USS *Arizona*.

When Ed reported to the *Arizona* in 1938, he first worked as a cook and pot-scrubber. It was the job that often befell new sailors when they reported to the ship. For many, it was considered a "rite of passage," before joining the ship's functional crew. After several months in the mess galley, however, Ed joined the ordnance crew on the *Arizona*'s forward gun batteries. He was now officially a "gun striker"—maintaining the black powder magazines below deck.

In mid-1939, however, there came an opening for an ordnance mate aboard one of the *Arizona*'s scout planes. "Everybody wanted to fly those planes," Ed recalled. The OS2U Kingfisher seaplane could be launched from the deck of any battleship, and recovered by a shipboard crane after landing on the sea. Ed won the coveted Kingfisher assignment through a combination of good luck and steady mentorship. With the help of an officer who had taken a liking to him, Ed was able to qualify as an Aviation Ordnance Mate Third Class, and found himself at the top of the recommendation list for the scout plane assignment.

Over the next few years, the USS *Arizona* shifted her home port from California to Pearl Harbor. In the years immediately prior to December 7, the ship spent most of its time at sea. In port, however, Ed recalled that the *Arizona* had a tremendous recreation program—"good baseball teams, football teams, wrestling, you name it. The crew spent all of its time together." Because the *Arizona* was a flagship, it also hosted a rear admiral, Isaac Kidd. "He was one of the orneriest admirals in the fleet," Ed remembered. "Everybody hated him. Our airplanes were on the

Ed Wenztlaff. The son of a bootleg saloon owner, Ed joined the Navy as a means to escape the Great Depression. He requested duty aboard a submarine, but was given a billet aboard the USS *Arizona*.

quarterdeck, and the admiral considered the quarterdeck his territory. He made us do all our work in dress whites. You tell me—how do you change the oil on an airplane in your dress whites?"

Grumpy admirals notwithstanding, Ed enjoyed his job on the *Arizona*; and he rose quickly through the ranks. In September 1941, he had passed the test to become an Aviation Ordnance Mate First Class. But the promotion itself would have to wait—"there were no first-class slots available at the time." Still, his duties aboard the Kingfisher aircraft remained the same: he took care of the plane's onboard weapons—"including the machine gun and bomb racks." As it turned out, maintaining the aircraft's machine gun was a daunting task. Just like the World War I biplanes, the Kingfisher's machine gun fired *through* its propeller. Thus, Ed became an expert at "synchronizing the machine guns so they wouldn't shoot off the plane's propeller." As an Aviation Ordnance Mate, Ed was also rated as part of the air crew, for which he drew flight pay.

December 7, 1941 began as a joyful day for Ed Wentzlaff. His four-year enlistment in the Navy was scheduled to end the following day. He and another friend were planning to leave the Navy and open a resort in Wisconsin. "It was a beautiful morning," he said. "As usual, I got up early to take a shower while there was still hot water, so I was probably up a half-hour before reveille. Just before 8 o' clock, I was up on the forecastle waiting for service to begin. I was Catholic, but they were having Lutheran service on our ship because the chaplain was Lutheran. They were just setting up the chairs. There were about 12 of us."

A few minutes before 8:00 AM, Ed looked out over the Harbor and saw an incoming airplane. "I could see the red ball on its side. It was coming right down the line of ships and strafing as it came. When it got to us, the bullets were hitting the teak wood on deck, and the wood and splinters were flying all over. Someone told us to get below. There was a kind of rule in the Navy that a ship was bombproof if you got down to the third deck."

But today, the *Arizona* would tragically disprove that theory.

On his way down to the lower decks, Ed roused a few of his shipmates from their sleep. "I told them they should get below," but his sleepy-eyed comrades refused to believe that the attack was real. They insisted that it was just the Army Air Corps simulating another attack; and that the Army staged these simulations regularly. "I told them to look out the porthole, and they'd see it wasn't a simulation."

Ed continued following his shipmates through the lower decks, down

The USS *Arizona* in 1931, after completing her upgrades and modernization.

to "what was thought to be an impregnable part of the ship." But as he approached the final ladder, he changed his mind. "I was the last one in the group," he remembered, "and they all went down below and I didn't." For some reason, Ed couldn't bring himself to hide in the bowels of the ship. "I don't know why I didn't follow them down there; I don't know. But my General Quarters station was up on the quarterdeck. Damn, don't you know, I just turned around and went back up."

That decision probably saved his life.

"There were some fires on the deck already, and a lieutenant commander told us to grab a fire hose. We got it out, and I told the other guy to stay at the valve until I was ready at the other end of the hose. When I had a good grip on it, I told him to hit the water, but nothing happened. I thought he might have opened the wrong valve, so we changed places and I tried to open the valve. But there was no water. We had already been torpedoed by that time."

As Ed was trying to open the valve, a Japanese Zero dropped its bomb through the upper decks of the *Arizona*, setting off the powder magazine at the forward edge of the ship. Most of the *Arizona*'s forward section disappeared in that horrific blast. "I was protected a little bit," he said, "but it burned off all my hair, my eyebrows." A nearby Marine had fared even worse. He was the commander of the ship's Marine detachment and, as Ed recalled: "he had a huge chunk missing on his forehead, and another chunk missing on his cheek." Yet this fatally-wounded Marine kept yelling, "We're going to get those SOBs!" until he expired a few moments later.

"Someone was yelling to abandon ship, but when I looked over the side, and saw all that oil burning, I didn't know if I wanted to jump into that. If I had jumped, I don't think I would have made it to shore." Thus, Ed and another sailor ran to the officer's gangway, where the admiral's barge was tied. Although the *Arizona* was sinking, the barge's line was still taut.

The sinking battleship was taking the barge down with her.

Ed yelled to the other sailor: "If you can get the engine going, I'll cut us loose!" Ed tried his three-inch blade on the mooring rope, but it was no use. "I went in the admiral's cabin and I found a flag staff that he used for official ceremonies. It had a metal device on the top of it, and I brought that out and started hacking at the line. I finally got it parted."

The other sailor got them underway. "We went down the side of the ship, and there was a group of men, they were just black from head to foot," Ed recalled. "So many men were burned, and they were burned all over because all they had on when the ship exploded were their shorts [skivvies]. We got them on board the barge, and brought them over to the hospital ship in the harbor, the USS *Solace*. If any of them lived, it had to be a miracle."

Ed spent the next several hours going in and out of Battleship Row, picking up survivors wherever he could find them. At one point, he ferried a group of badly-burned sailors to the onshore Navy Hospital.

"All those guys wanted were cigarettes," he recalled.

Somehow, these wounded sailors preferred nicotine over morphine.

"We hauled them over to the hospital, but there was no room inside, and we just had to put them on the lawn. The doctors would come around…but if you didn't look like you were going to make it, they just didn't bother." Indeed, these Navy doctors had to make the painful decision to bypass the fatally-wounded, and focus their energies on those who *could* be saved.

Moreover, Ed was astounded by how quickly the chain of command had broken down after the opening shots. "On the *Arizona*, nearly all of the senior officers were killed in the blast," including the maligned

The *Arizona* burns after being struck by Japanese bombs during the attack on Pearl Harbor.

Admiral Isaac Kidd. "We were all orphans out there," Ed remembered. "In fact, there was no command at all."

Still, Ed tried to help wherever he could.

At one point, he found himself on the USS *West Virginia*, as part of an ad hoc team desperately trying to save the ship. They knew they couldn't stop the ship from sinking, but they wanted to save it from capsizing. For if the ship could sink straight down, the Navy might have a chance to salvage it. "I remember talking to one guy who served on the *West Virginia*," Ed recalled. "He was a friend of mine. He said that he had been ordered to flood some compartments, but he refused to do it because he knew some of his shipmates were in those compartments. They made him do it. He had to kill them. A month later, he was dead [from suicide]. He never recovered from that." Later in the day, Ed joined a group of servicemen digging gun pits along the shore. The Americans were certain that the Japanese would launch a second wave, and that an invasion of Oahu was on its way.

By nightfall, Ed and the other survivors had been hoarded into the shipyard, where they spent the night in the naval base recreation building.

"They gave us a rifle, some ammunition, a blanket, soup and a sandwich. We painted all the windows black." Around this time, however, these shell-shocked survivors committed their first case of fratricide. A group of planes from an American carrier flew over Pearl Harbor that evening. Ironically, these carriers had been the primary target for the Japanese High Command when planning the attack on Pearl. Fortunately, the carriers had been away on maneuvers that morning. But when these carrier-borne planes appeared over the devastated remains of Pearl Harbor, the spooked survivors opened fire. "We thought they were Japanese," Ed lamented, "and we were all firing at them with rifles and everything else we had. We shot five of them down. Two of the pilots were killed. We felt terrible. But that's just how it was that day. For a while, I was carrying two .45s in my belt."

Two days later, Ed and the other survivors were taken to the local Post Office. "We were allowed to send a post card saying: 'I am okay, and I will write later.' There was an officer with us to make sure that's all we wrote. My parents were first informed that I was 'missing in action,' and that was the truth. Nobody knew where anybody was."

After the attack on Pearl Harbor, Ed Wentzlaff knew he couldn't leave the Navy. The country was at war; and he had witnessed the opening shots. He remained on active duty for another four-and-a-half years. He served in a variety of postings throughout the war, including a temporary stint on the USS *Yorktown* before its sinking at Midway. While fighting the Japanese, Ed continued to rise through the ranks, and had become a chief warrant officer by the war's end.

Rather than become a career sailor, however, Ed returned to his native Minnesota. "For a year, I just relaxed and drank," he said. Given the horrors of combat, one could hardly blame him. It would take time to decompress from the psychological traumas of war.

Although America emerged victorious from World War II, many veterans and social commentators have criticized the War Department's lack of attention to the long-term psychological health of its servicemen. These men, like those who fought before them, suffered the long-term effects of "battle fatigue" (a condition that has since been rebranded as "Post-Traumatic Stress Disorder"); and there were no effective care or rehabilitation systems to help them re-integrate into postwar America. They were left largely to their own devices. Perhaps tacitly, these veterans were expected to find catharsis in the fact that they'd *won* the war and had defeated the forces of Fascism.

Ed later attended law school at the University of Minnesota; but the large classes, pompous professors, and lack of personal attention quickly turned him off to the legal profession. Instead, he turned to farming, a career that he held for the next 38 years. He also ventured into local politics, serving as the Mayor of Butterfield, Minnesota (west of St. Paul) and later became the Watowan County Commissioner.

Throughout his life, Ed found comfort in attending the various Pearl Harbor reunions with his surviving shipmates. He also travelled with a panel of World War II veterans, discussing their experiences at various venues across America. "There was one guy who was on the *Indianapolis*," he said. The USS *Indianapolis* was torpedoed by a Japanese submarine on July 30, 1945, resulting in the greatest loss of life suffered by a single American ship. "They [the panel] billed us as being on the first ship that was sunk [Ed on the *Arizona*] and the last ship that was sunk [the sailor from the *Indianapolis*] during the war."

And like many survivors, Ed Wentzlaff cast a critical eye on the Hollywood renditions of Pearl Harbor. He recalled *Tora! Tora! Tora!* as one of the best representations of the event. He also visited the USS *Arizona* Memorial at least eight times before his death. "I just look at all the names," he said. "There were so many good friends of mine."

In the twilight of his life, Ed reflected heavily on being one of the last living survivors from the Arizona. "I can't explain why I've lived so long," he said. "It's like the good Lord is saying: 'I'm going to keep him here until he gets it straightened out.'"

Ed Wentzlaff passed away on September 11, 2013.

True to his intentions, his ashes were interred aboard the USS *Arizona* during a commemorative ceremony on December 7, 2013. Seventy-two years after witnessing the attack on Pearl Harbor, Ed Wentzlaff had finally rejoined his 1,200 shipmates in their place of immortality.

5
AMERICAN SPITFIRE

FLOYD "ROD" RODMYRE,
USAAF SPITFIRE PILOT

ew Americans can claim to have flown a Supermarine Spitfire—
the crown jewel of the RAF's Fighter Command. Lieutenant Floyd
"Rod" Rodmyre was one of those lucky few. "A lot of people
think it was the best fighter made by any country in World War II," he
said. "I know what it was built for; it was perfection."

Growing up on a farm near Hector, Minnesota, Rod Rodmyre
enjoyed the simple routines of Midwestern life. One of his most
memorable childhood moments was the day a local resident started a
school bus service. "My mom was so elated because it meant I'd get
home from school in time to help out around the farm," he said. But, for
as well-intentioned as this bus entrepreneur may have been, his vehicle
of choice seemed to be a deathtrap. "It was built on a Ford Model A
axis," Rod remembered. "The exhaust pipe fed into another pipe that ran
through the length of the bus. That was our heater."

Graduating from high school in 1939, Rod attended Augsburg College
for two years. Following the attack on Pearl Harbor, Rod approached his
father, who was serving on the local draft board. "We had a little heart-to-
heart," said Rod. "I asked him what my chances were [of being drafted],
and he said I'd be the first to go." Rod was now 21 years old, in good
health, and had no criminal record. Thus, he was a prime candidate for
being classified "1A" for the draft.

In February 1942, Rod enlisted in the Army air cadet program. "But
the way the military was in those days," he said, "they just sent us home
on vacation." Indeed, the Army did not yet have enough airfields to
accommodate the influx of new cadets. "So, I just collected my $30 a
month at home."

But this homestead vacation wouldn't last long.

Barely one month later, he was recalled to Minneapolis and put on a train to Randolph Field, Texas. "We got on the train, and they put us in sleeping cars. I thought this was pretty nice and assumed that everyone got the same treatment. Later, I found out it was because we were air cadets, and we were future officers, so they were treating us like officers."

For the young Cadet Rodmyre, however, Flight School was a challenge like none other. "We went through a series of check rides, and I was not doing well. I took the first check ride and I flunked, and the second check ride and I flunked that. It didn't look good."

Failing two consecutive check rides had put him on notice with the flight instructors.

"I assumed I didn't have much chance to make number three, and so I figured it would be my last flight in the Army. I was as relaxed as an old shoe. I had given up completely; it was kind of shameful." But, that level of relaxation seemed to help his performance. He flew this third check ride without incident and made a picture-perfect landing. "We got out of the plane," he said, "and the officer…looked at me and said, 'Cadet Rodmyre, I don't know why I'm doing this, but I think I'm going to let you go on.' I almost gave him a hug," he laughed. "From that time on, I never had any problems in the air. I started acting like I had some potential." His hard work paid off; Rod earned his wings in November 1942. "Nothing I had done in my lifetime up to that date could compare with the feeling of accomplishment, pride, and happiness."

He then received orders to attend fighter training in Oakland, California. "That was another experience," he said. "It seems our flight commander didn't have much to do except drink. But, of course, the sergeants ran the place, and they got us into our training schedule." Throughout the course, Rod piloted the P-39 Airacobra. "We thought it was a wonderful plane," he said. "It had the tripod gear, and you could almost land it blindfolded. And, unlike our training planes, this one could actually shoot bullets." The P-39 itself had somewhat of a checkered reputation among the Allied air forces. Although the plane was easy to handle, it was typically derided among the Western Allies for its poor combat record.

Because he was on a West Coast training station, Rod anticipated being sent to the Pacific. Instead, his entire training class received bulk orders to Fort Dix, New Jersey, and soon found themselves on a troop carrier to England. "But after a few days at sea," he noted, "the weather was getting warmer. That shouldn't happen if we're going to England."

As it turned out, they had been diverted to North Africa.

"That was a serious change. All the nylons the guys had bought for the women in England were now excess baggage," he chuckled. Soon, the official announcement came that they were headed to Casablanca. "We were all joking that we would see Humphrey [Bogart] there." The real-life Casablanca, however, bore little resemblance to the soiree setting of Rick's Café. "It was hot," Rod remembered, "and it was stinky." The young pilots then took a bus some 30 miles to the Moroccan town of Berrechid. "You didn't have to slur your words too much to make it sound like something else."

Arriving at the airfield, however, Rod was puzzled to find British Spitfires—"the fighter plane that many credited with winning the Battle of Britain"—branded with American roundels and markings. Rod soon discovered that these Americanized Spitfires had been escorting P-39s on various missions over the Mediterranean. "We wondered about that," said Rod. "Fighters being escorted by fighters." At first, it didn't make sense. "It soon dawned on us that our P-39 wasn't much of a fighter plane."

Rod had been assigned to the 308th Fighter Squadron, 31st Fighter Group. "It was one of the best-known groups in the war," and was the first American air group to arrive in England in 1942. However, because their planes were deemed inferior to the German fighters, the Yankee pilots had swapped most of their P-39s and P-40s for Spitfires.

A few days later, Squadron headquarters asked for any volunteers interested in flying the Spitfire. "We looked at each other for about three seconds, and then it was a mad rush to sign up," said Rod. The volunteers were assigned to an RAF officer, Major Rusty Gates, who had fought in the Battle of Britain, and was now training Yanks to pilot the Spitfire. "He had a real Cockney accent," Rod remembered. "He told us everything about the Spitfire."

Of course, the Spitfire was much different from the American planes. "The most significant difference was that everything was run by air pressure [i.e., pneumatics], including the firing of the guns."

Still, Rod was happy to be flying the Spitfire. "We realized that our life expectancy had just increased many-fold. It was such an easy plane to fly, it felt like it became part of you. We had a stupid grin on our faces for days." But the Spitfire wasn't the only piece of British equipment they were using. In fact, it seemed that the entire 308th Squadron had been equipped by His Majesty's armed forces. "We had RAF helmets, life vests, parachutes, boots, overalls, you name it."

Moreover, Rod was impressed by the cool nonchalance and derring-do of RAF pilots like Rusty Gates. For example, near the end of a training flight, Gates was on final approach when Rod spied a group of camel riders crossing the runway. "Gates just cruised in like nothing was there," Rod recalled, "and his landing wheel hit one of the camel drivers in the head…killed him instantly." Naturally, an irate Army Air Forces officer soon confronted Gates about the runway casualty.

Gates simply replied: "*By jove, I thought I felt a bump there.*"

"I later learned," said Rod, "that the government gave $25 to the family of the camel driver. Life in wartime is very cheap."

In July 1943, Rod flew his first combat missions during the Invasion of Sicily. The 308th Fighter Squadron arrived in Sicily on D-Day+4, and began flying missions in support of Allied ground operations. The rules of flying in combat suddenly became real. "There wasn't any horseplay, or any useless radio chatter," he said. "There were two main commands. One was 'break right' and the other was 'break left.' Our squadron's radio name was 'Helpful.' So, you'd hear on the radio, 'Helpful, break right,' and you'd make this sudden, almost violent turn to the right," vectoring themselves into the direction of an enemy formation.

The Americans would maintain their tactical formations for as long as they could. "But once the dogfighting began, it was a mass of swirling planes, turning, diving, climbing, sometimes upside down," he said. "The dogfights rarely lasted more than a minute or two, but it seemed like an hour."

Still, the Spitfire held up remarkably well in a dogfight.

One of its few drawbacks, however, was its line of sight. "When it was on the ground, it was impossible to see straight ahead because of the angle of the plane." As Rod remembered: "For that reason, you always saw Spitfire pilots zig-zagging down the runway so they could look out the side windows and see what was in front of them."

At times, however, it seemed that the Spitfire jocks had more to fear from Allied vessels than enemy planes. During one mission, for example, Rod's flight was fired upon by an American cruiser off the northern coast of Sicily. Luckily, there were no casualties; but the encounter left him shaken. "I guess the rule was: 'If you can't identify it, shoot it down.' We got out of his range as fast as we could and continued patrolling."

As the Allied troops moved forward, so too did the airmen, "jumping from one airfield to another." But life on the airfield was by no means easy. Pilots would go for days without a shower or a change of clothes. "We would stuff our mattresses with wheat straw, so of course we got lice," said Rod. "We learned that we could soak our mattresses and clothes in

Floyd Rodmyre poses in front of his Americanized Spitfire. Rodmyre was one of the American few pilots in history to fly a Spitfire in combat.

aviation gas, and that would get rid of the lice."

The aviation gas could not, however, stave off malaria—which Rod contracted during his first few weeks in Sicily. "First the chills, then the fever, then the chills again," he said. "When I had the chills, they could put seven wool Army blankets on me and I'd still be shaking. When I had the fever, I was just sweating all the time." Still, his fellow pilots never missed an opportunity to inject their own dark humor into the healing process. For instance, Rod's friend, Les Schult came to his bedside with an accordion. "He sat down on the next bunk and played every funeral song he knew, and then left without saying a word."

Rod yelled after him: "I'm going to get well just so I can kill you!"

While stationed in Sicily, Rod also had a chance encounter with General George Patton. "I was walking past this bombed-out hangar where the walking-wounded troops were being cared for," Rod remembered. "Walking-wounded" referred to any wounded soldier who was still ambulatory. "All of a sudden," he continued, "Patton's car came roaring up with all the stars on the fender and the red flags flapping. I stood at frozen attention, hoping that he would just think I was a statue."

By now, Patton's reputation preceded him wherever he went. His bombastic and larger-than-life persona had won him several admirers (and enemies) throughout the Army. And today, the young Lieutenant Rodmyre would see Patton's colorful antics on full display. "The Jeep passed the hangar," he continued, "and then stopped and backed up at about 30 miles an hour. I didn't think Jeeps could go that fast in reverse. And out came Patton and he went into the hangar."

Rod braced himself for the tirade he knew was coming.

"He used every cuss word in the vocabulary of a whole division, and far more," Rod recalled. "He didn't seem to think the men were dressed right." The wounded soldiers hastily (and perhaps reluctantly) pulled their uniforms over their casts and bandages. Patton, eyeing the spectacle before him, said: "Now you look like soldiers. I'm proud to lead you, and I salute you."

The verbose General then saluted his troops, and stormed off in his Jeep.

Rod remembered that this hangar visit was only a few days before the infamous "slapping incident" with a shell-shocked GI...the incident that nearly derailed Patton's career.

As the action moved onto the Italian mainland, the 31st Fighter Group followed. The Spitfire jocks stayed at various airbases, following the path of Allied ground forces as they pushed the Germans farther north. For this portion of the Italian campaign, Rod and his wingmen often flew bomber escort missions, accompanying B-17s and B-24s on their various runs. But even the most aggressive fighter escorts couldn't prevent the occasional loss of a heavy bomber.

"When a [B-17] got hit, he usually made it back to base. But when those [B-24s] got hit. *Oy-yoy-yoy*. I saw one get hit, and watched four guys get out, but then the plane went into a spin and the centrifugal force kept anyone else from bailing out. I know the B-24 had a great reputation with some people, but nobody asked me." Indeed, heavy bomber crews had among the lowest life expectancies of any Allied personnel in the ETO.

Of course, Rod had his own near-brushes with death. During one mission, while serving as the flight leader's wingman, Rod felt a sudden jolt that rendered him unconscious. "All of a sudden, everything went black," he said. "I didn't know where I was. I was out, and when I came to, my plane was at about 6,000 feet in a very steep dive, going very fast." Jerking back on the stick, he pulled the Spitfire out of its dive just moments before hitting the ground. When he returned to base, however, the ground crew pointed to an 11x16-inch hole in his canopy.

He had been hit by a German bandit.

"The fragments of the shell had penetrated my leather helmet and entered my scalp," he said. "The other guys said I was talking gibberish on the radio before I came to." The flight surgeon removed the shrapnel from Rod's scalp, and he was flying the next day.

By this time, Rod Rodmyre had flown dozens of missions, but had yet to down an enemy fighter. "It seemed like most of the time in air battles, the enemy was shooting at me, and not the other way around," he lamented.

However, his fortunes changed on January 29, 1944.

"It was a one-on-one deal with a Focke-Wulf 190," he recalled. "We got going round and round, but I could out-turn him…I was making my turns as sharp as I could without stalling. Eventually, I came up behind him. He tried to out-dive me, but he had used up all his altitude. I just went after him and got him." Rod's victory was quite impressive given the reputation of the Fw 190. It was among the fastest and most powerful fighters in the *Luftwaffe*, but the Mark V Spitfires (and their latter-day variants) could easily out-turn the Focke-Wulf at lower and medium altitudes.

Eventually, the 308th received an upgraded variant of the Spitfire, and the pilots were finally given permission to name their planes. His friends chose a variety of colorful nicknames, but Rod prophetically nicknamed his crate the "Flying Viking"—a seemingly clairvoyant nod to the future Minnesota Vikings football team. "I was twenty years ahead of the football team in picking that name," he chuckled.

In March 1944, Rod's fighter group was transferred to the 15th Air Force. "It meant more spit and polish," he said, "but the barracks were better and the food was better." Indeed, he no longer had to contend with lice, straw mattresses, or the lingering smell of gasoline-soaked linens. "And there was one other major change: The group was assigned the American P-51 Mustang fighter to replace the Spitfires."

It was quite possibly the last news he wanted to hear.

"They called us all together in a big tent and told us we had to give up our Spitfires. We were just incredulous. We knew we were flying the best airplane in the world. We didn't think any American plane was as good." Given their experiences with the P-39 and P-40, one could hardly blame them.

But, as they soon found out, the P-51 Mustang was in a class all its own. It was fast, nimble, and could stand toe-to-toe against any Axis fighter. "It could fly for hours, whereas the Spitfire could only go an hour or an hour-and-a-half." Before long, Rod and his fellow pilots realized that the P-51 was "quite an airplane."

Still, the P-51's performance metrics couldn't save it from a pilot's bad judgement. Such was the case in the fall of 1944, when Rod was flying wingman for Les Schult, the flight leader of a four-plane formation. "There was some fighting," said Rod, "but it was not compelling, and we were headed home."

On the way back, however, Rod's radio died.

"I pulled alongside Les and indicated by tapping on my headphones that my radio wasn't working. So, I formed up on his wing. He was going to have to fly for both of us."

One of the other pilots in their formation, however, was about to make a fatal mistake.

This other pilot, whom Rod identified as a "goofball," saw a flight of enemy bombers below, and dove after them—"without checking the surrounding skies or letting Les Schult, the formation leader, know what was happening." Rod and Les reluctantly dove after the wayward wingman, trying to give him some top cover. "And of course, as he approached the bombers," said Rod, "the [Bf 109s] sprung the trap."

The "goofball" pilot was immediately shot down, and the remaining P-51s came face-to-face with *nine* German Messerschmitt fighters. "It just went on and on," said Rod. "It was probably a 15-minute air battle, but it seemed like hours...and I was staying on Les' wing. I was kind of useless without the radio."

Luckily, Les Schult and Rod Rodmyre escaped the melee and landed safely at their base. But the surprise dogfight had taken its toll on Rod. "I taxied to the parking spot and started to walk to Operations. All of a sudden, I couldn't walk anymore. My knee was shaking too badly. It was the only time I ever experienced that, and boy was it shaking."

Rod was showing the first signs of "battle fatigue."

Later, when the ground crew inspected Rod's plane, they discovered that two of his exhaust pipes had completely melted off. "And there was no gas, not one drop, left in the plane. I don't even know how I taxied in." He must have been running on fumes. "It was the closest thing to a miracle I've ever felt."

Whenever a pilot returned from a brutal mission like Rod Rodmyre's, the flight surgeons would often give them a fifth of whiskey. Although the libation was *technically* prohibited while in theater, flight commanders often looked the other way. Most pilots knew from experience that a quick shot of alcohol (in any form or fashion) could quiet their nerves and slow their adrenaline after a painful mission. Rod had little tolerance for alcohol, but he often took solace in nicotine, as did many of his peers. "I smoked incessantly," he said. "Cigarettes were free. Even the Red Cross girls were handing them out." Elsewhere on the frontlines, American GIs were typically rationed two cigarettes per soldier, alongside their typical C and K-Rations.

Finally, after completing 130 missions, Rod was summoned to the flight surgeon's office. "He told me that I was showing signs of fatigue, and that I was losing weight. I went to the Isle of Capri for some R&R." Upon his return, Rod Rodmyre flew an additional 30 sorties, bringing his combat mission tally to 160, whereupon he was ordered to take more R&R. "They said they were going to send me home for 90 days' rest."

Rod presumed the Army Air Forces would send him back to Europe, or maybe to the Pacific so he could diversify his combat experience. However, by this point in the war, the Army had churned out so many pilots that Rod was no longer needed on the frontlines. Thus, Rod Rodmyre finished the war stateside, as an instructor pilot for the P-47 Thunderbolt.

After the war, most of his friends continued to fly as commercial aviators. Rod, however, chose to hang up his wings. After his discharge from the US Army, he never flew again. "I had flown the best fighter planes of World War II, and any other flying would be boring." Returning to Minnesota, he finished college on the GI Bill. During that time, an old childhood friend introduced him to Miss Margaret Boehmlehner, whom he married in 1948.

Rod began his professional, post-war career in the home appliance industry. After 38 years, he retired as a senior manager at the Whirlpool Corporation. Both before and after his retirement, Rod remained an active volunteer in his community. He devoted several hours to the Pilgrim Lutheran Church in Minneapolis, serving on its School Board and mentoring its Boy Pioneers program. He also served on the Board of

Regents at St. Croix Lutheran High School.

Floyd "Rod" Rodmyre passed away on September 17, 2014 at the age of 92. He was the last surviving American Spitfire pilot.

6
EYEWITNESS NORMANDY

Paratrooper Jim Carroll Recalls the D-Day Invasion.
June 6, 1944.

Jim Carroll was an unlikely hero. A native Minnesotan, he joined the Army after he and three friends had seen a movie about paratroopers. Fascinated by the concept of parachute infantry, Jim and his buddies decided to visit the Army recruiter the following Monday. It was November 1942, and the US had been at war for nearly a year. "I got to where we were supposed to meet," Jim recalled—but his friends were nowhere to be found. "I was the only one who showed. I guess the rest of them had a change of heart over the weekend." He thus went to the recruiting station alone.

The next day, Jim was sent to Jefferson Barracks in St. Louis, Missouri where, not surprisingly, he spent his first day in the Army peeling potatoes. It was the stereotypical, mundane task that often befell new recruits and unlucky privates. It wasn't long, however, before he found himself in Basic Training and Jump School at Camp Toccoa, Georgia. To earn the coveted jump wings, he had to make five qualifying parachute jumps from a C-47 at an altitude of 1,300 feet. Lining up along the inside of the fuselage, Jim and his fellow paratroops would hook their "static lines" to an overhead wire that ran the length of the plane. The static line was generally a fifteen-foot cord attached to the parachute on a trooper's back. Once the trooper jumped from the plane, the static line would extend until taught, at which point it would deploy the parachute from its pack as the trooper continued falling towards the ground.

"The first one was the easiest one," he said, "because I didn't know what was happening." Still, that first jump was a nerve-racking experience because the jumper in front of him broke his leg upon hitting the drop zone. "I could hear his leg snap when it hit the ground," said Jim. "I could hear it crack. That made me tense up a little bit."

Jim was assigned to the 501st Parachute Infantry Regiment, 101st Airborne Division. The regiment spent most of 1943 training at Camp Mackall and conducting maneuvers in Tennessee. "I remember one time, everybody's paycheck was shortened 11 cents," he said. "They told us later it was to pay the farmer back for the chickens we [the regiment] stole. I never even got a smell of those chickens." That November, Jim's regiment was sent to Boston and loaded onto a transport to England. "I was seasick every day," he recalled. "I've always had trouble with motion sickness and it was a rough crossing." Soon, however, Jim and the rest of the 501st, were camped at Newberry, England, where their training intensified. They were preparing for the invasion of mainland Europe. Nearly every day, Jim and his fellow paratroopers had to study the unit's "sand tables," scaled mockups of the terrain in Normandy.

By the first of June, the 501st had been marshaled into the airfields from which they would take flight. While the Allied ships stormed the beaches of Normandy, Jim and his fellow paratroops would jump into the Axis-held territory farther inland. "There were 490 planes in the 101st Airborne, with over 6,600 paratroopers. The standard plane was the C-47, the military version of the DC-3." As Jim Carroll described it: "It was the workhorse of the Army." During this first wave of the invasion, every paratrooper would be carrying nearly 100 pounds of equipment.

During their final preparations on the evening of June 5, he noticed some commotion from the other side of the airfield. As it turned out, General Eisenhower had come to meet with several of the paratroopers, wishing them well as they embarked upon the "Great Crusade." The resulting photograph from that meeting became one of the most iconic images of World War II. Jim could see and hear the bustle of activity, but he couldn't get close enough to see Eisenhower. "We wanted to go over and see what was happening but, of course, we couldn't leave our areas."

Nearly an hour after sunset, the first wave of aircraft carrying the 501st departed the British airfield. "England was on double daylight savings time," he recalled, "so it was still light after 10 o' clock at night." Each plane departed the runway at 7-second intervals. "The planes circled for a while as they got into the correct formation…and then headed off over the English Channel." There was still some lingering daylight in the sky as the planes reached their cruising altitude; and Jim recalled seeing faint traces of the invasion fleet below. By his estimate, there must have been thousands of ships headed to the coast of Northern France.

Suddenly, an eruption of anti-aircraft fire shattered the silence of their

Jim Carroll. Paratrooper in the 101st Airborne Division.

predawn flight. As soon as the C-47s vectored over the coast of Normandy: "That's when the fireworks started. Now and then, you could hear a piece of shrapnel hit the side of the airplane." Ironically, Jim admitted that he was too physically ill to be nervous. Motion sickness had once again rendered his stomach unreliable. "There was a slop bucket on the plane for those who had to throw up, but a couple of the guys didn't make it to the bucket. That stench didn't help. Plus, you were carrying all that equipment and you had your parachute harness on as tight as you could get it. I was so miserable; I just didn't care what happened."

Normally, the C-47s would slow down as they approached the drop zone. And Jim could deduce the change in speed by the sound of the planes' engines. "But out plane never slowed down at all," he said. Given the intensity of the *ack-ack* fire, he could hardly blame the pilots for maintaining their top speed.

Slower planes, after all, made easier targets.

"The men formed a line in the middle of the plane and attached their cables to the static line above their heads. It was up to the man behind you to make sure your cable wasn't tangled in your gear." Every paratrooper on board kept his eye on the glowing red light above the fuselage door. Once it turned green, every soldier would jump through the hatch, one after another. Jim recalled the very moment at which the indicator light switched from red to green: "Once the line starts moving, that's it. It's just pushing, pushing, pushing." Within seconds, Jim and his fellow jumpers were out the door.

Seconds later, Jim felt the violent jolt of his canopy opening. And the blast of cold air, as he later recalled, was enough to cure him of his motion sickness. Unlike his training missions in the States, this combat jump was executed from a mere *500 feet*—"and the first hundred feet were spent hoping your parachute was going to open." Of course, Jim's parachute did open, and he landed on the drop zone unscathed.

"The first thing you do is get out of your parachute, and then you have to put your gun together." They had to field strip their rifles for the jump, and had practiced putting them back together in the dark. "I had just got mine together," said Jim, "when I could see these dark forms coming at me."

But these dark forms didn't quite look human.

Not wanting to take a chance, Jim Carroll drew his rifle and pointed it in their direction. Prior to the invasion, every paratrooper had been issued a clicker—"so we could find each other in the dark." One click would be answered by two clicks, thus indicating a fellow trooper. Jim used his clicker, but got no response. The slow-moving forms continued in his direction. His finger was pressed against the trigger when the shapes finally came to light. "Then all at once I could see them. Oh my gosh, they were cows! With all the shells exploding and the airplanes roaring… they were scared and wandering in the field."

Shaking off the bovine encounter, Jim checked his gear and himself. "I wanted to see if I was all in one piece," he said. Luckily, his gear had survived the jump…and he had no visible wounds. "I could barely see a little patch of woods over in the distance, and I headed for that. I felt like I was all alone. I couldn't see even one other trooper around me." But as Jim crept farther into the woods, he began to hear muffled sounds. Not sure if they were humans or more cows, he pulled out his clicker and clicked it. "The response was immediate"—a dozen other clickers rang out in the night.

He had found his comrades.

Unfortunately, these comrades were from a different company. During the chaos of the Normandy invasion, the Allied airborne troops had been scattered across northern France, many of them landing miles away from their intended drop zones. "I didn't know where the rest of my guys were," said Jim, "so I stayed with this group." Together, they marched for nearly a mile to the regiment's objective, "which was to set up a roadblock near Carentan."

Their mission was to block the roads and bridges to prevent the Germans from reinforcing the beaches at Normandy. "It was an interesting four days," he recalled. "We didn't have to worry so much about what was ahead of us…our real problem was with the Germans that were retreating from the beaches. There were firefights all the time." At the end of those four days, however, the airborne troops were relieved by the US infantry units that had broken out from Omaha Beach. "Were we ever glad to see them," he recalled. "They had fresh water and they had food."

After being relieved by the straight-leg infantry, Jim and his fellow paratroopers were sent back to Cherbourg, mopping up pockets of German resistance and wrangling POWs. Then it was back to England for refitting, and a follow-on combat jump into Holland. Like many in the 101st, Jim later found himself in Bastogne for the Battle of the Bulge. When the Third Army finally reached the beleaguered paratroopers, Jim had a fortuitous reunion with his younger brother, Jackson, who was currently serving under Patton's command. In many cases, the war had drawn entire families into its service. Indeed, it wasn't uncommon for every brother within a single family to be drafted into the military. Running into a sibling overseas was always a welcome break from the deadly routines of wartime service.

In all, Jim Carroll made eleven combat jumps with the 101st Airborne Division. When Germany surrendered in May 1945, Jim was alerted that his unit would redeploy to the Pacific. But while training for the possibility of island-hopping combat (and an invasion of the Japanese homeland), Jim was relieved to hear that Japan had surrendered.

After the war, Jim returned to Minnesota and settled into a quiet life as a machinist. For more than twenty years, he was the shop foreman for Durkee-Atwood, a prominent manufacturer of industrial V-belts and other automotive products. Upon his retirement, however, he transitioned into a *second* career as a school bus driver and charter bus driver—jobs he held until the early 2000s.

For most of his adult life, Jim never spoke of the war. However, one day in 1980 when he was ice fishing with his daughter, she asked him why he never shared any of his wartime experiences.

"No one ever asked," he replied.

But in the years that followed, more people began to ask about his experiences in Normandy. This, in turn, led to a number of speaking engagements. These included appearances at schools, community functions, in documentary films, and TV/Radio interviews. In 2014, Senator Amy Klobuchar and the French Council awarded Jim Carroll the French Legion of Honor, recognizing his service in the liberation of France from Nazi occupation.

Jim Carroll passed away on March 28, 2017 at the age of 93.

7
BATTLEGROUND: CBI

Denzel Alexander (US Army) and Bob Maynard (US Army, OSS)
in the China-Burma-India Theater

The China–Burma–India (CBI) theater was, in many ways, the forgotten battlefront of World War II. "There are no infantry divisions here," said one soldier, "only detachments, special units, makeshift outfits, and made-over GIs. All the big divisions are in Europe or on Pacific islands. This is the forgotten war. This is where you fight and die, and nobody seems to give a damn whether your corpse is picked up for a halfway decent burial."

By most accounts, Burma was the epicenter of this human misery. "One day is just like all the others. You climb over vines and see things slither out of the way before you put your foot down. You walk around the thick things that hang from branches because you think you see them move." Indeed, every vine seemed to resemble a snake.

The worst offenders, however, were the leeches.

"They cling to your pants and leggings and squirm to get inside at your blood," said one GI. "Every few minutes you stop and scrape or burn the lousy parasites off your skin. Sometimes, you have to cut them off with a knife because their heads are buried under flesh…sucking your blood. You dig for their heads. If you don't get them out, you'll have a lump the size of a plum. So, you get them, even if it means taking some meat with it."

These sentiments would be echoed by the young Private Denzel Alexander when he arrived in Burma as a combat engineer. Born in Kentucky in 1924, he moved to Detroit when his father became a layout engineer in the automotive industry. On December 7, 1941, Denzel was listening to the afternoon radio when the announcer broke in, saying: "We interrupt this program to announce that Pearl Harbor has been attacked by a large Japanese force." There was no indication of how many had been killed, or what the extent of the damage had been.

But he knew the country was going to war.

"I was almost 18," he said. "I knew I was going to be graduating in a few months and perhaps be drafted."

Initially, Denzel wanted to join the US Army Air Forces. He had been attracted to the pilot lifestyle and, given the manpower needs of the war, the pathways to becoming a pilot had been greatly simplified. "I went to the Air Force induction center to enlist; they gave me an all-day exam"—consisting of a written portion and a physical evaluation. "I passed the written test, and I passed the physicals…but I was five pounds *under*weight."

To his surprise, the Air Force had rejected him for being too skinny.

"And I thought a pilot had to be lightweight!" he chuckled.

"So, a few months later, I was drafted into the Army and put into the Engineer Corps." But while completing his Basic Training at Camp McCoy, Wisconsin (now Fort McCoy), Denzel had one last opportunity to become a pilot. An announcement appeared on the bulletin board, stating that the Air Force needed more pilots to support the upcoming invasions of Italy and France. "They said if you're already in the service, we'll count you as being physically fit," Denzel recalled. "So, if you can pass the written exam, we'll transfer you to the Air Force cadets."

Denzel took the written exam and passed it, again.

"They sent me down to Miami Beach with the cadets and booked me into the New Yorker Hotel." From there, Denzel and his fellow air cadets began pre-flight training, until the cruel mistress of fate (and the Army's bureaucratic myopia) foiled his plans yet again. While he was attending the USAAF ground school, the invasion of Europe was already underway. The Allies had secured a foothold on the Italian mainland and were preparing to descend upon Occupied France. Thus, as Denzel recalled, the Air Force essentially told him: "The invasion has gone so much better and so much faster than we had expected. We've taken in way too many [soldiers] from the regular force [for pilot training]. So, if we took you from the Army after such-and-such date, you will be returned to your unit."

Denzel missed that cutoff date by one week.

"So, there was the *second* time I missed the Air Force!"

The Army then sent him to Fort Bragg, North Carolina, where he was assigned to the 1304th Engineers—"and I went to Burma with that outfit."

Denzel Alexander.

At first, however, he had no idea where the 1304th was going. Europe seemed like the logical destination, given the trajectory of the Allied campaign and the "Europe First" Policy. But as their troop ship, the USS *Anderson*, left Newport News, Virginia, Denzel and his shipmates were surprised to see her steer through the Panama Canal, down to Australia, and up to Bombay, India. And the *Anderson* had made her journey alone. "We weren't part of a convoy," he said, "and the *Anderson* was sleek and fast; we could outrun any submarine."

The 1304th Engineers unloaded at Bombay and boarded a train

eastbound to Burma. "If you ever went across India by train, it was terrible," he said. "You see, India at that time was under British rule. And there were three big sections of India, each controlled by a Maharaja, kind of like a dictator." Each of the three Maharajas had used a different railroad company to lay track within his respective part of the country.

Thus, all three Maharajas had railroads, but the tracks were incongruent to each other.

"They were all different gauges!" Denzel laughed.

So, at various parts of the journey, the 1304th Engineer Battalion had to be ferried across the river by rowboat, two men at a time. At that capacity, it took an entire day for the battalion to cross the river. "It was really something," he said, "I wouldn't want to do it again. But we got into Burma, and we were there to build the Ledo Road"—later known as the famous "Stillwell Road."

"Burma was a lot like Florida," Denzel recalled—"a long and narrow nation. The old Burma Road ran all the way up Burma into the Himalaya Mountains and over into China. Well, the Japs had conquered Burma. And for us to try to come up *through* Burma, well, that would have taken us a long time and a lot of expenses. So, we came from the north, through the jungles of Burma and built the Ledo Road to hook up with the old Burma Road."

Specifically, Denzel's unit had been tasked to build tactical bridges along the road. "We built three kinds: wooden bridges for smaller streams; pontoon bridges for medium-sized streams; and Bailey bridges for large rivers. We built those all across Burma. The jungle had a lot of streams flowing down out of the mountains, and there had to be a bridge there, otherwise you couldn't get trucks and tanks through it."

But the bridge-building operations were fraught with peril... particularly from the prying eyes of the Japanese. "Merrill's Marauders had driven all the Japanese out of North Burma," he said, "but they would come up the river at night." Denzel knew that the Japanese still had spies in the area; and if a bridge were about to be finished, "they would come up the river at night and try to blow it up." As Denzel recalled: "We had machine guns set up on both sides of the river and hidden in the jungle"—ready to open fire at the first sign of enemy movement.

Thankfully, the Japanese never reached any of Denzel's bridges.

"And we did sink an awful lot of their boats!"

At times, however, it seemed that Denzel had more to fear from the local wildlife than the Japanese. "A lot of things happened in the jungle," he said. "The jungle is not like a forest. A forest has trees; the jungle has *everything*. And at certain times between building a bridge, we'd have some free time and we could pretty much do what we wanted. So, three of us decided to go out and explore the jungle."

Denzel and his two friends hit the trails until they came upon a fallen tree.

One of his more daring comrades jumped atop the fallen trunk, using the low-lying branches to hoist himself up. His climbing expedition was cut short, however, when he came face-to-face with a cobra.

"And this one was *big!*" Denzel recalled.

By his recollection, its body was as thick as a human arm. "It was leaning over the tree, spitting at us." Denzel's buddy fell from the tree in a panic, but Denzel quickly shot the snake with his M1 rifle. "We decided not to go any farther."

A few days later, while sleeping in his tent, Denzel awoke feeling an odd sensation on his chest. Each tent could hold three soldiers, sleeping on their standard-issue Army cots. "I woke up sometime in the middle of the night…the moon isn't shining and its cloudy, pitch black. I couldn't see a thing, but I kept feeling something on my chest." From what he could deduce, this foreign object had a long, thin body with a wider mass at its top.

"*I was convinced it was a cobra.*"

Snakes were cold-blooded, and often slipped into warmer areas to maintain their body heat. This cobra had likely crawled through the tent flap and slithered into his cot.

"What in the world am I going to do?" he thought to himself.

"My first thought was, well, just stay here all night," and perhaps the snake would slither away on its own. But then he realized if he fell asleep, and inadvertently shifted his body, the snake would bite him. "To be bit by a cobra in the jungle…forget it! I figured the snake was over my left arm, but my right arm was free." Thus, Denzel reasoned that he could grab the cobra by its hood with his right hand, lift it up, and grab its lower body with his left hand, incapacitating the snake long enough for his friends to kill it with their bayonets.

Silently, Denzel began to psych himself up.

"Ok, on the count of three…1, 2, 3…I couldn't do it. Second time: 1, 2, 3…I *still* couldn't do it." He kept thinking the snake would bite him in the neck.

"Finally, I said I've got to do it. So…1, 2, 3…and I grabbed it!"

As Denzel screamed and strangled the offensive snake, he realized that this "snake" was, in fact, his own left arm. His left arm had fallen asleep and he hadn't even realized it. Still, the commotion had been enough to awaken his tentmates, both of whom scrambled for their flashlights.

"Denzel! What's the matter?!"

But Denzel, now realizing he was ahold of his left arm, wasn't going to admit that he had mistaken his own appendage for a venomous snake. "If I tell them," he thought, "I'll be known as the 'snake man' for the rest of my time here." He thus turned to his tentmates and said: "Sorry, I guess I just had a bad dream. Go on back to sleep."

Imaginary reptiles notwithstanding, Denzel's most memorable story from his time in Burma involved a seemingly ill-fated cargo pilot trying to navigate the "Hump" of the Himalayas. "The Himalayas are the highest mountains in the world; and the Burma Road weaved around through the Himalaya Mountains into China." But until the Allies could retake those sections of the Burma Road, the only way to get supplies into China was by air. "And we called it 'flying over the 'Hump.'" The Allied cargo planes, however, were often so heavily-laden that they couldn't gain enough altitude to fly over the Himalayan peaks. They had to fly at lower altitudes between and amongst the mountainsides and jagged escarpments. As expected, maneuvering a utility plane among these imposing obstacles required a high degree of airmanship.

"We had one pilot," said Denzel, "who had some heavy equipment and had to take two or three extra men to come along and show the Chinese how to operate it." The pilot, his crew, and the additional tag-alongs took off from Burma and went flying through the mountains. But as he rounded the plane between two peaks, he suddenly realized he had made a wrong turn.

"He was in a box canyon," Denzel recalled.

This problematic piece of terrain had steep walls on three sides, and only *one* point of egress…which was now behind them. "He couldn't park anywhere, and he couldn't turn around," Denzel continued. "So, he started trying to climb over that [canyon wall] at the end." The not-so-nimble cargo plane began climbing so steeply, rattling and trembling, that the pilot was certain his engine would stall.

Miraculously, however, the plane made it over the canyon wall, but not without scraping its underbelly against the jutting rocks. "It tore out the bottom of the fuselage, ripping a hole about six feet wide along the bottom," whereupon the plane started losing altitude. Meanwhile, the errant pilot turned to his crew and said: "Men, we're not going to make it. The only thing we can do is this: If you five men will bail out"—pointing to the five heaviest crewmen aboard—"you can make it back to northern

Bob Maynard.

Burma by tonight." The pilot insisted that he would try to stay airborne with the equipment operators in tow.

"If I can make it [into China], fine. If not, I'll have to bail out, too," said the pilot.

The five heavier airmen reluctantly strapped on their parachutes and did as they were told. "Five heavy men," said Denzel, "could weigh close to half a ton," thus reducing the plane's overall weight, and giving the pilot a chance to land at his destination in China.

The five parachuting airmen made it back to the Allied airfield, "but we never heard whether the pilot had made it," said Denzel. "We kept asking, and every time we'd see an airman, we'd ask: 'Did you hear about that pilot?'" Yet nobody seemed to know what had happened to the pilot or his plane. "There were three or four landing bases on the other side of the mountain," Denzel recalled. So, there were no guarantees of finding an airman with knowledge of the seemingly-doomed cargo plane.

Yet, several years later, a chance encounter with a VA doctor in Florida revealed the fate of that wayward pilot. After the war, Denzel was ordained as a Baptist minister and pastored a church in Palm Bay, Florida for several years. Before his final relocation to Minnesota, Denzel was chatting with his young VA doctor:

"Hey Denzel," said the young doctor, "I never did ask you; where did you serve?"

"Burma…near the Himalayas."

"Oh, my father was over there."

"Oh?" said Denzel. "Was he working on the road?"

"No, he was in the Air Force; but let me tell you an interesting story."

The young doctor proceeded to tell him the story about how his father had been flying a plane (carrying a load of heavy equipment) whose bottom was torn off by a canyon cliff, which in turn precipitated an early bailout for the five heaviest crewmen on board.

"You gotta be kidding me!!" Denzel exclaimed. "I've been trying to get the answer to that for years. Did he make it?"

"Oh yea, he made it," the doctor beamed. "He's here in Florida with me and my mother…they live about two doors down."

After several decades of preaching, Denzel Alexander retired from the pulpit in the early 2000s. Now at the age of 97, he lives quietly with his family in Chanhassen, Minnesota.

On December 7, 1941, Bob Maynard was an Ivy League student, enjoying his life as a college baseball player at Princeton University. In 1943, however, he left the comforts of academia and joined the US Army at Fort Bragg, North Carolina. Having some college under his belt, he applied for and was accepted to Officer Candidate School (OCS) at Fort Sill, Oklahoma. Commissioned as a Field Artillery officer in May 1944, he was made a forward observer (FO).

The FO, as he described it, was a liaison of death.

He could ensure delivery of deadly-accurate cannon fire. "But, if you make a mistake in your mathematical calculations, you can bring fire down on yourself."

As a newly-minted artilleryman, he arrived at Fort Jackson, South Carolina—one of the primary hubs for personnel going to the European Theater. However, he had barely set foot on Fort Jackson when he was cornered by a Major Weiner, who was compiling a list of the top-rated artillery officers coming through the stateside Replacement Depot. "He asked me a series of questions," Bob recalled.

"Do you have any college?"

"Any foreign language experiences?"

"Do you have any objections to taking parachute training?"

"Do you have any dependents?"

Bob grew more uncomfortable with each passing question…until Weiner asked him: "Would you prefer being in an outfit where you have some degree of discretion over your own destiny, and plan innovative things on your missions?"

Weiner was recruiting for the Office of Strategic Services (OSS).

Bob liked the idea of having autonomy…and being in a unit where creativity was rewarded rather than punished. One week later, he received orders to Washington, DC.

"The people at Jackson thought it was a very strange order," he said, "because you normally got orders to go from base to base," and almost never to DC. His orders included a message to call a Washington-based telephone number. "I called it and they told me that the next morning, I would be taken in for psychological training."

It was perhaps the most peculiar experience of his young life.

For psychological training, each of the OSS candidates were hoarded into the same building and, regardless of rank, were dressed in unmarked Army fatigues. "You didn't know if the guy next to you was an Admiral, or a private, or a sergeant…and we all had false names and backgrounds." Indeed, each of the candidates had been given a character role, and was told to keep that identity while mingling with his comrades. As Bob recalled: "I was supposed to be from Kansas, and my dad was supposed to be a college professor out there." In reality, Bob was from New Jersey, and his father had *no* ties to academia. Throughout this role-playing exercise, "psychiatrists would observe if you were a good leader or a good follower," said Bob, "because you don't need all leaders, you need some followers."

Five days later, Bob and the other candidates progressed to the physical evaluation trials. To his surprise, this portion of the training took place in a "great big mansion," he said, "without much furniture." Apart from the OSS trainees, Bob noticed that many of the mansion's residents were GIs who had been wounded in combat. Unbeknownst to Bob, however, this "mansion" was the former Congressional Country Club. "It had gone bankrupt, and General [Bill] Donovan had rented it as a rest home for people coming back from overseas duty, and for those training to go overseas." The physical portion of the OSS training included a lot of "creeping and crawling under barbed wire, jumping off practice towers for parachute training, and explosives going off all over the place." Curiously, the man in charge of the physical regimen was Wes Fesler—a college football Hall of Famer who later became head coach for the University of Minnesota.

Upon completing the physical module of his OSS pre-selection, Bob reported to OSS Headquarters, near the Old Naval Hospital in Washington, DC. He was one of five OSS selectees reporting to Headquarters that day—"and the man in charge said we were very lucky because '109' was in town, and he wanted to talk to new arrivals."

Bob had no idea who this "109" may have been; but he sounded important.

"So, we all went over to the next building…and there was '109'— it was Major General Bill Donovan." Known as "Wild Bill," General Donovan was already a legend within the American defense community. He had been awarded the Medal of Honor, the Distinguished Service Cross, *and* the Croix de Guerre for his service in World War I. He had also been an Assistant Attorney General under Calvin Coolidge. His colorful personality (and candid bluntness), however, didn't always sit well with the Washington establishment. "He was an expert at stepping on toes," said Bob, "and people said he had as many enemies in Washington as he did overseas."

Today, Donovan wasted no time. When he met the young Bob Maynard, he asked him: "Lieutenant, do you know why you're here?"

"No sir," Bob replied.

"Well, I don't either," said Donovan. "But we'll find something interesting and worthwhile for you to do."

Bob later said that this exchange was illustrative of how the OSS recruited its personnel. In the military, established units were sent on missions according to their function—for example, a fighter squadron or an armored division. In the OSS, however, units were formed *ad hoc* from a "pool" of specialists. "We had doctors, radio operators, demolition experts, map readers, and even people we'd gotten out of Alcatraz who were good forgers…because we had to forge a lot of documents in the work we were doing."

At first, the OSS had tapped Bob for duty in the Philippines, where he'd be spying on enemy ship movements. But it soon came to light that any OSS operatives within General MacArthur's territory would be transferred directly to his command.

"And that was unacceptable to Bill Donovan," said Bob.

In fact, Donovan and MacArthur had been professional rivals and "frenemies" since serving together under General John Pershing during the hunt for Pancho Villa. As a result of this bureaucratic rivalry between the OSS and MacArthur's Southwest Pacific Area command, Bob Maynard soon found himself reassigned to the CBI theater.

"I was put on the slow boat to China, down around Australia, and into Calcutta," he said, where he boarded the train to the Chabua Airfield in India. It was the primary hub for flights going "over the hump" of the Himalayas to deliver supplies into China. By now, Stillwell's men had driven the Japanese back to the Burma Road, but the enemy's air defense capabilities over the Himalayas were still going strong. "They shot down an awful lot of C-47s and their escorts," Bob recalled. "And if the Japs didn't get them, the air currents and bad weather got a lot more. That passageway through the Himalayas was called 'The Aluminum Graveyard,'"—but Bob's flight over the hump was surprisingly pleasant. "We didn't have any attacks, and we landed in Kunming."

Reporting to OSS Detachment 202, Bob met Colonel Richard Heppner, the officer-in-charge. Heppner said that he had looked through the records of his incoming personnel, and found a job that might suit Bob well. "It was coordinating missions," said Bob—ensuring that the field agents got what they needed, and that their intelligence data was passed along to the right venue.

"It was, I think, the best job in the OSS for the CBI theater," said Bob.

As a rule of thumb, everything in the OSS was on a "need-to-know" basis. No information was shared among the different operational sections unless it facilitated their unique missions. For example, an agent in the OSS Propaganda Section didn't know what the Sabotage Section was doing, or what the Air Operations Section was doing. "They were all separate," Bob remembered.

Coordinating spy missions was a monumental job for a young lieutenant, and Bob was certain that there were more-qualified individuals than he. "But I had three qualifications that no one else had," he recalled. "First, I was available…most of the people who arrived [in Det 202] already had assignments. Second, they noticed I came out of the Field Artillery,"—Colonel Heppner and his executive officer, Major Bill Davis, were both artillerymen. "But the clincher was that Heppner, Davis, and I had all played baseball at Princeton. That's what did it!" he laughed.

Taking stock of his new responsibilities as an intelligence coordinator, Bob had his work cut out for him. "China was chaotic," he remembered. "There were espionages on all sides…even amongst the Allies!" As Bob recalled, Chiang Kai-shek, Mao Zedong, the British, and the French were all spying on each other. To make matters worse, Chiang and Mao seemed to be more interested in killing each other than fighting the Japanese. From what Bob could deduce, the collective attitude between Mao's Communists and the Kuomintang was: "Let the Westerners defeat the Japanese. In the meantime, we're going to hoard things so we can fight each other and gain control of China after the war."

In April 1945, a few months into his duties as an intelligence coordinator, Bob received an unexpected visit from Wild Bill Donovan, the commanding general whom he'd met in Washington prior to arriving at Detachment 202.

"He came to China for a surprise visit," said Bob, "and he didn't bring an aide."

However, remembering Bob from their prior meeting at OSS Headquarters, Donovan tapped him to be his aide. "I got to know him and had some amusing but meaningful experiences with him."

One such experience included Donovan's need for a barber. On his first day at the OSS station, Donovan asked:

"Do we have a barber here, Lieutenant?"

"Yes sir. We can have him here in the morning."

"Good, because I need a haircut and a shave."

Detachment 202 had a young corporal who provided haircuts as a hobbyist barber. But when Bob approached him with a request to cut General Donovan's hair, the corporal refused. "I couldn't cut his hair; I'd be too nervous."

But luckily, Bob had a contingency plan.

As it turned out, the OSS staff also got their haircuts from a local Chinese man—"tall, about 60 years old, with a smock and a scraggly beard." The Chinese barber arrived as requested, and sat down in front of Donovan, opening his pigskin satchel to reveal a full complement of barber tools—including scissors and a straight razor.

"Is this one of our men?" asked Donovan.

"Well," said Bob, "he cuts our hair, sir."

"Has he been cleared for security?"

Bob Maynard (left) stands with Major General William Donovan and the members of OSS Detachment 202.

"I don't think so," Bob winced.

"And you're going to let him near my neck with *those*?" Donovan asked, pointing to the scissors and razor. Indeed, no one in Detachment 202 had vetted this Chinese barber to ensure he had no enemy connections. Luckily, the young corporal was standing by, and quickly jumped in to give Donovan a fresh haircut and a smooth shave.

All the while, Bob sat nervously, expecting that once the haircut was complete, he'd get a severe reprimand, or possibly terminated from the OSS. But to his surprise (and his relief) Donovan simply stood up from his chair and said: "The corporal would have been a better first choice, don't you think so, Lieutenant?"

Bob nodded in agreement.

But such was the way Donovan handled his subordinates. Simple redirections got better results than terse reprimands.

The next morning, Donovan was inspecting the grounds of the OSS station when he asked Bob how the staff maintained physical security of the compound. "Well, the compound has walls around it," said Bob, "we have an Officer of the Day, with guards, and we have Doberman Pinchers" on roving patrols.

"Well," said Donovan, "I'm holding *you* personally responsible."

Donovan was only kidding, but the young Bob Maynard thought he was serious. Still, Bob took Donovan's playful admonition to a curious extreme. Indeed, the next morning, Donovan found Colonel Heppner.

"You know what this kid did last night?" he told Heppner, referring to Bob.

"I was kidding when I told him about the security," Donovan continued. "But I tried to get out of my room last night to use the bathroom and I couldn't get out…he had moved his bed against the door!" Apparently, Bob had barricaded Donovan's door in case the high walls, roving guards, and Doberman Pinchers failed to stop an advancing intruder. But by the same token, Bob hadn't realized that the impromptu barricade would have also prevented Donovan's easy egress from the room.

Donovan and Heppner just laughed.

Donovan's trip to China had three objectives, all of which were top secret. "He knew about the Atomic Bomb, the timing, and what the plans were," Bob remembered. As such, Donovan's first order of business was to meet with Allied commanders in the CBI and ask them: "If this war ended soon, who do you anticipate taking over from the Japanese in Burma, Laos, and China?" Although Donovan had posed the question as a hypothetical, Bob said Donovan already knew the answer: Given the trajectory of this conflict, there was no way the European powers could hold onto their colonial possessions much longer. Nationalist forces were already on the rise in India, Burma, and French Indochina.

Second, Donovan had to compile data for President Roosevelt, outlining permanent functions for the OSS after the war. "But FDR died and Truman put it on the backburner," said Bob. Still, Donovan's memos outlined the doctrinal precepts for what would become the modern CIA…including espionage and propaganda. "There were two kinds of propaganda," Bob continued, "*white* propaganda, which was just the news; and *black* propaganda, where you make things up that are to your benefit, lies included. That's what our OSS propaganda section did." Part and parcel to Donovan's theories was to collectivize intel data into a "central intelligence" apparatus that could easily relay information to different field agencies. "Prior to that," said Bob, "the Army had its own intelligence staff; the Navy had its own staff; the FBI had theirs"—and these agencies rarely spoke to one another.

Third, Donovan had come to China to organize teams to rescue Allied POWs in Manchuria and elsewhere throughout the CBI because, as Bob recalled: "Intelligence showed that the Japanese pattern was to either execute POWs at the end of the war, abandon them, or put them on another Death March."

However, Donovan nearly lost *all* the paperwork for these top-secret missions when the Kunming OSS station flooded. During a torrential downpour, the rising water (polluted by raw sewage and street litter) had seeped into the compound, thereby forcing Donovan and his staff to eat their meals at a local Chinese restaurant until the flood receded.

Naturally, Donovan wouldn't leave his briefcase containing his top-secret documents behind at the compound. After all, it contained critical data about the rescue of prisoners and details about the Atomic Bomb. "It was too secure to leave back at Headquarters, so he carried it himself into the restaurant."

After lunch, though, as Donovan, Heppner, and Bob Maynard got back into the car, Donovan turned to Heppner and said:

"Dick, do you have the briefcase?"

"No sir," he replied.

"Lieutenant, do you have it?"

"No sir."

It was then that they realized Donovan had left his briefcase under the restaurant table. "And none of us had the guts to tell him 'Sir, you had it.'" Bob recalled with a chuckle. "And so, we drove back and I ran into the restaurant," said Bob, who was relieved to see that, even among the lunchtime crowd, the briefcase was still under the table.

Bob quickly retrieved it and darted back into the car.

After a brief period of silence, Donovan broke the tension, saying: "I won't tell anyone if you won't." All three of them laughed.

Bob's tour as Donovan's aide also put him in contact with another OSS agent, Paul Cushing Child, "who was in charge of the secret war room, where they had a map and they moved pins," said Bob. "All he did, all day, was move pins wherever we had agents and operations going on," allowing Donovan and the station chiefs to have real-time situational awareness of where the OSS teams were operating within the CBI.

Bob soon discovered that Paul had a girlfriend: another OSS operative, Julia McWilliams.

Standing at 6'2," she was decidedly tall for a woman. So tall, in fact, that she had been rejected by the WACs and the WAVES. Casting her lot with the OSS, McWilliams eventually arrived at the Kunming station alongside Bob Maynard, where she catalogued the high volume of classified data coming in from field agents. As Bob recalled, if an OSS team needed to blow up a bridge on the Yellow River, "they would go to Julia, and she'd know how many Japanese were nearby; what the bridge construction was; what its weak points were; and how many aircraft might be available." After the war, McWilliams married Paul Child, taking his surname and becoming "Julia Child," the famous chef and American TV personality.

After the war, Bob returned to Princeton, graduating with a degree in international relations. He elected to stay in the Army Reserve, and simultaneously earned a law degree from Harvard. With the outbreak of the Korean War in 1950, Bob was recalled from the Army Reserve and placed in the Counterintelligence Corps. After his final release from the Army in 1953, Bob worked as a corporate attorney: first for the United Shoe Machinery Corporation in Boston; then for Honeywell in Minneapolis. He retired in 1985 as the Senior VP of Legal Affairs for Honeywell. He continued to reside in the Minneapolis–St. Paul area until his passing in 2017, at the age of 94.

8

FROGMAN

DAVID GOULD,
NAVY COMBAT DIVER

limbing to the edge of the black water, Dave Gould readied himself for the oncoming plunge. The muffled gurgling of the PT boat's engine seemed to egg him on as he waited for the signal… "Gould. Get set! Ready, now! Go!"

Dropping over the side, and into the balmy waters of the South Pacific, he re-surfaced just in time to hear the revving of the PT's engine fade into the distance. Just above the waves, barely visible in the moonlight, was the dim outline of Eniwetok—the menacing atoll that had just become the latest target in the "island hopping" campaign.

Swimming towards the amorphous land mass, Dave took stock of the items strapped to his body—Colt .45, a graph paper mapping board… and his cyanide capsule. The training manual had made this poisonous pill sound so matter-of-fact: "If about to be captured, break the capsule in your teeth. Death will be quick and painless"—a fair alternative to what the Japanese would do to him.

Dave Gould was a combat diver—a "Frogman"—but not by choice. In fact, he had become a frogman in the most old-fashioned way: Instead of volunteering, he had been volun-*told*. When he enlisted in the Navy, he had requested to become a Seabee—the Navy's combat engineers. The term "Seabee" came from the abbreviation "CB," referring to the Navy's construction battalions. This rating seemed like a good fit, considering he had been a metalworker before the war. But a seemingly-innocent disclosure on his Classification Card had roped him into the world of combat diving. Under the heading labeled "Hobbies," he wrote "Swimming." After all, he had grown up on the beaches of Long Island, where swimming was a way of life.

Having been tapped for dive training, the Navy quickly hastened him to Underwater Demolitions (UD) school in California. UD was an integral part of the Frogman's repertoire. If he wasn't laying sea mines, he was diffusing them. He was expected to be, in equal parts, a demolitions expert *and* a reconnaissance specialist—taking note of the enemy dispositions, capabilities, and strongpoints. Frogmen like him were part of an elite subculture—the burgeoning "special operations" community. These Frogmen would become the forefathers of the modern-day Navy SEALs.

Tonight was January 6, 1944, his first plunge into the waters surrounding Eniwetok. "It would be six weeks yet before the vast invasion force hit the beaches here," he recalled.

And tonight, Dave wasn't alone.

Elsewhere along the atoll, other Frogmen were treading through the perilous waters, preparing to clear the way for the Allied ground troops that would storm the beaches. This would be the first of four visits Dave Gould would make to the remote atoll. He would come again ten days before the invasion. Then, a third visit the night before D-Day. "And then, hit the beach with the assault wave on D-Day itself"—guiding a platoon of Marine infantry to key points along the enemy's redoubts.

On this first night at Eniwetok, however, he stopped about 100 yards offshore, treading water as he studied the Japanese fortifications in the moonlight. "If there were sentries or guard posts," he said, "they were well-concealed." Swimming over to the edge of the reef, he realized that the landing craft could easily ride over it during high tides. Trafficability of the reef as a function of tides was a critical detail for mission planning— "a matter of life and death," he said, for the Marines and soldiers who would soon be storming the beach.

Wading into the shallows, Dave pulled the mapping board from his leg. Extracting a small grease pencil from his sheath, he began to annotate the enemy fortifications on his map. Under a nearby palm grove stood the telltale figure of a pillbox. "There, off to the right a bit," he said, "a roundish mound indicated a gun pit—a long barrel jutted over it, close to the ground. Nearby were other emplacements, probably for machine guns to sweep the beach." All told, he was confident that the pre-invasion bombardment would make short work of these defenses.

As he waded back and forth across the beach, he was careful to avoid the ominous sea mines bobbing in the water—"ready to set off a blast on contact." But these mines weren't the only obstacles awaiting the Allied landing force. "Metal boat traps loomed silently under the shallows. Trip wires etched faint lines along the sand."

Suddenly, a crouching noise rang out from the beach.

Ducking down into the shallows, Dave saw the faintly luminous silhouette of two Japanese sentries walking along the shore. They were so close that Dave could hear them talking, even over the sound of the breaking waves.

"That had been close!" A little too close for comfort.

In fact, these close calls reminded him how ironically fortunate he was to have the cyanide capsule. If the Japanese captured him, they would gleefully torture and kill him—but not before extracting as much information as possible.

His watch now read 3:00am. "Time to start back." A Frogman had only *one* chance to rendezvous with his pickup boat. For if he missed the incoming PT boat, it wouldn't risk another pass to look for him in the darkness. "That might tip off the whole invasion approach," he said. Thus, if a Frogman missed his boat, he had two options: (1) swim out to sea, hoping to find a friendly base before the sharks got to him, or (2) swim ashore and evade the enemy by living in the bush. "That was damn unlikely on a small island like Eniwetok," he said. "No place to hide!"

It was nearly dawn when Dave reached the pickup point, one mile out from the beach. In the pre-dawn darkness, he could see the heads of his fellow Frogmen, bobbing along the water as they waited for the pickup boat. Suddenly, the PT boat appeared over the horizon, piercing the charcoal-gray aura of the morning darkness with its rambling Packard engine. As the boat came nearer, Dave could see the pickup man seated at the bow.

"A heavy loop was slung around his shoulder," he recalled, "trailed down over the side."

What ensued was a carefully-rehearsed choreography wherein the pickup man would lower the loop down to the surface, ready to catch the extended arm of the nearest frogman, hoisting him aboard.

When the pickup man got to Dave, he caught the loop with such brute force that it felt as though his shoulder might rip off. Tumbling back onto the deck of the PT, Dave thought to himself:

"Visit Number One is nearly over—thank the Lord!"

The PT boat raced out to its destroyer escort. Once aboard, Dave would be debriefed by the shipboard intelligence officers, examining his maps and asking him what he'd seen along the nighttime shores.

Four weeks later, Dave returned to Eniwetok for his second visit. "This was no mere reconnaissance trip," he said.

This time, he was laden with explosives.

"A string of wires, detonators, and sub-surface buoys" trailed behind him as he swam through the night. Tonight, he was putting his demolition skills to the test.

As he swam up the ring of floating mines, he carefully taped blocks of TNT between their deadly spikes, fastening the lead wires with a tailor's dexterity. Nimble, steady hands were a necessity in this line of work. One false move could detonate the sea mine, killing him and alerting the Japanese to other Frogmen's presence. While fastening the TNT to some of the floating mines, Dave successfully disarmed others—slowly but deftly unscrewing the Japanese detonator caps.

For the underwater tank traps, Dave intermittently taped them with alternating quantities of high explosive charges and a dollop of plastic explosives. Either of these demolition assets would suffice to disable the tank traps. Fastening the lead lines and trip lines, he strung them out to the deeper waters beyond the reef, securing each one to a marker buoy. He then dove down, anchoring the buoy, and preparing it for the "electric plunger detonator," that he would attach the night before D-Day.

On the eve of the invasion, he prepped the last of his offshore demolitions before wading back to the atoll. Tonight, he would reconnoiter the inland Japanese outposts *on foot*. The Intelligence staff wanted him to "find lanes of access off the beach and into the island"—presumably without getting captured.

As he quietly ambled onto the beach, his skin crawled as he beheld the sight in front of him. The displaced sand revealed an unmistakable pattern of anti-personnel mines.

The Japanese knew the invasion fleet was on its way.

Moving like a shadow amongst the trees, Dave spied a narrow road leading up from the beach. Several yards inland, the road ended at a cluster of buildings—barracks for the Japanese defenders. "An attack down the road would run right into them," he said, "flat, open areas good for flanking attacks."

From his shadowy redoubts in the jungle, Dave could hear the muffled staccato of enemy voices piercing through the night. "The place was crawling with Japanese." Not wanting to press his luck any further, Dave slowly withdrew towards the beach, back into the surf, and out to his designated pickup point.

"D-Day was tomorrow morning," he said. And the American task force would initiate its pre-dawn bombardment within a few hours.

Marines storm the beaches of Eniwetok as an SBD Dauntless flies overhead.

"Off the shores of Eniwetok, a vast fleet of American warships lay in the darkness. Thundering guns of warships made the night one roaring bedlam. Deep in their dugouts and pillboxes, the Japanese defenders cowered as all hell raged roaring above them."

On the morning of D-Day, Dave Gould stood aboard the transport USS *Middleton*, conferring with the Marine infantrymen whom he'd be guiding along the beach. "Get up the beach and through the narrow strip of woods fast," he said. "Set your machine guns up damn fast. Then you can sweep the road and open space in front of the barracks—what's left of them. That's as far as I can lead you. Beyond that, it's up to you guys."

Climbing down into the landing craft, he crouched down near the helmsman. It was up to Dave to guide this helmsman around the reef and point out significant landmarks along the shore. And for this mission, Dave had traded his normal scuba gear for the full complement of battle regalia—"Helmet, pistol, ammo belt, and full combat kit, ready for the assault." He had no rifle, but his Colt 45 could inflict *some* damage on the enemy. Then, too, it was an unspoken rule that he could pick up any rifle or machine gun from the nearest fallen comrade.

As the landing craft neared the reef, naval gunfire was thundering overhead, pounding into the shore to keep the enemy's head down. Just outside the reef, their landing craft stopped long enough for Dave to jump over the side and fasten his plunger detonator to the pre-set buoy. Treading water while the sea rattled from Allied naval guns, Dave fastened the lead wires and rammed down on the plunger. The beach erupted into a "boiling wall of water, coral fragments, and pieces of flying metal," he said. "It was done, the way was open." His pre-set demolitions had cleared the way for all landing craft in their sector.

Eager Marines happily pulled him back onboard. Checking his personal gear one more time, he signaled to the helmsman:

"Okay. All clear. Come on in!"

The landing craft crunched into the surf just moments after the naval bombardment lifted from the beach. "Flights of planes screamed in, overhead, raking the battered area beyond the beach with bombs and guns." Along the beach, the lush palm trees had been reduced to charred and battered stumps. But from among these destroyed palms and peppered pillboxes, a few surviving Japanese began returning fire. Somehow, they had survived the naval onslaught, and they were determined to make the Americans pay for it. Clouds of sand erupted as bullets and mortars rained down along the beachhead.

"Down ramp!" a voice cried out.

As the mechanical ramp dropped into the surf, Dave and his Marines ran headlong into the fiery beach. "That way—around the side of the pillbox!" he yelled, pointing to the structure he had mapped on his first visit. "The men ran heavily up the beach," he recalled, "and dove to earth in the edge of the shattered tree stumps."

All seemed to be going well…until Dave felt the fiery sensation of a Japanese bullet slamming into his left leg. His entire leg seemed to have been jerked out from underneath him. Feeling the onrush of blood, however, Dave was somewhat relieved to see that his leg was still intact, but a pulsating wound had just emerged from above his knee. Digging for his First Aid pouch, he unsheathed the field dressing for a hasty but effective tourniquet. As he pulled himself up from the sand, he faintly heard a voice shouting:

"Goddamnit! Gould, where the hell are you?!"

In the opening rounds of the melee, his platoon had lost sight of him. Hobbling half-erect up the slope to his immediate front, he told himself:

"You can navigate boy! Get off this damned beach!"

Dave found his Marines as he descended into the tangled mess of fallen trees at the crest of the slope. They were maneuvering their way to the edge of the road, but the Japanese were likewise taking up their own positions, ready to lay down some deadly return fire. Dave hobbled over to the two closest Marines, a machine gunner and his assistant gunner (AG). The two-man machine gun teams were a deadly duo: one man firing while the other fed his ammunition into the gun, changing barrels as needed.

But before they could open fire, the gunner was killed by an enemy bullet.

His shocked AG sat there in a dazed, catatonic stupor until Dave crawled up behind him.

"Snap out of it, Mac!" Dave thundered.

"Keep the belt feeding smooth. They'll be here any second now."

Dave's words were uncannily prophetic. For within moments, another Marine farther down the line yelled: "Here they come!" But Dave was ready. He knew the area well. "Good field of fire, right across the flat."

From across the open field, a hoard of Japanese soldiers came thundering towards the American lines. "An officer led them," Dave recalled, "swinging a glistening samurai sword in circles over his head. They were screaming hysterically as they came."

It was the classic *Banzai* charge.

"Keep that belt feed smooth!" he yelled to the AG.

Dave hammered down on the trigger, sweeping the machine gun from side to side.

He was aghast at how many Nipponese warriors were falling under the fury of his automatic fire—medleys of pink and red mists spouted into the air as innards and brain matter were littering the battlefield. And Dave was even more aghast at how many of them kept charging the line with unflinching fanaticism, unfazed by the blood and carnage erupting all around them.

"A red glow began to show as the barrel became overheated."

But there was no time to change it now—the enemy was closing in fast. The barrel shimmied and rattled as Dave kept the trigger pressed tightly against its well. But just when it seemed the barrel would explode from overheating, the last *Banzai* charger fell from view. "The field was full of twisted, sprawling bodies." Dave grimly wondered how many of them had been killed by his own gun. But he didn't have too long to consider the carnage. For within a few moments of the last gunshot,

Dave's wounded leg finally caught up to him—he passed out from the loss of blood.

He regained consciousness two days later aboard the *Middleton*; he had been patched up by a local corpsman. His leg was stiff, but not broken. Aside from the loss of blood, he was otherwise intact. "Able to fight another day!" the corpsman told him.

And David Gould would fight for many more days…swimming recon missions at Kwajalein, Palau, and Leyte Gulf. After the war, he returned to his native New York and re-entered the metalworking industry, eventually rising to become a Fabrication Superintendent. Like many from the Greatest Generation, Dave Gould often stayed mum about the war, and was unimpressed by his own deeds. "Look," he said, "the war was a dirty job that had to be done. So we did it. I was suited for Frogman combat, so that's why they put me in. That's all." Dave Gould passed away in 1983.

9

IWO JIMA: THE SHADOWS OF SURIBACHI

GILBERTO MENDEZ:
FROM THE MEXICAN ARMY TO THE US MARINE CORPS

Gilberto "Gil" Mendez was the youngest of *seventeen* children (nine boys; eight girls) born to Sebastian and Maria Arroyo Mendez. His parents had fled Mexico during the Revolution of 1910, settling in San Antonio, Texas, where Gil was born. "They were legal residents," he emphasized, "and what they knew best was agriculture." Like many others who had fled from the Revolution, Gil's parents sought refuge across the border in Texas. "So, they settled down, and they worked in seasonal agricultural crops…fruit and vegetables, they were the most abundant crops to be harvested."

Although money was tight, Gil recalled that his family was exceptionally close. The older children were expected to work, while the younger siblings attended school. Growing up on the rural outskirts of San Antonio, Gil recalled that there were "no hospitals, no clinics, no nothing"—thus facilitating the use of natural remedies handed down through generations of Mexican tradition. Gil proudly recalled that each of his siblings were born at home with the assistance of a midwife. No doctors or fancy obstetrics needed.

"Unfortunately, when we came of age," said Gil, "the Depression had already started." This led to a severe backlash against Mexican immigrants living in the American Southwest. Known as the "Mexican Repatriation," the US government deported more than 80,000 Mexicans, many of whom were legal residents like the Mendez family. "I was never able to comprehend how you can expatriate an American citizen,"—Gil and many of his siblings were, after all, American-born. "We were repatriated to Mexico [but] we were not *citizens* of Mexico." Gil claimed Mexican heritage, of course, but not Mexican citizenship. Yet, because his parents were Mexican-born, the Mendez family had no choice but to accept deportation. "The government should never have sent us back to Mexico," he said.

Following their forced repatriation, the Mendez family re-settled in Michoacan. Gil eventually went to live with his uncle in Monterey, where he continued his formal education until Mexico declared war on Germany in May 1942. Until then, Gil had never given much thought to Pearl Harbor. He saw it as a tragedy, to be sure, but it was an *American* problem. By this point, he had been living in Mexico for more than ten years, speaking mostly Spanish, and he thought that this new conflict would run its course without Mexico's involvement. "Mexico was very sympathetic toward the Germans at first," said Gil, "and prior to the war they did a lot of business with Germany." But when the *Kriegsmarine* started targeting Mexican ships on the high seas, the Mexican government promptly declared war on the Axis Powers. "When the Mexican President declared the war," Gil continued, "they instituted conscription, or the draft."

Gil was a few months shy of his 18th birthday, the minimum age for duty in the Mexican Armed Forces. "They called it the '1924 Class,' which was the year that I was born. They drafted everybody that was eighteen. And they used the lottery system," which ultimately selected Gilberto Mendez as one of its earliest draftees. But his uncle was quick to say: "You don't have to go because you are a United States citizen. It's up to you…but if you don't want to go, we'll go to the authorities here, and we can go to the US Consulate, and tell them the situation."

Gil thought it over.

"Well," he said, "everybody that was born in 1924 is volunteering to go. I think I'll go." After all, the designated term of service was only *one* year. Thus, Gilberto Mendez enlisted in the Mexican Army.

He was sent with his fellow conscripts to Jalisco, where they were issued their new equipment, uniforms, and rifles. "For new recruits," he said, "we were embedded with the regular army but we were separate." And at the end of his 90-day training cycle, Gil was promoted to the rank of second sergeant. "The Mexican Army only has two types of sergeants," he explained, "second sergeant and a first sergeant." His designation as "second sergeant" put him in charge of the company's administrative functions.

"We stayed six months in Guadalajara," he said. "And we used to just drill all day long…took a break for lunch, and then in the evening we'd have at least two hours of lectures, tactics, and classroom training. After six months [in September 1942], we went to Mexico City in a convoy and participated in the parade on the Sixteenth of September...Mexican Independence Day." After the parade, Gil's unit was sent to Queretaro. "We went to stay at a convent that was part of a church taken over by Benito Juarez [the famous 1800s-era Mexican president] and we spent six months there doing the same thing that we did in Guadalajara. Training, exercises, and classroom training."

Gil was discharged on Christmas Day 1942.

It was an uneventful end to a seemingly uneventful conscription. Still, his brief service in the Mexican Army taught him a lot about the fundamentals of military science. And the Mexican Armed Forces served with distinction during the war, most notably the 201st Fighter Squadron of the Mexican Air Force. Dubbed the "Aztec Eagles," these P-47 pilots were attached to the US 58th Fighter Group, flying some 96 combat missions over the Pacific.

Meanwhile, back in the States, Gil's eldest sister received an interesting letter in the mail. She had been allowed to stay in Texas because she was already married to an American citizen. "The Draft Board had gotten in touch with her," said Gil—asking for his whereabouts and demanding that he register for the draft. "Well, he's in Mexico," she told them. "He was deported with the rest of my family." But the Draft Board was clear: "If he doesn't appear within thirty days, he is going to lose his citizenship."

Gil and his family were dumbfounded.

Despite being an American citizen by birth, the US Government had cast him down to Mexico; and now they were threatening to revoke his citizenship if he didn't come back and register for the draft.

Gil didn't know what to do.

Did the US have any legal basis to revoke his citizenship? Or was it all a scare tactic?

Going to his uncle, Gil said: "I have to go back, because I might lose my citizenship if I don't." The uncle, who was likely just as perplexed as his nephew, said: "It's up to you. Whatever you want, I told your mother that I would help you." Thus, Gil Mendez returned to the US to accept conscription. He reported to the Induction Center on March 31, 1943.

"We were shipped to San Diego," he said, where he and his comrades were given their options of service. His older brother, Vincent, had joined the Navy two years earlier and was serving as an aerial photographer.

"Try to get into the Navy," his brother told him.

"At that time," said Gil, "it was supposedly the best branch of the service." Gil asked for naval service, but a Marine Corps gunnery sergeant quickly burst into the room: "I need ten volunteers," he said. "You will be Navy personnel, but you will be in the Marine Corps, which is the infantry of the Navy. And you will be the fighting force, land, sea, and air, and you will be at the disposal of the President of the United States."

The gunnery sergeant's dress blue uniform definitely added to the showmanship.

"This sounds pretty good," Gil thought to himself. "So, I was one of those volunteers." Within the next few days, he reported to Camp Pendleton in San Diego for recruit training. As he described, Marine recruits went through "boot camp" followed by "line camp." Boot camp, of course, taught the fundamentals of warfare and military life. "They just drilled you to death," he said. Line camp, however, was a more advanced level of training. "Night patrols, simulated combat against dummies," interspersed with survival training, demolitions, and anti-tank weapons.

Gil found that his prior service in the Mexican Army had prepared him well for the rigors of boot camp. Although the 1940s Mexican Army was small, Gil remembered that they were tough and highly professional. "They were very disciplined," he said. Thus, when he arrived at Camp Pendleton, "I didn't suffer because I had the discipline already embedded in me from the Mexican Army." After line camp, Gil and his fellow Marines arrived in Hawaii. "We continued more advanced training, night patrols, and [training maneuvers with] landing craft,"—the famous Higgins landing boats.

From Hawaii, they boarded a troop ship, en route to whatever Marine ground units would take them. "We were replacements," he said. None of them had yet been assigned to a unit. "We went as a 'nobody' group," he continued. "Because, as replacements, we were here…there… wherever we were needed." Such was the life of a replacement. Indeed, a replacement was sent to any unit where a fellow Marine had been killed, and would literally replace that fallen comrade in the ranks of his unit.

After a few days at sea, the troop carrier met up with an invasion convoy. Gil didn't know it at the time, but he was in the convoy headed for Iwo Jima. "Hundreds of ships," he recalled. And on February 19, 1945, Gil could see the faint silhouette of the craggy island jutting up from the horizon. "Now, the Air Force and the Navy had bombarded that island for *nineteen* consecutive days, day and night," he lamented—but they hadn't killed a thing.

The Japanese had gone underground, determined to wait out the shelling.

And now that the bombardment was over, the Rising Sun had emerged

The iconic flag raising on Iwo Jima. February 23, 1945.

from their spider holes and were ready to return fire on the incoming task force. The convoy was under fire but, as Gil recalled, "we stayed on the ship because...we were being held in reserve as replacements for the other units." Indeed, the first wave of Marines were expected to suffer heavy casualties; and they needed a steady stream of replacements to sustain the momentum of the attack.

Still, most of the Allied commanders were anticipating a quick victory on Iwo Jima. "We were told that the operation, the whole operation, would only take three to four days," Gil remembered. "And then it turned out that it was 36 days of pure hell." But during the opening rounds of the battle, Gil was more concerned with being on a big ship than being on the beaches. The troop carriers presented bigger targets; and one well-placed shot from an onshore battery could take the ship, and its Marines, to the bottom of the sea.

When the first wave of Higgins boats descended onto Iwo Jima, "all hell broke loose," said Gil. From the deck of his troop carrier, miles offshore, Gil remembered: "You could see the Higgins boats receiving direct hits, going sky high. That's when I got scared." For the next few days, he saw the muzzle flashes of American and Japanese forces flickering across the landscape, most of which were punctuated by violent explosions from the supporting artillery. He saw a glimmer of hope, however, on the fifth day of the battle. From the top of Mount Suribachi, the highest point on Iwo Jima, a group of Marines raised the American flag.

"We saw it from the ship."

Joe Rosenthal, an embedded photographer from the Associated Press, captured the moment in his iconic photograph, *Raising the Flag on Iwo Jima*. The photo itself came to represent the Pacific War, and has since become a symbol of Marine Corps heritage. But for Gil Mendez, seeing the Stars & Stripes raised in real time was a thrill like none other. "Your heart was beating a thousand times a minute," filling him with pride, and even giving him goosebumps.

After six days of waiting along the coastal waters, Gil's troop carrier finally began making its way to the shore. The beachhead had been secured, but even at D-Day +6, Gil Mendez still did not have an assigned unit. As replacements, Gil and his friends wouldn't be sorted out until they made landfall.

Wading off the Higgins boat, the new Marines assembled onto the black volcanic sand. One by one, a personnel sergeant called names from a roll sheet, assigning each new replacement to a rifle company. When Gil answered to his name, he was directed to I Company, 23d Marine Regiment (part of the 4th Marine Division).

His first week in the 23d Marines, however, was marked by feelings of dread. Statistically speaking, a GI stood the greatest chance of being killed during (a) the first few months of his tour, or (b) the last few months of his tour. And Gil Mendez didn't want to fall on the wrong side of that statistic.

In fact, he was so hypervigilant that he couldn't sleep.

He was running on pure adrenaline.

He refused to let go of his rifle, even while eating or using the latrine. "I felt that if I dropped my rifle…I would be killed." For fear of lingering snipers, he often told himself: "Gilberto, don't get up." Enemy snipers were, after all, a persistent threat. And they enjoyed taking aim at a GI's head. "And I didn't sleep because of the stink of the blown-up bodies. Bodies torn to pieces."

"Our mission was to take the main airfield," he said—the infamous Airfield One. And the Japanese were defending it with their customary fanaticism. Part of the airfield was guarded by an enormous bunker. "We called it the Meat Grinder," said Gil, "because it played hell on our troops."

Indeed, a medley of Japanese mortars, machine guns, and anti-tank guns wrought havoc on any one trying to gain access to the airfield. "They had everything they could throw," Gil added. "And they had the advantage to be close. They were on the highest part [of the hill]."

While moving forward to take the airfield, Gil's company was pinned down by heavy gunfire. "We were pinned down," he said, "for a number of hours…we couldn't move, because every time somebody got up, or exposed himself, he was gone." But during the opening rounds of this firefight, Gil had taken cover behind a thick slab of volcanic rock. "It was an act of God," he said, because the shape of the rock allowed him to prop his rifle into a good firing position, while still providing good cover from the enemy's counterfire. And, as it turned out, this rock would play a critical role in saving Gil's life. For within the next few hours, Gil Mendez would have his first encounter with a Japanese *banzai* attack.

It was about 7:00 AM, and Gil remembered that "there were about twenty of us [three infantry squads] pinned down along that section of the battlefield when we saw something glistening in the sunlight." Whatever it was, he could tell by its luster that it had a highly-reflective surface. "I thought it was a mirror," he said, "because they had showed us in line camp how to communicate with a mirror," using the reflective sunlight to flash communiques in Morse Code.

But these flashes didn't resemble any type of naval code.

In fact, they seemed erratic…and almost panicky.

That's when Gil realized it was no mirror…*it was the blade of a samurai sword*. A Japanese officer had emerged from one of the caves, rallying a group of wild-eyed soldiers behind him.

And Gil could hear them shouting: *"Banzai! Banzai!"*

By now, the bullets were flying in both directions, but Gil remained perfectly concealed behind his rock, ready to line up his first shot against the fanatical *bushido* warriors. At that moment, the fear and nerves left him; all his focus was directed into picking off the Japanese troops…one by one.

"I was shooting until I ran out of ammunition," he said. But rather than sprint back to the ammo point, "I decided to crawl." And, just as he had done during his first week on Iwo Jima, he told himself *not* to get up. "Because I had seen the bodies with shots in the head," he recalled, "they got up…they exposed themselves, and they were gone."

The mantra continued as he shimmied on his belly:

"Don't get up, Gilberto. Don't get up."

He belly-crawled over to two fellow Marines on his left, asking for a bandolier. Each of them happily obliged, tossing Gil a single bandolier. Thus, with two full bandoliers, Gil crawled back to his rock, ready to take aim at the next wave of incoming troops. "And here…the Japanese, kept on coming out of the cave."

Kneeling back behind his rock, Gil drew a bead on a Japanese soldier who was slowly cresting a rise in the terrain. At first, all he could see was the helmet, but it soon morphed into the unmistakable visage of a Japanese infantryman.

Aiming for his neck, "I pulled the trigger…pow."

But surprisingly, the enemy soldier didn't die. The bullet had only wounded him. Nearly a minute later, Gil was aghast to see this *same* soldier crawling up a rise in the terrain, "trying to push himself forward." Without hesitation, Gil readied his rifle for another shot.

"Bang! Bang! Bang! And the clip jumps up and out of the rifle."

Gil reloaded just in time to see the Japanese soldier expire. "They found thirteen holes in his body." Gil didn't know it at the time, but this was the same officer, who had led the *banzai* charge with his samurai sword. "They found his sword right beside him."

"Anyway, they kept on coming," Gil continued. "I stayed behind that rock ten hours." By the end of that firefight, however, Gil was credited with *twenty* confirmed kills. In total, the platoon had killed nearly 70 Japanese soldiers.

But this battle for Iwo Jima was far from over.

The following day, Gil recalled: "we started moving out and all hell broke loose again." Mortar fire, machinegun fire, rifle fire, an anti-tank fire pelted the American positions. Of the enemy's ordnance, the anti-tank guns seemed to be the worst. Gil described the Japanese anti-tank guns as somewhat comparable to the US 37mm pieces—deadly when used against armor *or* dismounts.

"One of the mortar shells landed pretty close to me," he said. "I was lucky because they later told me that a large piece of shrapnel was embedded in my pick shovel on my back. So, I could imagine, and anybody could imagine, had it not been for that [shovel] it would have hit me probably somewhere in the spine." Still, the impact of the mortar had been close enough to knock Gil clear off his feet—"and with a terrible ringing in my ear, my right ear."

To make matters worse, the shock wave had disrupted Gil's equilibrium to the point that he was now choking on his own tongue. A corpsman and a fellow Marine tried to pull his tongue out with a safety pin. "They pierced my tongue and they were pulling my lip," he recalled, trying to get his tongue from becoming his own demise.

"Get up," they pleaded.

But Gil couldn't even stand.

For that matter, he could hardly hear.

"And that terrible ringing in my ear," he said. "It took about six months after I was discharged to get rid of the thing." Deducing that Gil had no physical wounds, the corpsman and other Marine hoisted Gil back to the field hospital. He had obviously sustained a concussion, but they had no idea how bad it may have been. "Then a nurse came over, gave me a shot, I don't know what, but it knocked me out."

When he woke up on February 28, 1945, he was on a hospital ship bound for Hawaii.

"We were dropped off in Maui…transferred to another ship and came back to the US, to the Oakland Receiving Hospital. We stayed in Oakland just a short while, maybe a day or two. Then we joined in a convoy by bus, went from Oakland to San Diego." After a brief stay at Balboa Navy Hospital, Gilberto Mendez was honorably discharged from the Marine Corps in November 1945.

Having served in combat, while wearing the uniform of his American birthland, Gil was certain that no one could argue for a *second* deportation. In fact, he never understood the legality of why he and his parents had been deported the first time. He was, after all, an American citizen by birth. And although his parents were not citizens, they were, nevertheless, *legal* residents. But such was the nature of the great Mexican Repatriation of the 1930s.

All told, however, Gil had no desire to return to Mexico.

In November 1945, he bought a bus ticket to San Antonio, where he remained for the rest of his life. "When I was discharged, I spent about two, three days just making applications," he said. "I made applications for every government installation that there was at the time. Lackland, Kelly, Fort Sam, Randolph, Brooks [Army Hospital], everywhere, the Post Office, the VA. And the first one to call me for an interview was the Post Office, but they wanted me as a postal clerk."

Gil wasn't impressed.

"No," he said, "I want to be outside. I want to *deliver* the mail."

"Well," said the postmaster, "we don't have a position available right now, but if you want postal clerk…you'll have a job."

Gil stood his ground.

"No, I don't want to be inside. I like the outdoors."

That's when he landed a job at Lackland Air Force Base. He remained a federal employee for the next several decades until his retirement.

Reflecting on his service in both the Mexican Army and US Marine Corps, Gil said: "If I had to do it again, I would gladly do it. By the grace of God, I'm here, and I have four children. Three girls and my son…and three out of four have worn a uniform of this country. I had a daughter in the Army, my son in the Navy, [and] my youngest daughter in the Navy making a career out of her service. I think that I paid my ticket."

Gilberto Mendez passed away on April 29, 2012, at the age of 87. He was buried with military honors at Fort Sam Houston National Cemetery in San Antonio, Texas.

10
COMBAT MAILMAN
FRANK CANNEY,
AN ARMY POSTAL WORKER IN COMBAT

By the standards of conscription warfare, Frank Canney was already an "old man." At 34 years of age, he was more than a decade older than most of his fellow GIs. He had been a postal worker in California prior to answering the call of duty in 1943. Owing to his service in the US Post Office, Frank was made an Army mail handler. "A year later," he said, "I went overseas as a replacement in the Army Postal Unit of the 24th Infantry Division." The bastion of these Army postal workers was the "Army Post Office"—the ever-popular APO.

By the summer of 1944, he had served all throughout the Pacific, manning APOs in Dobodura, Wakde, and Hollandia.

And he had never heard a shot fired in anger.

All this changed, however, on the morning of October 20, 1944, when Allied forces invaded the Philippine Islands at Leyte Gulf. "My outfit, on the Liberty ship *Marcus Daily*, was shaken up when Japanese bombs hit a forward 75mm gun position," he said, "killing every member of the armed guard." Liberty ships were a class of cargo ships used to transport men and materiel to the frontlines.

Frank's unit hit the beach on October 25. "There followed two months of bombing and torrential rains while we were stationed in a Chinese-owned rice warehouse in Tacloban"—the provincial capital. From there, his APO sailed to Mindoro as part of the Western Visayan Task Force. "I was aboard LST 741," he recalled, "in a convoy of twenty-five ships." It was in this convoy, as it steamed into the Sulu Sea, that Frank Canney would have his first sustained look at the carnage of naval combat.

"Before getting underway," he said, "we GIs descended to the tank deck and secured the ambulances, Jeeps, six-bys [utility trucks], weapons carriers, and other vehicles by running heavy chains around their wheels, and attaching them firmly to the deck." Advanced elements of the 24th Infantry Division and the 503d Parachute Infantry Regiment had departed days earlier. "These were led by the ill-fated cruiser *Nashville*," he said, "carrying the Task Force commander, Brigadier General William Dunckel"—along with a bevy of other high-ranking Allied officers.

The *Nashville* had been crippled by a *kamikaze* attack on December 13, killing 133 sailors and wounding an additional 190. These *kamikaze* attacks were a fairly new (and incredibly disturbing) tactic in military aviation. Japanese pilots would deliberately ram their aircraft into the oncoming Allied ships—hoping to sink them or kill as many sailors as possible. "It was terrifyingly effective…and hard to cope with." Indeed, it showed what little regard the Imperial Japanese forces had for human life.

Frank's convoy set sail on December 19, 1944. A motley crew of Victory, Liberty, and LST ships, this convoy numbered twenty vessels in total—not including the eleven destroyers that formed their protective screen. "They darted around our flanks like nervous watch dogs," he said. "So great was their speed, sometimes reaching thirty or more knots, that when turning, their port or starboard rails almost touched the water line." For the first two nights at sea, their voyage had passed without incident. "The weather was ideal, with a calm sea marked by gentle, rolling swells."

However, Frank and his fellow GIs were not merely "passengers." Indeed, aboard every troop carrier, the soldiers were expected to be gainfully employed, helping the ship's company with their critical tasks. In that regard, Frank Canney had become an "assistant gunner" of sorts. During General Quarters, he would load ammunition into a port-side .50 cal anti-aircraft gun.

On the morning of December 21, the men aboard LST 741 had endured two calls to General Quarters, both of which had been false alarms. There had been no enemy ships on the horizon; and there had been nothing in the skies except a few scattered clouds.

But the third call to General Quarters would be the proverbial charm.

One of the destroyers spotted a seemingly out-of-place junk ship. "The junk must have been motorized, though, as it quickly sailed towards a far-off island." The destroyer gave chase, signaling for the junk to turn about. But this junk, obviously an enemy recon ship, ignored the warning and tried to flee the scene. Though small and agile, the speedy junk could neither outrun the destroyer, nor outmaneuver its gun batteries. Following a quick salvo from the forward gun battery, the junk disappeared under a cloud of billowing smoke and raging fires.

But the junk obviously had time to report their position.

LST 741, the landing craft that carried Frank Canney onto the beaches of the Philippine Islands.

For within minutes, a dozen Zeroes came thundering over the horizon, silhouetted against the red glow of the setting sun. Aboard LST 741, Canney's unit shared its billets with an Australian detachment. Wearing their signature khakis and floppy hats, Canney recalled one of them shouting "Here come the bloody Nips!" as the all-too-familiar droning of Japanese aircraft filled the air.

General Quarters sounded.

"My hands were sweaty and I had a queasy feeling in the pit of my stomach as I ran to my station. By this time, the sun was low on the western horizon and I hoped for the shelter of darkness that comes so quickly in these waters only twelve degrees above the Equator."

Sadly, it was not to be.

Almost immediately, the Japanese planes descended upon the convoy, hitting one of the more vulnerable support ships, causing it to lose its place in the convoy. "Every gun on LST 741 started firing. I carried magazines from the locker to the twin .50 while the gunner blazed away at low-flying aircraft. Soon, the air overhead was filled with ack-ack bursts." Suddenly, one of the offending Zeroes swooped down along the port side of LST 741. "My gunner and the ones nearby sprayed .50 cal rounds towards it," Frank recalled—many of which met their mark, shearing off the bandit's wing, and sending his plane headlong into the sea.

Three more planes were quickly shot down—"two of them bursting into flames"—but the third Zero had just been inspired to turn himself into a suicide bomber. Going into a long glide, the pilot set his sights on the neighboring LST 460. Frank watched in horror as the fanatical pilot plowed his Zero into the ship's main deck, crashing into the cargo hold, whereupon he detonated all the 105mm and 155mm artillery shells onboard. Within moments, LST 460 was ablaze from its bow to its stern. The artillery shells, cooking off from the intense heat, rocketed into the air, leaving a fiery trail of smoke and gunpowder in their wake.

"It seemed like a madman's Fourth of July celebration," said one sailor.

The sky was red, and parts of the sea were ablaze, as a growing mass of sailors desperately swam away from the flaming LST. But among the shell-shocked and badly-burned survivors lay several of their less fortunate comrades, bobbing face-down in the water as their lifeless bodies drifted with the current.

"I saw hundreds of sailors and soldiers leaping overboard," said Frank. Some tried to launch lifeboats while others simply threw life rafts over the side. "Some crewmen, stricken by panic," he continued, "leapt into the sea. They dropped upon the heads of other men, resulting in additional casualties." Some of the more able-bodied survivors swam towards LST 741. The skipper then ordered the ship into rescue mode.

"Now it was time for saving instead of killing," said Frank.

Hoisting the "mercy flag" up its main mast, LST 741 signaled that it was now picking up survivors. A slew of Higgins LCVP landing boats soon descended from LST 741, motoring gingerly among the mass of ill-fated sailors and GIs. Frank and his port-side comrades, meanwhile, cast lines off the rail to survivors struggling to reach 741. "We hauled up burning and screaming men," he said. "Medics and corpsmen, with many a Yank and Aussie volunteers, placed stricken survivors on litters and carried them into the wardroom for medical attention. This part of the ship was to become a combination hospital and mortuary."

Some of the men, however, were too badly wounded to climb up the lifelines under their own power. For these ailing survivors, Frank and his comrades tied belays to the strongest swimmers aboard LST 741, lowering them into the sea. The strong swimmers stayed afloat by treading water as they tied their lines under the armpits of the bobbing wounded. "They, too, were, hoisted aboard for medical care."

As LST 460 began its fiery descent into the black tepid waters, Frank noticed something peculiar—"tiny lights," as he described them, blinking on the surface of the sea. "These belonged to naval personnel swimming towards the rescue ships. Each sailor had a blinker attached to his Kapok life jacket." These pulsating lights would facilitate easier rescues during the hours of darkness.

"But what about the soldiers?" he asked himself.

Army personnel had no such beacons on their life jackets. "How could they be found when the quick tropical darkness settled over the ocean?" How many would survive until daybreak? "Hundreds of soldiers could have died," said Frank, "because the Army failed to have the foresight to put signal lights on its men's life jackets. That was one occasion where it was better to be a sailor instead of a soldier!"

The following morning, December 22, the Western Visayan Task Force made landfall at Mindoro. Frank Canney and the rest of the GIs on LST 741 landed unopposed at Red Beach. Ironically, Frank's landing party suffered only *one* casualty while storming the beach: a soldier was trampled by an angry water buffalo. "But," he said wryly, "our casualties in the sea battles had been heavy."

Frank spent the remainder of the war manning the 24th Infantry Division's APO on Mindoro. "I was stationed in the barrio of San Jose, about five miles inland." But even at the APO, he found little relief from the enemy. "Our units went through many bombings," he said, "both day and night, from the Japanese bases north of us."

But the Allies had begun clearing their own landing strips on Mindoro, and their combined air forces were determined to give as much as they had gotten. The closest airstrip to the APO was occupied by the Royal

Australian Air Force—running daily sorties of Aussie and American aircraft. Their ranks included B-24 Liberators; P-47 Thunderbolts; P-51 Mustangs; P-38 Lightnings; and a squadron of P-61 Black Widows (deadly night fighters); and US Marine F4U Corsairs. Frank remembered that this aerial armada was highly effective in clearing the way for the upcoming invasion of Luzon.

Christmas Day 1944 was as enjoyable a holiday as one could have in the forward area of Mindoro. "Filipinos from the surrounding barrios were invited to share a feast of roast turkey, mashed potatoes, gravy, pie and coffee," said Frank. "We filled our mess kits and our cups, talking about how fortunate we had been so far." Even in light of the carnage they had witnessed on the high seas, Frank and his fellow GIs were grateful not to have endured the meat grinder battles or Tarawa, Saipan, and the Mariana Islands.

"But our luck was too good to last."

The very next day, Allied Intelligence detected a Japanese naval task force headed straight for Mindoro—"a cruiser and two destroyers."

Under the cover of darkness, the 24th Division and the 503d Parachute Infantry started digging in near the beach. "Those of us in the rear echelon outfits received orders to fall back to the inland hills." Frank grabbed his hammock along with as many C and K Rations as his shoulder pack could carry. With a full clip of ammunition for his carbine, he began the long hill-ward march to the high ground of Mindoro.

Trudging along the narrow roads under the bright moonlight, Frank saw a caravan of ambulances and supply trucks pass him by, vehicles belonging to the 2d Field Hospital and the 13th Station Hospital. If and when the enemy hit the beach, these medics would be the first support soldiers dispatched to the shores of Mindoro. Behind them were a steady stream of Filipino refugees, eager to avoid the anticipated bombardment. "Many of these Filipinos, most of them loyal to the Americans, had been through this kind of exodus before," Frank remembered. The Japanese had forced many from their homes in 1942; the Filipinos then returned jubilantly to the beaches when the Western Visayan Task Force arrived; now they were on the move again to take shelter farther inland. "Hundreds of refugees passed us," carrying what few possessions they owned. "One boy held a bicycle frame by an arm. Others trundled wheelbarrows and small carts, filled with everything from cooking utensils to blankets and small carts."

After nearly an hour into their march, Frank and the others heard the sound of aircraft overhead. It couldn't have been Allied, as their own

The ill-fated LST 450, which came under fire and sank in route the Philippines. Frank Canney witnessed the ship's demise from his position aboard LST 741.

fighters and bombers had taken flight from Mindoro to search for the enemy fleet. Frank's suspicions were confirmed when a Japanese spotter plane began dropping flares above the tree line.

"We hit the ditch," he said.

A young lieutenant came into view.

"Pass the word," he told Frank. "Watch out for enemy paratroops."

After dropping more flares over the island, the Japanese recon plane returned to sea, likely to be picked up by the incoming cruiser. "We clicked the safeties off our carbines, holding them in readiness for the enemy's next move."

Paratroopers?

Aerial bombardment?

An amphibious landing?

The GIs wouldn't have to wait long to find out. For within moments, Frank was greeted by the rushing, crackling sound of incoming naval shells. "I had been under much strafing and bombing," he said, "but this was the first time that I experienced heavy shellfire from a battle cruiser and two destroyers."

But the shelling stopped almost as soon as it had started.

"For over an hour, we stayed in the ditch, relieved by the silence and total darkness." After getting the "All Clear," Frank and his comrades were ordered to move back down towards the beach.

"The next morning, I learned that American and Australian forces had been saved by our PT boats." The prowling PTs had crept up on the Japanese task force undetected. "They dropped their torpedoes and sped away into the night…putting the destroyers out of action and seriously damaging the armored warship [cruiser]. That was my experience under fire."

Frank Canney remained on Mindoro until December 1945, three and a half months after Japan's formal surrender. While loading his APO back aboard the troop ship, he beheld a poignant, yet saddening sight. At the temporary Allied cemetery, a Graves Registration unit was digging up the bodies of the men who had lost their lives during the convoy sea battles en route to Mindoro, "and also during the subsequent bombings and the one night of shellfire." Dead or alive, every member of the Western Visayan Task Force was going home.

Frank Canney returned to the United States on January 2, 1946. He was honorably discharged from the United States Army shortly thereafter. He and his wife, Lauretta, settled in Salinas, California, where he returned to his job with the US Postal Service. He was happily employed as a letter carrier for the next several years, until he earned his eligibility for retirement. He passed away in 1990.

11
ONE HALF ACRE OF HELL

Avis Dagit Schorer with the
56th Evacuation Hospital in Anzio

Avis Dagit was one of eleven children growing up on a farm in
Iowa. "With all those kids," she said, "you just can't stay at home."
Thus, after graduating from high school in 1937, she went to Des
Moines for nurse training at the Methodist Hospital. She took readily
to the medical profession, and signed an agreement with the American
Red Cross, pledging her service to the country if a war or other "crisis"
erupted. "With Europe already at war," she said, "and the world situation
deteriorating, that crisis seemed likely."

And the crisis finally arrived on December 7, 1941.

"I knew on December 7," she said, "that I was all in." Following the
attack on Pearl Harbor, Avis took the next four months to settle her
personal affairs before reporting to the Army Induction Center in Des
Moines on March 17, 1942—her 23d birthday.

Sworn into the ranks of the Army Nurse Corps, Avis was commissioned
as a Second Lieutenant. But she and her fellow nurses received no formal
basic training. They simply went to work...and were expected to learn
Army customs along the way. "You had to learn as you go," she said. "It
was a whole new language for me. I'd never heard of a latrine, or a chow
line, or a mess hall."

Reporting to Camp Chaffee, Arkansas, she was quickly assigned to
the infirmary. But, at this early stage in the war, Camp Chaffee was a faint
wisp of a military post. "When we got there, it was nothing but a few
scattered buildings and some dirt roads," she said. "Not long afterwards,
though, the troops started pouring in." Indeed, within a year, its ranks had
swollen to more than 100,000 troops, and the Camp Hospital had grown
to a 1,000-bed capacity. "It was unbelievable how quickly it developed."
Years later, Camp Chaffee would become the primary hub for Cuban

refugees during the Mariel Boatlift of 1980.

While learning the art of military nursing, Avis and her comrades were ordered not to fraternize with enlisted men. "But that was easily broken," she said. "Some women broke it just to see if they could get away with it." Still, the Army Nurses were happy to be part of the Regular Army, not the Women's Army Corps (WACs). "We didn't want to be called WACs." During World War II, each branch of the military had its own segregated service for females. The Army had its WACs; the Navy had its WAVES; the Army Air Forces had their WASPS; the Coast Guard had SPARS; and the Marines had their Women's Reserve.

Still, her duties at Fort Chaffee were strenuous, and often heartbreaking. "I remember one time a soldier was brought into my ward with pneumonia. We didn't have antibiotics in those days, and the head nurse told me I should report to this other ward when the soldier died. Well, I was determined he wasn't going to die on my watch, and I stayed with him for several nights. He finally did recover." But soon thereafter, another soldier in her ward died from pneumonia. "You learned that soldiers didn't have to get shot up to die," she said. "They died just from going out on maneuvers."

In February 1943, the nurses at Camp Chaffee were ordered to Fort Sam Houston, Texas, where they joined the 56th Evacuation Hospital—"made up mainly of doctors and nurses from Baylor University." The 56th was a motley crew of 48 direct-commission doctors, 49 nurses, and 310 enlisted medics. It was, however, a self-contained and self-sufficient unit, with its own x-rays, laboratories, cots, and shelter tents. Being from the Midwest, Avis quickly learned that Texans had a culture all their own. "They're so proud of their state. I sure learned all the songs of Texas," she chuckled.

Two months later, the 56th Evacuation Hospital loaded its medical gear and personnel onto a troop ship in New York City. "They didn't tell us where we were going, but when they started teaching us the language and customs of North Africa, it became pretty clear. We landed in Casablanca." In the spring of 1943, Allied forces were chasing Rommel out of North Africa. It was a hard-fought campaign, during which the US Army paid a heavy price before turning the tides against Rommel and his *Afrika Korps*.

When the 56th Evacuation Hospital arrived in-theater, they boarded a truck convoy for an eight-day trip to the front. "It was not a nice ride," Avis recalled. "It was hot, and we had to carry our own food, which was C-rations. We got a quart of water every day. There were no baths, there

Avis D. Schorer, Army Nurse.

were no slit trenches, and there was no sightseeing." But as the convoy rode onward, Avis began seeing the unmistakable signs of war. "Shell holes…blown-up tanks and vehicles littered the landscape."

The 56th eventually reached Bizerte, Tunisia, where they set up shop in an old French colonial garrison. "One night," Avis remembered, "there was an air raid." But because it was nearly July 4th, Avis and her fellow nurses cheered the bomb blasts "like it was a fireworks display," she added. "But then hundreds of casualties started coming in."

After that, the nurses weren't cheering anymore.

Several more of these early casualties were victims of malaria. "Those were some of the sickest men I've ever seen in my life." Luckily, most made a full recovery with the proper intake of atabrine.

As Avis soon found out, duty in the field hospital was exhausting work. She worked 12-hour shifts, with frequent day-night shift differentials. "As the front moved, the hospital units would leapfrog over each other." The hospitals closest to the front would treat the most casualties, while the hospitals in the rear would be able to rest and refit before rotating back to the front. But even during their so-called "rest cycles," there were plenty of casualties that needed treating. The GIs coming in from the battlefield had some of the worst injuries Avis had ever seen—burned flesh, severed limbs, missing scalps, bullet holes, and the like.

By September 1943, Avis's unit had been tapped for duty in Italy. "The Italians had surrendered by that time," she said, "and some thought we might be going on a sightseeing tour, but the Germans didn't give up and they were there to meet us." Avis and her comrades waded ashore at Salerno, and got back to work. "From that point on, we usually just wore coveralls. We had long ago forgotten about the white shoes and white dresses. We wore what the men were wearing." And by the time Avis's unit had set up at Avellino, "our tents were overflowing with the wounded." The fighting among the surrounding hills was *that* bad.

Treating the casualties (even those who had no chance to survive) was hard enough. But the oncoming winter made their job even worse. As Allied forces pressed on towards Rome: "It rained and rained…for days on end. It was muddy everywhere, and all the tents leaked. We waded in mud wherever we went. The casualties began to change as the men came in with trench foot. If they had been wounded, they were caked with mud and blood. It was a terrible situation."

But little did Avis know that the collective situation was about to get worse.

In January 1944, their hospital was ordered to prepare for the invasion of Anzio. The Allies were determined to end-run the German forces by landing behind their positions. "We boarded a British LCI at night, and were put down in a [cargo] hold. Our bathroom was a bucket in the middle of the floor. With that, and with the fumes from the ship, you could hardly get your breath. We had no blankets. Some of the nurses got sick just at the sight of the ship. I didn't, but it was miserable. The seas were vicious and tossed us around like a cork. Some of the nurses would just throw up in their helmets…lie on their bunks and moan and groan."

At one point during the trip, the nurses were offered a chance to transfer from the British LCI onto another ship. Twenty-six of the nurses who were healthy enough to do so (i.e., those not rendered immobile from seasickness), made the hasty rope ladder transfer. This second ship was more stable, but it was laden with several tons of explosives and high-octane gas. Adding to the tension (and the fear of riding aboard a floating powder keg), these nurses endured a 36-hour air raid, with Axis bombs landing within mere feet of the ship. And when the ship made landfall, these same nurses found themselves running ashore onto a beachhead that was still under enemy fire.

Still, these 26 ladies were the first nurses to land on Anzio.

Scrambling off the beach, the nurses got a few miles inland before a male officer stopped them: "What are you women doing here? This place is hot. Get out of here!"

Avis later described her arrival in Anzio as a nightmare. "I'm sure that anybody who was at Anzio has it seared in their minds forever. It was just crazy. We were so tired. We'd had no sleep for several days." And the Nazis weren't going to let the GIs take Anzio without a fight. "The Germans had this long-range gun we called the Anzio Express," she continued. "It had a screeching sound and it just got louder and louder as it approached. Your heart would stop until you heard it hit on the other side. You'd be relieved, but then you'd realize that it probably hit somebody else."

Meanwhile, getting the 56th consolidated was a chore unto itself. "The task was made more difficult because the unit had been split up on five different landing ships." But as soon as the 56th Evacuation Hospital opened for business, it was flooded by the onrush of casualties. "It was much worse than anything we had seen before. Instead of one wound, these men would have multiple wounds." Because the 56th was so close to the front, they saved many a soldiers' lives. But despite their prominent Red Cross markings, the hospital itself was frequently under attack. As Avis recalled: "The hospital was surrounded by fuel dumps...ammo dumps and motor pools"—making it a prime target for the *Luftwaffe* and German artillery. "The bombing was constant," she continued, "and the night was often lit up brighter than sunshine by those white flares. Sometimes, when the men were brought in, they'd ask to be allowed to go back to their foxholes where it was safer. There wasn't much protection in a tent."

To make matters worse, there was a shortage of blood, which precipitated the doctors, nurses, and medics of the 56th to donate their own blood on a regular basis. Still, Avis and her fellow nurses worked at breakneck speed to heal the ever-growing influx of casualties. "We got their wounds cleaned and did some operations," she said. "We watched out for gas gangrene and other complications. Our goal was to get them into a condition where it was safe to move them."

But no one was truly safe at Anzio...not even the nurses.

In fact, six of her fellow nurses were killed on Anzio Beach, including one of Avis's close friends whom she had known from the Methodist Hospital in Des Moines. "She was killed in an air raid. It was dreadful, but you didn't have time to break down. Your attitude was: 'Well, this is going to happen to all of us.'"

Ironically, one of their only sources of entertainment was listening to Axis Sally. Despite the anti-American broadcasts, Hitler's propaganda DJ actually played the best music. One day between songs, however, Axis

Sally said that there would soon be "happy days" for the 56th Evacuation Hospital. Avis didn't know what to make of the remark. How did Sally know about their unit? And who had told her? Moreover, what did she mean by "happy days?" Were the Germans planning a massive counteroffensive? Was the hospital itself on the target list?

"We didn't know what she was talking about; but the next day, we were relieved [from duty in Anzio]."

Avis and her comrades had been on the Anzio beachhead for a grueling 76 days. During that time, she had seen some of the worst carnage of the war. "It sounds crazy, but we didn't want to leave. We didn't want to be called quitters."

But alas, the 56th Evacuation Hospital had no choice in the matter. They were rotated off Anzio Beach and sent south to the Cassino front—just in time to treat casualties from the Battle of Monte Cassino. On June 6, 1944, however, the Allies entered Rome. "But it was kind of an anticlimax," she said. "The D-Day landings happened the same day. We were all so excited."

Still, it was a long road ahead for the Americans fighting in the Italian campaign. Indeed, as the 56th moved farther along the Italian Peninsula, they began seeing evidence of another deadly weapon—land mines. "Some of the mines would blow off a foot, but they also had these 'Bouncing Betties.' They were vicious things. They would kill and maim the civilians, the children, even the farm animals."

Towards the end of 1944, the hospital crossed the Arno River and moved into Florence. The following spring, the Allies made their final push into the Po Valley. "I don't think one square foot of that valley didn't have a shell hole or bomb crater in it. But it was a gorgeous spring, and the German Army was finally beginning to disintegrate. They were giving up by the thousands." Soon, too, would Adolf Hitler—although he elected suicide over capture. Hitler's death was a clarion call for the 56th. In many ways, Hitler's demise took the edge off the grief they shared over President Roosevelt's death earlier that month. "Roosevelt died and it was very traumatic. It was just devastating to lose him."

A week after Hitler's suicide, however, the German Army surrendered and the news of V-E Day rang throughout the world. By this time, the 56th Evacuation Hospital had spent 25 months in theater, and had seen more than 73,000 patients. With the war in Europe effectively over, Avis and her friends were excited to be going home.

"But as usual, the Army had other plans."

Her unit was sent to Udine, Italy, near the Yugoslavian border. And there was muffled talk of a pending deployment to Japan. Fortunately, the Japanese surrendered in September 1945, and the 56th Evacuation redeployed to the US that October. She was discharged from the Army Nurse Corps in February 1946, completing nearly four years of active service.

Reflecting on her wartime service, Avis said: "When you're going through something, sometimes you just can't comprehend it all. You just take it a day at a time and hope later you can sort it all out." Even during her later years, Avis's memories remained sharp. "I can still see the faces that I saw then. They still flash in front of you."

Returning to civilian life, Avis went back to school on the GI Bill, receiving her certification as a nurse anesthetist. In 1950, she married Dr. Calvin Schorer (a fellow GI), with whom she had three children. She worked at hospitals in Detroit and Iowa City before moving to Minneapolis in 1968. She became one of the leading nurse anesthetists at Lutheran Deaconess Hospital until her retirement in 1982.

Avis later wrote of her experiences in the book, *A Half Acre of Hell*, initially as a project for her children. And like many other projects in life, Avis attacked the book with a great sense of purpose. Still in print, the book has continued to garner positive reviews. "I was surprised," she admitted. "I never had any idea anybody would find it interesting except my family."

Avis Dagit Schorer passed away on August 31, 2016 at the age of 97.

12

GROUND ZERO: GUADALCANAL

BOB JOHNSON,
A MARINE ARTILLERY OFFICER IN THE SOUTH PACIFIC

B ob Johnson was a hero of the college gridiron. From 1936-38, he played defensive tackle for the University of Minnesota—two seasons punctuated by a National Championship and two Big Ten Conference titles. In fact, during one game against Washington State in 1937, he ran an interception for some 86 yards. Despite these impressive plays, however, professional football would not be in his future. Instead, he graduated with a business degree, and began the arduous task of looking for work in Depression-era Minnesota. "The only job I could find was as a grease monkey down at the Standard station in Anoka [his hometown]. I decided to look for something else."

Thus, he enrolled at the University of Minnesota School of Law, where he befriended future US Marine and Minnesota Governor, Orville Freeman. While learning the art of jurisprudence, Bob was shocked to hear of the attack on Pearl Harbor. Both he and Orville had registered for the draft, and both men knew that they had high lottery numbers— meaning that they stood a high chance of being drafted into the first wave of conscripts. Given the severity of Pearl Harbor, and the realization that America would be fighting a two-front war, Bob and Orville had a choice: They could wait to be drafted, or leave school and join voluntarily.

They chose the latter.

"If we were going to fight, we wanted to fight with an outfit that knew how to fight. So, we both joined the Marines."

Upon his induction, Bob was sent to Quantico, Virginia for Officer Candidate School, with follow-on training at Camp Elliott in San Diego. As one of several "shake-and-bake" Marine officers—hastily trained to meet manpower needs—he was assigned as the Executive Officer (XO) of an artillery battery in the 10th Marine Regiment, 2d Marine Division.

The battery's standard weapon was the pack howitzer—"a 75mm cannon that could be dissembled and moved by hard work from place to place, even in the jungle."

In the summer of 1942, the Marine Expeditionary Force deployed to the South Pacific. Bob's unit made the voyage, unescorted, aboard a commercial sea liner. Their first stop was New Zealand, where they trained in the mountains near Wellington. "We tried to make the training as realistic as possible," he said. "When we got into combat, it was a different animal altogether." Their eventual destination would be Guadalcanal.

It was America's first major offensive of the war, fought mostly by GIs with "too little experience and too little training."

Still, Guadalcanal would be the first step on the bloody road to Tokyo. Barring the exception at Midway, the Japanese had seen nothing but success throughout 1942. In May, however, a system of "Coastwatchers" (set up by the Australian Defence Force), reported to the Allies that the Japanese were building an airbase on Guadalcanal, a small island on the western edge of the Solomons. "Such an airbase would extend the Japanese ability to attack to the west, and threaten the major sea lanes to Australia." Thus came the idea for Operation Watchtower, the plan to retake Guadalcanal and capture the enemy airbase. "Because of the low priority of the Pacific campaign, compared to Europe, the operation became known to those involved as Operation Shoestring."

The 1st Marine Division led the charge, landing on Guadalcanal in August 1942. "The Marines were ashore, but they were on their own. There was no air support or sea support, and every day their four-mile beachhead was attacked from the air and shelled from passing Japanese ships." Nevertheless, the beleaguered Marines captured the airfield. By August 20, the first American planes touched down on Guadalcanal. The Japanese, meanwhile, fled into the jungle, determined to regroup and drive the Allies back into the sea.

The arrival of American air support was fortuitous, since the Japanese were planning to retake the airfield. Indeed, that night, a 1,000-man enemy task force set ashore at Taivu Point. "Either out of supreme overconfidence…or a gross underestimation of the US strength, the Japanese attacked immediately in the dead of night. The result was disastrous. By morning, 800 Japanese were dead, and their commander killed himself." The following month, the Battle of Bloody Ridge was almost just as costly. Although the Japanese had pushed the American lines back to within a thousand yards of the airfield, the Marines dug in and beat back the enemy advance.

Bob Johnson (center, wearing lip balm) poses with his fellow artillerymen on Guadalcanal.

In November 1942, Bob's unit with the 2d Marine Division landed at Guadalcanal. "We were there to relieve the troops that were on the line," he said. "The airfield had been secured by then, and it was our job to drive the Japs off the island." But the Americans' slapdash training, and their atrophied supply system, was now coming back to haunt them. Indeed, on one of Bob's first missions, he recalled: "Our maps were so bad, we couldn't use them. I went up ahead to be a forward observer so we could hit what we were supposed to hit. Sometime later, I realized I was two or three hundred yards away from our troops."

Moreover: "We seemed to always be short on supplies, and there was a constant food shortage. Our cook used to go down to one of the little bays and toss in a hand grenade. We'd have plenty of fish for supper." The Marines also scavenged barrels of rice that came floating ashore. "The rice was cast off Japanese ships for their own troops, but the troops' location had been miscalculated."

As an artillery unit, Bob's battery didn't have quite the same frontline exposure as the infantry…but the cannoneers' lives were far from easy. "I remember it was very hot, and it rained all the time. I don't think we ever got mail." Sometimes, it seemed that the local insects posed a greater threat than the Japanese. There were mosquitos, flies, leeches…and other creepy crawlers that most GIs had never heard of. In fact, during his time on Guadalcanal, more Marines died from malaria than enemy fire.

But nothing could have prepared him for the brutality (and borderline insanity) of a Japanese *banzai* attack. Bob witnessed three separate *banzai* attacks during his time in the Marine Corps, the first of which happened on Guadalcanal. "The Japanese would get all sake'd up as the night went on," he said. Saké was their drink of choice - an alcoholic beverage that, even when diluted, could lead to a quick state of inebriation. "Then they would charge en masse, yelling '*banzai*,' and screaming like you've never heard before."

That *banzai* attack came about 3:00 in the morning.

In fact, at one point during the battle, Bob's artillerymen had to lower their gun tubes, and fire their howitzers directly into the advancing enemy. "The resourcefulness of our men was incredible," he said. "I didn't have to give one order. They knew what to do. The fuses were set for the minimum and we just kept firing. I don't know how many rounds we fired." But by the end of the attack, some 300 Japanese soldiers lay dead, killed senselessly in a fit of drunken rage. "*Banzai* attacks are not something you learn about growing up on a farm outside of Anoka."

But this *banzai* charge wouldn't be his last near-brush with death. One day, the Marine howitzer crews noticed a group of heavy bombers flying overhead. Because the Americans had already taken the airfield on Guadalcanal, Bob and his fellow artillerymen assumed that the planes were Allied. "As they got close, though, all of a sudden we could see the Rising Sun on the bombers," followed by the dreadful opening of their bomb bay doors. "You can't believe how fast we got into our foxholes.

They bombed the daylights out of us, but not one guy got hurt."

Another near-death experience occurred during an unassuming Jeep ride. "The Japanese would send planes over regularly and we got to know them," he remembered. "One was 'Washing Machine Charlie,' and you could tell by the putt-putt-putt of its engine [likely a Nakajima A6M2-N or Aichi E13A]. All we had was rifle fire, and I told our guys not to even bother to shoot at him. It was just wasted ammunition. The other plane that would come over was known as 'Pistol Pete' [also a nickname given to the Japanese Type 92 artillery]. The driver and I were near the beach went Pistol Pete flew over. We watched as a couple of bombs hit nearby, with the second one closer than the first."

Bob turned to his driver, intending to tell him to vector off the road.

Bob Johnson, during his later years as an attorney. Bob continued litigating cases well into his 80s.

But before he could even get the words out, the third bomb landed next to the Jeep.

"I'll never know if I dove out of the Jeep, or if I was blown out of it," he said. All he knew was that, when he regained consciousness, he was still alive. "I wasn't injured except my ear drum was blown out. I was worried about the driver, and it turned out he was cut up pretty badly. The Jeep was destroyed."

Before Bob left Guadalcanal, he took part in a memorial service for the thousands who had died on the island. Among the seemingly endless rows of white crosses, he was startled and saddened to find a familiar name. It belonged to one of his former roommates and best friends from the University of Minnesota. "I didn't even know he had gone into the service," he said, "but it turns out he had joined the Army Air Corps and had been shot down. That shook me up a little bit."

The 2d Marine Division returned to New Zealand to rest, re-fit, and conduct more training. Thereafter, Bob Johnson fought his way through *three* additional Pacific battles—Tarawa, Saipan, and Tinian. Each island was its own brand of Hell. Tarawa, as he recalled was the worst landing. Naval Intelligence had miscalculated the tides, and the Marines had to wade through neck-high water as the onshore batteries cut them down. Saipan, however, was a personal nightmare. On his way to the beachhead, Bob's amtrack took a direct hit, wounding him and several others. "There was blood all over the place. It was just spurting out of my arm. It must have hit an artery."

When the ailing amtrack got to the shore, Bob ordered his Marines to get out, "but they were hesitating," he said. "I got to the front and dove out, and as I dove, a hand grenade went over my right head into the amtrack. I landed right on top of the Jap who had thrown the grenade. I had to get rid of him, that's all I knew." Bob killed that enemy soldier on the spot. "I've never talked about that at all until a few years ago."

As the Marines stormed Saipan, Bob was evacuated to a hospital ship, where they treated his arm and found a piece of shrapnel lodged in the cranial nerve of his neck. "I got patched up and rejoined my outfit a few days later."

Bob was preparing for the invasion of Japan when Emperor Hirohito announced the surrender in late August 1945. As part of the Occupation detail, Bob was sent to Kyushu, the southernmost Japanese island, where he went from town to town, "accepting the surrender of the local militia."

After the war, he returned to law school and was accepted to the Minnesota State Bar. Rekindling his friendship with Orville Freeman, the two served as 'Best Man" at each other's weddings. His graduation from the University of Minnesota's Law School was the start of a long and distinguished legal career. In 1948, he became a municipal judge; and from 1950–82 he was the Anoka County District Attorney. Even during his later years, he refused to retire. After leaving the DA's office, he entered private practice, where he continued litigating cases well into his 80s. When asked, at age 81, if he ever intended to retire, he simply shrugged and said: "I just come to work every day. I enjoy it."

But time eventually caught up to Bob Johnson. After a long and fulfilling legal career, he passed away in November 2010, at the age of 93.

13

COMMANDO KELLY

CHARLES E. KELLY,
MEDAL OF HONOR RECIPIENT

O n June 30, 1957, Charles E. Kelly appeared on an episode of *The Mike Wallace Interview*. Wallace opened his segment with the following monologue:

"My guest tonight was a hero of the Second World War. He's Commando Kelly, winner of the Congressional Medal of Honor, whose exploits included killing forty Germans within twenty minutes in the Battle of Salerno. Charles "Commando" Kelly, in just one of his battles, manned machine guns, rifles, and an anti-tank gun in a virtual single-handed defense of an ammunition dump and emerged unscratched. But in peacetime, Commando's been hit hard by bad-luck, ill-health, and financial misfortune."

Although hardly a dignified set-up, Charles Kelly nonetheless conducted himself with grace and poise throughout the interview. He had earned the nation's highest award for valor, but was quick to point out: "I don't think I deserve any more than any other GI just because I won the Medal of Honor. That don't make me a hero, it was just something that had to be done, and I was one of the fortunate ones."

Charles Kelly was born on September 23, 1920 in the working-class suburbs of Pittsburgh. As a kid from the "wrong side of the tracks," he spent most of his youth in a local street gang, and had numerous run-ins with the law. Despite his background as a juvenile delinquent, however, Kelly was accepted for military service in May 1942. By the following year, he was a corporal serving in the 143d Infantry Regiment, 36th Infantry Division.

In September 1943, Kelly's unit (L Company, 3d Battalion) was preparing to invade Salerno. The North African campaign had been a resounding success, and the Allies had just conquered Sicily. Taking Salerno would be the next step to conquering the Italian mainland, and getting a toehold on the European continent. Adding to the sense of good fortune was Italy's surrender on September 8, 1943. Hoping to exploit the newfound surrender, the Allies began their initial strike on Salerno the following day.

The Nazis, however, had anticipated their arrival.

They knew, as the Allies did, that the Gulf of Salerno was a critical crossroads between Sicily and Sardinia, the latter of which had just been vacated by the Axis.

Moreover, the Nazis had anticipated Italy's defection to the Allies. Although Mussolini and a few of his hardcore loyalists stayed within the Axis fold, creating the Italian Socialist Republic (an *ad hoc* splinter state), it would do nothing to stem the tide of an Allied invasion. As such, Field Marshal Albert Kesselring had the 16th Panzer Division dig in along the shores of Salerno, lying in wait for the Allied task force.

That morning of September 9, Charles Kelly waded ashore with other elements of the 36th Division. As he slogged inland, Kelly beheld the sight of his first fallen comrade: "A dead GI lying peacefully, as if asleep, with his head on his pack, his rifle by his side."

He averted his gaze, trying not to let the sight of a dead comrade faze him.

After clearing their way around a drainage ditch, Kelly's platoon met the raking gunfire of a German machine gun nest.

Kelly ducked to the ground as the whizzing bullets arced over his head.

He had narrowly escaped a premature death, but his staff sergeant hadn't been so lucky. "He went down with bullets in his head," recalled Kelly. To make matters worse, during the chaos of maneuvering around the machine gun nest, Kelly got separated from his unit.

Trying not to panic, he remembered the all-encompassing advice from his unit's leadership: "When you get on the beach, keep moving forward." It was enough to give any disoriented soldier a sense of direction. In wartime, it wasn't uncommon for soldiers to be separated from their units in the fog of combat. Thus, a general direction might help re-orient them towards an eventual rendezvous.

Taking his Browning Automatic Rifle (BAR) with him, Kelly followed a path until he came upon another group of GIs. They were mixed in from among two other companies in the regiment, and they were likely in the same situation as Kelly—separated from the main body

Charles E. Kelly.

of their respective units.

"Once more, I started looking for my outfit."

Striking down a new path, Kelly stumbled upon an abandoned farmhouse, picking peaches and grapes off the vine to satiate his hunger and stop the flow of adrenaline. "I figured I had walked about eight hours and must be about twelve miles inland." Factoring both the time and relative distance travelled, Kelly knew that he was likely in the vicinity of "Mountain 42"—a critical piece of high ground that his unit was expected to occupy. But before he could regain his bearings, he spotted a German Panzer IV rumbling down the road.

Diving into a nearby ditch, Kelly took aim and fired his BAR at the tank's slit openings. Of course, his 7.62mm bullets had no effect on the Panzer. And the Germans didn't even seem to notice that Kelly was shooting at them. Considering the noise of the tank's engine, and the mechanical droning from within the turret, the Panzer crew likely never heard the gunfire. "They rumbled and clanged by," he said, "and I kept walking down the highway, coming at last to a little creek, where I drank, took my shoes off, and bathed my feet."

While wringing out his socks, he suddenly spied the outline of Mountain 42. While hiking in the direction of the distant crag, he came upon a winery that, from what he could see, was now occupied by his regiment's 1st Battalion. Elated to have found a friendly unit, he knew that his own battalion had to be nearby. He briefly considered walking up to the 1st Battalion outpost. Surely, one of them would know where 3d Battalion had settled.

But as he drew nearer to the 1st Battalion foxholes, he quickly changed his mind.

These soldiers were a little too trigger-happy.

"They were shooting at sounds and dimly-seen movements," he said. Not the time for a social call. And certainly not the time to become a "friendly fire" statistic. Still, he couldn't blame them for being jittery. "Both sides had infiltrated into and behind each other," he said, "so that you had to be on alert each minute and watch every moving thing on each side of you." Rather than risk spooking his comrades, Kelly crawled under a nearby bush and got some sleep.

The next morning, he started down the highway, searching for anything that resembled a cluster of GIs. "It would have been nice to fill my canteen with water," he said, "but my canteen had picked up a bullet hole somewhere along the way." As he ambled down the country highway, German gunfire punctuated the long hours of silence, and Kelly eventually found his unit. As he recalled, they were "dug in among scattered, shallow holes"—hastily-prepared fighting positions dug into the countryside, waiting for the next wave of German counterattacks.

"Where the hell have you been?" they greeted him.

As it turned out, L Company had taken a tremendous beating. By the time Kelly rejoined their ranks at Mountain 42, they had been taking heavy artillery fire for the past few days. By now, the growing list of casualties had taken its toll on the unit's morale. The surviving soldiers now envied the dead. When Kelly reported to his platoon leader at Mountain 42, the lieutenant's only words were: "I sure wish they'd got you." Even among the officers, the better-off-dead mentality had infected the ranks.

Defeatist and Doomsday attitudes notwithstanding, Kelly and his comrades knew they had a job to do. "After a time, we started down the road," he said, en route to their next objective. As a rank-and-file soldier, Kelly often knew little about the broader context of their movements. When orders came to occupy a new piece of terrain, or move a certain number of miles inland, he did so without question. As they displaced from their foxholes, and marched tactically down the road, Kelly and his friends soon came upon a little Italian boy. But from the look on his face, they could see that this young boy was frightened and agitated.

"Germans! Germans! Germans!"

One of Kelly's friends who spoke fluent Italian tried to calm the boy, hoping to get more information on the whereabouts of these purported Germans. "But the kid was frightened and didn't make much sense," said Kelly. But just then, the lieutenant saw the Germans to which this boy had been referring.

"Here come some Heinie scout cars!" he shouted. "Get off the road!"

Kelly dove for cover as the enemy scout cars (likely Sd.Kfz wheeled variants) opened fire. The Americans returned fire, and two of Kelly's friends were hit. "All of a sudden, one of our boys got his bazooka on his shoulder," said Kelly, "and let go with a tremendous, crashing 'Boom!'" As the bazooka round drilled into the first enemy scout car, another GI jumped onto a nearby wall, leaping atop the second scout car, dropping his hand grenade into its crew compartment. That second car then shimmied to a halt.

The other scout vehicles quickly sped up, trying to envelop the dismounted GIs. The German crews might have succeeded, if not for a nearby anti-tank platoon. Indeed, one of 3d Battalion's anti-tank units had set up their 57mm recoilless rifles, and were taking aim at the incoming recon vehicles. "It was chancy stuff," said Kelly, "for if that 57mm had missed its target, it would have gotten us." But the anti-tank gunners engaged the remaining mounts with deadly accuracy. "The bazooka kept on booming, and, quicker than it seemed possible, that whole small reconnaissance detachment was knocked out. The place was a shambles. Scout cars were going up in flames. Tires were burning with a rubbery stink, and bodies were burning too." Kelly recalled one German leaping out from his disabled vehicle, attempting to flee the battlefield. "When we went after him," said Kelly, "he put his revolver to his head and killed himself. We had thought that only the Japs did that, and for a moment I was surprised and shocked."

But these feelings of shock soon gave way to what Kelly described as a "deep-rooted GI habit"—they started collecting souvenirs. One of his friends wrangled a German Luger; others were happy to find knives, insignias, and German Reichsmark notes. "Looking back at it," he recalled, "I can remember no feeling about the German dead except curiosity. We were impersonal about them; to us they were just bundles of rags."

About two hours later, Kelly and his unit moved into another nearby town. "The townspeople were out waving at us and offering us water, wine, and fruit," he said. Kelly also remembered it was the first time he had seen an Italian jail. "A woman had told us it was where they kept the Fascist sympathizers. The leading Fascist citizen of the town was in there, mad as blazes, and yelling his head off behind the bars."

Later that night, Kelly's platoon sergeant organized a mission to the nearby town of Altavilla. Division intelligence estimated a sizeable German contingent operating within the vicinity. "See that town over there?" said the platoon sergeant. "That's where I'm going, and I want some volunteers to go with me. I'm taking the second platoon and some sixty-millimeter mortars"—which included Charles Kelly.

As they drew closer to Altavilla, the platoon came upon an Italian man. Second Platoon was fortunate to have *three* Italian-speaking GIs within their ranks—Gatto, Survilo, and La Bue—all of whom intently listened to the local man. "The Italian didn't seem to know where the Germans were," said Kelly, "or whether they were in the town or not, but we took what he had to tell us with a cupful of salt." Italy had formally surrendered the day before the invasion, "but we had been told not to believe it, for our officers didn't want us to feel relaxed and spoil the fighting edge we had worked up."

Still, Altavilla seemed to be friendly, and devoid of any Axis sympathizers. "They were all out shaking hands with us, and telling us they came from St. Louis or Brooklyn or other towns and cities all over the United States. They kept saying, 'I speaka Engleesh,' and bringing out bottles of wine and glasses. But we didn't have much time for that; we were busy trying to find places to set up our weapons." The company commander then ordered Kelly to carry the unit's water and ammunition stores into the mayor's house—"a big, solidly-built, very beautiful building," Kelly remembered. "But first, he wanted me to be sure that the house was free of Germans. We checked every room on the first floor, leaving a man in each room. Then I went up the stairs, and found a girl ducked down under some blankets on a bed"—presumably the mayor's daughter. "I pulled the blankets back and motioned for her to get out," to which she complied, but not without yelling and cursing up a storm. Understandably, the young girl was irate at the sight of American GIs taking over her family's home. "Still yelling, she went downstairs to join her family. Men began hauling ammunition in through the door and setting up machine guns in the courtyard and in the windows. Before it grew dark, we had changed that building into a fortress-arsenal."

During the night, however, the Germans occupied a nearby hill, one-half mile away. Their position on that hill gave them an excellent redoubt over the American positions in Altavilla. The town itself was on the slope of a hill which, as Kelly recalled, featured a road at its base, leading ten miles out to the beach. "The mayor's house fronted on the town square, and both were in the uphill half of the town," said Kelly, "near its outskirts and overlooking the road." This meant that the Germans atop the nearby hill would have a clear line of fire to the mayor's house and the American outposts. During the ensuing battle, Kelly recalled that the Germans came down their hill, "and also down the slopes of the hill upon which the town was located."

The next morning, just as Kelly was preparing to eat breakfast, the German machine gun nests opened fire. "They had a beautiful field of fire," he said, "and knocked out one of our machine guns in the courtyard." Enemy bullets ripped into the GI machine gunners, and Kelly was aghast as he remembered that "the gun itself was sticky with blood, and had small nicks where the bullets had bitten into its metal. The men who had manned it lay around dead."

And, at this point, Kelly didn't even have a weapon. He had lent his rifle to a lieutenant the day before. "I had picked up two or three since then," he said, "but now I didn't have a gun. I felt naked without it." With enemy gunfire erupting all around him, he bolted upstairs looking for any available firearm.

As luck would have it, he found a BAR lying on the floor.

"I also found a pair of field glasses and, kneeling at a window, I could see men walking on Hill 315. The fire directed at us was coming from that hill, so I knew the men on it must still be Germans. I loaded my gun, waited a second to make sure my aim was true, and fired. When I picked up the field glasses again and took a look, three of the men who had been moving before were lying still. A fourth, who had fallen into a foxhole, was still moving one foot, so I upped with the BAR and let it chatter once more. When I peered through the glasses, that foot slowly straightened out and lay flat on the ground."

During a brief lull in the battle, a fellow GI (a lone machine gunner), plunked himself down at a window next to Kelly's, ready to lay down additional fire. "We spotted Gerry machine guns in the distance," Kelly continued. "Every time I'd duck down to load my BAR, the Gerry machine gun went into action. When I popped up ready to squirt lead, Gerry was busy loading."

The friendly machine gunner in the next window, however, wasn't so lucky.

He was hit through the shoulder, and began crying for a medic. But this wounded gunner wasn't the only soldier in peril. From the other rooms in the house, several more GIs joined the chorus of "Medic!" as they too were being hit by the incoming fire. Surprisingly, one of the first "medics" on the scene was a German POW who had been a doctor before the war. The GIs wrangled him over to the wounded, ordering him to render medical aid. "That Kraut doc really knew his trade," said Kelly. "In no time at all, he was fixing up two of our wounded for every one [that] our own medic was repairing."

By this time, Kelly had fired his BAR so much that it literally ceased to function. "When I put the next magazine load of cartridges in it, it wouldn't work anymore."

Kelly was dumbfounded, but he had no time to troubleshoot the weapon.

He had to keep returning fire.

"I laid it against a bed, went into another room to get another BAR, and when I got back, the bed was on fire. That first gun was so hot that it touched the bed off like tinder." Unfazed by the sudden inferno, Kelly took aim and began firing his new BAR until its barrel lit up with the reddish-orange glow of an overheated weapon.[1] With the barrel now warped from the excess heat, Kelly discarded the BAR, and began searching for another.

No luck. But he did find a fully-loaded Thompson submachine gun.

"So, I went upstairs...went to the window and gunned for some more Germans. There was no assurance that we would ever get away from that house. Any of us. We seemed a hell of a small island in an ocean

---

Kelly or one of his comrades must have extinguished the bed fire at some point during the battle. Or the bed may have been small enough to burn itself out, sans igniting the entire house.

of Germans. Yet I don't think any of us thought much about it. Not then, anyhow." To make matters worse, the Germans were descending into the town, and the battle was devolving into a close-quarters street fight.

By now, Kelly had burned out two Browning Automatic Rifles, and was using all the ammunition he could find for his Thompson submachine gun. When his Tommy gun ran dry, he picked up the next available weapon he could find—a bazooka. "Now, I picked up a bazooka," he said, "and crawled among our dead men in the upper floor, looking for bazooka shells. Those shells weighed about four pounds each. I brought down six of them, and put one in…but it wouldn't go off. I worked on that bazooka for a while, then poked it out of the window and pulled the trigger. The men in the house thought an 88-mm shell had hit the place. All the pressure came out of the back end of that tin pipe, along with a lot of red flame, and the house trembled and shook."

Kelly fired that bazooka four times before he spied a box of dynamite on the floor. He asked his platoon sergeant if they could use it, but to no avail—"we had no caps or fuses." Lying beside the dynamite, however, was a small incendiary device. "I threw that at the roof of a nearby building the Germans were holding," he said. "It exploded there and the house started to burn." Capitalizing on that momentum, Kelly picked up a 60mm mortar shell, pulled out the safety pin, and tapped it on the window ledge, making it a live round—"or, the way I planned to use it, a live bomb." For if the mortar shell landed on its nose, it would provide the necessary percussion weight to detonate on impact. As Kelly looked out the window, he could see a handful of Germans coming up a small ravine by the rear of the house. "I whirled that shell around and let it drop among them. I did the same thing with another shell. As each of them landed, there was a cracking roar, and when I looked out again, five of the Germans were dead."

With no mortar rounds left, Kelly went searching for yet another weapon. Grimly, he found his third BAR in the hands of a dead comrade on the third floor of the house. "His ammunition was lying in the belt beside him," he recalled, "but he didn't have much of it left." Thus, Kelly found some machine gun cartridges of the same caliber, and put them into the BAR magazines. "Then, I took it down to the front room and started to squeeze its trigger. Another man, three or four feet away, had an M1 rifle. Every once in a while, he got excited and stood up to shoot. But he tried it once too often. Peering from my window, I could see a stream of tracers coming from off in the distance," one of which hit the rifleman next to Kelly, passing right through his shoulder. "He slumped down to the floor, blood poured from his shoulder," followed by the inevitable cries for a medic.

Kelly, meanwhile, continued to bullseye German soldiers with his *third* BAR of the day. "Snipers were touching up the men down in the kitchen," he said, "and someone sent for me to go down and help." When Kelly got there, however, he was aghast to see his fellow GIs *cooking spaghetti*, nonchalantly as if nothing else was happening. They were gingerly going about their kitchen routines, "just as if they were chefs in a ravioli joint back home and food was all they had to think about." Kelly continued: "They had spread tablecloths, had laid out knives and forks, had sliced bread, watermelon and honeydews, and had put out grapes and tomatoes."

Kelly was beside himself.

Here they were, in the middle of a life-and-death firefight, and these GIs were setting up meals as if it were a five-star restaurant. They didn't even seem to care that the German snipers were drilling holes into the kitchen windows. "I don't mind people doing screwy things," he said, "it helps to let off steam sometimes when things are so tight that otherwise you'd go off your rocker, but to see them readying that meal made me mad."

Kelly blew up at his comrades, but his remarks didn't faze them.

"Ah, quit blowing your top, Kelly," they said as they continued stirring their spaghetti. "So, I thought, the hell with it. Maybe they've got a good idea there."

With a shrug, Kelly found the nearest box of champagne, broke the neck off a bottle, and took a hearty gulp. "Then I took the straw off a big basket, got out three or four eggs, broke them into an empty C ration can and drank them raw. Still tasting those eggs, I went over to the window through which those snipers' bullets had been coming. Nobody had been paying much attention to the snipers; they had been having their own way and had grown careless about concealment. I saw one of them in a tree, and drew a bead on him. His rifle dropped from the tree first; then, after a few seconds, he toppled down limply to the ground himself. While I was squatting there, one of the men from upstairs came down with about fifty BAR magazines, lay beside me and began feeding me ammo. On a distant hill, tanks were firing at us. I took a look at them through a pair of field glasses, and saw a Heinie on top of a turret, shooting at us with a 20mm cannon. I fired about twenty magazine loads at him."

After firing the first 15 magazines in rapid succession, this gun's barrel, too, was turning red. But Kelly fired the remaining five clips for good measure. Looking through his field glasses once more, he could see that the turret was down, and one of the Panzers had fled the scene. Deciding to give his red-hot glowing BAR a rest, Kelly took a swig of champagne—the first he'd ever had. "To me, it tasted like soda pop, and after drinking it I felt full of gas bubbles." Back at the window, he spotted a lone German soldier coming towards the house by way of a small gully. By now, the BAR had cooled off, and the barrel had returned to its normal graphite hue. But when Kelly pulled the trigger, the BAR wouldn't fire.

"I pulled it again, but it still wouldn't fire."

Even when he threw a bullet into the firing chamber, the BAR couldn't produce enough pressure to ignite the propellant, "so I had to let that German come ahead," he said wryly. "He was coming from where our troops were supposed to be, and it dawned on us that the Germans had separated Company K from Companies I and L, and built a circle around them. We were running low on ammo and we had almost given up hope of relief. Our only communication with the world outside the mayor's house was our radio, and the Germans had jammed that. They had gotten hold of one of our radios, tuned to the same frequency we were using, and all we could hear over our set were Germans talking."

Miraculously, the house-bound GIs found a hand-set phone radio, and re-established contact with 3d Battalion Headquarters. After a few minutes of back-and-forth radio chatter, Battalion agreed to let the GIs in the mayoral home withdraw after nightfall, escaping under the cover of darkness. "In the meantime," however, "we were to stay there and fight."

As daylight faded, Kelly and his comrades gathered up the remaining ammunition and started a decoy firing pattern on one side of the house while the GIs escaped out from the other side, six men at a time. "There were about thirty of us left alive," Kelly remembered. "The lieutenant broke us down into groups of six men each, and at intervals those groups drifted away." Those who remained behind kept firing to cover the retreat. "I offered to stay as part of the rear guard," said Kelly, "and Bill Swayze, a six-foot-five GI from Trenton, New Jersey, said, 'I'm going to stay, too.'" Kelly remembered Bill as a "fast talker" with a perennially cheerful disposition. Even in the heat of combat, "he had grinned all through the battle," said Kelly, "and he was good company."

After the last group of GIs had exfiltrated the house, Kelly crawled out with Bill Swayze, the lieutenant, and another GI from K Company. "We took with us the wounded who could travel. The ones who were hit too badly to move we left there. We heard Germans coming into the house behind us. Then I heard guns going off upstairs. Our guns. The wounded had saved a few rounds for a last fight. The Germans yelled 'Surrender!' but the firing didn't stop short; it gradually flickered out."

Stealthily sneaking their way out of town, Kelly and his friends came upon their unit's communication wire. "It was like finding a street you know after wandering around lost in a big city," he said. All they had to do was follow the landline…and they'd eventually find the unit's command post. "Miles farther along, we heard somebody yell the word, 'Hollywood!'" said Kelly—the challenge to which they would have to provide the password. The so-called "challenge" and "password" was a long-standing tradition in the Anglophone armies. It was a security measure to verify any unknown persons lurking beyond a unit's perimeter. A sentry would yell the challenge word—in this case, "Hollywood"—to which the other soldier, if he were in the same unit, would know the password reply. "Luckily, I remembered the answer to that challenge," said Kelly, "and called back, 'Theater!'" As a general rule, passwords were carefully selected based on phonetics that the enemy would have difficulty pronouncing. For example, Germans typically pronounced "th" as if it were a "z." This gave rise to using passwords like "Theater" and "Thunder." For if a password were compromised, and a German tried to use it in hopes of gaining entry into an American position, the GIs could spot the imposter by hearing him say "*Zeater*" or "*Zunder*." The same logic held true in the Pacific, where passwords were deliberately chosen by the letter "L" (i.e. lollipop) because the Japanese pronounced the letter "L" as an "R."

"Sixteen of our men had been waiting with their rifles on us, ready to let us have it, if we'd given the wrong countersign," Kelly continued. Among them were several of the men who had escaped from the mayor's house in the earlier groups of six. After taking a quick head count, the lieutenant in charge gathered up the survivors and ran towards the nearest confirmed Allied position.

But for his actions on September 13, 1943, Charles Kelly was awarded the Congressional Medal of Honor. It was the first Medal of Honor awarded to a soldier in the European Theater. After receiving his medal, Kelly returned stateside, where he toured the US as part of the Army Ground Forces "Here's Your Infantry" demonstration team. It was, by all accounts, a PR "Dog-and-Pony Show"—selling war bonds and demonstrating various battle techniques. When the tour ended, he was assigned to the Infantry School at Fort Benning, Georgia. He received his Honorable Discharge in the summer of 1945 at the rank of Technical

Sergeant.

Years later, Kelly reflected on his actions at Altavilla. "I've had people ask me what a man thinks of at a time like that." Most people expected him to say that a soldier thinks of home, or wonders if his soul is ready to meet the Almighty. "The truth is," said Kelly, "once a man is in action, he thinks very little about home or the hereafter…and most of his thoughts are focused on finishing the job at hand."

As Kelly recalled: "A GI has to work out his own philosophy of fighting." Early on, Kelly adopted a mindset of continuous positive affirmation. In other words, he *refused* to die. "If I ever let myself go into battle thinking, 'This is one battle I'm not going to come out of,' I'd be no good as a soldier, and I probably wouldn't come out of it. Once in a while, anybody gets scared. But if you don't think about it, it doesn't last. One of the things that helps drive away fear is actually seeing, the enemy. It's patrol work and fear of the unknown that gets on your nerves. Then, too, having a buddy killed snaps men out of the jitters."

Unfortunately, Kelly's return to civilian life was marked by personal tragedy. In 1946, he opened a service station in his hometown of Pittsburgh. However, he was forced to sell it the following year after a robbery and a downturn in business. That same year, his first wife Mae was diagnosed with cancer, which ultimately took her life in 1951. The cost of her radiation treatments eventually drove the Kellys into foreclosure, and they lost their home. After Mae's death, Kelly's sister said: "He went out of control after that and was never the same again."

Having lost his wife and his business, Kelly took a series of odd jobs—working as a security guard, house painter, and construction worker—none of which he held for very long. However, a reprieve of sorts came in 1952, when General Dwight D. Eisenhower ran for president. The former Supreme Allied Commander asked Kelly to help him on the campaign trail. While at a campaign stop in Louisville, Kentucky, Kelly met Ms. Betty Gaskins.

They were married six weeks later.

Still, he couldn't ignore the harsh realities of civilian life. He was running out of money, and was being rejected by every potential employer he sought. In a 1952 interview, Kelly admitted: "When you're in combat, you have a job to do; you know how to do it; and you know you can do it. But these years have been rough. Your hands are tied. You have a thing to do, but you can't do it. You go in and ask a man for a job. It's a job you never had before, and you're asking for it. And you get so many 'No's.'"

However, the story of Kelly's plight as a hard-luck war hero became a media sensation. Newspapers throughout the country ran stories about him, drawing attention to the fact that a Medal of Honor recipient should never have this much trouble finding gainful employment. Money donations poured into the family, along with more than 100 job offers. Kelly purportedly accepted a job with a scrap iron company in St Louis, whose owner provided financial assistance for Kelly to purchase an eight-bedroom home. However, Kelly quit the job before his family even had a chance to move in.

But soon thereafter, Kelly seemed to have gotten another lifeline. Kentucky Governor (and former Senator), AB "Happy" Chandler, arranged a job for Kelly as an inspector in the State Highway Department. It was a steady job, and one that paid $340 a month ($3,514.35 in 2022 money). Still, by the time of his appearance on *The Mike Wallace Interview*, Kelly's wife Betty said: "Chuck deserves a better deal from his country; he did something special as a soldier, and now he should get some kind of special consideration."

But things only got worse for Charles "Commando" Kelly. He kept his position in the State Highway Department until April 1961, when he called Betty to say that he was going to Cuba to fight Fidel Castro. He ended the call with a promise to set up a trust fund for her and the kids, but instructed her not to try to find him.

Charles Kelly never returned home.

For the next 15 years, Betty had no idea of his whereabouts. In 1962, she divorced him in absentia, and raised their children as a single mother. During his self-imposed exile, Kelly began to drink more heavily, and became an itinerant worker, moving from Kentucky to California to Texas, and finally re-settling on the East Coast. Sometime in the 1970s, Kelly was involved in an auto accident in Washington, DC, whereafter he was hospitalized for nearly a year with a fractured skull and broken legs.

In 1984, Kelly resurfaced at the VA Hospital in Pittsburgh. After several decades of hard drinking, his kidneys and liver were failing. He had taken the bus to the hospital and told the VA clerk that he had no living relatives, even though his children and five of his brothers were still alive. On January 11, 1985, Charles Kelly facilitated his own death by deliberately pulling the treatment tubes from his body.

He was 64 years old.

He was buried at Highwood Cemetery in Pittsburgh. To this day, no one knows the whereabouts of his medals.

14
THE LONGEST WINTER

CHARLIE HAUG:
A REPLACEMENT IN THE "BLOODY BUCKET" DIVISION

A native of Sleepy Eye, Minnesota, Charles "Charlie" Haug enlisted in the Army on February 19, 1943. He completed Basic Training at Camp Wolter, Texas; and was initially assigned to the 92nd Infantry Division at Fort Leonard Wood, Missouri, before leaving overseas as a "replacement." Being a replacement was inevitable for many soldiers during times of conscription. As the name implied, their job was to *replace* an individual soldier who'd been killed in action. However, that fallen soldier often had strong ties to the comrades he'd left behind. Thus, the "replacement" was often seen as an outsider—someone who had to prove his worth, and try to make friends among the battle-hardened veterans in his company. Very often, replacements came and went so quickly (i.e., killed or wounded) that their platoon mates avoided getting to know them. Charlie Haug expected as much when he departed the US aboard a troop carrier on September 12th, 1944.

In fact, every GI on that ship was a designated "replacement," not knowing where he'd ultimately be assigned. They only knew that they were headed to Europe. "Each man had just been issued new clothes and a new rifle, and all 4,000 on the ship were being sent as replacements in units that had been shot up during the Allied advance across northern Europe to the gates of Germany." By September 1944, Italy was firmly in Allied hands, and the invasion of France had been rolling back the tide of Nazi aggression. In fact, it seemed that the Allies would be in the Fatherland by Christmas. But little did they know that certain pockets of the *Wehrmacht* were about to catch their second wind, and launch a counteroffensive in the Ardennes Forest.

Haug's group landed at Omaha Beach near the end of September. Although it had been three months since the Normandy invasion, the beach still bore the unmistakable scars of combat. "In either direction," he said, "all we could see were wrecked ships and landing barges." The torrential rain that greeted them as they arrived on Omaha Beach only added to the somberness. And, as they stepped onto the steep cliff leading from the shore, Charlie caught his first glimpse of the American cemetery. "As we looked at these thousands of crosses, we realized for the first time just how many men can be killed in a single battle." Each one of these graves marked the body of a man who had fallen on D-Day.

Following a series of marches, truck rides, and a five-day journey inside a cramped "Forty & Eight" boxcar, Charlie arrived at the frontlines near the German-Belgian border on Veterans Day—November 11, 1944. His final destination was Company B, 112th Regiment, 28th Infantry Division. Known as the "Keystone Division," the 28th was Pennsylvania's federalized National Guard unit. More recently, they had earned the nickname "Bloody Bucket," owing to their bright red, semi-trapezoidal unit patch. The 28th Division was among the hardest-hit units during the bloody, brutal fighting in the Hurtgen Forest. The battle had cost them more than 6,000 casualties, hence the need for replacements like Charlie.

When he reached the survivors of Company B, however, it was a "pitiful sight." As Charlie remembered: "They had been in the attack for eight constant days, and there was only a handful of them left. Their clothes were all caked with mud, their faces were all dirt and grease. None of them would say a word to us. They just sat there and stared. Occasionally, one would drop his head between his knees and sob like a baby. They had had enough. They didn't want us to replace their buddies whom they had just seen fall, because this meant that they would have to go up into it again. They immediately made each of these poor men a sergeant, and they put them in charge of us green replacements."

The reluctant sergeants made Charlie a "platoon runner"—a messenger between his platoon and the company command post. The 28th Division then moved north into Luxembourg, relieving a unit that had been on the line for nearly a month. By this time, the weather was getting colder, and the first snowfalls had begun. Still, Charlie didn't find life on the frontlines all that bad, minus the occasional artillery attack. Company B was, after all, facing a portion of the Siegfried Line, and the Germans were hunkered down inside a network of well-constructed pillboxes.

Charlie shared his foxhole with two other "runners," but the three of them made their earthen abode livable with a layer of straw; and they burned bark inside an old oil drum for warmth. Throughout the night,

Charlie Haug.

each of them stood guard in two-hour shifts. Their twice-daily meals were served only during the hours of darkness (9:00PM and 4:00AM), so the enemy couldn't see them walking around. "As December began, the extreme cold forced the company to move into the small German town of Lutzkampen," which was much closer to the *Wehrmacht's* main line of resistance. The Division's outpost in Lutzkampen was fairly secure— "except for one day when a German patrol wandered into town and killed a GI who was souvenir hunting." Charlie then had the unenviable task of hauling his dead comrade back to the rear. While carrying the body of his deceased friend, Charlie's pants were soaked by the blood. And it would be two months before Charlie could get another pair.

Being from Minnesota, the cold weather didn't bother Charlie much, but trench foot was a persistent problem in the ranks. Some men found that when they removed their boots, they were unable to put them back on because their feet had swollen so badly. "The troops were issued new socks and overshoes that were two sizes too big." After a few weeks, however, the collective swelling went down, and the men returned to wearing their normal sizes.

There was very little action in Company B's sector until the pre-dawn hours of December 16, 1944. The previous night, December 15, Charlie had stood guard from 10:00PM until Midnight, and got four hours of sleep before rotating back onto his guard shift. "Little did I know," he said, "I had just had my last real sleep for the next ten days."

Suddenly, at 5:10AM, the sky erupted with the sights and sounds of German flares. "The whole sky had become light, just like dawn was breaking and it was two hours early. What the hell happened? Who turned on the light switch? It took about a minute before we finally got out mouths closed again." The artillery battery supporting Company B responded, firing multiple volleys into the suspected German positions, but with little success. Shortly after 6:00AM, the Germans initiated their own counter-battery fire, punctuated by an infantry advance on Lutzkampen. Two American outpost were quickly overrun as the sounds of German gunfire filled the air. "This was our initiation into the famous Battle of the Bulge," said Charlie. "We didn't realize it yet, but we had been caught directly in the middle of a German attack."

The gunfire waned at around 7:00 AM as the Germans consolidated their forces around Lutzkampen. By 7:30, however, they renewed the attack. "Out of the still darkness came the awfullest screaming and yelling you would ever want to hear. The Germans were coming. They were screaming, and they were less than 100 yards in front of us. How they got so close without our hearing them, we'll never know. There was a steady stream of lead pouring from their guns. Many of their bullets were tracers, and the red streaks snapped in every direction."

Still, the GIs had the upper hand.

They were concealed by their foxholes, and the Germans were exposed, offering clear and silhouetted targets. "During the first half hour of the battle, our men had some pretty easy pickings." But Company B had suffered some serious casualties as well. Their company commander was killed in action, as were the two medics who tried to save him.

By 10:00 AM, the Germans' hasty counterattack had failed. Those who had survived began waving their white handkerchiefs. As Charlie began wrangling the first of these German POWs, he was surprised to see that many of them were just young boys. "The oldest was perhaps about 18 and the youngest about 14." Moreover, these young conscripts began to pelt the GIs with numerous questions, like: "Will I be sent to New York City?" These German boys seemed anxious to see America.

In this opening firefight, the Germans had lost 135 men. Company B had held their ground, but their sister companies on either flank had been cut down. This left the 90 surviving men of Company B to spread out over a defensive front nearly one mile long. "We still had some faith left in the American Army though, and we prayed that other outfits in the rear would be able to stop the Germans and push back up to us. We had lost contact with our division, but we didn't have any orders to withdraw, so we had to sit tight."

By 3:00 PM on December 16, the main body of the German attack force reconsolidated at Lutzkampen. Company B hunkered down, but they no longer had "priority of fires" for artillery support. To make matters worse, all of their machine gunners had been killed. Later that evening, the Germans renewed their assault, this time with half a dozen Panzers in the lead. The first Panzer came within 50 feet of the outpost American foxhole; but this was no garden-variety German tank—it was a *Flammpanzer 38*, a flame-throwing combat vehicle. And it wasted no time unleashing its fiery death onto the first two GIs in its path. "The two kids sat there helplessly as a gigantic stream of roaring fire shot in on them. Their worries were over. All of us on the hillside [Company B's current position] saw this, and we knew we were next. It terrified our guys, and many of them jumped up from their holes and ran back over the hill into the thick woods behind."

Charlie and a few others stood their ground, but to what possible avail?

They had no anti-tank weapons in the foxholes, and certainly nothing that would stop a *flamethrower* tank. But as the lead Panzer got within 200 yards of Charlie's foxhole…a miracle happened. From another hillside nearly a quarter-mile away, an anti-tank gun from a sister unit began to fire on the incoming Panzers. "The first few shells missed, but suddenly the lead tank burst into flames. Soon, the second and third tanks were hit, and a few seconds later the fourth and fifth tanks were burning." The final Panzer beat a hasty retreat.

Saved by the anonymous angel gunner, Charlie sprang to his feet, going from foxhole to foxhole to count the living and the dead.

His numbers were heartbreaking. Of the 90 men in Company B, only 18 had survived.

And the one remaining lieutenant (who was now the company commander by default) told his men to keep standing strong. As night fell, the young lieutenant surmised that a quick artillery strike might eliminate the German ground troops in Lutzkampen.

It was a solid idea. But at this point, could the artillery even support it?

Given the high volume of fire missions, the howitzer batteries had likely run out of ammunition. Still, it was worth asking. But with all their communications down, the GIs' only method of inquiry was to send a runner…a job that inevitably befell Charlie. "Ken Jenne [a fellow trooper] and I were ordered to contact the artillery," he said. Normally, Ken and Charlie would have no issue sending the request. But today, their anticipated path to the artillery unit would take them through enemy-held territory…in broad daylight.

Not surprisingly, Ken and Charlie had walked barely 200 yards before the Germans opened fire. "They started firing mortar shells on the hillside we were climbing," said Charlie. "About 15 shells landed around us, but we were not hit by shrapnel."

It was the second miracle Charlie had experienced that morning.

A few moments later, Ken and Charlie came upon the Forward Observers' outpost…but all he found were their discarded rifles, helmets, and cartridge belts. "The men had evidently been captured just hours before"—thus robbing the howitzer batteries of their essential spotters. Dismayed but not discouraged, the two runners headed farther west to find the gun batteries. But as they made their way across an open field, they were quickly greeted by a hail of grazing gunfire, and the unmistakable roar of a Panzer's engine. Neither Ken nor Charlie attempted to gauge the direction of the gunfire; *they just started running.* "The machine gun bullets were kicking up snow…and the shells from the tank's gun were ripping up the treetops." With so many friendly and enemy units intertwined along the Ardennes front, it was often hard to gauge who was firing at whom. But given the intensity of the fire, and the telltale sound of German equipment, there was little question as to who was firing. Years later, at a Battle of the Bulge reunion, Charlie recalled that: "Jenne told the group that normally when a person runs, their legs go one in front of the other. But as we crossed the field that day, he said mine were going all the way around."

After what seemed like an eternity, Ken and Charlie reached the thick of the woods, out of sight and range from the German ground fire. A few hours later, they ambled into the fire base of the 229th Field Artillery. Surprisingly, at the fire base, Charlie found several of his comrades from Company B who had fled from the previous day's Panzer attack. The bad news, however, was that the artillery battalion had, in fact, run out of ammunition. Ken and Charlie briefly considered walking back to Lutzkampen, but decided it would be a "suicide mission." Instead, the remnants of Company B, along with the 229th Artillery, headed farther west at nightfall.

The ragtag GIs travelled through the open country until they came to a road, which they followed for nearly a mile. The road led to a bridge, guarded by two German sentries at its entrance. The GIs killed the guards and crossed over the bridge, but the presence of these two guards was a telltale sign that there were other Germans nearby. Thus, the Americans dispersed into the woods, heading west at their own pace.

A few hours later, they came upon an abandoned town where other American stragglers had congregated. "We now had a few men from every company in the 112th Regiment, and they all told the same story," Charlie recalled. "They had been attacked on December 16, and most of their men had been killed or captured." Still, these battered Americans decided to form a defensive perimeter around the town. Charlie was put in charge of running ammunition to the outpost machine gun teams. Later that same day, however, the Germans advanced on the town. Charlie made only *one* round trip to the machine gun team before it was overrun by enemy Panzers. Realizing it had become a "no win" situation, Charlie and the other GIs made a break for the forest.

They escaped farther west, keeping a steady pace until the afternoon of December 18. By now, they were fighting off exhaustion and the much-maligned adrenaline dump. "As we lay there, we realized for the first time that we were mighty hungry. Some of our guys had not had a bite to eat for three days now." Some of the retreating soldiers had scavenged food from the town they had just departed; and Colonel Gus Nelson (the ranking officer in the group) ordered the remaining food to be divvied up among the men. "Each of us got a little something to chew on," said Charlie.

As the group hunkered down for the night, they were unexpectedly joined by five other GIs from Company B. As it turned out, these five wayward soldiers were all that remained of the sixteen men whom Ken and Charlie had left behind at Lutzkampen. Now, this hodgepodge of GIs from the 112th Infantry and 229th Artillery huddled together, trying to conserve body heat. "It began to snow during the night, and it was still snowing when dawn broke on the 19th of December." Under the cover of this snowfall, Charlie and his comrades moved out along the first road they came upon. The following day, they came upon another American unit where they dug in and repelled a series of German attacks throughout the 20th and 21st.

The battered GIs were holding their own, but the bigger question was: "Where was the rest of the Army?" These isolated pockets of soldiers seemed to be all alone in the Ardennes, fighting off whatever German probes came their way. "There seemed to be no help coming from anywhere," said Charlie. "We ourselves had now retreated about 30 miles since the first day of the attack, and it looked like the only thing we could do was retreat again." More to the point, their morale was falling. Two of Charlie's comrades had shot themselves in the foot, hoping to earn a ticket home. Instead, the two men were left behind with their self-inflicted wounds as the rest of the group retreated farther into the woods. "Everybody was hungry and tired and cold. Whenever two or three of us got together, we would always find ourselves talking about whether or not we should give ourselves up the next time we were attacked." There was no sign of help; and every day the Germans seemed to be gaining more strength. "We thought the Germans were winning the war."

With few options left, the officers of the group decided to leave a dozen troops at every major crossroad to slow down the Germans' advance, and perhaps buy more time for the main body of retreating American forces. As they came to the third crossroad, Charlie was among the next dozen selected to stand guard. "We were scared, and as we watched the rest of the guys head down the road, we were wishing we could be going with them. Soon they were out of sight, and we were left to our fate.

Two hours later, an American M3 halftrack zoomed by—but this halftrack was carrying German troops. It was another piece of captured Allied equipment. During the drive to the German borderlands, both sides had captured and impressed vehicles from the other. And this formerly American halftrack was followed by a long convoy of enemy trucks.

Charlie and his friends, realizing they were outnumbered and outgunned, beat a hasty retreat into the woods. Part of the German contingent caught up to them near a village on the other side of the woods, whereupon two of Charlie's friends were felled by machine gun fire. Charlie himself was running so hard that he lost his helmet as he dashed into another thicket of trees. "We must have run for an hour steady," he said, "and then we were so exhausted we all stopped, threw ourselves on the ground and rested. Our lungs ached."

By now it was dark, and the men suddenly realized it was Christmas Eve. "We didn't have the slightest idea where we were," he said, but they decided to continue west. Soon they came upon a river, which they estimated to be nearly 100 yards wide. Not keen to making a river crossing in the dead of winter, the men looked for a bypass…until they heard the incoming mortar attack. The shelling, however, was American. Indeed, the rounds were passing over their heads, and landing in the opposite direction. Charlie and his friends then realized that they were getting closer to friendly lines, and thus waded across the river.

A short time later, the ten GIs came upon a Belgian farmhouse, whose occupants gave them bread, but warned them that several thousand German troops were in the area. Once back on the road, Charlie met the first other Americans he had seen in days. As luck would have it, a small convoy of Jeeps came around the bend, picking up Charlie and his battered friends.

But their luck ran out nearly as soon as they had found it.

For within only a few moments, the convoy was intercepted by a German patrol. Two of Charlie's friends, Frankie Jordano and Warren Quimby, were riding in the lead vehicle and were taken prisoner. However, when the Germans noticed that Warren was missing a leg from a prior battlefield injury, they decided to kill him rather than tend to his wounds. "They saw Quimby's leg was gone, and a German pointed a rifle at Quimby's head." Panicking, Quimby raised his arms and shouted "No! No!" but it was no use—"there was a loud crack and Quimby's body bounced back on the ground. He felt no more pain."

Charlie himself was a bit luckier. His Jeep was farther down the line, far enough to give his driver time to throw it in reverse. But as the Jeep crested a nearby hill, the driver met an enemy bullet. Charlie and a few others fled into the woods, but two of their number were wounded during the escape. One comrade caught a bullet to the neck, but was still alive; the other caught a bullet to his gluteus muscles. The latter could walk, but he could no longer sit down. Another man in the group, Lieutenant

Mayer Goldstein, one of the few surviving officers, was nursing earlier wounds in both of his legs.

"Our three wounded guys were exhausted," he said. "The kid that was shot in the neck kept falling down all the time, and was getting awfully weak from the loss of blood. We knew that we couldn't keep going like this much longer, so we decided to head for town. If the Krauts were in town, we'd give ourselves up."

Given the circumstances, it seemed like their only option.

"No matter which way we went, we ran into Germans," said Charlie. "The woods were full of small groups of Americans trying to survive." Because Charlie was the only man in the group who still had a rifle, the senior sergeant ordered him to go into town and make the overtures for surrender.

Racked by hunger pangs and lack of sleep, Charlie stumbled towards the nearest house in the village. As he got nearer to the house, an angry voice rang out from the darkness.

"Halt!"

Charlie threw down his weapon and raised his arms, signaling his surrender.

But that same angry voice then cried out: "Who the hell are you?"

Charlie had just surrendered to a paratrooper from the 82d Airborne Division. Indeed, Charlie and his battered friends had accidentally wandered into the 82d's area of operations. Nearly 1,000 paratroopers had occupied the town, making their final preparations for an eastward counterattack. "Three of the wounded were transported to an aid station, and the other five were debriefed on where they had seen the German concentrations." Charlie and his friends were then sped to the rear, where each of them ate the "biggest meal you'd ever want to lay your eyes on. We really ate."

Charlie spent the next few weeks recovering from his ordeal while more replacements flooded into the 28th Division—"filling up the depleted ranks." On January 5, 1945, the reconstituted 112th Infantry Regiment (now manned mostly by replacements), was sent back to the frontlines, ready for an attack on the German-held town of Spineux, Belgium. The Americans quickly gained the upper hand, and the Germans began to fall back. "It was the first time some of us had ever seen the Germans back up, and it did us a lot of good," said Charlie.

Unfortunately, many of the new replacements were "trigger happy" (i.e., nervous and having trouble adjusting to the newfound stress of combat). As a result, "several GIs were killed by their own comrades." Still, the enemy was on the run. The following day, after a 12-minute artillery barrage, Charlie's unit took Spineux. "The fighting was house to house, but by nightfall, the town was held by the battalion and 200 German prisoners had been taken."

And it would be the last hurrah in the ETO for Charlie Haug.

"This was the last combat action we saw in the Bulge," he continued. "Our 28th Division was now ordered to a rest area in France."

As the Allied campaign dragged on, Charlie's unit was then ordered south to attack the German-held city of Colmar, a city on the River Rhine, just north of the Franco-Swiss border. Charlie would have participated in the attack, but the torturous winter of 1944-45 had taken a toll on his feet. Indeed, by March 1, a debilitating infection had rendered him unable to walk. It was the consequence of his feet being frozen, thawed, and re-frozen several times throughout the campaign. While convalescing at an Allied hospital in Paris, however, Charlie heard the news of V-E Day. The Nazis had quit; and Charlie's unit had now been designated part of the "Army of Occupation." He rejoined the remnants of Company B, serving this time as the company clerk until the unit returned stateside in July 1945.

After the war, Charlie returned to his hometown of Sleepy Eye, Minnesota, taking a job at First Security Bank of Sleepy Eye. Two years later, on August 4, 1947, he married the former June Enebo in a small ceremony at the Lake Hanska Lutheran Church. Charlie and June made their home in Sleepy Eye, where they ultimately raised five children. Charlie, meanwhile, continued working in the finance industry. In 1968, he became President of the First Security Bank, a position he held until his retirement in 1990. But even in retirement, he spent the next several years preparing Income Tax Returns for the bank's depositors. Charlie Haug passed away on May 4, 2017 at the age of 94.

15
GI JACK OF ALL TRADES

Tom Stafford: From Quartermaster, to Combat Engineer, to Rifleman, to Career Officer

Tom Stafford was the eldest of two children born to a small-town agricultural family. Born in rural Virginia in 1923, Tom came of age during the Great Depression. And, like many families in his community, he had grown accustomed to *both* parents working to support the family. Said Tom of his mother: "She was a housewife until the Depression hit and then she went to work. My dad, he owned and operated four farms"—three of which were contiguous to each other. "The other farm, the fourth one, was about a mile up the road." Each farm yielded a variety of crops and livestock—including hogs, cattle, chickens, tobacco, and corn. Still, even during the worst of economic times, the Staffords fared better than most. "As far as the Depression was concerned, we always had plenty of food and as I remember our clothing was always good; and my dad was able to hold on to all the farms."

Like many of the Greatest Generation, the New Deal was a defining aspect of their lives. The so-called "Alphabet Soup" of New Deal programs (including the CCC, TVA, and WPA) sought to put Americans back to work and improve their quality of life. At times, however, it seemed like many of the New Deal programs were "make-work" projects. "I remember one time sitting out on the front porch of our house…looking across the street, and there were a group of men cutting the grass," he recalled. "There were nine people and they had two lawnmowers. And they were cutting the grass with those two lawnmowers." Finally, a neighbor went up to the man who appeared to be in charge and said: "I want to know why you need nine people to cut the grass when you only got two lawnmowers." The man replied: "Well, ma'am, this is a WPA project; and we have to have two to come and two to go, two to sit, and two to mow."

"Well, that's only eight," she replied. "What's the ninth person do?"

"That's me," he said, "I'm the supervisor."

Tom graduated from high school in May 1941, with the goal of attending Virginia Tech. But even with a solvent family, tuition rates along with room-and-board would be a steep cost. Tom's dad said: "Well, you know it's a pretty expensive proposition," but he offered his son a deal. If Tom was willing to spend a year at home, working and saving enough money to cover the first year of college expenses, the elder Stafford would pay for the remaining three years. "So, I stayed out of school, went to work for Brown & Williamson [a prominent tobacco distributor], worked a year, saved all my money," and enrolled at Virginia Tech in September 1942.

The attack on Pearl Harbor the previous December, however, had modified his plans. "I remember hearing about it," he recalled, "and we went down to the Gulf Oil station and everyone was saying, 'Well we'll whip those Japs' ass inside of a week.' Damn fools." It seemed that no one was anticipating a four-year struggle in the Pacific that would end with the first nuclear weapons ever used in warfare. But, with war on the horizon, Tom joined Army ROTC and enrolled in the Corps of Cadets. Virginia Tech was among a half-dozen Senior Military Colleges, or "citizen-soldier" schools, who hosted a Corps of Cadets separate from the general student population. Each member of the Corps was required to participate in the ROTC program, and many took commissions as officers in the Armed Forces.

But his ROTC career was cut short when he was unexpectedly drafted in March 1943. The draft age had been 21 until mid-1942, when President Roosevelt lowered it to 18. Given his ROTC background, Tom was familiar with at least some of the military customs and courtesies. "When I got drafted it was in March of 1943, and I lived in Petersburg, Virginia. They shipped me down to Camp Lee [present-day Fort Lee]… it was a Quartermaster Center but they had a basic training center there." After completing his basic training, he applied for OCS, but "I was told I was too young to lead troops in the Quartermaster Corps." As somewhat of a consolation, however, the Camp Lee cadre offered to make him an NCO through the proverbial "shake-and-bake" Non-Commissioned Officers School—where in as little as 90 days, a high-performing soldier could earn the stripes of a technical sergeant. "So, I went in and took that course and it turned out that the NCO course was almost identical to the basic OCS." Just another example of the Army's bureaucratic inefficiency.

From Camp Miles Standish outside of Boston, Tom boarded the HMS *Empress of Australia* (an old British cruise ship turned troop carrier), and set sail for England in November 1943. "We landed in Liverpool," he said, "and then from there I went down to Birmingham," to the Replacement Depot in Lichfield where he awaited orders to a gaining unit. As luck would have it, Tom arrived at perhaps the *worst* Replacement Depot in the Allied footprint. "This place became infamous," he said, "and, in fact, the commander was later court-martialed for the horrible conditions [within his camp]. His name was Killian; and they called it Colonel Killian's Concentration Camp." Killian was a notoriously toxic leader, and many a GI dreaded spending any amount of time within his Replacement Center.

Normally, incoming GIs like Tom were supposed to stay 4-5 days at the depot before getting their follow-on orders. But after a week had gone by with no orders, Tom took matters into his own hands. He and his friend, Mel Sadler, went down to the Replacement Center bulletin boards, looking for any announcements of units seeking volunteers. "We saw this notice on the board for volunteers for a particular unit. It didn't say what kind of unit; but, hell, we'd have done anything to get out of there. So, we put our names in, and we were told to load up everything in our duffle bags and be ready to move out early that evening." Tom and Mel then climbed aboard the two-and-a-half-ton troop carrier truck, eagerly anticipating their new unit…and equally anticipating a reprieve from Colonel Killian's toxic command climate.

"It seemed like we drove all night long but…when they finally stopped and it was daylight, and when they opened that tarp [the covering on the back of the truck] and I looked out, I thought I was in Florida—palm trees, tropical foliage, and everything else. We wound up in Torquay, England, down in Devonshire…the southern tip of England; and we found out later that the reason that all this tropical vegetation existed was because the Gulf Stream came up the east coast of America and went across the North Atlantic. That warm water helped the tropical vegetation grow." Stepping off into the seemingly out-of-place tropical landscape, Tom and his buddy learned that they had volunteered for the 6th Combat Engineer Amphibious Special Assault Brigade.

"It was a top-secret outfit," said Tom. And three such brigades had been assigned to the European Theater. Of course, as a trained Quartermaster, Tom knew *nothing* about being a Combat Engineer. But he was certain that he could learn anything with the right amount of on-the-job training. All incoming members were assigned to live in British homes. "There was no barracks, no mess hall, no nothing," Tom remembered. "Everyone lived in private homes, two of us to a home." Tom and his buddy Mel were assigned to live with a greengrocer. "This guy owned a little grocery shop that specialized in vegetables and canned goods."

Seven days a week, Tom and his fellow GIs would assemble at different locations throughout the English countryside, learning the fundamentals of combat engineering—demolitions, obstacle emplacements, and hasty fortifications. Typically, every GI got the evening to himself, and was free to do what he pleased, so long as he remained within a certain mileage of his home billet. Tom and his friends used it as an opportunity to mingle with the British residents. He soon discovered, however, that the English language seemed to be the only thing they had in common with the British.

One evening, for example, Tom attended a local dance catering to American GIs and British Tommies. After the dance was over, the band played the *Star-Spangled Banner*, to which the GIs stood at ramrod attention. Then, the band broke into a chorus of *God Save the King*. At first, no one took offense; but the American GIs heard the tune and mistook it for *My Country 'Tis of Thee*, unaware that *God Save the King* had the same melody. Thus, when the GIs started singing *My Country 'Tis of Thee*, it started a fight between the Americans and the indignant British troops. "We didn't know the difference," Tom admitted, "but we soon found out."

Diplomatic gaffes and cultural ignorance aside, the GIs spent many a week training alongside their Allied partners for the upcoming invasion of Europe. By the summer of 1944, most of Italy was in Allied hands, but to truly effect the conquest of Europe, the Allies would have to invade Northern and Southern France. By all accounts, Northern France had to be the priority. And Normandy was the focus of the Allied entry.

During the lead-up to the invasion, Tom and his fellow sappers conducted a number of rehearsals at Slapton Sands on the shores of Devonshire. Slapton Sands inadvertently became a flashpoint during the war because of the disastrous invasion rehearsals. During these dry-run invasions, several Allied troops were killed by friendly fire, and a handful of US naval vessels were sunk by German PT boats. In all, these poorly-executed invasion rehearsals cost the Allies more than 700 casualties before D-Day even started.

By the fifth of June, however, Tom felt that many of the growing pains, false starts, and hiccups had subsided. They were ready to invade Normandy. From their launch point in Weymouth, Tom's brigade had initially taken off on the night of June 4, among the designated "first wave" of troops to hit the beach. "We got half-way across," he said, but "the channel was so rough that they decided to turn around and come back." Realizing they had lost the element of surprise, the Allied Command decided to wait another day, launching late on June 5, with anticipated landfall on the morning of June 6, 1944.

"We were supposed to land on Omaha," said Tom, and at a draw called Les Moulins…and that was about 1,000-1,200 yards, from our first objective which was a little village called Saint Laurent-Sur-Mer." Tom and his platoon of sappers were expected to hit the beach shortly after H-Hour (6:30 AM). Like most troops going ashore, Tom's platoon was riding aboard a tactical landing craft, a British variant. "Wasn't very long as I recall, couldn't have been more than 100 feet. It was big enough to carry several deuce-and-a-half trucks, and some jeeps, couple of platoons of infantry and combat engineers." The landing craft itself was crewed by US Coast Guardsmen—"two sailors and an ensign," recalled Tom.

Because Tom and his fellow sappers were crouched behind the landing ramp, they couldn't see the gut-wrenching carnage of the Normandy landings.

But they could certainly hear it.

The bombs, bullets, and artillery shells, punctuated by blasts of water, were a stark reminder that they were headed into harm's way.

But just as the coxswain got ready to lower the ramp, he decided against it.

From his spot at the helm, the coxswain had a front row seat to the blood and carnage playing out on Normandy beach. And he didn't want his men to become a statistic before they even left the beachhead. As Tom recalled: "he wasn't going to lower that ramp because we'd have been slaughtered getting off." Instead, he winched the boat back into the shallows, and vectored farther down the beach, out of range from the heaviest machine gun fire. Thus, instead of getting off at Les Moulins, Tom's platoon landed farther down the beach near Vierville-Sur-Mer.

"I recall that we waded about 100 yards or so through the surf," said Tom, "and all I remember is making a mad scramble getting up to a sea wall," which in turn led to a paved road running parallel to the beach. As Tom got halfway across the road, however, he encountered his first friendly casualty. "I saw a body lying there," he said, "an American face-down, and decided to pull him over to the side of the road." Grabbing the fallen comrade by his shoulder straps, Tom dragged him to the edge of the road, but when he turned him over: "Lord, half of the guy's face was shot off." Tom noticed, briefly, that this dead GI was a Ranger captain. "That surprised me," he said, "because the Rangers were supposed to land at Pointe Du Hoc. I couldn't figure out why there would be Rangers there." Years later, Tom discovered that the fallen captain was part of a Ranger company that had somehow gotten separated from the rest of the Ranger Battalion.

Scrambling to the top of a nearby hill, Tom looked back to the beaches of Normandy, now several yards below. "I'll tell you, it was just mayhem and bedlam. German artillery was coming in and mortars, etc., and I remember seeing one lone American 105 howitzer that had been able to get ashore. There were a lot of amphibious tanks that were supposed to get ashore but very few of them made it. This one howitzer, boy, I thought it was an automatic cannon. These guys were firing, it looked like they were firing 10-15 rounds a minute"—an impossible feat for even the most experienced cannon crew. Years later, Tom discovered that the furious 105mm howitzer was, coincidentally, one of two guns commanded by his cousin, Brad Stafford, an artillery officer in the 29th Division. He survived the war, too," said Tom, "but he's long since passed on."

Also coincidentally, Tom's unit was tasked to support the 29th Division, helping them get across the beach and supporting them as they moved farther inland. "I remember a couple of days after we got ashore, a British commando, believe it or not, showed up." He had been separated from his unit at one of the other beaches, "I guess on Gold or Juno Beach," Tom added. "He joined up with us and stayed with us for several days."

After the breakout from Normandy, Tom's career as a GI took an interesting detour. As a reward, of sorts, for having survived the D-Day invasion, Tom was inexplicably reassigned to a POW stockade, guarding German prisoners. But after three weeks of babysitting indignant Nazis, "I got fed up with that," he said, "and I went in and told them I wanted to go back to a regular unit, either back to my old unit [the special engineer brigade] or some other unit, but I didn't want any more of that POW guard business." The stockade commander granted Tom's wish, but told him that he would likely end up in a regular infantry division.

"That's OK by me," Tom replied.

Thus, Tom Stafford was thrown back into the replacement network, and by December 1944 he was a new rifleman assigned to the 87th Infantry Division. "I don't know exactly where we were at the time" he said, "but I recall landing in Luxembourg City to join the 87th, and found out that the Bulge had just broken out. We were told we're going to hold you here [at the replacement depot] in Luxembourg City in case the

Germans break through and attack." And that's where Tom stayed until early January. The rest of the 87th Division, meanwhile, had been pulled from Metz and attached to the Third Army for the relief of Bastogne.

Finally, in January 1945, Tom joined the 347th Infantry Regiment, "and I was assigned to L Company…2d Platoon." From there, Tom spent the remaining winter months manning a number of frozen outposts along the western battlefront. They went from Bastogne to Bonnerue, then back into Luxembourg along the Sauer River, then to St. Vith, and finally Belgium, where they managed to drive the *Wehrmacht* back into Germany. "Things were rough," he recalled. "When I got to 2d Platoon, I don't think there were more than 20-25 men in the platoon. Normally, the strength of a platoon is 41 men, one officer and 40 enlisted men." Yet, throughout his tour in the 87th Division, he never saw the platoon's end-strength exceed more than 30 men.

Like many of the units that had been thrown into the Battle of the Bulge, Tom's platoon was manned almost entirely by replacements. Most of the original non-commissioned officers in the company had been killed or wounded. And among the replacements, "none of them had had any prior combat experience." The new non-commissioned officers were enthusiastic but, as Tom said: "They just didn't know how to lead. I found that out in a hurry. We had a fairly good lieutenant but he didn't last too long." Indeed, the lieutenant was killed in action and, to make matters worse, the platoon sergeant sustained a critical wound, which led to his evacuation. This left Tom Stafford as the senior-ranking sergeant in the platoon. "And so, the company commander, Captain Kidd, told me to take over the platoon as acting platoon leader." As a young sergeant with less than two years of service, Tom Stafford, the young quartermaster-turned-sapper-turned-rifleman was now an acting platoon leader. "I remained acting platoon leader until the end of the war," he said bluntly. "Got a battlefield commission right there at the end."

By the end of March 1945, Tom's unit had broken through the Siegfried Line and crossed the Rhine River at Koenigstuhl. They had expected the river crossing to pass without incident, but Tom's unit met fierce resistance on the opposite side of the Rhine. At a nearby town called Braubach, Tom instantly recognized the source of his troubles: "There was a big castle on the other side of the river overlooking Braubach," he said. "We were told, at the time, not to fire on the castle because it was one of the few castles that hadn't been destroyed in all the wars the French and Germans fought. The castle was called Marksburg Castle." Despite its protected status as a historical landmark, the Germans had been using it as an artillery observation post. "They had complete command of the river," said Tom—for miles in either direction.

Tom's platoon was barely halfway across the river when the Germans opened fire. "They were dug in right there on the banks of the river," he said. "They had dug trenches and covered them over with turf and bushes and there were machine gun nests in there and they had...this observation from the top. They had put 20mm anti-aircraft guns on the hills overlooking the town, and they had depressed those things and they were firing those at us." His platoon fared well, losing none of its men during the river crossing—"but a couple of the other platoons didn't fare as well," he added. "We lost one of our best platoon sergeants. At this time, all four platoons in L Company, with the exception of one, were being led by the platoon sergeants."

L Company succeeded in taking Braubach, while their neighboring K Company stormed the Marksburg Castle. Tom, in the meantime, captured two Germans in Braubach who were overlooking the Marksburg Castle redoubt. After a brief interrogation, one of the captured Germans revealed the location of their commo line, which Tom's platoon hastily cut, thereby severing all communication between the castle-bound forward observers and the artillery guns along the hills.

"Then from Braubach," he continued, "we moved to a little town called Bad Ems, then from Bad Ems I captured a German general." It appeared to be a stroke of good luck; for it wasn't every day that an American GI captured a Nazi general. Moreover, this general was dressed in civilian attire; and, at first, he gave no indication that he was a high-ranking officer in the *Wehrmacht*. The clandestine general might have avoided detection, but as the GIs were searching his home, Tom found the general's uniform.

"He admitted that it was his," said Tom. "I think he was home on leave or something."

But whatever the reasons for his out-of-uniform appearance, Tom made the general put on the uniform and marched him back up the road to the L Company commander.

Not far ahead, Tom had another surprise encounter.

"We found a POW camp," he said, "had a bunch of American prisoners, British prisoners," the most senior of which was a British Sergeant Major.

After liberating the multi-national POW camp, Tom recalled that "we began to move pretty fast, going across Germany." In fact, he called it somewhat of a "merry chase." For by now, the *Wehrmacht* was in full panic as the Americans were closing in from the west, and the Soviets from the east. "We got on the autobahns,"—the legendary superhighways that indirectly inspired the US Interstate System—"and that was one of the very few times I can remember loading up in trucks, or on tanks, and riding. Finally got to a place, Zella-Mehlis, I remember. Then we began to run into resistance at a place called Saalfeld. Lots of resistance there." Indeed, from Saalfeld, the Germans were blowing up every bridge behind them, doing whatever they could to slow the Allied advance.

By now, it was April 1945, and "most of the units we encountered were *Wehrmacht*, which was the German regular army, and sometimes we'd run into SS." But on other occasions, they ran into the *Volkssturm*. Literally translated as "People's Storm," the *Volkssturm* was a national militia levied by the Nazis during the latter months of World War II. "Most of them were old men," said Tom, "and when I say old, most of the guys had fought in World War I. The rest of them were 14- and 15-year-old boys. We called them 'Hitler's secret weapon.' They were 14- and 15-year-olds armed with *panzerfausts*…the German version of the bazooka."

From Saalfeld, Tom's battalion led the regimental attack on Plauen. "My Company L was given the mission of leading the way into Plauen," he said. "We got halfway into Plauen and Captain Kidd [the company commander] got a message from an artillery spotter plane." These observers had just spotted a platoon of Germans preparing to demolish the one remaining bridge over the Elster River—the tributary running through the heart of Plauen. "As Captain Kidd got the message that the Germans were setting demolitions under the bridge," Tom continued, "he called me on the radio and told me to move my platoon through… and to see if I couldn't keep the Germans from blowing up the bridge."

To affect the capture of Plauen, a section of tanks (two Shermans) had been attached to L Company, providing direct fire support to the infantry. "Kidd gave me the two tanks," said Tom, "and I put a couple of squads right in front of the tanks." As they made their way to the site of the suspected demolition, however, they were surprised to see very little resistance. "We were really surprised," Tom added, "because this town had a lot of factories and ordnance plants"—one of which was manufacturing tanks. To boot, there were several warehouses where the German Army had purportedly cached weapons and equipment. "We figured the Germans certainly would put up a fight to try to keep us from capturing that," Tom explained, "because that stuff was sorely needed by them."

But this piecemeal resistance had grown to a deafening crescendo by the time they reached the river. Seeing the Germans on the bridge, Tom directed both tanks to open fire on the German dismounts, "to try to scare them," as he said—"scatter them so we could get across the bridge and keep them from blowing it." The German sappers, realizing they were outgunned and overmatched, beat a hasty retreat across the river, leaving their detonation assets where they lay. "I cut the wires that were leading down to the demolitions they had placed under the bridge." Tom discovered later that, by preserving the bridge, he had saved a historically-significant piece of engineering. "That old bridge had been built 250 years before Columbus discovered America," he said. "It was the oldest stone-arch bridge north of Italy."

Having saved the bridge, captured the fleeting Germans, and secured the city of Plauen, L Company then moved into the town of Theuma, near the Czech border. At around this time, Tom had his first look at the Buchenwald concentration camp. Buchenwald was nearly 30 miles from their current location, and had been liberated by the Allies only a few days earlier. "General Eisenhower wanted every division that was close enough to Buchenwald to go there," said Tom, and see just how horribly its inmates had been treated.

At first, Tom didn't know what to expect.

Was this "Buchenwald" just another POW camp?

When Tom came through the front gates, however, his jawed dropped. "I tell you, that was one horrible, horrible sight…bodies stacked up, dead bodies…everything you read about, all the pictures you see of Buchenwald, they were absolutely correct. The bodies stacked up, and I remember also…seeing a bunch of German civilians from the town of Weimar ordered into the camp to take a look at what the Nazis had done."

Tom quickly realized that this was no POW camp.

But he couldn't immediately deduce the camp's purpose. At first glance, the prisoners seemed to have nothing in common. There were Jews, Poles, Gypsies, Slavs, political dissidents, and handicapped persons. Moreover, there was nothing in their background that should have warranted their imprisonment. Tom soon discovered, however, that the Nazi regime had imprisoned them for being "undesirables," and liabilities to the Aryan race.

By mid-April, Tom's regiment had been ordered into a holding position. "We were told to hold up, not to move it any further, wait for the Russians." Indeed, on the Eastern Front, the Soviet war machine had been beating back the tide of Nazism. From Moscow to Stalingrad, the Red Army had reclaimed its territory lost during the early days of Operation Barbarossa. Through Ukraine, Belarus, and Poland, Soviet forces had overrun the *Wehrmacht* and were striking into the heart of Germany.

"Finally, we got the word right after the first of May to move out again," said Tom, "and so L Company's objective was a town called Jaegersgrun," which they occupied with relative ease. As they secured the town, L Company was elated to hear the news of Adolf Hitler's suicide, followed soon thereafter by the news of V-E Day.

But although the war in Europe had officially ended, L Company had no time to celebrate. "We had our hands full taking care of all these German prisoners," said Tom. At one point, however, Captain Kidd gave Tom permission to take a truck across the border into Czechoslovakia and find any brewery willing to sell beer in exchange for German *Reichsmarks*. Luckily, Tom didn't have to go far to find an obliging brewmaster. "We went into Czechoslovakia," he said, and got three or four kegs of beer"— all in exchange for a wad of German *Reichsmarks*.

On May 12, 1945, Tom wrote the following letter to his father in Virginia:

"Dear Dad,

Just a few lines to say hello and to let you know I'm well and OK and hope that you're fine and feeling all right these days, too. I've been planning to write for the last few days but honest, Dad, we're really keeping on the go.

Since I wrote you last, lots has happened, hasn't it?

Yes, what I've been praying for a long time finally made up its futile mind to happen. Now when you shoot a Kraut, they call it murder, which all goes to show just how nonsensical war really is. Just by signing a little piece of paper a man can change the life and destiny of millions, and those who yesterday had the sole purpose of killing his fellow man can now laugh, joke, smoke and give food and shelter to those same people.

Well, it's beyond me.

I suppose the American Army and the rest of the Allies have become so powerful that they can afford to forget some of their original purposes…

Dad, this may be a little hard to believe, but your son had two complete German infantry divisions surrender to him, as well as a number of other assorted enemy organizations. I'd always wanted to see what the enemy really looked like; so the day before the peace was signed, my jeep driver and I took off, and we wound up at a general staff meeting where one Lieutenant General surrendered his division and then we went on through the lines where another General surrendered also.

Dad, I've always thought of your advice, and as far as that's concerned, the war hasn't changed me one bit. So, without further fanfare, I come to you for some more of it. I don't know whether I mentioned it or not, but I've been put in for a battlefield commission. That's well and good, but I also understand that officers don't count in the point system. As an enlisted man, I probably stand a good chance of staying away from the CBI [China–Burma–India Theater] and prospects for a discharge. If you were in my shoes, what would you do? I've just about made up my mind, but I'll wait to hear from you; what you think? So, write soon.

Lots of love,

Tommy."

Tom Stafford ultimately accepted that battlefield commission, although the process of receiving one was rather morbid. To earn a battlefield commission, the existing lieutenant had to have been killed in action, or permanently evacuated from the battlefield. Taking command of the platoon (or what remained of it), the next-senior sergeant would become the acting platoon leader and, if his performance warranted it, he was recommended for a commission.

"The recommendation would have to be endorsed by the battalion commander, and the regimental commander…then it would go on up to the division commander, and that's where the final decision was made. I think the division commander had been given authority by the War Department to promote people to commissioned rank. I had my bars pinned on by General [John] McKee who was the assistant division commander." Ironically, McKee was a graduate of the Virginia Military Institute (VMI), which had a long-standing rivalry with Virginia Tech. And McKee, well-aware that he was pinning bars on a former Virginia Tech student, said with a chuckle: "I never thought I'd see the day when I'd be giving anybody from [Virginia Tech] anything."

Accepting the commission allowed Tom to stay with his unit longer. By now, he had already amassed enough "points" to earn his ticket home. The points system (officially, the "Adjusted Service Rating Score") determined when a GI could earn his eligibility for an early discharge. "You needed at least 85 points," Tom recalled. "You got points for the number of months you'd been on active duty. You got points for the number of days you'd been in combat." A GI could also earn points through various decorations like the Bronze Star, Silver Star, etc.

But accepting his commission took him out of the points system, and he never regretted it. "I wanted to stay with my men." Typically, however, if a soldier earned a battlefield commission, they would transfer him to another regiment. "They certainly wouldn't allow you to stay in the same company or even in the same battalion."

But Tom refused to leave the men with whom he had shed blood.

In fact, Tom had made it a non-negotiable condition of his acceptance. He told his chain of command: "Hell, I'm not going to leave these guys, and if I can't stay with them as a commissioned officer after having led them for four months in combat, then keep the damned commission." Surprisingly, the regiment yielded to his demands.

But although the fighting in Europe had ended, the Pacific War raged on. "We were the first division pulled out of Europe in order to make the invasion of Honshu," said Tom. "In fact," he continued, "we were brought back to the States in July and we were given a 30-day leave…then we went down to Fort Benning…to be re-outfitted and get replacements and get re-equipped." They were about to be loaded on a train westbound to California, then depart San Francisco for the anticipated invasion of Japan.

Fortunately, the war ended before Tom could steam out of San Francisco Bay. After his division was deactivated in October 1945, Tom Stafford decided to stay in the military. In his first postwar assignment, he was selected to be the Aide-de-camp to General Phillip Gallagher, Commanding General of the 25th Infantry Combat Team at Fort Benning.

The following year, Tom accompanied General Gallagher to Occupied Germany, again as his Aide-de-camp when the latter became Deputy Commanding General of the US Constabulary. This assignment gave Tom a front-row seat to the burgeoning "Cold War"—a war to be fought not necessarily with bombs and bullets, but with words and ideas. The "hot" battles would be fought mostly by proxy, and at the farthest corners of the earth. Words like "Mutual Assured Destruction;" "Nuclear Holocaust;" and "Balance of Power" would steer American foreign policy for the next forty-plus years.

When Tom Stafford returned to Germany as part of the US Constabulary, he saw the harsh realities of the post-war Reich. Many within the Nazi High Command were put on trial at Nuremberg for their part in the Holocaust. Understandably, most Germans were still shocked and embittered by their defeat at the hands of the Allies. To make matters worse, their country had been partitioned along ideological lines. East Germany was now a Communist state and West Germany was a fragile, ailing democracy. The economies of both nations were in shambles, millions were starving, millions more were homeless, and several had taken to a life of crime.

Upon his promotion to Captain in 1950, Tom was awarded command of a rifle company in the 1st Infantry Division, whose regular mission was to secure the German–Czechoslovakian border. In 1953, he began his first tour in Korea, taking command of a Headquarters Company in the 7th Infantry Division. The following year, he became the Civil Affairs Officer for the 25th Infantry Division, and oversaw the division's redeployment to Hawaii. Tom stayed with the 25th until his next tour in Korea, from 1960-61, as the Budget Officer for the Eighth Army. His final assignment was in the Office of the Comptroller, Military District of Washington, where he served until 1963. Having completed twenty years of active service, Tom Stafford retired at the rank of Major.

But even in retirement, he continued to serve the Department of Defense, working as a civilian comptroller until his final retirement in 1987. At this writing, Tom Stafford and his wife, Gayla, are living quietly in Fairfax, Virginia.

16

BLOOD ALLEY

PETER WIRTH (USMC)
AND THE BATTLE OF OKINAWA

I
t was the last losing battle for the Imperial Japanese Army. But it was a long, grueling fight for the soldiers and Marines who pummeled the island into submission. On June 5, 1945, Company L (3d Battalion, 5th Marines) was in a tight spot. They were pinned down under heavy fire from *two* Japanese machine gun nests. As the casualties began to mount, the situation seemed hopeless. Company L could not advance, and they had nowhere to hide. But one of the young Marines, PFC Peter Wirth, suddenly decided that he had had enough.

"I could sit there and die, or I could go out and do something about it."

Without orders, he grabbed his rifle and charged the machine gun nests. His actions freed the company from its peril and earned him the Navy Cross.

Peter Wirth was another child of the Great Depression. Born on December 6, 1926 in the suburbs of Chicago, Pete spent most of his formative years in Iowa. Amidst the economic hardships of the era, he quit school after the 8th Grade. Not one for being idle, however, he joined the National Youth Administration (NYA)—one of the various New Deal agencies that aimed to mobilize America's young work force. Through the NYA, Pete trained as a machinist, landing jobs with International Harvester and the Rock Island Arsenal.

When he turned 17, however, he decided to join the war effort.

"I knew I'd be drafted eventually," he said. "I probably knew a few people who had joined the Marines, but to be honest, I didn't know one branch of service from another." At the age of 17, however, he was still a minor, and needed a parent's permission to enlist. His mother, perhaps reluctantly, signed his consent form; and in January 1944, he departed

Iowa for Camp Pendleton, California.

As expected, boot camp was an unpleasant experience. "I didn't care much for that," he said, "but it didn't last long." After graduation, the Marines offered him a 10-day furlough, but he turned it down. He had briefly considered going home to Iowa for his ten days; but he soon realized that the travel time would eat up most of his furlough. "It didn't seem worth it. I remember I had a grand total of $10 in my pocket, and I gave it to a buddy so he could go home."

Soon, Pete boarded a troop carrier to the western Pacific. Their final destination was Guadalcanal, where the new Marines underwent training for jungle and amphibious operations. Shockingly, part of the training included an exercise to see how long the Marines could withstand dehydration. "Well," said Pete, "the fact is you can't go very long without water no matter how much training you've had. But I suppose they did that for discipline."

He also recalled doing several hikes on Guadalcanal. "One time, we had to cross a river that was in full flood stage. Trees were going down all over the place." The trick to getting across this river, however, was to have two Marines wrap their gear into two separate poncho halves, snapping them together. The two Marines would then swim across the river, pushing the semi-buoyant poncho raft in front of them as they swam along. "The idea was to avoid anything like a tree bumping into you." But crossing a river under these conditions was a perilous task. Several Marines perished that day while trying to cross the river, three of whom were in Pete's company. "They drowned. Plus, guys were panicking and leaving their gear behind. We lost hundreds of rifles that day. And then when we got to the other side, they gave us some C-rations, and then marched us back to camp over a bridge that was just down the river. I'll never know for sure how many died that day. You don't get a lot of information out of the military."

The training on Guadalcanal was severe; but so was the situation that lay ahead. His next stop was Okinawa.

As the island-hopping campaign drew closer to the Japanese mainland, the Allies narrowed their gaze onto Okinawa. Located some 340 miles south of the mainland archipelago, Okinawa was the ideal location for an Allied airfield and staging area for the anticipated invasion of Japan. For their part, the Japanese High Command had also recognized the salience of the island, and committed 117,000 troops to its defense.

Peter Wirth as a young Marine in the Pacific.

Pete, meanwhile, had been assigned to the 5th Marine Regiment, and boarded another troop carrier en route to their new mission. At first, none of the onboard Marines knew where they were going. "Then Tokyo Rose came on the radio and told us...she said we were going to Formosa or Okinawa." The Marines couldn't figure out how this propaganda DJ got the information before they did; but based on their direction of travel, they knew she was likely correct.

But whether it was a lucky guess, or information delivered through the backdoor spy network, Tokyo Rose was correct that the Marines were headed to Okinawa. Along the way, however, Pete's unit made a daylong pit stop on a sandbar island, where the Marine Corps provided one last kegger before the invasion. "After a while," said Pete, "it got to be a problem. It was 110 degrees in the shade, and a lot of those people were not used to drinking beer. There were a lot of fights, but it didn't amount to much." But after they had all sobered up, the Marine expeditionary force returned to its ships, and stormed the beaches of Okinawa on April 1, 1945.

"I was up early, and they gave us the best breakfast I've had in the military. I don't know where they got fresh eggs out of the Pacific," he marveled. But the culinary euphoria was short-lived. For within moments, Pete flung himself over the side of the ship, descending down the rope ladder to the landing craft below.

"As soon as we got loaded, we barreled for the shore."

The undulating motion of the landing craft was made worse by the sudden onset of enemy mortars. Rounds began plummeting into the waves, splashing the innards of the landing craft with tepid seawater. "The guys driving the boats had their time just right," Pete continued. "The front end of the boat hit the beach, the front came down, and we took off out of the boat. The idea was to disperse as fast as possible so one mortar doesn't get you all. As soon as we were off the boat and lightened the load, he [the landing craft helmsman] was able to back up and go get more troops." Piloting the landing craft was a dangerous gig unto itself; the helmsmen often had to make multiple trips to deliver all the Marines to the shore. Naturally, this made them easier targets for the Japanese onshore batteries.

But aside from these mortar rounds, there was surprisingly little Japanese resistance on the beach. Operationally, the Army and Marine Corps had split the island in half, hoping to facilitate a "divide and conquer" of Okinawa. After a few days of reconsolidating, the Marines headed northeast, where they encountered only light resistance. Said Pete of these opening rounds: "I remember that we stalled around until we headed south to relieve the Army unit." In fact, the 1st Marine Division was conducting a relief-in-place with the US Army's 27th Infantry Division.

"I'm sure we had a lot more soldiers than the Japanese, but we hit tough resistance as soon as we went south. I think more Marines were killed and more ships went down in the battle for Okinawa than any

Pete Wirth poses with his uncle, who was also in military during World War II. Ironically, Pete's uncle was killed at the Battle of Okinawa, not far from where Pete's unit had made landfall."

other battle. At any time of night, you could look out and see Navy ships going down."

Seeing this action unfold before his eyes, Pete was admittedly nervous.

This was, after all, his first time in combat.

"I was kinda scared. But everybody else was in the same position." And it was not an easy position. "It was hilly, and very tough to go down…lots of fire, lots of casualties. It kind of came in spurts. I remember there was one hill near Naha [the prefectural capital of Okinawa] that we took twice, and got knocked off of it twice. The third time, we got to the top."

By June 2, the Marines had succeeded in pushing the Japanese to the southern end of the island, but not without heavy cost. It was on that day when Company L found itself under fire from two raging machine gun nests. With his fellow Marines dying all around him, Pete said: "It's hard to just stand there with people dying all around you. It's hard not to do anything. But we were pinned down. It was a quick decision. Either stay and die, or go out and die fighting."

He chose the latter.

Armed with his rifle, six grenades, and a .38 Special, the young Pete Wirth began his charge to the enemy positions. "I found that a short gun is handier when you're crawling on the ground. I had bought the .38 from somebody. Once you were over there, you carry anything you can get ahold of. Nobody cared." At first, another Marine accompanied Pete on his daring dash. But after a few yards, the comrade fell back under enemy fire. "It was probably about 200 yards I had to go," said Pete. "But of course, it felt like a couple or three miles to me."

As Pete came within striking distance of the first machine gun, he maneuvered to the side, out of the gun's traversing range. The Japanese had dug this machine gun nest into a cave; thus, the cave's walls provided Pete with all the flanking defilade he needed. "I pulled out a grenade, let the spoon go, and waited. If you throw it too fast, they'll just throw it back at you. You have to judge the time, but I'd thrown a lot in practice." Pete used up all his grenades to silence the first machine gun nest. But, in a stroke of derring-do, Pete sprinted back to L Company's position, running through the same gauntlet of fire from which he had come, and gathered *more* grenades to use on the second nest.

The second nest, however, would be more problematic than the first. It was higher up on the cliff, occupying another cave, thus making it harder to stay out of the machine gunner's sights. But with the help of some covering fire from L Company, Pete made it back up the hill to within sight of the second nest. At one point, he drew his pistol, and emptied it in the general direction of the enemy machine gunner.

"I didn't hit anything, but I didn't think I would."

Undeterred, Pete crawled up to the top of the cliff and shimmied his way over to the machine gun nest. Just as he had done with the previous nest, Pete ripped the pin from his hand grenade and tossed it into the cave's opening.

Thus ended the machine gun fire.

Climbing back down the cliff, however, Pete realized his work wasn't done. Back at the first nest, he discovered that two Japanese soldiers were still alive, which he quickly remedied with his M-1 Garand rifle.

Company L was now free to advance.

"At the time, you're too busy to be scared. When it's all over, the fear settles in. I was shaking a bit."

For his actions that day, Pete's commanding officer recommended him for the Navy Cross. In the Navy and Marine Corps, the Navy Cross was awarded for extraordinary heroism, second only to the Congressional Medal of Honor. Two weeks, later, however, Pete received an early exodus from the war, courtesy of a battlefield wound. "I was pursuing a couple of Japanese soldiers down by the beach. By this time, we were gathering up prisoners, but these guys didn't want to be prisoners, I guess. They went behind a boulder, and I didn't realize that one of them had doubled back and climbed on top of the boulder." The treacherous Japanese soldier shot Pete from above. The bullet struck his right shoulder, exiting through his back. The wound wasn't fatal, but it was enough to get Pete's attention. Yet, without missing a beat, the young Marine turned and killed his Japanese assailant. "I didn't feel any pain at all," he said. "It was just like someone hitting you in the shoulder. I never even dropped my rifle."

Still, his wound was enough to warrant a trip to the aid station. "There were bubbles in the blood coming out, so I knew it must have nicked my lung. Later on, it got to be more painful, and they shot me up with morphine, of course. There was a lot of pain as it was healing." Pete was then evacuated to a hospital in Guam, where he stayed until V-J Day.

Pete Wirth remained on active duty until 1946. For a time, he considered becoming a career Marine, but decided he had seen enough action for one lifetime. Ahead of his discharge, he traveled home aboard an aircraft carrier, where he recalled a funny story involving a sailor and his bicycle. This sailor, perhaps one of the deck handlers, was enjoying the postwar idyll by riding his bicycle along the perimeter of the flight deck. But whether he lost his balance, or was hit by a sudden gust of wind, this cyclist inadvertently rode his bike right over the edge of the carrier deck. "They fished him out—still holding the bicycle."

When he returned to Iowa, there were no bands, no ticker-tape parades, no homecoming events of any sort. His hometown newspaper ran a short story about his Navy Cross. But beyond that token acknowledgement, there was no fanfare for the returning war hero.

All told, it mattered little to him. Pete was proud to have served his country; moreover, he was happy to be alive.

After the war, Pete Wirth returned to his vocation as a machinist. He spent the next several years working for Mansfield Industries, tooling components for photographic equipment. He later worked for the Control Data Corporation; but when the company relocated, Pete negotiated to buy their tool and die machinery. With these new assets, he opened his own machine shop, running the business for nearly two decades before his retirement in 1988.

While building this career as a machinist and latter-day entrepreneur, Pete married Berthana Bergsrud in 1951, with whom he raised four children. Pete and Berthana were married for sixty-four years until his passing on December 3, 2015—just three days shy of his 89th birthday. He was proud of his service, but never attended any reunions. He likewise never wore his Navy Cross, and rarely spoke about his wartime experiences. But even in the twilight of his life, Pete never missed the opportunity to poke fun at his battlefield injury. His shoulder made a full recovery, but now and again, he could feel a tinge of pain where the bullet had dug its path. "When the weather changes, I can feel it," he joked. "I suppose there's some arthritis getting in there."

ABOUT THE AUTHOR

Mike Guardia is an internationally-recognized author and military historian. A veteran of the United States Army, he served six years on active duty as an Armor Officer. He is the author of the widely-acclaimed *Hal Moore: A Soldier Once...and Always,* the first-ever biography chronicling the life of LTG Harold G. Moore, whose battlefield leadership was popularized by the film *We Were Soldiers*, starring Mel Gibson.

He was named "Author of the Year" in 2021 by the Military Writers Society of America, and has been nominated twice for the Army Historical Foundation's Distinguished Book Award.

As a speaker, he has given presentations at the US Special Operations Command, the George HW Bush Presidential Library, the First Division Museum, and the US 7th Infantry Division Headquarters at Fort Lewis.

In 2022, he appeared in the History Channel series, *I Was There*, cast as a featured historian in the episodes on the Johnstown Flood of 1889, the Chernobyl Disaster, the Battle of Stalingrad, and the Oklahoma City Bombing. His other media appearances include guest spots on *National Public Radio (NPR)*; *Frontlines of Freedom*; *Armada International*; and *Military Network Radio.*

His work has been reviewed in the *Washington Times, Military Review, Vietnam Magazine, DefenceWeb South Africa*, and *Soldier Magazine UK*. He holds a BA and MA in American History from the University of Houston; and an MA in Education from the University of St. Thomas. He currently lives in Minnesota.

Printed in the USA
CPSIA information can be obtained
at www.ICGtesting.com
LVHW011959070224
771230LV00004B/64

POST-RACIAL CONSTITUTIONALISM AND THE ROBERTS COURT

Post-Racial Constitutionalism and the Roberts Court: Rhetorical Neutrality and the Perpetuation of Inequality provides the first comprehensive Critical Race Theory critique of the United States Supreme Court under Chief Justice John Roberts. Since being named to the Court in 2005, Chief Justice Roberts has maintained a position of neutrality in his opinions on race. By dissecting neutrality and how it functions as a unifying feature in all the Court's race jurisprudence, this book illustrates the consequences of this ostensible impartiality. By examining the Court's racial jurisprudence dating back to the Reconstruction, the book shows how the Court has actively rationalized systemic oppression through neutral rhetoric and the elevation of process-based decisional values, which are rooted in democratic myths of inclusivity and openness. Timely and trenchant, the book illustrates the permanence of racism and how neutrality must be rejected to achieve true empowerment and substantive equality.

CEDRIC MERLIN POWELL is the Wyatt, Tarrant & Combs Professor of Law and Distinguished Teaching Professor at the University of Louisville Brandeis School of Law. His extensive publications in articles, essays, and book reviews explore the connections between neutrality and structural inequality.

Post-Racial Constitutionalism and the Roberts Court

RHETORICAL NEUTRALITY AND THE PERPETUATION OF INEQUALITY

CEDRIC MERLIN POWELL

University of Louisville, Kentucky

Louis D. Brandeis School of Law

CAMBRIDGE
UNIVERSITY PRESS

CAMBRIDGE
UNIVERSITY PRESS

University Printing House, Cambridge CB2 8BS, United Kingdom

One Liberty Plaza, 20th Floor, New York, NY 10006, USA

477 Williamstown Road, Port Melbourne, VIC 3207, Australia

314–321, 3rd Floor, Plot 3, Splendor Forum, Jasola District Centre, New Delhi – 110025, India

103 Penang Road, #05–06/07, Visioncrest Commercial, Singapore 238467

Cambridge University Press is part of the University of Cambridge.

It furthers the University's mission by disseminating knowledge in the pursuit of education, learning, and research at the highest international levels of excellence.

www.cambridge.org
Information on this title: www.cambridge.org/9781108839945
DOI: 10.1017/9781108878227

© Cedric Merlin Powell 2023

First published 2023

A catalogue record for this publication is available from the British Library.

ISBN 978-1-108-83994-5 Hardback

To my family: Annette, Coleman, and Ellu. Thanks for your support, encouragement, and love.

And to the memory of my parents, Annie Kate McCalebb Powell and Marcus Garvey Powell, Sr.

Contents

Tables

Preface

America's pernicious history of racial subjugation has always been neutralized by the Supreme Court. The most recent iteration of this neutrality is the Roberts Court's post-racial constitutionalism. Embracing post-racialism as a normative principle in its constitutional decision-making, the Roberts Court's race jurisprudence rationalizes oppression with neutral rhetoric that belies the devastating impact of structural inequality.

My intention in writing this book is to explore how the Court's neutral rhetoric advances post-racial constitutionalism and how this is antithetical to the constitutional mandate of the Reconstruction Amendments (the Thirteenth, Fourteenth and Fifteenth Amendments). I argue that neutrality unfolds in a myriad of ways, emphasizing the complexity of race and racism and how neutral rhetoric legitimizes racial subordination. The central point is that the Roberts Court uniformly favors process over substantive equality, and its narrative advances neutrality in various forms to eliminate race from decision-making. This is post-racial constitutionalism. *Post-Racial Constitutionalism and the Roberts Court* assesses the narrative framework of neutrality.

To describe the analytical and narrative structure of the Roberts Court's opinions, I introduce the concept of Rhetorical Neutrality – the neutral narrative deployed by the Court to advance post-racial constitutionalism – to conceptualize three interlocking myths: historical, definitional, and rhetorical that advance colorblindness (race neutrality). Revising history in post-racial terms, the Roberts Court emphasizes societal progress in order to transcend race (the historical myth); it defines racial discrimination so narrowly that it only can be established upon particularized proof and there is no analysis of structural inequality (the definitional myth); and because there rarely is any proof of discrimination, the persistence of inequality is rationalized as a natural societal outcome that is irremediable (the rhetorical myth).

Additionally, the Court propagates neutral themes throughout its race jurisprudence. Neutrality functions to advance post-racial constitutionalism in a number of ways: (i) the Roberts Court employs neutral process rhetoric as the Constitution protects equal opportunity (not equal results) to underscore the fact that race is insignificant because the process is fair and neutral; (ii) this leads to a set of neutral rationales (the process functions well and very rarely malfunctions) and process values (states as laboratories of democracy) to explain the limits of racial progress – since formal inequality has been eliminated, post-racialism must be the guiding principle of our polity; and (iii) because the Court is skeptical of race, in any form, the results in its race cases are virtually predetermined: "the judiciary presumes the unconstitutionality of all uses of race within law – even those that are designed to benefit historically disadvantaged racial groups"[1] – this is post-racial determinism.

The Roberts Court plays a central discursive role in American society. In concert with the post-racial sentiments of the polity, there is a doctrinal and political movement fortified by retrogression and retrenchment to preserve white supremacy. My hope is to give readers the critical tools to identify, assess, and then dismantle structural inequality wherever they find it. A critical place to start is with the post-racial constitutionalism of the Roberts Court.

---

[1] KHIARA M. BRIDGES, CRITICAL RACE THEORY: A PRIMER 109 (2019).

Acknowledgments

This book project has been a revelation to me. I have been inspired by many friends and colleagues who have supported me, offered compelling insights, and pushed me to be a better scholar and teacher. Matt Gallaway of Cambridge University Press has been a gracious, patient, and supportive publisher and editor; I was honored that he truly understood what I was saying, believed in my work, and helped me to express myself in a meaningful way. I was especially fortunate to have colleagues both at my home institution and across the country who were extraordinarily generous with their time, candid, kind with their comments, and so enthusiastic that they bolstered my confidence. They are true friends who happen to be great and gracious colleagues: Khiara M. Bridges, Charlton Copeland, Audrey McFarlane, Laura McNeal, and Enid Trucios-Haynes. I would also like to thank all my brother-colleagues of the John Mercer Langston Writing Workshop, especially Mario Barnes, who has always been interested in my work on neutrality; I have learned so much from his work. Thanks also to Gregory Parks, who invited me to present a chapter of my book at Wake Forest University School of Law. Katie Davidson, University of Louisville Brandeis School of Law Class of 2021, provided excellent research support. Finally, *Cleveland State Law Review* graciously allowed me to draw on my article 'Rhetorical Neutrality: Colorblindness, Frederick Douglass, and Inverted Critical Race Theory,' 56 *Cleve. St. Univ. L. Rev.* 823 (2008); *Saint Louis University Public Law Review* permitted me to adapt portions of my article 'Harvesting New Conceptions of Equality: Opportunity, Results, and Neutrality', 31 St. Louis Univ. Pub. L. Rev. 255 (2012); and *Utah Law Review* granted me permission to use portions of my article 'The Rhetorical Allure of Post-Racial Process Discourse and the Democratic Myth', 2018 Utah L. Rev. 523.

Introduction

Post-Racial Constitutionalism and the Roberts Court offers the first comprehensive Critical Race Theory examination and critique of how the Supreme Court advances post-racialism as a normative principle in constitutional doctrine, namely an illusion that racism no longer exists; equal opportunity is not affected by race; and racial discrimination claims should be viewed skeptically in a colorblind or post-racial society. In advancing process values such as equal opportunity and non-racial decision-making, the Court perpetuates structural inequality through neutral process rhetoric and illusory democratic ideals. Because the Court stands for principles embodied in the legitimacy of the rule of law and societal cohesion, the citizenry must embrace its constitutional rulings. As this book will illustrate, the Court has instead perpetuated a democratic myth that so much societal progress has been made that race has been transcended. Through ostensibly neutral rationales, the Court advances false or contrived judicial narratives undermining the confidence that historically oppressed minorities can have in the Court as an institution.

During his confirmation hearings, Chief Justice Roberts proclaimed that judges should act as "neutral umpires" in adjudicating cases. Far from calling balls and strikes, the Roberts Court has perfected a manner of judicial umpiring that is deceptively neutral – it advances formalism and adherence to a process-based reasoning that is ostensibly democratic but reinforces inequality. At this moment, the United States is witnessing the devastating effects of racist hate rhetoric in the public square, impacting people of color and other excluded communities, and a largely unexplained aspect of this societal phenomena is how the Court is actively engaged in rationalizing oppression. This jurisprudential dialogue is largely hidden from public view, by the doctrinal camouflage of neutral rhetoric.

Its impact, however, is devastating for the nation and no less (or particularly) on the subjugated communities it affects, whose oppression is rationalized by the democratic myth.

The Roberts Court's race jurisprudence has advanced post-racialism premised on a rhetorical stance of adhering to a legal principle of neutrality that is often disingenuous yet disconcertingly effective and disruptive. Predictably, whenever race is a factor in decision-making, there are set assumptions that guide the reasoning and shape the outcomes of the Court's race decisions. Indeed, in race cases, the results can be said to be virtually pre-determined. This post-racial determinism means that race-conscious remedial approaches like affirmative action, school integration plans, employment hiring and promotion practices, voting rights, and fair housing initiatives will be struck down.

All the Court's race decisions are unified by post-racial constitutionalism – racial oppression is rationalized through a series of doctrinal myths that shape the core of the Court's jurisprudence. The Roberts Court represents the current manifestation of post-racial constitutionalism. When it comes to acknowledging the salience of race as an organizing principle of subordination in American society, the Court has always been post-racial. We are in the Third Reconstruction,[1] a period of fleeting progress followed by retrenchment and retrogression after the two-term presidency of the first African-American president, Barack H. Obama.[2] However, the starting point for analyzing the Court's post-racial constitutionalism is the neutrality inherent in its doctrinal rationales in the *Civil Rights Cases* and *Plessy v. Ferguson*. Both decisions are rooted in formalistic equality.

It is important to frame the Roberts Court's post-racial constitutionalism in reference to the Courts that preceded it. The Burger Court is post-racial in its transitional position[3] between the liberal Warren Court and the colorblind conservatism of the Rehnquist Court.[4] Both Courts actively seek to move beyond race by embracing neutrality and formalistic equality. None of the Courts embrace substantive equality, so race is either discarded to preserve white entitlements and privilege or balanced so as not to disturb it.

Under the Roberts Court's doctrinal approach, neutrality has nothing to do with fairness, as it serves as a rationalization of systemic oppression. Because race is inherently suspect, in the Roberts Court's worldview, there is no place for it as a factor in governmental decision-making: accordingly, context is irrelevant, history is disconnected, and the present-day effects of past discrimination are dismissed as mere societal discrimination. Today's Court equates neutrality with colorblindness as an absolute ideal and thus post-racialism means that the United States is over race – race has been transcended and racism is over in America unless it is so blatant as to be obvious. In fact, to point to race as explicative of a discriminatory outcome is to in fact be guilty of racism. Thus, the Roberts Court's doctrine of neutrality – that

[1] The Rev. Dr. William J. Barber II, and Jonathan Wilson-Hartgrove, The Third Reconstruction: How a Moral Movement Is Overcoming the Politics of Division and Fear (2016).

[2] Keeanga-Yamahatta Taylor, From #BlackLivesMatter to Black Liberation 136–52 (2016); Peniel E. Joseph, Dark Nights, Bright Days: From Black Power to Barack Obama 203–08 (2010).

[3] Michael J. Graetz and Linda Greenhouse, The Burger Court and the Rise of the Judicial Right 8–9 (2016).

[4] Craig Bradley, The Rehnquist Legacy 369–81 (2006).

"the way to stop discrimination on the basis of race is to stop discriminating on the basis of race"[5] – advances several post-racial themes in its jurisprudence: (i) so much racial progress has been made that race-conscious remedies are obsolete (and unfair to whites in a neutral process); (ii) race neutrality means that there is an universality to the experiences of all racial groups, so that racial discrimination claims are viewed skeptically because oppression is not analyzed structurally (the Constitution protects individuals, not racial groups); (iii) because race is inherently suspect, there can be no distinction between state-mandated oppression and race-conscious remedial measures to eradicate caste; and (iv) the significance of anti-discrimination law is diminished by distancing language employed by the Court.

In a recent book review of Joan Biskupic's *The Chief: The Life and Turbulent Times of Chief Justice John Roberts* (Basic Books 2019), Adam Cohen notes that "Roberts, in fact, regularly opposes the rights of blacks, gay people, the poor and other relatively powerless groups."[6] There is no moderating influence here; the only question now is how far the Court will go in diluting or undermining substantive equality and the implications for traditionally marginalized groups. This is the hallmark of the Roberts Court's post-racial constitutionalism; Cohen describes it as "a bias against the weak." This is what makes the Court's pronouncement of the illusory process values underlying the democratic myth so treacherous.

Post-Racial Constitutionalism has four defining goals. First, it identifies and critiques how the Roberts Court has actively rationalized systemic oppression through neutral rhetoric and the elevation of process-based decisional values. By placing the Roberts Court in historical context to the Reconstruction, Burger, and Rehnquist Courts, it is clear that the Supreme Court has always been post-racial. Second, it unpacks how the Court advances neutrality by embracing process values rooted in the democratic myth of inclusivity and openness. Third, it connects the Roberts Court's post-racial rhetoric to its decisions to illustrate the doctrinal concepts of post-racial constitutionalism. Finally, the book builds on and refines the Critical Race Theory tenet of the permanence of racism by connecting this proposition with current public discourse around race. The Roberts Court's post-racial constitutionalism legitimizes structural inequality through ostensibly neutral rhetoric. A core principle of the Roberts Court's post-racial constitutionalism is its strict allegiance to process-based values. This means that the Court consistently favors neutrality over substantive outcomes that advance substantive equality. Substantive equality, or the eradication of all systemic oppression, is discarded in favor of flawed normative principles that simply confirm the persistence of inequality without addressing it.

---

[5] Parents Involved in Cmty. Schs. v. Seattle Sch. Dist. No. 1, 551 U.S. 701, 747–48 (2007).

[6] Adam Cohen, *The "Enigma" Who Is the Chief Justice of the United States*, N.Y. TIMES, www.nytimes.com/2019/03/18/books/review/joan-biskupic-chief-life-turbulent-times-chief-justice-john-roberts.html.

The Supreme Court has played an essential role in the maintenance of white domination and advancement of anti-Black racism. It legitimizes structural inequality and all its devastatingly oppressive manifestations mainly by utilizing neutrality as a rationale for its decision-making and tacit acceptance of inequality as the natural state of affairs of subjugation. The roots of this perspective and its pernicious effects go back to the nation's failed Reconstruction.

Emerging from the immoral savagery of slavery and the nation's failed attempt at redeeming its promise of substantive equality, the U.S. Supreme Court was readily predisposed to post-racialism. Because America was built on a series of constructed myths that serve to obscure and revise the sheer brutality of its oppression of non-white peoples, substantive equality has remained elusive.

In fact, the Court has always been post-racial, throughout its history to the present day. The Court has skillfully crafted legal rationales, doctrines, and neutral narratives that diminish the centrality of race in American society and instead advance neutrality as the touchstone of equality. It is virtually impossible, under the Court's race jurisprudence, to advance the anti-discrimination and anti-subjugation principles embodied in the Fourteenth Amendment and anti-discrimination statutes. This is the essence of post-racial constitutionalism: singular events like the end of slavery and Reconstruction; the eradication of *Plessy v. Ferguson's*[7] separate but equal colorline in *Brown v. Board of Education;*[8] the passage of the Civil Rights Act of 1964 and the Voting Rights Act of 1965, a century after the original promise of full citizenship under the Reconstruction Amendments; and, in 2008, the election of President Barack Obama, all denote transformative societal progress to the Court so that race is irrelevant and race-conscious remedial measures are constitutionally invalid. The history of progress for the formerly oppressed is linear and unbroken to the Court. Each societal epoch marks the end of formalized oppression, and neutrality is then deployed to rationalize the persistence of racism – or to simply move on because focusing on race is exhausting and divisive.[9]

"Post-racialism denies that the nation today is in any important way proximate to its historical past."[10] Because racism is rare, the Court espouses the rhetoric of progress: the eradication of all systemic oppression is discarded in favor of the normative principle of post-racial constitutionalism, which simply explains the persistence of inequality without addressing it.

The U.S. Supreme Court has always protected whiteness as a political and property interest, which meant that post-racialism was the guiding principle of analysis during the First Reconstruction and continues to be so to this day. That is, the Court reflects the mood of the political community that sufficient societal progress

---

7   163 U.S. 537 (1896).
8   347 U.S. 483 (1954).
9   Darren Lenard Hutchinson, *Racial Exhaustion*, 86 Wash. U. L. Rev. 917 (2009).
10 Khiara M. Bridges, Critical Race Theory: A Primer 5 (2019).

has been made, and that any further race-conscious remedial efforts are illegitimate racial outcomes. When formalized oppression ended, post-racial systemic oppression took its place and transcending race was integral to the sustainability of white dominance. Since the abolition of slavery and the overruling of *Dred Scott v. Sanford*[11] by the Civil War, the Court has aggressively limited substantive equality by advancing formalism and neutrality through Reconstruction, *Brown* and the civil rights era to the present day.[12]

Historically, colorblindness (or ignoring race while simultaneously acknowledging it) and post-racialism (embracing ephemeral progress to transcend race) have always animated the Court's race jurisprudence. Post-racial constitutionalism is the culmination of these two conceptual propositions. Chapter 1 canvases the doctrinal underpinnings of the *Civil Rights Cases*[13] and *Plessy*. What is striking about these post-Reconstruction decisions is how modern they are in neutralizing the present-day effects of past discrimination, and in formalizing equality rather than advancing it substantively.

The Roberts Court is not only linked to the post-racial historicism identified in the *Civil Rights Cases* and *Plessy*, but the thread also continues to the Burger and Rehnquist Courts' conceptions of transitional equality and post-racial colorblindness. Chapter 2 posits that the Burger and Rehnquist Courts' efforts to neutralize race led to the Roberts Court's post-racial constitutionalism.

There is a discernible doctrinal pattern in the Burger Court's (1969–1986) race jurisprudence – it moves from sweeping affirmations of remedial power to eradicate structural inequality[14] to neutral rationalizations of the subordinating dynamics underlying the status quo.[15] Post-racial colorblindness depicts the Rehnquist Court's (1986–2005) jurisprudential enterprise of neutralizing race so that history, and its present-day effects, is never acknowledged; discrimination is narrowly defined with an emphasis on lessening any burden on white interests;[16] and, dismantling structural inequality and racial subordination is not a feature of the Court's interpretation of the Fourteenth Amendment, which seeks only to rationalize formalistic equality.[17]

All the Courts – Burger, Rehnquist, and Roberts[18] – are post-racial, but they seek to transcend race in distinct ways based upon neutrality. The Burger Court eschews

---

[11] 60 U.S. 393 (1856).
[12] LAURENCE H. TRIBE, AMERICAN CONSTITUTIONAL LAW § 5–12, at 330 n. 3 (1988).
[13] 109 U.S. 3 (1883).
[14] *Swann v. Charlotte Mecklenburg Bd. of Ed.*, 402 U.S. 1 (1971).
[15] *Milliken v. Bradley*, 418 U.S. 717 (1974); *San Antonio v. Rodriguez*, 411 U.S. 1 (1973).
[16] *Grutter v. Bollinger*, 539 U.S. 306 (2003).
[17] *City of Richmond v. J.A. Croson Co.*, 488 U.S. 469 (1989).
[18] ADAM COHEN, SUPREME INEQUALITY: THE SUPREME COURT'S FIFTY-YEAR BATTLE FOR A MORE UNJUST AMERICA xviii (2020) ("In the five decades since [Chief Justice Burger] arrived, there have been only conservative chief justices: Burger, William Rehnquist, and John Roberts. Since January 1971, when the last two Nixon justices arrived, these conservative justices have consistently had conservative majorities behind them."). "The Court, overall, has done much more harm than good

race in order to dilute the constitutional mandate of *Brown v. Board of Education*;[19] it erects a nearly insurmountable standard of proof by requiring discriminatory intent by the state;[20] it re-conceptualizes affirmative action so that white interests and privilege are not unduly burdened by positive remedial measures for Blacks and other historically oppressed groups;[21] and it adopts a neutral marketplace analysis of Title VII, preserving the entitlement interests of white workers at the expense of true structural change in employment.[22]

This is the Burger Court's transitional equality, an incrementalistic interpretation of anti-discrimination law, and its remedial potential, so that any significant societal progress is relative and subject to the limits imposed by the Court. Equality ebbs and flows based on how persuasively the Court can articulate neutral rationales for any divergence from the status quo that benefits African Americans and disrupts the settled expectations of white privilege. This is the essence of retrenchment and retrogression.

The Rehnquist Court goes even further in its post-racial neutrality. Essentially, the Rehnquist Court, with its strict adherence to colorblind constitutionalism, advances formalistic equality. Scholars have referenced this as a shift from the Fourteenth Amendment's anti-subordination principle to an anti-differentiation principle that, devoid of history and context, mandates that African Americans and whites be treated the same because the Constitution protects individuals, not racial groups.[23] There is no viable distinction, to the Court, between oppressive state action and race-conscious remedial action by the state. Liberal individualism, then, serves as a key rhetorical component in constitutionalizing white privilege by privileging reverse discrimination claims, concluding that anti-discrimination law is outdated (or should be given a temporal limit), and expanding colorblindness so broadly that this leads to post-racial constitutionalism. Neutrality means that race is so subsumed amongst other neutral factors that it is irrelevant – the Rehnquist Court consistently advances the rhetoric of post-racial colorblind neutrality. An example of this is how the Rehnquist Court, in an opinion authored by Justice O'Connor, reaffirms the diversity principle, in *Bakke*, by concluding that it is a compelling interest and that race, among many factors, can be considered in enrolling a diverse law school class. A "critical mass" of diverse students would provide educational *benefits* to the institution. This is a neutral conception of equality with no mention of eradicating structural inequality; the Court is post-racial in its assessment of the remedial

---

with regard to race. The beneficial decisions during the seventeen years of the Warren Court cannot outweigh the horrendous ones in the century and a half before that or the troubling ones since. There is a strong case against the Supreme Court in the area of race." ERWIN CHEMERINSKY, THE CASE AGAINST THE SUPREME COURT 53 (2014).

[19] 347 U.S. 483 (1954).
[20] *Washington v. Davis*, 426 U.S. 229 (1976).
[21] *Regents of the Univ. of Ca. v. Bakke*, 438 U.S. 265 (1978).
[22] *Firefighters Local Union No. 1784 v. Stotts*, 467 U.S. 561 (1984).
[23] CASS R. SUNSTEIN, THE PARTIAL CONSTITUTION 340 (1993).

purpose of diversity. Many scholars have referenced this post-racial effect rooted in the protection of white interests.[24]

The Roberts Court (2005–) goes the furthest. A core principle of the Roberts Court's post-racial constitutionalism is its strict allegiance to process-based values. Post-racial constitutionalism shifts the analysis from anti-subordination to anti-differentiation to anti-remediation because all state-sanctioned racial oppression has been abolished. This means that the Court actively ignores structural inequality and rationalizes this approach by adopting new standards of proof which are ostensibly neutral, but which make it virtually impossible to prove discrimination. The Court has decided that discrimination, in large part, no longer exists so any consideration of race means that decisions are being made on the impermissible basis of race.

The Burger Court leads directly to this result, setting the stage for both the Rehnquist Court's post-racial colorblindness and the Roberts Court's post-racial constitutionalism.

The Burger Court is generally conceptualized as a transitional institutional bridge between the liberalism of the Warren Court and the hard swing to the right of the Rehnquist Court, but this is an incomplete assessment of the Court's doctrinal role in fashioning colorblind constitutionalism as antecedent to post-racial constitutionalism.[25] Canvassing the Burger Court's race jurisprudence in school integration cases, the doctrinal evolution of the discriminatory intent standard, the early affirmative action decisions, and its disjointed Title VII decisions protecting the expectation interests of white employees, Chapter 2 explores the doctrinal themes embodied in these decisions to illuminate the connection between the Burger Court's transitional equality and the Rehnquist Court's post-racial colorblindness. This vein of colorblindness leads directly to the Roberts Court's post-racial constitutionalism.

Since formalistic equality is the touchstone of the Court's race jurisprudence, the Rehnquist Court actively crafts decisions that neutralize race by ignoring history and context, defining discrimination so narrowly that it does not exist, and offering neutral explanations for inequality. Rationalization of oppression and structural inequality is a defining characteristic of Rhetorical Neutrality. In every permutation of the Court's race jurisprudence, there is a conscious attempt to conceptualize race as irrelevant, so that neutral principles define the Court's decision-making. This ultimately leads the Roberts Court to be actively engaged in dismantling anti-discrimination law.

---

[24] *See, for example,* Osamudia James, *White Like Me: The Negative Impact of the Diversity Rationale on White Identity Formation,* 89 N.Y.U. L. REV. 425, 450 (2014); Eboni S. Nelson, *Examining the Costs of Diversity,* 63 U. MIAMI L. REV. 577, 582 n. 22 (2009); Bryan K. Fair, *Re(caste)ing Equality Theory: Will Grutter Survive by 2028?* 7 U. PA. J. CONST. L. 721, 761 (2003).

[25] MICHAEL J. GRAETZ AND LINDA GREENHOUSE, THE BURGER COURT AND THE RISE OF THE JUDICIAL RIGHT (2016).

Building upon the previous chapters' deconstruction of neutrality, Chapter 3 turns to the Roberts Court and its post-racial constitutionalism. Justice Kennedy, the chief author of the Court's post-racial constitutionalism, consistently tries to transcend race in the Court's race jurisprudence by emphasizing race neutrality as a guiding principle. The doctrinal shift is from the Rehnquist Court's balancing of interests, so as not to disrupt white privilege while pursuing process-based equality through neutrality, to the Roberts Court's explicit dismissal of race as a relevant consideration and the inevitable conclusion that anti-discrimination law is unnecessary. Each subsequent chapter explores a distinct conceptual feature of the Roberts Court's post-racial constitutionalism.

Conceptualizing the Roberts Court's post-racial process discourse, Chapter 4 highlights how the Court's post-racialism was used to weaponize participatory democracy and allow political majorities to undermine positive remedial approaches to structural inequality. In *Schuette v. Coalition to Defend Affirmative Action*,[26] the Court upheld a voter initiative to amend the Michigan Constitution to prohibit the consideration of race in state decision-making. By empowering the voters to "interpret" the anti-discrimination principle of the Fourteenth Amendment, the decision not only radically revises established precedent focusing on the structural dimensions of race-based subjugation, but it also constitutionalizes post-racial discourse against affirmative action. Instead of protecting discrete and insular minorities[27] from an unconstitutional restructuring of the political system, the Court promotes a democratic myth: a direct democracy movement advancing the tenets of post-racialism and formalistic equality is privileged over the anti-subordination principle of the Fourteenth Amendment. Process neutrality reinforces inequality.

Examining the Roberts Court's conception of race, diversity, and education, Chapter 5 offers a critique of the fraught concept of diversity. Diversity relies heavily on difference, an open marketplace of ideas, and the educational benefits accruing from it, but this educational enhancement is skewed toward developing the tolerance of white students rather than disrupting the structural barriers of exclusion that isolate and oppress students of color. Writing for the Court in *Fisher I*[28] and *Fisher II*,[29] Justice Kennedy's opinions embody the doctrinal shift from post-racial colorblindness to post-racial constitutionalism. Where post-racial colorblindness sought to explain the insignificance of race by neutralizing it (Rehnquist Court), post-racial constitutionalism advances the view that race has been transcended in light of the full attainment of formal equality (Roberts Court).

---

[26] 572 U.S. 291 (2014).
[27] United States v. Carolene Products Co., 304 U.S. 144, 152 n. 4 (1938).
[28] 570 U.S. 297 (2013).
[29] 579 U.S. 365 (2016).

An animating feature of the Roberts Court's post-racial constitutionalism is its radical reinterpretation of anti-discrimination statutes, so that their very purpose is neutralized or gutted altogether. Chapter 6 posits that the Roberts Court transplants a new discriminatory intent standard, borrowed from its equal protection jurisprudence, into Title VII. A hallmark of the Roberts Court's post-racialism is the protection of the expectation interests of whites. The Court turns Title VII law inside out to protect white privilege. In yet another decision by Justice Kennedy, in *Ricci v. DeStefano*,[30] the Court re-conceptualizes disparate impact liability under Title VII to require a "strong basis in evidence" that an employer would be subject to a disparate impact lawsuit if it fails to adopt a race-conscious remedial approach. Notwithstanding the city of New Haven's attempt to redress the disproportionate exclusion of African Americans from the fire department officer's corps, the remedial decision to throw out skewed test results is viewed as intentional discrimination (disparate treatment) by the employer. The Court's approach legitimizes the reverse discrimination suit brought by white firefighters who passed the officer's examination, and views the structural inequality evinced in the disproportionate failure of African-American candidates as statutorily irrelevant.

The Roberts Court has extended its devastating reach to housing discrimination law as well. Exposing the doctrinal tension in the Court's novel conceptualization of disparate impact, Chapter 7 dissects the reasoning in *Texas Department of Housing and Community Affairs v. Inclusive Communities*,[31] which ostensibly reaches a good result, holding that disparate impact claims are properly cognizable under the Fair Housing Act. At first glance, the opinion restores the statutory primacy of disparate impact analysis where it had been casually discarded in *Ricci*. But there is much more at work here. A jurisprudential calling card of the Roberts Court is to deploy neutral principles that promote openness, accessibility, and inclusion while substantially undermining the very framework that would provide for such substantive equality. Structural inequality is rationalized, and substantive equality is illusory because it is completely limited by neutrality.

In the same manner that Justice Kennedy did in his decision in *Ricci*, eviscerating disparate impact liability under Title VII, he constructs a novel conception of disparate impact, which is deferential to the neutral operations of the housing marketplace. So, economics and profit determine the viability of disparate impact claims under the Fair Housing Act. There are neutral reasons for disproportionate housing disparities for the poor and people of color, and the Court is all too eager to find them. This means that the Court ignores both the racial and structural factors underlying housing segregation. The Court emphasizes the limitations on disparate impact liability more than the actual substantive protections embodied in the Fair Housing Act.

---

[30] 557 U.S. 557 (2009).
[31] 576 U.S. 519 (2015).

Starting with its post-racial pronouncement in *Shelby County v. Holder* that history did not end in 1965, the Court has prioritized returning power to the states to determine how elections are conducted, ignoring the lasting impact of voter discrimination and suppression against people of color and the poor. Chapter 8 focuses on three recent decisions – *Shelby County v. Holder*,[32] *Husted v. A. Philip Randolph Institute*,[33] and *Rucho v. Common Cause*[34] – that effectively undermine participation in the democratic process. Each decision disempowers African Americans in a manner that suggests that the Court is actually targeting them, so as to ensure that they remain a subjugated group and any relative social justice progress is overturned: in *Shelby County*, the Court discards the Voting Rights Act as unnecessary because of the "progress" made by Blacks in the political process and the fact that "old" discrimination has been effectively eradicated; *Husted* permits the removal of nearly 1 million voters from Ohio's voting rolls based on the Court's hyper-technical reading of a law crafted to prevent voter fraud where none existed; and *Rucho* insulates the political process from any judicial scrutiny concluding that partisan gerrymandering is a non-justiciable political question.

Recently, during the devastating outbreak of the COVID-19 virus, with confirmed cases and deaths rising exponentially across the United States and globally, the Court, in a *per curiam* opinion, intervened to block an extension to receive absentee ballots for an additional six days after an election primary in Wisconsin. Ignoring the well-documented anxiety and fear caused by this historic pandemic, the Court glibly concluded that such an extension "fundamentally alters the nature of the election."[35] The Court's decision gave Wisconsin voters a stark, existential choice – either go to the polls and risk contracting the deadly virus or forfeit their constitutional right to vote. Such rank partisanship undermines the legitimacy of the Court.[36]

All of this points to how, under the Roberts Court's post-racial constitutionalism, the Court is re-envisioning federalism and the structural Constitution so that states have more power to enact legislation designed to address ostensibly neutral concerns like voter identification fraud, access to the polls, and election procedures. However, these serve to displace people of color, especially African Americans, who have been consistently targeted for exclusion.

Essentially, this book accepts Derrick Bell's trenchant insight about the permanence of racism;[37] and, examines how ostensibly neutral doctrines and decisional outcomes, articulated by the Roberts Court, have not only failed to incorporate the

---

[32] 570 U.S. 529 (2013).

[33] 138 S. Ct.1833 (2018).

[34] 139 S. Ct. 2484 (2019).

[35] *Republican Nat'l C'tee v. Democratic Nat'l C'tee*, 589 U.S. __ (2020) (April 6, 2020), 140 S.Ct. 1205, 1207 (2020).

[36] Linda Greenhouse, *NYT Opinion: The Supreme Court Fails Us*, N.Y. Times, April 9, 2020, www .nytimes.com/2020/04/09/opinion/wisconsin-primary-supreme-court.html.

[37] Derrick Bell, Faces at the Bottom of the Well (1993).

reality of race and racism in American society but have instead served to legitimize structural inequality and caste-based oppression. While it can be said that this has been the modern institutional mission of the Court since the end of the Civil War, the Roberts Court stands uniquely apart for being openly hostile to the rights of oppressed minorities under the thinly veiled guise of neutrality.

Concluding with a conceptual vision for dismantling structural inequality in this never-ending struggle for liberation and substantive equality, the Conclusion argues for a Third Reconstruction of transformative social change. The Third Reconstruction would seek to dismantle structural inequality and systemic racism by identifying disproportionate impact as a constitutionally cognizable injury and dispensing with an unduly rigid discriminatory intent requirement; disrupting neutral rationales in decision-making that preserve and perpetuate subordination and inequality; integrating the Thirteenth and Fourteenth Amendments so that they are re-envisioned as legislative mandates to eradicate the badges and incidents of slavery in American society; and acknowledging the permanence of racism in any analysis of structural inequality so that the possibility of retrogression and retrenchment is a factor in analyzing claims of discrimination.

1

Rhetorical Neutrality and Post-Racial Historicism

After the American Civil War, the course of the nation's racial destiny was set by how the Supreme Court interpreted the Reconstruction Amendments. Ironically, instead of embracing a broad constitutional mandate eradicating caste-based oppression, securing full-fledged citizenship in an inclusive democracy, and the right to vote as a fundamental component of equal citizenship, the Court constitutionalized the badges and incidents of slavery that had been formally abolished by the amendments. The myth of democracy was born. Even in the immediate aftermath of the Civil War, the Court was post-historical and post-racial. Post-racial historicism references the Court's attempt to neutralize race while simultaneously transcending it. The Court plays a central role in constructing the narrative of racial progress in this country, and it has done so in a manner that either ignores history or substantively revises it, all in the name of moving beyond race.

Rhetorical Neutrality unpacks the narrative structure of the Court's race jurisprudence. It is a means of describing the underlying neutral rhetoric of the Court's race decisions and how these rhetorical moves perpetuate subordination. By distorting the historical mandate of the Reconstruction Amendments, redefining discrimination so that its existence must be established through nearly impregnable burdens of proof, and then rationalizing inequality as an ostensibly neutral systemic outcome, the Court preserves the status quo of structural inequality. This leads the Court to adopt a formalistic view of equality where discrimination claims of historically oppressed minorities are ignored.

American society has always been post-racial because it actively seeks to erase or ignore communities of color through neutral rhetoric of progress and process. The Court has actively engaged post-racial rhetoric since the end of the Civil War to the present-day Roberts Court. Only eighteen years after the Civil War, in the *Civil Rights Cases*, the Court, ignoring history, context, and the historical mandate of the Reconstruction Amendments, stated that "When a man has emerged from slavery, and, by the aid of beneficent legislation, has shaken off the inseparable concomitants of that state, there must be some stage in the progress of his elevation when he takes the rank of a mere citizen and ceases to be the special favorite of the laws."[1] It is astonishing that the Court frames the "beneficent legislation" as a sort of jurisprudential windfall affording the recently emancipated slaves a "special" privilege of citizenship. This judicial embrace of formalistic equality is rooted in a neutralizing narrative that is a defining feature of the Court's race jurisprudence.

Rhetorical Neutrality is the narrative doctrinal structure that is the fulcrum of the Court's race jurisprudence. The Court advances three interlocking myths that resonate to this day. The first is an historical myth, which is deployed to ignore the legislative mandate of the Reconstruction Amendments. Second, a definitional myth reinforces this historical distortion by disconnecting race from social context and defining discrimination so narrowly that it is virtually nonexistent. Finally, the rhetorical myth serves to rationalize the existence of discrimination and to suppress any remedial efforts as unduly burdensome on whites.

THE HISTORICAL MYTH

The historical myth, underlying Rhetorical Neutrality, essentially erases any connection between the legislative history of the Civil War Amendments – the Thirteenth,[2] Fourteenth,[3] and Fifteenth Amendments[4] – and race. The Reconstruction Amendments were race-conscious amendments based upon a theory of group empowerment of African Americans who endured centuries of subjugation under a racial caste system.[5] These Reconstruction Amendments were debated, drafted, and ratified to bring the newly emancipated slaves into the American polity;[6] thus, the American racial caste system was dismantled, and African Americans were accorded the full benefits of citizenship, and the unabridged right to vote.

But what emerged, even from the Court's early race jurisprudence, was a singular focus on the formalism of equality, its underlying neutrality, and a shift from the

---

[1]   109 U.S. 3, 25 (1883).

[2]   "Neither slavery nor involuntary servitude, except as a punishment for crime whereof the party shall have been duly convicted, shall exist within the United States." U.S. Const. amend. XIII, § 1. "Congress shall have power to enforce this article by appropriate legislation." U.S. Const. amend. XIII, § 2.

[3]   "No state shall ... deny to any person within its jurisdiction the equal protection of the laws." U.S. Const. amend. XIV, § 1. "The Congress shall have power to enforce, by appropriate legislation, the provisions of this article." U.S. Const. amend. XIV, § 5.

[4]   "The right of citizens of the United States to vote shall not be denied or abridged by the United States or by any State on account of race, color, or previous condition of servitude." U.S. Const. amend. XV, § 1. "Congress shall have power to enforce this article by appropriate legislation." U.S. Const. amend. XV, § 2.

[5]   Eric Schnapper, *Affirmative Action, and the Legislative History of the Fourteenth Amendment*, 71 Va. L. Rev. 753 (1985); Eugene Gressman, *The Unhappy History of Civil Rights Legislation*, 50 Mich. L. Rev. 1323 (1951).

[6]   Bryan K. Fair, *The Acontextual Illusion of a Color-Blind Constitution*, 28 U.S.F.L. Rev. 343, 348 (1994) (reviewing Andrew Kull, The Color-Blind Constitution (1992)); Bryan K. Fair, *Foreword: Rethinking the Colorblindness Model*, 13 Nat'l. Black L. J. 1 (1994).

anti-caste and anti-subordination principles, rooted in the Fourteenth Amendment, to a post-racial anti-differentiation principle.[7] The anti-differentiation principle, meaning that the similarly situated should not be treated differently because of race,[8] is a neutral principle premised on formal equality.

Fundamentally, the Court's race jurisprudence is about a concern for the "similarly situated" – those who must be treated the same. The rhetoric of neutrality becomes especially appealing because everyone can be viewed as similarly situated along some post-racial metric of individualism. Thus, history can be ignored (or revised) in the name of colorblindness (history is neutral and without a racial context); race can be decontextualized so that it becomes an institutional value so that benefits are not distributed based on race; and neutrality is preserved through a series of doctrinal tenets which invert the central meaning of the anti-subordination principle and entrench structural inequality.[9]

Because the present-day effects of past discrimination are constitutionally irrelevant to the Court, history has no significance in the Court's race jurisprudence in the absence of a clearly identifiable discriminatory perpetrator. This failure of proof rationale has long been a defining feature of the Court's race decisions (even if disproportionate impact or societal discrimination is identifiable, it is constitutionally irrelevant without proof of discriminatory intent). The historical myth ignores the legislative history of the Civil War Amendments – the Thirteenth, Fourteenth, and Fifteenth Amendments – and instead focuses on the neutral principle of colorblindness.

Rhetorically, recasting the Fourteenth Amendment in liberal individualist terms, the Court emphasizes the language of personage (essential individualism) in the Fourteenth Amendment,[10] and this disconnects the Fourteenth Amendment from the anti-caste[11] and anti-subjugation[12] principles underpinning the Thirteenth and Fifteenth Amendments. Personal rights displace the rights of the oppressed. The historical myth distorts the legislative mandate of the Reconstruction Amendments.

The Court neutralizes race by prohibiting formal discrimination – any dissimilar treatment because of race by the state – rather than state-mandated

---

[7]   CASS R. SUNSTEIN, THE PARTIAL CONSTITUTION 340 (1993).

[8]   *Ibid.*

[9]   Kimberlé Williams Crenshaw, *Race, Reform, and Retrenchment: Transformation and Legitimation in Anti-Discrimination Law*, 101 HARV. L. REV. 1331, 1345–49 (1988).

[10]   John E. Morrison, *Colorblindness, Individuality and Merit: An Analysis of the Rhetoric against Affirmative Action*, 79 IOWA L. REV. 313, 328–29 (1994).

[11]   Cedric Merlin Powell, *Blinded by Color: The New Equal Protection, the Second Deconstruction, and Affirmative Inaction*, 51 U. MIAMI L. REV. 191, 227 (1997).

[12]   LAURENCE H. TRIBE, AMERICAN CONSTITUTIONAL LAW § 16–21, at 1516 (2d ed. 1988) (discussing and quoting *Strauder v. West Virginia*, 100 U.S. 303, 308 (1880) as the "first postbellum racial discrimination" that stands for the proposition that the Equal Protection Clause was meant to remedy racial subjugation – the clause is an "exemption from legal discriminations implying inferiority," which are "steps toward reducing [African-Americans] to the condition of a subject race.").

oppression and its continuing effects. Embracing this colorblind mandate, the Court reframes the Reconstruction Amendments so that race is read out of them, and formalistic equality becomes the guiding principle of the Court's race jurisprudence. The Reconstruction Amendments formally eradicated the subordination of African Americans, but the Court preserved state autonomy and the subjugation of the newly emancipated slaves by its cramped interpretation of anti-racist legislation enacted pursuant to Congress' enforcement power embodied in the amendments.[13]

The Court's erasure of the legislative history of the Reconstruction Amendments and the present-day effects of past discrimination means that structural racism is nearly never mentioned in its race decisions. The Court defines discrimination non-structurally so that it is simply a singular occurrence unrelated to any identifiable state-mandated discriminatory conduct.[14] The Constitution protects individuals, not racial groups, so history is irrelevant because the focus is exclusively on individualized acts of discrimination, not state legitimized oppression.[15]

THE DEFINITIONAL MYTH

Just as the historical myth strips the historical core from the Civil War Amendments, the definitional myth reinforces this historical distortion by disconnecting race from its social context. This rhetorical move essentially diminishes the scope and impact of structural racism by defining discrimination narrowly.

Drawing upon colorblindness as a trope for neutrality, and post-racial historicism to transcend race while preserving white privilege, the Court ingeniously crafts ostensibly neutral rationales for dismantling legislation enacted pursuant to the Reconstruction Amendments.[16] The Court's definitional mythology advances several "neutrally" oppressive doctrinal themes, the most significant of which is the public–private distinction[17] which is deployed to expand state power in the name of principled federalism; there are local and private matters that should be beyond the reach of the federal government.

---

[13] *Ibid.*

[14] Powell, *supra* n. 11, at 217 ("Consequently, the analysis is shifted from principles of anti-subordination and anti-caste to a search for 'individuals' who openly practice racism. By focusing on the protection of individual rights, race becomes meaningless – individuals are not components of racial categories. … it is not racism that accounts for [structural inequality], but some 'misguided' individual.").

[15] Tanya Lovell Banks, *What Is Community? Group Rights and the Constitution: The Special Case of African-Americans*, 1 U. Md. L. J. Race, Religion, Gender, and Class 51, 64–68 (2001) (discussing how the Constitution and anti-discrimination law is premised on liberal individualism without addressing the group dynamics of oppression and subjugation).

[16] Sumi Cho, *Post-Racialism*, 94 Iowa L. Rev. 1589, 1609–11, 1609 n. 7 (2009).

[17] Neil Gotanda, *A Critique of "Our Constitution is Color-Blind,"* 44 Stan. L. Rev. 1, 5 (1991) ("Race discrimination is unconstitutional only in the realm marked out by the doctrine of state action.").

In its early race jurisprudence, the Court defines discrimination by conceptualizing state power in a manner that expands and insulates it from judicial review. Essentially, in the absence of clearly identifiable discrimination by the state, there is nothing to remedy. Private discrimination is out of the reach of the Constitution. The public–private distinction functions in concert with formal race and disconnectedness.[18] If the state is acting in a "neutral" manner toward both races (Black and white), then the only discrimination that is left is "private" discrimination, which cannot be reached by the Fourteenth Amendment.[19] In the absence of some specific evidence of state-mandated racial discrimination, the Court is free to assume (and it invariably does) that the alleged discrimination is illusory or irremediable because it is merely societal discrimination. This ultimately insulates anti-Black racism from judicial review.[20]

Because formal discrimination has been eradicated, anti-differentiation (the similarly situated must be treated the same) – not the anti-subordination principle – is the guiding principle of the Fourteenth Amendment.[21]

The definitional myth is a post-racial explanation for why anti-discrimination law is severely limited in addressing the structural dimensions of systemic racism. Defining discrimination as intentional state action, the narrow focus is on a discriminatory perpetrator. The *Civil Rights Cases* and *Plessy* are clear examples of this component of post-racial constitutionalism – both decisions reify the colorline.

Under the definitional myth, discrimination is defined in a manner that perpetuates systemic racism. Devoid of history or context, "Black" or "white" are simply societal labels through which the state, by its actions, distributes benefits or burdens. In his classic article "A Critique of 'Our Constitution is Color-Blind,'" Professor Neil Gotanda explains how the Court's early race decisions were grounded in a perverse symmetry designed to preserve American apartheid and shows this definitional framing as using formal race to disconnect social context.[22] Here, the colorline is maintained by interpreting legislation on either side of the line as "neutral"; that is, subordination was not constitutionally cognizable because both races were treated equally. For example, Homer Plessy, an African American who could "pass," was not forbidden from riding the streetcar; he simply had to observe the social convention of the colorline – he was free to ride, but the only 'limitation' was where. Because race is neutral, "Black" and "white" are simply classification labels without history or context; the fact that Blacks were a subordinate class was not constitutionally cognizable.

---

[18]   *Ibid.* at 5–7.
[19]   *The Civil Rights Cases*, 109 U.S. at 17; *Plessy*, 163 U.S. at 534.
[20]   Cho, *supra* n. 16, at 1607–08 (noting how the Court promoted whiteness, by effectively undermining the Reconstruction Amendments and Acts with neutral rationales to overturn civil rights legislation and the constitutional protections embodied in them).
[21]   Ruth Colker, *Anti-Subordination Above All: Sex, Race, and Equal Protection*, 61 N.Y.U. L. Rev. 1003, 1005 (1986).
[22]   Gotanda, *supra* n. 17, at 6.

The Court defined discrimination narrowly to accommodate the racist sentiment of the day;[23] and, in many ways, little has changed. This is the essence of post-racial constitutionalism – to move beyond race based on a contrived societal notion of progress.[24] The Court's narrow framing of discrimination helps to advance this contrivance.

The definitional myth, by redefining what discrimination is under the Reconstruction Amendments, literally defines discrimination out of existence. Individual rights are elevated over those of the descendants of the newly emancipated slaves for whom the amendments were passed by Congress. Since the Equal Protection Clause protects individuals, not groups, then finding state-sponsored racial discrimination is an almost insurmountable task. The Court has "privatized" discrimination since its early race decisions as in the *Civil Rights Cases* and *Plessy*. Privatization, then, means that the personal rights of innocent whites are protected whenever the state employs race to their "disadvantage," unless the use of race can be legitimized in context. To this day, incremental progress is permitted, to a significant degree, only when the interests of African Americans and other people of color specifically align with white interests. This is interest convergence. Professor Derrick Bell deploys this concept in his interpretation of the *Civil Rights Cases*:

> With the political benefits to powerful political and corporate interests in maintaining Republican control in Congress secured, blacks over time became victims of judicial interpretations of the Fourteenth and Fifteenth Amendments and legislation based on them so narrow as to render the promised protection meaningless in virtually all situations. For example, in the *Civil Rights Cases*, the Supreme Court found the amendment inadequate to protect Negroes' entitlement to nondiscriminatory service in public facilities. The Reconstruction Amendments, particularly the Fourteenth's guarantee of equal protection and due process, wrought a major reform of the Constitution with measurable benefits for every citizen. And yet, when policymakers' interests no longer aligned with those of the recently freed blacks, the protection was withdrawn from the blacks, who needed them more than ever.[25]

Once the history of racial oppression has been erased or stylized into a mythical narrative of societal progress, and discrimination has been decontextualized so that it means any encroachment on an individual right, then there must be a narrative tool that explains why inequality is a natural outcome of a neutral societal marketplace. The rhetorical myth supplies the rationale for structural inequality.

---

[23] Cho, *supra* n. 16, at 1611 ("In this way, white power, white privilege, and white supremacy benefited from an incredibly efficient synergy between law and society. In the pre-civil-rights era, courts played a key role in enabling unreconstructed whiteness.").

[24] *Ibid.* at 1645 ("... what is new and distinct about post-racialism (as compared to say, colorblindness) is that the state's retreat from race-based remedies is only possible in a society that is perceived as having made significant strides in racial equality, at least symbolically.").

[25] Derrick Bell, Silent Covenants: Brown v. Board of Education and the Unfulfilled Hopes for Racial Reform (2004).

THE RHETORICAL MYTH

The rhetorical myth is the final prong of Rhetorical Neutrality. It functions as a post-racial narrative to de-legitimize any slight deviation from the preservation of white privilege – since race has been transcended, any progress by people of color is unduly burdensome. The historical and definitional myths, erasing history and neutralizing the present-day effects of past discrimination, lead directly to the rhetorical myth, which rationalizes subordination as a natural result of a neutral societal marketplace. Because race is irrelevant and identifiable discrimination by the state is rare, the rhetorical myth serves to legitimize formalistic equality, white privilege, and forward-looking approaches to the eradication of structural inequality.[26]

Essentially, the forward-looking approach rejects race-conscious remedies to eradicate systemic racial oppression. The emphasis is on some future (colorblind) remedial benefit, which leaves structural inequality intact because there is no connection to the persistent effects of past discrimination. The *Civil Rights Cases* and *Plessy* are early examples of the Court's post-racialism. Even in the direct shadow of slavery, the Court focused on neutrality, an expansive conception of state power that insulates its oppressive impact from judicial review, contrived societal access, and a cramped conceptualization of the enforcement power of Congress to eradicate caste. But what is particularly devastating about both decisions is that they set the course for the Court's modern-day race jurisprudence – the anti-subordination principle is supplanted by a post-racial conception of formal equality rather than substantive equality.[27]

In this vein, it is striking that both decisions presume that equality is firmly established for African Americans because equality is defined and explained literally. That is, since slavery has been abolished, equal citizenship has been obtained, and the right to vote granted, then any consideration of the badges and incidents of slavery is superfluous.[28] The rhetorical myth rationalizes this by advancing a contorted notion of access and equality notwithstanding the second-class citizenship decreed by Jim Crow and structural inequality.

The rhetorical myth supplies the narrative rationale for explicating the Court's post-racial determinism.[29] By ignoring history, narrowly circumscribing the definition of discrimination so that it is devoid of any structural component, and then

---

[26] Charles R. Lawrence III, *Passing and Trespassing in the Academy: On Whiteness as Property and Racial Performance as Political Speech*, 31 HARV. J. RACIAL & ETHNIC JUST. 7, 10 (2015) (discussing how white privilege and structural racism are actually legitimized by the absence of explicit state-mandated oppression because, in this post-racial context, race is irrelevant).

[27] Darren Lenard Hutchinson, *"Unexplainable on Grounds Other Than Race": The Inversion of Privilege and Subordination in Equal Protection Jurisprudence*, 2003 U. ILL. REV. 615, 622–23 (2003).

[28] Jennifer Mason McAward, *Defining the Badges and Incidents of Slavery*, 14 U. PA. J. CONST. L. 561, 583–84 (2012).

[29] Cedric Merlin Powell, *Justice Thomas, Brown, and Post-Racial Determinism*, 53 WASHBURN L. J. 451, 452 (2014).

neutralizing the persistence of systemic racism, the Court virtually predetermines the result in all its race decisions. The Court formalistically adheres to a set analytical formula: all claims for transformative racial justice are presumptively invalid, so the current social order dictates how far the Court will go in protecting constitutional rights; the Reconstruction Amendments, and any legislation enacted pursuant to Congress' enforcement power, must be construed narrowly because formal equality has been achieved; and post-racialism is the goal of the Court's race jurisprudence – because race has been transcended, any remedial reference to race is unconstitutional.[30]

The rhetorical move is to traverse race and advance a neutral explanation for a result that offers an incremental and ephemeral gain, or a dramatic reversal of substantive rights for African Americans and people of color. This ultimately leads to outcomes that are merely process based and non-substantive or that dismantle anti-discrimination law and totally obliterate the constitutional rights of oppressed minorities. This is the essence of post-racial constitutionalism: societal progress is exaggerated so that substantive equality is limited, and structural inequality is preserved to advance white supremacy. This legacy of the *Civil Rights Cases* and *Plessy* is engrained in the Court's race jurisprudence. And the Roberts Court is particularly adept at dismantling constitutional rights and statutory protections while extoling the incremental progress legitimized by the rhetorical myth.

The *Civil Rights Cases* and *Plessy* are post-racial in the sense that both decisions dismiss race, racism, and stigmatization as irrelevant, and instead rely on a formalistic interpretation of equality. The rhetorical myth is buttressed by the conception of formalistic equality – the existence of discrimination is rationalized because, after the formal eradication of oppression, and in the absence of an identifiable state actor, everyone is 'equal' and there is nothing to remedy.

FORMALISTIC EQUALITY

Formalistic equality is a defining feature of the Court's post-racial historicism. The Court actively neutralizes or ignores the historical significance of past discrimination and the persistence of its continuing effects. In essence, the Court consistently avoids any consideration of the structural aspects of racism. Given the nation's sordid racial history – social change has been transformational only incrementally and substantive change is always limited – the Court has consistently advanced decisions

---

[30] David Schraub, *Post-Racialism and the End of Strict Scrutiny*, 92 Ind. L. J. 599, 601–02 (2017) (Conservatives, and indeed the Supreme Court, have "successfully converted the historical link between race and power into a transcendent critique of any and all uses of race – sabotaging race-conscious progressive reform efforts. Today, strict scrutiny is almost exclusively deployed against progressive efforts to ameliorate racialized injustice.").

that move beyond race and leave structural inequality intact. This explains the permanence and intransigence of racism.

The post-racial constitutionalism of the Roberts Court attempts to transcend race, but it is impossible to do so. Race and racism are indelible components of our society and polity.[31] After 400 years of subjugation dating from the landing in Port Comfort, Virginia,[32] a Civil War and the Black Codes, a brief Reconstruction period, decades of Jim Crow, a civil rights movement (the Second Reconstruction), and a new period of white backlash[33] and the emergence of a new empowerment movement seeking to dismantle structural inequality (the Third Reconstruction), the salience and centrality of race cannot be denied.[34]

Post-racial constitutionalism references the Court's presumptive approach to racial discrimination; the Court presumes that race-conscious remedial approaches are inherently suspect[35] and, as such, are unconstitutional because they violate color-blind neutrality and illegitimately focus on race because sufficient societal progress has been made. Formal equality means that racial considerations are unnecessary because discrimination has been officially eliminated. Society is post-racial, so the historical myth obscures the salience of race underlying the Reconstruction Amendments; discrimination is defined so narrowly that its existence is virtually mythological; and the rhetorical myth explains the persistence of subordination in neutral terms. Rhetorical Neutrality is the doctrinal narrative structure of the Court's race opinions that advances its post-racial constitutionalism.

The rhetorical structure of the early race decisions of the *Civil Rights Cases* and *Plessy* portend the post-racial constitutionalism of the modern-day Roberts Court. Both decisions ignore history and the present-day effects of caste-based oppression; they redefine discrimination so narrowly that it is unrelated to systemic oppression or structural inequality; and, finally, they rationalize oppression so that extant inequality is explained as natural so as not to burden white privilege. Both decisions uphold social conventions built on racism.

Indeed, any racial progress must be justified with neutrality in mind. The core of the modern Roberts Court's post-racial constitutionalism begins with the *Civil*

---

[31] Mario L. Barnes, Erwin Chemerinsky, and Trina Jones, A *Post-Race Equal Protection?* 98 Geo. L. J. 967, 969–70 (2010) (discussing the *Civil Rights Cases* and *Plessy* as post-racial decisions); C. Vann Woodward, The Strange Career of Jim Crow (1957); Brian Purnell and Jeanne Theoharis with Komozi Woodard, The Strange Careers of the Jim Crow North: Segregation and Struggle Outside of the South (2019).

[32] The 1619 Project, www.nytimes.com/interactive/2019/08/14/magazine/1619-america-slavery.html.

[33] Terry Smith, Whitelash: Unmasking White Grievance at the Ballot Box 6 (2020) ("Viewed as a vector of white racial resentment, whitelash is not a uniquely American problem, yet America has a unique role in its spread and deterrence. A nation that boasts of its ability to encourage democracy throughout the world must be mindful of its similar ability to foster racist ideology.").

[34] Khiara M. Bridges, Critical Race Theory: A Primer (2019).

[35] Schraub, *supra* n. 30, at 601–02.

Rights Cases and *Plessy*, as both decisions seek to diminish the applicability of the Reconstruction Amendments to state mandated inequality. In the Court's early race decisions, it is ironic that discrimination is defined so narrowly in the immediate aftermath of slavery. It is as if once the Thirteenth Amendment abolishes slavery, and this is even debatable given the expansion of the carceral state through the punitive exception,[36] then any other discrimination must be identifiable as state action; or it is outside of the remedial power of the Thirteenth and Fourteenth Amendments, or any legislation enacted by Congress to enforce these constitutional amendments. The Roberts Court has fully expanded this conceptual approach in all areas of anti-discrimination law.

The farther we move away from historical oppression to the more subtle, but equally devastating, forms of subjugation, the less receptive the Court is to affirming the power and viability of anti-discrimination law in dismantling structural inequality. The unifying normative principle of the Roberts Court is post-racial neutrality, and this can be traced directly to the *Civil Rights Cases* and *Plessy*. Indeed, the Court's modern race jurisprudence begins with these post-racial decisions.

THE *CIVIL RIGHTS CASES*: THE STATE ACTION REQUIREMENT AND THE IRRELEVANCE OF SLAVERY

Exercising its enforcement power under Section 2 of the Thirteenth Amendment, Congress enacted the Civil Rights Act of 1866, which bestowed citizenship on the liberated slaves. Next, the Civil Rights Act of 1875, enacted pursuant to the Fourteenth Amendment's Section 5 power, conferred upon African Americans all the rights of citizens to move through and participate fully in society, thereby obliterating the newly created shackles of the colorline. The Civil Rights Act of 1875 prohibited discrimination in all public accommodations, opening society to African Americans previously enslaved and excluded by the colorline.[37]

Declaring the Civil Rights Act of 1875 unconstitutional,[38] the *Civil Rights Cases* is the death knell of Reconstruction legislation, and Congress' attention to racial subordination and its exercise of enforcement power, under the Thirteenth and

---

[36] Michele Goodwin, *The Thirteenth Amendment: Modern Slavery, Capitalism, and Mass Incarceration*, 104 CORNELL L. REV. 899, 935–52 (2019); MICHELLE ALEXANDER, THE NEW JIM CROW: MASS INCARCERATION IN THE AGE OF COLORBLINDNESS 185–200 (2010).

[37] "Sec. 1. That all persons within the jurisdiction of the United States shall be entitled to the full and equal enjoyment of the accommodation, advantages, facilities, and privileges of inns, public conveyances on land or water, theaters, and other places of public amusement; subject only to the conditions and limitations established by law, and applicable alike to citizens of every race and color, regardless of any previous condition of servitude." *The Civil Rights Cases*, 109 U.S. at 9.

[38] *Ibid.* at 25.

Fourteenth Amendments, would remain dormant for nearly a century afterward. The *Civil Rights Cases* and *Plessy* effectively inter the first Reconstruction.[39]

By overturning this comprehensive legislative attempt to eradicate America's racial caste system, the Court not only reflected the popular attitudes of the time but constitutionalized them by providing a post-racial narrative that legitimized the persistence of racism. Given this, it is no surprise that the decision is nearly unanimous with Justice Harlan as the lone dissenter.

The post-racial historicism of the *Civil Rights Cases* is breathtaking: the decision not only erases the brutal legacy of chattel slavery, but it also diminishes the constitutional primacy of the Thirteenth and Fourteenth Amendments, and it rationalizes the continued subjugation of African Americans for generations as 'mere citizens' unworthy of constitutional protection in the absence of direct state action. Insulating private discrimination from congressional remedial power and judicial review, the Court encourages private discrimination and enhances an enduring remnant of slavery – the power to exclude and stigmatize. It is extraordinary that the Court would declare that African Americans were "mere citizens," after centuries of oppression, while simultaneously dealing the final devastating blow in eradicating the short-lived gains embodied in the Reconstruction statutes.[40]

The *Civil Rights Cases* provide the doctrinal conception of state action and how the Court will define discrimination, which is a defining feature of post-racial constitutionalism. Concluding that there was no violation of the Fourteenth Amendment because there was no intentional discrimination by the state, the Court offers a cramped interpretation of Congress' power to eradicate subjugation and subordination under the Constitution. In fact, in the absence of identifiable state action, it would be a constitutional overreach for Congress to legislate in matters deemed to be purely private.[41] To the Court, it is state action that actualizes the operation of the Fourteenth Amendment's prohibitive power because the amendment is based on "[s]tate laws and acts done under State authority."[42] Since there is no state action, Congress is without power to prescribe local codes of conduct; private racist conduct and its ubiquitous harms are out of the reach of Congress' enforcement power.[43] This aggrandizement of state power – where Congress' enforcement power shrinks

---

[39] JOHN HOPE FRANKLIN, RECONSTRUCTION AFTER THE CIVIL WAR 215 (3d ed. 2013) ("The Civil Rights Act of 1875 was a dead letter from the day of its enactment, and white Southerners boasted that it was not being enforced and could not be enforced anywhere in the South."); Francico M. Urgate, *Reconstruction Redux: Rehnquist, Morrison, and the Civil Cases,* 41 HARV. C.R.-C.L. 481, 496 (2006) ("Through the *Civil Rights Cases,* the Supreme Court dealt the final and most decisive blow to Reconstruction and the nineteenth-century struggle for racial liberation."). The Court supplies the doctrinal narrative for this racist intransigence; the same is no less true today.

[40] IBRAM X. KENDI, STAMPED FROM THE BEGINNING: THE DEFINITIVE HISTORY OF RACIST IDEAS IN AMERICA 264–65 (2016).

[41] *The Civil Rights Cases,* 109 U.S. at 13–14.

[42] *Ibid.* at 13.

[43] *Ibid.* 13–14.

as inequality is normalized – runs through post-racial constitutionalism – the Court consistently narrows or limits legislative power whenever it is exercised to eradicate structural inequality and systemic racism.[44]

The Court has never fully embraced substantive equality for people of color generally, and African Americans specifically. Even in an early race decision like the *Civil Rights Cases*, the Court ignores the legislative history of the Fourteenth Amendment and neutralizes and distorts the anti-subordination principle. After erecting the state action requirement and ignoring the race-based oppression that the Civil Rights Act of 1875 was enacted to remedy, the Court fashions a formalistic conception of the scope of Congress' remedial power under section five of the Fourteenth Amendment.[45]

Under this narrow conception of congressional power, Congress' enforcement power is limited to only corrective or curative actions, those which counteract or redress clearly identifiable and prohibited state action.[46] Anything other than this narrowly defined category of enforcement power remedial authority is impermissible under the Constitution because it is "primary and direct" legislation rather than corrective legislation to remedy prohibited state conduct.[47] In the absence of state action, Congress is devoid of direct and plenary power to legislate to eliminate discrimination in all public accommodations in the states.[48] Because the Civil Rights Act of 1875 does not specifically reference "adverse State legislation" that is discriminatory in nature, it unduly expands congressional power by "supersed[ing] and displac[ing] State legislation in the same subject. ... It ignores such legislation, and assumes that the matter is one that belongs to the domain of national regulation."[49]

This post-racial interpretation of legislative power can only be explained by reference to the historical, definitional, and rhetorical myths that animate Rhetorical Neutrality. The legislative history of the Fourteenth Amendment is completely ignored by the Court.[50] With no reference to the legislative history of the Fourteenth Amendment, the Court reinterprets the enforcement power of Congress.

---

[44] Smith, *supra* n. 33, at 159 ("In short, the Supreme Court in 1883 was as fed up with attempts to secure equality for blacks as the Supreme Court was in 2013. And just as the *Civil Rights Cases* set the stage for 75 years of Jim Crow, *Shelby County* unleashed America's racist potential like no other modern decision of the Court. The decision forecasted the age of Trump and has made more imperative than at any time since Jim Crow the need for structural reforms to protect people of color against voter whitelash."). *Shelby County* and its legacy is discussed at length in Chapter 8.

[45] *The Civil Rights Cases*, 109 U.S. at 18–19.

[46] *Ibid.*

[47] *Ibid.* at 19.

[48] *Ibid.* at 18.

[49] *Ibid.* at 19.

[50] TRIBE, *supra* n. 12, § 5–12, at 330 ("The Supreme Court restrictively construed or simply invalidated much of this legislation, acting to preserve in law the autonomy that the states had largely lost politically in the wake of the Civil War.").

The Court defines discrimination and caste-based oppression so narrowly that this effectively eviscerates the Section 5 enforcement power of Congress under the Fourteenth Amendment. Congressional power can only be exercised correctively to remedy state mandated discrimination, not to legislate directly to eradicate private discrimination. This upside-down depiction of federalism serves to expand state power, which was actively targeting African Americans for new forms of subjugation only eighteen years after the abolition of slavery, and contract federal power to intervene where states failed to protect the rights of freed slaves who were now full-fledged citizens of a flawed democracy. Under this reasoning, Congress would take its legislative cues from the very states that were prohibited from discriminating against their citizens.

But the Court does not stop here in limiting Congress' remedial enforcement power; the Court offers a formalistic definition of slavery and thereby narrowly defines discrimination and limits the scope of congressional remedial power. Notwithstanding the fact that the Thirteenth Amendment has no state action requirement, the Court nevertheless applies its novel corrective legislation limitation to Congress' Thirteenth Amendment enforcement power as well. Because there is no state action under the Fourteenth Amendment, and there is a bright-line distinction between actual bondage in shackles and mere private denials of access to public accommodations, the Thirteenth Amendment offers no grant of authority to remove all structural barriers to public accommodations.

Acknowledging that the Thirteenth Amendment reaches private discriminatory conduct, because there is no state action requirement, the Court defines the badges and incidents of slavery formalistically by making a facile distinction between involuntary servitude and an "ordinary civil injury, properly cognizable by the laws of the state."[51] The Court can advance this contrived distinction because it frames the issue under the Thirteenth Amendment in decidedly post-racial terms. The issue presented is about class, not race.[52] Other than a reference to the Thirteenth Amendment "simply abolish[ing] slavery,"[53] the Court does not discuss the legislative history of the first Reconstruction Amendment.[54] Rather, the analytical posture of the Court is to limit the scope of discrimination the Thirteenth Amendment can reach.

The definitional myth in the *Civil Rights Cases* is that slavery, and its persistent effects in all avenues of society, is erased, and the constitutional validity of class legislation is analyzed in its place. Discrimination is defined out of existence

---

[51] *The Civil Rights Cases*, 109 U.S. at 24; Urgate, *supra* n. 39, at 498 (discussing how the opinion constructs a distinction between civil and political rights, which would later lead to the "separate but equal" rationale in *Plessy*).

[52] "Many wrongs may be obnoxious to the prohibitions of the Fourteenth Amendment which are not, in any just sense, incidents or elements of slavery." *Ibid.* at 23.

[53] *Ibid.* at 23.

[54] Barnes, Chemerinsky, and Jones, *supra* n. 31, at 975.

so that African Americans are presumptively equal to whites only eighteen years after slavery ended. Thus, the issue is not the continued subjugation of African-American citizens, but rather whether the customs and practices of a racist society should be upheld since there was no 'formal' involvement by the state itself and slavery had been abolished. Of course, the state is composed of its citizenry and their collective political will, a fact that the Court conveniently rationalizes to normalize second-class citizenship for African-Americans. The Court refers the aggrieved and excluded African-American citizenry to the very state structures that continue to oppress them in the shadow of slavery. The Court's reasoning is extraordinary:

> … [W]e are forced to the conclusion that such an act of refusal has nothing to do with slavery or involuntary servitude, and that if it is violative of any right of the party, his redress is to be sought under the laws of the State; or, if those laws are adverse to his rights and do not protect him, his remedy will be found in the corrective legislation which Congress has adopted, or may adopt, for counteracting the effect of State laws, or State action, prohibited by the Fourteenth Amendment.[55]

The history of slavery, and its present-day effects, is neutralized by the Court's post-racial class rhetoric, and the badges and incidents of slavery, the stigmatization and exclusion that is the hallmark of oppression, are redefined as the mere 'civil' injury of being refused admission to an amusement park, opera house, or theater.

Rhetorically, the Court advances the myth of racial progress as a rationale for being exhausted[56] by the prospect of continuing to focus on the rights and unearned benefits of African Americans. In post-racial terms, it is time to move away from race:

> It would be running the slavery argument into the ground to make it apply to every act of discrimination which a person may see fit to make as to the guests he will entertain, or as to the people he will take into his coach or cab or car, or admit to his concert or theater, or deal within other matters or intercourse or business.[57]

Noting that innkeepers and public carriers are bound to provide service to 'unobjectionable persons',[58] the Court concludes with a statement that is breathtaking in its formalism and absolute rationalization of structural inequality – there were some "free colored people,"[59] during slavery, who did not enjoy the full benefit of an inclusive society, so now that slavery has been abolished, why should these "mere citizens" be afforded anything "special"?

---

55   *Ibid.* at 24.
56   Darren Lenard Hutchinson, *Racial Exhausation*, 86 WASH. U. L. REV. 917, 922–23 (2009).
57   *The Civil Rights Cases*, 109 U.S. at 25.
58   *Ibid.*
59   *Ibid.*

> When a man has emerged from slavery, and by the aid of beneficent legislation has shaken off the inseparable concomitants of that state, there must be some stage in the progress of his elevation when he takes the rank of a mere citizen, and ceases to be the special favorite of the laws, and when his rights as a citizen, or a man, are to be protected in the ordinary modes by which other men's rights are protected.[60]

This is a fantastic proposition in 1883, and no less so in 2022, because it presumes a process that is neutral, functional, and uninfluenced by the structural dynamics of inequality. In the *Civil Rights Cases*, the Court ignores the present-day effects of the history of slavery; it redefines caste-based oppression emanating from slavery as mere societal inconveniences; and it rationalizes all of this by portraying the limited and incremental racial progress of Reconstruction as post-racial (so much progress has been made that African Americans should not receive a "windfall" as "special favorites" of the laws). This post-racial trope runs through the Court's entire post-racial constitutional jurisprudence. The Court exhibits unbridled confidence in the very systems and processes that produce structural inequality, and this is why the "ordinary modes" for protecting the rights of the historically oppressed are so appealing to the Court.

The majority opinion ignores the fact that there is no state action requirement under the Thirteenth Amendment, deftly acknowledging the brutal institution of slavery while simultaneously distinguishing its vestiges as normal products of "voluntary" social interactions amongst citizens. Under this contrived formalism, whites, and the newly emancipated citizenry of African Americans are free to engage each other, as they see fit, if they adhere to the colorline. *Plessy* would reaffirm this constitutionally noxious principle and its subordination of African Americans thirteen years later.

What is particularly striking about the *Civil Rights Cases* is that there is no structural conception of inequality. Slavery is something that occurred eighteen years before and, apart from being formally abolished by the Thirteenth Amendment, has no constitutional relevance to the Court. Justice Harlan's dissent offers an early example of the structuralism that is glaringly absent from the Court's post-racial constitutionalism.

JUSTICE HARLAN'S *CIVIL RIGHTS CASES DISSENT*: EARLY STRUCTURALISM

While Justice Harlan's colorblind constitutionalism dissent in *Plessy* is more widely known and heralded, his dissent in the *Civil Rights Cases* is particularly compelling because it is the first structural critique of the Court's nascent post-racial constitutionalism. He identifies the salient features of neutrality

---

[60] *Ibid.*

and post-racialism that continue to animate the Roberts Court's jurisprudence: he rejects the historic myth by focusing on the color-conscious legislative history of the Reconstruction Amendments; he critiques the contrived neutrality of formalistic equality; and he emphasizes that it is structural inequality – the badges and incidents of slavery – that was to be eradicated by the Reconstruction Amendments.[61]

Dissenting in the *Civil Rights Cases*, Justice Harlan offers a wide-ranging and forceful critique of the Court's Rhetorical Neutrality, exposing the Court's obliviousness to the legislative history of the Thirteenth and Fourteenth Amendments; how the Court misconstrues slavery and its continuing impact on African Americans; and, finally, how the Court rationalizes the persistence of oppression by characterizing remedies necessitated by slavery and the Black Codes as "preferential" treatment for Blacks. Justice Harlan's structural critique advances three major premises: a critique of the absence of legislative history, specifically, the fact that the Reconstruction Amendments were drafted to afford the newly freed African-American citizens the full attributes of citizenship;[62] the complementary connection between the Thirteenth and Fourteenth Amendments;[63] and the present-day effects of slavery and its underlying badges and incidents.[64]

Rejecting the Court's formalist view of equality and its inherently narrow depiction of Congress' enforcement power, Justice Harlan underscores the complementary relationship between the Thirteenth and Fourteenth Amendments. His analysis is structural; he defines how slavery has been reified by its underlying badges and incidents of stigmatization, state complicity in subordination, and publicly supported segregation.

The Thirteenth and Fourteenth Amendments are legislatively intertwined: freedom is meaningless without the full panoply of substantive constitutional rights that permit citizens to determine their own political destiny. To be truly free, a citizen must have equal protection under the laws, substantive access to all public places in society, and the right to vote. Thus, Justice Harlan concludes that Congress has the power, pursuant to Section 2 of the Thirteenth Amendment and Section 5 of the Fourteenth Amendment, to eradicate structural inequality considering the

---

[61] In this vein, Justice Harlan offers a prescient comment on how the colorline that is constitutionalized by the Court in *Plessy* is the present-day effect of *Dred Scott*: "In my opinion, the judgment rendered will, in time, prove to be quite as pernicious as the decision made by this tribunal in the Dred Scott case." *Ibid.* at 558 (Harlan, J., dissenting).

[62] *Ibid.* at 26–37 (Harlan, J., dissenting).

[63] *Ibid.* at 32–51 (Harlan, J., dissenting).

[64] *Ibid.* at 35 (Harlan, J., dissenting) ("That there are burdens and disabilities which constitute badges of slavery and servitude, and that the power to enforce by appropriate legislation, the Thirteenth Amendment may be exerted by legislation of a direct and primary character, for the eradication, not simply of the institution, but of its badges and incidents, are propositions which ought to be deemed indisputable.").

country's centuries-old history of racial caste-based oppression.[65] Congress' enforcement power is affirmative and broad,[66] and not limited to purely corrective remedies for prohibited state action.[67]

Exposing the central components of neutrality as antithetical to the abolition of caste based oppression by the Thirteenth Amendment and the anti-subordination principle of the Fourteenth Amendment, Justice Harlan explicitly critiques the perpetuation of oppression by the majority's narrow reading of congressional power;[68] he unpacks the historical myth by centering the Thirteenth and Fourteenth Amendments as specifically concerned with the eradication of slavery and the granting of *full* citizenship rights to African Americans; he rejects formalistic equality by defining slavery not simply as an institution abolished by the Thirteenth Amendment, but as a set of subordinating stigmatisms and incidents that serve to continually exclude African Americans from society;[69] and he forcefully rejects the post-racial formalism that animates the majority's reasoning with African Americans as "mere citizens" who deserve no special favors under law. Justice Harlan concludes with a direct retort to the majority's post-racial constitutionalism:

> It is ... scarcely just to say that the colored race has been the special favorite of the laws. The statute of 1875, now adjudged to be unconstitutional, is for the benefit of citizens of every race and color. What the nation, through congress, has sought to accomplish in reference to that race is – what had already been done in every State of the Union for the white race – to secure and protect rights belonging to them as freemen and citizens; nothing more. ... The one underlying purpose of congressional legislation has been to enable the black race to take the rank of mere citizens. The difficulty has been to compel a recognition of the legal right of the black race to take that rank of citizens, and to secure the enjoyment of privileges belonging, under the law, to them as a component part of the people whose welfare and happiness government is ordained.[70]

Recognizing that systemic racism separates African Americans from the "component part of the people," Justice Harlan's dissent unpacks the ostensibly neutral majority

---

[65] *Ibid.* at 35–37; 43–47 (Harlan, J., dissenting).

[66] *Ibid.* at 45–51 (Harlan, J., dissenting).

[67] *Ibid.* at 46 (Harlan, J., dissenting) ("The assumption that this amendment consists wholly of prohibitions upon State laws and State proceedings in hostility to its provisions, is unauthorized by its language.").

[68] "Reading section 2 of the Thirteenth Amendment and section 5 of the Fourteenth Amendment together, it becomes readily apparent that Congress has the power to eradicate caste and its incidents as well as to secure equality." Powell, *supra* n. 11, at 230; Douglas L. Corbert, *Liberating the Thirteenth Amendment*, 30 HARV. C.R.-C.L. L. REV. 1, 33–34 (1995).

[69] 109 U.S. at 37 (Harlan, J., dissenting) ("... the power of Congress under the Thirteenth Amendment is not necessarily restricted to legislation against slavery as an institution upheld by positive law, but may be exerted to the extent at least of protecting the liberated race against discrimination, in respect of legal rights belonging to freemen, where such discrimination is based upon race.").

[70] *Ibid.* at 61–62.

opinion and reveals it for what it is – a post-racial rationalization for retrenchment and retrogression following a stunted period of Reconstruction.

Doctrinally, the *Civil Rights Cases* stand for the proposition that is a major tenet of post-racial constitutionalism: African Americans do not deserve "special treatment" because formalized oppression has been eradicated; to do more would lead us to a racially polarized society. When it comes to racial progress, it is not an overstatement to say that the Court has been actively engaged in a rhetorical balancing act – espousing the constitutional mandate of anti-subordination and substantive equality while simultaneously seeking to first neutralize it, and then ultimately dismantle it – ignoring the present-day effects of past discrimination, narrowly defining discrimination, and then articulating a rationale for the persistence of inequality or why anti-racist legislation or policies are superfluous. In his canonical work, *Stamped from the Beginning*, historian Ibram X. Kendi describes this as a duality of two distinct historical forces: "a *dual* and *dualing* history of racial progress and the simultaneous progression of racism. … the antiracist force of equality and the racist force of inequality marching forward, progressing in rhetoric, in tactics, and policies."[71]

Post-racial constitutionalism is the latest incarnation of this duality: it combines the aspirational appeal of colorblind neutrality while simultaneously impeding antiracist efforts because so much incrementally relative progress has been made. This forms the basis of the Roberts Court's active judicial agenda to dismantle anti-discrimination law.

By constitutionalizing the colorline, the *Civil Rights Cases* and *Plessy* animate the racist force underlying inequality. *Plessy*'s ostensibly neutral and symmetrical approach to equality, and Justice Harlan's famous colorblind dissent, are both rooted in this tense duality of equality and inequality.

PLESSY v. FERGUSON: NEUTRALITY AS SUBORDINATION

Upholding a Louisiana law that required railroad companies to provide separate but equal accommodations for whites and Blacks partitioned by a colorline dividing the races, the Court concluded that there was no violation of the Fourteenth Amendment because the legislation was a "reasonable regulation."[72] Thus, the Court held that the state action here, judged under an inherently deferential standard of review, did not violate the anti-subordination principle of the Fourteenth Amendment because the law simply codified the "usages, customs, and traditions of the people"[73] with an emphasis on "the preservation of the public peace and good

---

[71] KENDI, *supra* n. 40, at x (emphasis in original).

[72] *Plessy v. Ferguson*, 163 U.S. at 550.

[73] *Ibid.*

order."[74] But this preservation of "good order" came with the price of continued subjugation of people of color.

Adopting a deferential approach premised on the rationality of the Louisiana Law, the Court rejected a central principle of the Fourteenth Amendment – state legislation cannot be based upon the presumption that African Americans are inferior and deserve to occupy a subordinate position in American society. Just as it had done in the *Civil Rights Cases*, the Court recognizes race, but does so in a manner that perpetuates caste: in the *Civil Rights Cases*, slavery and its devastating legacy disappear so that there is no prohibited state action because access to public accommodations is a private matter based upon local racist customs; likewise, in *Plessy*, there is no discriminatory state action because "equal" access is provided to all with the only condition being adherence to the colorline. If this is stigmatization or oppression, it is purely imaginary, the Court concludes:

> We consider the underlying fallacy of the plaintiff's argument to consist in the assumption that the enforced separation of the two races stamps the colored race with a badge of inferiority. If this be so, it is not by reason of anything found in the act, but solely because the colored race chooses to put that construction upon it.[75]

Thus, the Court's inverted reasoning is not of recent vintage. One hundred and twenty-four years ago, the Court embraced a 'neutral' construction of the racist law that it upheld in *Plessy*. Because the state's conduct toward the "colored race" and whites was equal and neutral – the colorline separates both races in Louisiana's railroad cars – then there was no subordination or caste-based stigmatization. It was all in the subjugated race's imagination.

The Court's post-racial rhetoric fits squarely within Rhetorical Neutrality: the history of slavery, and how subjugation is advanced based on a theory of bestial inferiority, is not even referenced because slavery has been formally abolished;[76] the historical myth supplies a neutral narrative of "progress" only thirty-one years after the end of slavery and a severely limited Reconstruction;[77] "separate but equal" is defined formalistically and symmetrically, so that whites and Blacks are equal on either side of the colorline, which is merely a societal "custom"; and, finally, while

---

[74] *Ibid.*

[75] *Ibid.* at 551.

[76] *Ibid.* at 543. Indeed, the majority opinion noted that simple distinctions between the white and non-white races, which was essential because whites were "distinguishable from the other race by color," *ibid.*, did not destroy the equality of the races, nor did it "re-establish a state of involuntary servitude." *Ibid.* The Thirteenth Amendment was cast aside in the *Plessy* opinion. Like the *Civil Rights Cases*, the *Plessy* decision emphasizes formalism rather than structural inequality.

[77] Citing the *Civil Rights Cases*, the Court concludes that refusing accommodations to African-Americans by innkeepers, or other owners of properties open to the public, is merely private conduct, not amounting to a badge or incident of slavery; because there is no identifiable state action, this is simply "an ordinary civil injury." *Ibid.* at 543. "If one race be inferior to the other socially, the constitution of the United States cannot put them upon the same plane." *Ibid.* at 552.

racial oppression is denied, it is also acknowledged as existing only in the minds of the oppressed. This is the rhetorical myth of racial progress, which is deployed to rationalize the continued subordination of African Americans. The duality of racial progress and racist oppression is what stamps African Americans from the beginning[78] to be buffeted around in a never-ending progression of evolving racist ideas crafted to perpetuate systemic racism. The Court is the primary purveyor of ostensibly neutral principles crafted to preserve inequality.

Plessy's articulation of colorblind neutrality is an early pronouncement of post-racial constitutionalism: African Americans are commanded to obey the societal conventions of the colorline, because the neutral law impacts African Americans and whites in the same way. Of course, this ignores the stigmatization inherent in state-mandated racial oppression. But it also underscores how the Court is post-racial – the former slaves can now ride the segregated railroad cars in Louisiana. It is of no constitutional moment that they cannot ride in integrated cars because "Legislation is powerless to eradicate racial instincts ... and the attempt to do so can only result in accentuating the difficulties of the present situation."[79] African Americans are part of society but excluded from it. That exclusion is not a violation of the Fourteenth Amendment because access to public transportation is not denied; it is only conditioned on the colorline. Therefore, there is no remedy for the caste-based oppression upheld in the decision.

JUSTICE HARLAN'S *PLESSY* DISSENT: THE DUALITY OF COLORBLINDNESS

In vivid contrast to the majority's willful dismissal of the primacy of the Reconstruction Amendments, Justice Harlan locates the constitutional connection between the Thirteenth and Fourteenth Amendments. He understands the present-day effects of past discrimination, and that the Reconstruction Amendments were enacted to fully integrate African Americans as citizens in the American polity:

> [The Thirteenth Amendment] not only struck down the institution of slavery as previously existing in the United States, but it prevents the imposition of any burdens or disabilities that constitute badges of slavery or servitude. ... But, that amendment having been found inadequate to the protection of the rights of those who had been in slavery, it was followed by the fourteenth amendment, which added greatly to the dignity and glory of American citizenship. ... These two amendments, if enforced according to their true intent and meaning, will protect all the civil rights that pertain to freedom and citizenship. Finally, and to end that no citizen should be denied, on account of his race, the privilege of participating in the political control of his country, it was declared by the fifteenth amendment that "the rights of citizens of

---

[78] KENDI, *supra* n. 40.
[79] *Plessy*, 163 U.S. at 551.

the United States to vote shall not be denied or abridged by the United States or by any state on account of race, color, or previous condition of servitude."[80]

The fallacy of the *Civil Rights Cases* and *Plessy*'s formalism is readily apparent in Justice Harlan's dissent. He critiques this formalism by noting that the Reconstruction Amendments "removed the race line from our governmental systems"[81] and that consequently, neutrality must be rejected. That is, there is no equality of public accommodations if access is partitioned on the colorline.[82] Concluding his structural analysis, Justice Harlan states that "[t]he arbitrary separation of citizens, on the basis of race, while they are on a public highway [or in a Louisiana railroad car] is a badge of servitude wholly inconsistent with the civil freedom and the equality before the law established by the constitution."[83] To Justice Harlan, there is a clear distinction between an "ordinary civil injury"[84] and a stigmatizing exclusion, rooted in slavery and surviving as a remnant of it, which is premised on racism and subordination.

Exposing how neutrality – the make weight premise evoked by the *Plessy* Court to conclude that there was no constitutional violation because both races had access to seats on the train – actually reifies and advances subordination, Justice Harlan posits that "[s]tate enactments regulating the enjoyment of civil rights upon the basis of race, and cunningly devised to defeat legitimate results of the war, under the pretense of recognizing equality of rights, can have no other result than to render permanent peace impossible, and to keep alive a conflict of races, the continuance of which must do harm to all concerned."[85]

Post-racial constitutionalism is the embodiment of this continuing conflict. Indeed, Justice Harlan's dissent, with all its critical references to systemic racism, nevertheless advances on a flawed premise of white supremacy. This is the duality of colorblindness: on the one hand, Justice Harlan categorically rejects ostensibly neutral state action that simply masks the American racial caste system;[86] but, on the other, he places this neutrality in the context of "equality" to both races with the white race preordained to be superior to the other "for all time, if it remains true to its great heritage."[87] The magisterial tenor of "There is no caste here. Our Constitution is color-blind"[88] rings less true.[89]

---

[80] *Ibid.* at 555 (Harlan, J., dissenting).
[81] *Ibid.* (Harlan, J., dissenting).
[82] *Ibid.* at 557 (Harlan, J., dissenting).
[83] *Ibid.* at 562 (Harlan, J., dissenting).
[84] *See Civil Rights Cases*, 109 U.S. at 24.
[85] *Plessy v. Ferguson*, 163 U.S. 537, 561 (Harlan, J., dissenting).
[86] *Ibid.* at 560–63 (Harlan, J., dissenting).
[87] *Ibid.* at 559 (Harlan, J., dissenting).
[88] *Ibid.* (Harlan, J., dissenting).
[89] Yet some have read this passage as a "direct plea" to whites to understand the perniciousness of the *Plessy* ruling. *See* STEVE LUXENBERG, SEPARATE THE STORY OF *PLESSY V. FERGUSON* AND AMERICA'S JOURNEY FROM SLAVERY TO SEGREGATION 486 (2019).

However, it is this colorblind mandate, with its anti-subordination and anti-caste underpinnings, that has been inverted and distorted by the Court. This is an inevitable doctrinal progression because Justice Harlan's dissent has some disconcertingly racist undertones steeped in white supremacy. Of course, Justice Harlan does not believe in the continuing effects of caste-based subordination,[90] but he does believe in the *dominance* of the white race "in prestige, in achievements, in education, in wealth, and in power."[91] He also believes in the lasting legacy and primacy of that dominance.[92]

Today, subordination is maintained through neutrality. The hallmark of Rhetorical Neutrality is its inversion of normative, substantive constitutional principles, like the eradication of caste and the rejection of subordination premised on race, into neutral non-substantive principles like an open political process, diversity, preservation of colorblind seniority in the employment marketplace, fair and open housing, and voting rights in the absence of clearly identifiable discrimination – all of which are explored in the succeeding chapters. None of these neutral themes engages structural inequality.

The Court's post-racial constitutionalism is not a historical artifact; its doctrinal resonance connects its early race decisions to the transitional equality embodied in the Burger Court's decisions; the post-racial colorblindness of the Rehnquist Court; and, finally, the post-racial constitutionalism of the Roberts Court. At each stage, the Court's neutrality expands to such an extent that race is displaced or transcended, so that the primary analytical concern of the Court is balancing incremental gains against their impact on white privilege, which it is actively engaged in maintaining.

---

[90] *Ibid.* at 563–64 (Harlan, J., dissenting).
[91] *Ibid.* at 559 (Harlan, J., dissenting).
[92] *Ibid.* (Harlan, J., dissenting).

The Burger and Rehnquist Courts

Transitional Equality and Post-Racial Colorblindness

The Burger Court is widely viewed as a transitional Court lodged between the liberal rights explosion ignited by the Warren Court[1] and the hard shift to the right of the Rehnquist Court's colorblind constitutionalism.[2] However, this is a misconception of the Burger Court's pivotal role in constructing the doctrinal edifice that ultimately leads to the Roberts Court's post-racial constitutionalism. "The [Burger] Court interpreted the equal protection guarantee itself as protecting against only deliberate discrimination action by the government; the need to prove intentional discrimination has cut off constitutional challenges to policies that have obvious, even foreseeably disparate, impacts on racial minorities or women."[3] Race-conscious remedies are not only unconstitutional, but unnecessary because discrimination has been largely eliminated.

The Burger Court fundamentally altered the historical legacy of *Brown* and narrowly circumscribed the remedial powers of federal courts,[4] and this will ultimately lead to the Roberts Court's evisceration of *Brown* and its post-racial proclamation to stop discriminating on the basis of race;[5] the Burger Court narrowly defined discrimination, building upon the formalism first articulated in the *Civil Rights Cases*, to require a particularized finding of discriminatory intent, which the Roberts

---

[1] Carol S. Steiker, *Keynote Address the Warren Court and Criminal Justice: Some Lasting Legacies and Unfinished Business*, 49 STETSON L. REV. 223, 224 (2020).

[2] Christopher E. Smith and Thomas R. Hensley, *Assessing the Conservatism of the Rehnquist Court*, 77 JUDICATURE 83, 83–86 (1993); Christopher E. Smith and Avis Alexandria Jones, *The Rehnquist Court's Activism and the Risk of Injustice*, 26 CONN. L. REV. 53, 54–55 (1993).

[3] MICHAEL J. GRAETZ AND LINDA GREENHOUSE, THE BURGER COURT AND THE RISE OF THE JUDICIAL RIGHT 8 (2016). *See* Jack M. Balkin, *Why Liberals and Conservatives Flipped on Judicial Restraint: Judicial Review in the Cycles of Constitutional Time*, 98 TEX. L. REV. 215; 216–20; 238–42 (2019).

[4] *See* Cedric Merlin Powell, *Milliken: "Neutral Principles," and Post-Racial Determinism*, 31 HARV. J. RACIAL & ETHNIC JUSTICE ONLINE 1 (2015).

[5] *Parents Involved in Cmty. Sch. v. Seattle Sch. Dist. No. 1*, 551 U.S. 701, 747–48 (2007) ("For schools that never segregated on the basis of race, such as Seattle, or that have removed the vestiges of past segregation, such as Jefferson County [Louisville], the way 'to achieve a system of determining admission to the public schools on a nonracial basis' is to stop assigning students on a racial basis. The way to stop discrimination on the basis of race is to stop discriminating on the basis of race.").

Court would later expand to create a nearly insurmountable barrier of proof in racial discrimination cases; the Burger Court also introduced the concept of diversity, which has proven to be an elastic and nearly meaningless term in the hands of the Rehnquist and Roberts Courts; and, finally, the Burger Court consistently and aggressively protected the settled expectation interests of white workers, and the Roberts Court would go even further by fundamentally redefining disparate impact under Title VII. All of this is to say that the Burger Court's race jurisprudence is discernibly post-racial.

In its school, affirmative action, and Title VII decisions, the Burger Court actively charted a post-racial course – race must be transcended, so that the settled expectations of whites will be undisturbed; or, at least, only temporarily impacted by a remedy limited in time and scope. Indeed, the Burger Court's Title VII jurisprudence leads directly to the Roberts Court's post-racial interpretation of the statute in *Ricci*, which is discussed in depth in Chapter 6. What is striking about all the Court's post-racial jurisprudence is how it privileges a white innocence (victim) narrative to disregard the plight of oppressed people of color. Any progress is conditioned on the impact on white interests. This is a unifying theme of post-racial constitutionalism.

THE BURGER COURT AND TRANSITIONAL EQUALITY

The School Decisions

There is a doctrinal and conceptual overlap between the Warren and Burger Courts in the school integration cases – both Courts, the Warren Court (1953–1969), at the end of its jurisprudential tenure, and the Burger Court, in the beginning of its ascendency, embraced a structural view of inequality and endorsed sweeping remedial powers to address it – but in the span of three years,[6] the Burger Court would effectively end any hope of substantive school desegregation, and this paves the way for the death blow that the Roberts Court delivers to school integration in *Parents Involved*.[7]

In one of the last landmark decisions of the Warren Court era, in *Green v. County School Board of New Kent County, Virginia*,[8] the Court rejected the contrived neutrality and formalism of a "freedom of choice" school plan that perpetuated segregated schools fourteen years after *Brown*. Concluding that "[t]he New Kent School Board's "freedom-of-choice" plan cannot be accepted as a sufficient step to "effectuate a transition to a unitary system, the Court rejects the dual school plan premised on illusory choice." In three years of operation not a single white child has chosen to attend Watkins school [a Black school on the west side of town]

---

[6] Cedric Merlin Powell, *From Louisville to Liddell: Schools, Rhetorical Neutrality, and the Post-Racial Equal Protection Clause*, 40 Wash. U. J. Law & Pol'y 153, 164 (2012).

[7] Girardeau Spann, *Disintegration*, 46 U. Louisville L. Rev. 565, 600–601 (2008).

[8] 391 U.S. 430 (1968).

and although 115 [Black] children enrolled in New Kent school [a white school on the east side] in 1967 ... 85% of the [Black] children in the system still attend the all-Black Watkins school. In other words, the school system remains a dual system."[9]

It is no small irony that the Warren Court began and ended with powerful pronouncements about the embodiment of America's racial caste system – segregated schools. But *Green* represented something different; it was a rare instance where the Court acknowledged systemic racism, structural inequality, and the attendant badges and incidents of slavery animating oppression, and what remedies were necessary to dismantle it.[10] As such, it explicitly rejected the state action requirement[11] and formalistic equality, and instead offered a scathing rebuke of *Brown II's*[12] constitutionally recalcitrant "all deliberate speed."[13]

Given the Court's post-racialism – its consistent posture of ignoring race and racism – *Green* is an extraordinary decision, fourteen years after *Brown*, the Court explicitly holds that the freedom-of-choice plan is quintessentially a badge and incident of slavery.[14] Its neutrality masks a pernicious attempt by the state to stigmatize and subjugate African-Americans on the basis of race.[15] *Green* rejects the formalism that the Court embraced in the *Civil Rights Cases*, only eighteen years after the end of slavery. Reaffirming *Brown*, the Court concludes that

> [s]chool boards, such as the County School Board of New Kent County, Virginia, operating state-compelled dual systems were nevertheless clearly charged with the affirmative duty to take whatever steps might be necessary to convert to a unitary system in which discrimination would be eliminated root and branch.[16]

This is a rare instance of the Court taking a structural view of caste based oppression: the Court readily invokes the history of delay since *Brown I* and *Brown II*;[17] there is a broad definition of discrimination in that any remedial approach should be designed to completely dismantle dual school systems to their core – "root and branch" – and all of their interconnecting tributaries of oppression; and, there was

---

9   *Ibid.* at 441. It is interesting to note that while there was no residential segregation in the county, there were only two hyper-segregated schools serving the entire county. *Ibid.* at 432–34.

10 Julius L. Chambers, *Race and Inequality: The Still Unfinished Business of the Warren Court* in THE WARREN COURT: A RETROSPECTIVE 25–26 (Bernard Schwartz, ed.) (1996).

11 *Ibid.* at 24 ("The Warren Court also supplied the theory for softening the effect of the 'state action' requirement that had been engrafted onto the Fourteenth Amendment in the *Civil Rights Cases* ... In theory and practice, the "state action" requirement limited Congress's role in giving force to the Fourteenth Amendment's broad provisions.").

12 349 U.S. 294 (1955).

13 *Green*, 391 U.S. at 438 (citation omitted) ("Moreover, a plan that at this late date fails to provide meaningful assurance of prompt and effective disestablishment of a dual system is also intolerable. 'The time for mere 'deliberate speed' has run out.'").

14 *Ibid.* at 435 ("In short, the State, acting through the local school officials, organized and operated a dual system, part 'white' and part 'Negro.'").

15 *Ibid.* at 432–36.

16 *Ibid.* at 437–38.

17 *Ibid.* at 438.

no attempt to rationalize the status quo of inequality and oppression. *Green*, then, rejects the historical, definitional, and rhetorical myths of Rhetorical Neutrality. There is an affirmative duty on school boards to end segregation in their schools. Exasperated with fourteen years of inaction, the Court concludes that "[t]he burden on a school board today is to come forward with a plan that promises realistically to work and promises realistically to work now."[18]

The Burger Court would briefly share the Warren Court's urgency of now, affirming *Green*'s call for substantive school integration remedies in *Swann v. Charlotte Mecklenburg*,[19] but this period would be short lived as the Court would chart a course that would ultimately doom school integration efforts. Indeed, in just three short years, the Burger Court moves from the most expansive articulation of federal remedial power to eradicate dual school systems to a conception that completely circumscribes federal power, insulates the suburbs, and all but guarantees the current re-segregation that plagues the nation's school systems today.[20] The Roberts Court would fully constitutionalize re-segregation in its *Parents Involved* decision.

Swann v. Charlotte Mecklenburg: *Broad Equitable Powers?*

In *Swann*, Chief Justice Burger, writing for a unanimous Court, reaffirms the mandate of *Brown* and the remedial imperative of *Green* in the broadest articulation of federal remedial power in the Court's school desegregation jurisprudence. Chronicling a history of resistance, retrogression, and intransigence seventeen years after *Brown*, the Court, quoting *Green*, emphasizes the affirmative duty of the school board to "come forward with a plan that promises realistically to work now … until it is clear that state imposed segregation has been completely removed."[21] Thus, *Swann* adopts the same structural approach espoused by the Warren Court in *Green* – the constitutional mandate was to eliminate dual school systems "root and branch."[22]

---

[18] *Ibid.* at 439.
[19] *Swann v. Charlotte-Mecklenburg Bd. of Ed.*, 402 U.S. 1 (1971).
[20] Gary Orfield, Erica Frakenberg, Jongyeon Ee, and Jennifer B. Ayscue, *Harming Our Common Future: America's Segregated Schools 65 Years after Brown*, May 10, 2019, civilrightsproject.ucla.edu/research/k-12-education/integration-and-diversity/harming-our-common-future-americas-segregated-schools-65-yearas-after-brown; Joseph O. Oluwole and Preston C. Green III, *Riding the Plessy Train: Reviving Brown for a New Civil Rights Era for Micro-Desegregation*, 36 CHICANA/O-LATINA/O L. REV. 1, 9 (2019) ("The judiciary has now effectively retreated from desegregation enforcement despite resegregation in schools."); Erika K. Wilson, *Charters, Markets, and Universalism*, 26 GEO. J. ON POVERTY L. & POL'Y 291, 302, nn. 22 & 78 (2019) ("The net result of the Supreme Court's retrenchment was a resegregation of public schools across the country."); Girardeau A. Spann, *The Conscience of a Court*, 63 U. MIAMI L. REV. 431, 434–48 (2009); Charles J. Ogletree, Jr., ALL DELIBERATE SPEED: REFLECTIONS ON THE FIRST HALF CENTURY OF BROWN V. BOARD OF EDUCATION 311 (2004) ("For all their clear vision of the need to end segregation, *Brown I* and *Brown II* stand as decisions that see integration as a solution that is embraced only grudgingly. Subsequent courts do not even seem to recognize integration as an imperative.").
[21] *Swann*, 402 U.S. at 13 (*quoting Green*, 391 U.S. at 439).
[22] *Ibid.* at 15.

Discrimination is defined broadly as the product of deliberate systemic resistance to the mandate of *Brown*.[23]

Building upon this definition, the Court sought to clearly delineate the affirmative duty imposed upon school authorities, by the Fourteenth Amendment, to completely dismantle dual school systems. Preserving discretionary authority in school officials to create plans to eradicate apartheid in public education, the Court specifically noted that federal courts could not intervene in the absence of a constitutional violation;[24] and, more specifically, that "the nature of the violation determines the scope of the remedy."[25] Thus, the Court preserves the local authority of the school board after seventeen years of virtually no progress in integrating the schools in Charlotte-Mecklenburg.[26] This illustrates the Burger Court's transitional equality – the Court reaffirms the constitutional primacy of *Green* while emphasizing that federal intervention was only permissible upon a finding that the school board failed in its affirmative duty to eradicate the dual school system.[27] Ironically, *Green*'s urgency is blunted by the Burger Court's conceptualization of desegregation remedies.

In *Swann*, the Burger Court posits definitive affirmative duties on the part of the local school board; and, in the absence of a viable plan to eradicate the dual school system, federal courts have equitable power and an affirmative duty to remedy constitutional violations. The Court readily rejects neutrality in the context of a *de jure* school system, and its remedial mandate for Charlotte-Mecklenburg is race-conscious. But the Court's neutrality and its affirmance of race-conscious remedial approaches comes with some doctrinal contradictions.

While the Court speaks broadly in terms of remedies, it articulates a broad and narrow conception of structural inequality. The Court references all of the components that perpetuate dual school systems – school construction and abandonment, student and faculty assignment plans, residential developments, and transportation plans – but nevertheless concludes that "one vehicle [school desegregation plans] can carry only a limited amount of baggage."[28] Apparently, this means that the primary remedial focus must be on the segregated school system itself, not other manifestations of racial subjugation "even when those problems contribute to disproportionate racial concentrations in some schools."[29] This narrow definition of discrimination means that the Court looks only to the school board, and not to a myriad of factors contributing to discriminatory decision-making like school zoning decisions, residential redlining, and financial allocations for specific districts,

---

[23] *Ibid.* at 13.
[24] "Judicial authority enters only when local authority defaults." *Ibid.* at 16.
[25] *Ibid.* at 16.
[26] *Ibid.* at 7.
[27] *Ibid.* at 5–6.
[28] *Ibid.* at 22.
[29] *Ibid.* at 23.

among other structural factors. This is, of course, the definitional myth at the core of Rhetorical Neutrality.

Rejecting colorblind neutrality and acknowledging structural factors like student assignments and construction of schools as reinforcing systemic inequality, the Court interprets the scope of permissible federal court remedial power by focusing on: (i) racial balance or racial quotas, (ii) whether one-race schools establish that there is a dual school system, (iii) attendance zones, and (iv) transportation of students. Essentially, the Burger Court balances local school board autonomy, the power of the federal courts to intervene based on a constitutional violation, and the permissible scope of the remedies mandated by the court on the school districts.

Concluding that federal courts could use mathematical ratios, as a starting point, to achieve an integrated school system, the Court noted that knowing the racial composition of a segregated school system was useful in remedying constitutional violations.[30] While there is no constitutional guarantee of absolute racial proportionality in school systems, the consideration of mathematical ratios, like the 71 percent majority to 29 percent minority ratio used in *Swann*, is not an unconstitutional racial quota and can be used in very limited circumstances.[31]

Even within the context of a *de jure* segregated school system, the Burger Court concluded that the existence of "some small number" of one-race (or virtually one-race) schools did not necessarily mean that there was a constitutional violation; or, at the very least, not one that was directly traceable to the state.[32] A true example of the Burger Court's transitional equality is its recognition that there should be a presumption against one-race schools in a district with a history of systemic racism. But it nevertheless accepts the existence of such schools if school districts can meet the burden of proffering a neutral reason for their existence. Of course, this would ultimately lead to neutral rationalizations like school choice, neighborhood schools, and signature curricular or sports identities unique to specific schools. Such rationalizations ultimately perpetuate dual school systems or lead to resegregation.[33] The Court mentions optional majority-to-minority transfer programs as a possible remedial avenue,[34] but optional choices in a system with a history of segregation, with present-day effects, promises very little in terms of results. Individual school choice would become the linchpin of the Roberts Court's school resegregation jurisprudence,[35] and it all started with the Burger Court.

---

[30] *Ibid.* at 25.
[31] *Ibid.*
[32] *Ibid.* at 26.
[33] Derek W. Black, *The Future of School Desegregation and the Importance of Goodwill, Good Sense, and a Misguided Decision*, 57 CATH. U. L. REV. 947, 966–67 (2008); Kevin Brown, *Has the Supreme Court Allowed the Cure for de jure Segregation to Replicate the Disease?* 78 CORNELL L. REV. 1, 29 (1992).
[34] *Ibid.* at 26–27.
[35] SPANN, *supra* n. 20.

Swann is a decision particularly emphatic in rejecting neutrality, noting that "an assignment plan is not acceptable simply because it appears to be neutral."[36] This is a clear indication that the Court is aware of how neutrality can perpetuate inequality, and that race must be considered to eradicate dual school systems. Thus, remedial altering of attendance zones could include connecting and pairing noncontiguous school zones, which means school district boundary lines should not be insulated from changes to advance substantive inclusion and integration. Noting that school busing is a valuable tool in pursuing integrated schools, the Court concludes that "Desegregation plans cannot be limited to the walk-in school."[37]

Yet after its comprehensive exposition of federal remedial power in school desegregation cases, the Burger Court ultimately limits it in deference to local decision-making by stating that there was no continuing obligation to make year-by-year adjustments to preserve the racial composition of integrated schools.[38] This, coupled with permitting neutral rationales for the existence of one-race schools, ultimately makes it easier for schools to re-segregate. This is an example of how the rhetorical myth explains the existence of persistent inequality.

Swann is an "easy" case because the dual school system is directly attributable to discrimination by the state. What becomes apparent is that *Swann* is a broad call for structural remedial relief, providing the remedial blueprint prompted by *Green*, in a limited context. Since there is an identifiable history of *de jure* segregation, the Court offers several remedial approaches that promote federal power in the absence of local plans to eradicate segregated schools. The Court has much more difficulty in acknowledging structural inequality in the North,[39] so the *de jure–de facto* distinction becomes the artifice to conceptualize and distinguish state-mandated discrimination from mere discrimination in fact. The legacy of the *Civil Rights Cases*, and even *Plessy*, resonates throughout the Court's race jurisprudence. In essence, *Swann* establishes a remedial colorline – expansive, unfulfilled remedies for the *de jure* segregated South, and formalistic relief for the *de facto* segregated North. Of course, this formulaic distinction is illusory.[40]

Only two years after *Swann*, the Burger Court will deliver the first of two death blows to school integration efforts. In 1973, in *San Antonio Independent School District v. Rodriguez*, the Court dilutes the constitutional imperative of *Brown* by conceptualizing education as a public benefit, with no reference to the structural

---

[36] *Swann*, 402 U.S. at 28.
[37] *Ibid.* at 30.
[38] *Ibid.*
[39] Derrick Bell, Silent Covenants: Brown v. Board of Education and the Unfulfilled Hopes for Racial Reform 108 (2004) (noting that after *Swann*, the Supreme Court, in its first northern school case, *Keyes v. Dist. No. 1 Denver, Colo.*, 413 U.S. 189 (1973), did not apply the same standards instead erecting what amounted to a discriminatory intent standard).
[40] *Cf.* C. Vann Woodward, The Strange Career of Jim Crow (1957) with Brian Purnell and Jeanne Theoharis with Komozi Woodard, The Strange Careers of the Jim Crow North: Segregation and Struggle Outside of the South (2019).

inequality and a skewed local tax funding system, that has stalled desegregation for twenty years. One year later, in *Milliken v. Bradley*, advancing a formalistic application of the *de jure–de facto* distinction, the Burger Court forever insulates suburban school districts from the burden of desegregation by constitutionalizing the inviolability of school district boundary lines.

What is striking about *Swann* is that it broadly focuses on structural inequality – the prevalence of one-race schools in Charlotte-Mecklenburg and the ostensibly neutral factors underlying them – while narrowly construing what discrimination is. The Court does not reach the issue of whether "other types of state action, without any discriminatory action by the school authorities, is a constitutional violation requiring remedial action by a school desegregation decree."[41] This issue is ready-made for the conclusion that, in the absence of clearly identifiable or *de jure* segregation, there is no constitutional violation to remedy. Three years after *Swann*, the Burger Court would expand this formalism in *Milliken*, and this will ultimately lead to the Roberts Court's post-racial pronouncement that school integration is dead in *Parents Involved*. But the first step to this formalistic expansion is the Court's decision in *San Antonio v. Rodriguez*.

San Antonio Independent School District v. Rodriguez: *Rhetorical Neutrality*

From the unanimous and unrealized constitutional mandate of *Swann*, the Burger Court, in its 5–4 decision in *San Antonio Independent School District v. Rodriguez*,[42] dramatically shifts from a broad conception of remedial power to a neutral posture rooted in post-racial constitutionalism. This class action challenged the state tax funding system for public schools in San Antonio, alleging that the substantial disparities between the poor and affluent school districts were tantamount to a dual school system depriving Mexican Americans of the education guaranteed by *Brown's* mandate.[43] The tax system produced stark disparities between the most affluent school district, Alamo Heights, and the poorest school district, Edgewood. The average assessed property value per student in the predominantly white Alamo Heights schools district was over $49,000, compared to Edgewood's assessed property value per student of $5,960.

Concluding that education is not a fundamental right, and that wealth is not a suspect classification,[44] the Court upholds a local property tax system rife with glaring economic disparities between the wealthiest and poorest school districts.[45] Indeed, it is not so much the constitutional claims of impoverished school students

---

[41] *Swann*, 402 U.S. at 23.
[42] 411 U.S. 1 (1973).
[43] *Ibid.* at 5–14.
[44] *Ibid.* at 33–44.
[45] *Ibid.* at 55.

that resonate with the Court, but rather whether the social and economic market-place is fair in distributing adequate resources, such as public education. The Court has great difficulty even finding a constitutionally cognizable injury.[46] This is yet another example of Rhetorical Neutrality: the Court deploys the historical myth to revise the history of *Brown* and its legacy; the definitional myth defines discrimination so narrowly that there is no structural analysis of the continuing effects of past discrimination; and the rhetorical myth explains the debilitatingly oppressive system upheld as a natural product of a neutral marketplace.

The Court's post-racial neutrality stands in stark contrast to the district court's structural analysis of the perpetually unequal property tax system which edifies San Antonio's dual school system. Concluding that wealth is a suspect class and education a fundamental right, the district court, applying strict scrutiny, held that the property funding system violated the Equal Protection Clause.[47] The district court's decision was a structural one, borne of its analysis of the systemic effects of the property tax funding apparatus in San Antonio. Indeed, the systemic effects of this structural inequality last to this day.[48] The Burger Court ignored the district court's findings and adopted a deferential approach, the rational basis test, which presumed the constitutionality of the Texas school finance system in the absence of a violation to a fundamental right or a suspect class.

Dismissing history and the present-day effects of past discrimination, defining discrimination formalistically and narrowly, and rationalizing "substantial inter-district disparities in school expenditures,"[49] the Burger Court upheld the taxing system as a reasonable exercise of state power.[50] *San Antonio v. Rodriguez* is a post-racial decision. Its reference to race is merely to identify the class litigants, and not their subjugation. The Court adopts a neutral narrative – Rhetorical Neutrality – to privilege a neutral economic and educational marketplace where inequality is an incidental burden caused by how resources naturally are distributed rather than by identifiable state action. Again, the doctrinal legacy of the *Civil Rights Cases* resonates here: in the absence of discriminatory state action, there is nothing to remedy. To the Court, the funding scheme, even with its stark taxing disparities impacting students of color, was not state action violative of the Fourteenth Amendment.

---

[46] *Ibid.* at 25.
[47] *Ibid.* at 15–18.
[48] Krista Torralva, *San Antonio's School Districts Still Struggle with the City's Segregated Past*, San Antonio Express-News, July 31, 2020, www.expressnews.com/news/education/article/San-Antonio-s-school-districts-still-struggle-15433318.php; Albert H. Kauffman, *Latino Education in Texas: A History of Systematic Recycling Discrimination*, 50 St. Mary's L. J. 861, 880–81, 881 (2019) (noting that Texas is the third most segregated state in the United States, with 53.7 percent of its Latino students in hyper-segregated, 90–100 percent non-white schools, and concluding that "Segregation of Mexican-Americans had a direct effect on the discrimination in the school finance system …").
[49] 411 U.S. at 15.
[50] *Ibid.* at 55.

Not only does the Burger Court conclude that there is no discriminatory state action, but it also concludes that there is nothing to remedy because there is no fundamental right or suspect class.[51] This is the historical myth: it is nearly twenty years after *Brown* and significant integration has been quite limited, yet the Court does not even acknowledge this fact. And this is particularly striking after its affirmation of *Green* in *Swann*.

By ignoring the comprehensive history of structural inequality and racial segregation in the San Antonio school system, the Court reinterprets history by focusing on the "historically rooted dual system of financing education,"[52] which is post-racial in that the concern is how the system functions, and not on the Brown and Black people it subordinates. Indeed, if it can be explained as a rational, functioning tax system then some inequality, no matter how breathtakingly jarring, is to be expected. The extreme economic gulf between the affluent school district of Alamo Heights and the poor school district of Edgewood is ignored by the Court,[53] as is the district court's structural decision emphasizing the systemic effects of the inequitable property tax funding apparatus in San Antonio.

What is particularly striking about the historical myth crafted by the Burger Court is that *Brown* has no direct doctrinal applicability to the skewed school property tax system. In fact, the Court's conclusion that wealth is not a suspect class – the undifferentiated poor are too hard to define and any remediable injury even more so – and education is not a fundamental right is a product of its historical revisionism. The Court focuses on the historical legitimacy of state taxing systems and a stylized notion of federalism,[54] rather than the twenty years of retrogression after *Brown*. Up to this point in time, *Brown* had been a substantive constitutional mandate to eradicate dual school systems – *San Antonio v. Rodriguez* constitutionalizes duality in school financing, thereby reifying the segregation and inequality between schools on either side of the district line.

The Burger Court's analysis effectively diminishes the significance of *Brown*. In fact, *San Antonio v. Rodriguez* is the first re-conceptualization of *Brown*. While *Green* and *Swann* acknowledge the primacy of *Brown* as a substantive constitutional and remedial mandate, *San Antonio v. Rodriguez* makes a passing reference to it as a unanimous decision but then characterizes education, which is "the very

---

[51] *Ibid.* at 25–37.

[52] *Ibid.* at 16.

[53] *Ibid.* at 54–55 (Analyzing the substantial interdistrict disparities, and concluding that "to the extent that the Texas system of school financing results in unequal expenditures between children who happen to reside in different districts, we cannot say that such disparities are the product of a system that is so irrational as to be invidiously discriminatory.").

[54] *Ibid.* at 44. I mean to suggest here that the Burger Court actually expands state and local power by failing to critically assess the existence of segregated schools, a history of residential segregation, and a property tax system predicated on substantial disparities between rich and poor. The facile approach is to "defer" to the expertise of the very institutions that have perpetuated inequality.

foundation of good citizenship,"[55] as a "service performed by the State."[56] This commodifies education, and leads to the natural conclusion that this "service" has to simply be provided adequately,[57] and that the level of that service cannot be constitutionalized because to do so would lead down the slippery slope of fiscal policy and a disruptive intrusion into education, which is an inherently local enterprise.[58] But this revisionism misinterprets the constitutional significance of *Brown*.

Indeed, a reading of *Brown* that rejects the historical myth would acknowledge education as a fundamental right[59] and wealth as a suspect classification. *Brown* itself embraces both propositions which are deeply rooted in the anti-subordination principle. Education is inextricably connected to voting and all the First Amendment freedoms in the Constitution; it is fundamental to the exercise of those rights.[60] Moreover, education, as expressive public action by the state, must be provided in a manner that comports with the anti-subordination principle of the Fourteenth Amendment. *Brown* can be conceptualized as a First Amendment opinion[61] – the state cannot privilege a message branding its citizens as inferior by stigmatizing them with a color-line designed to effectuate a racial caste system. This means that underfunded, poorly resourced, and hyper-segregated schools – the shadow institutions buttressed by the noxious "separate but equal doctrine' – must be eradicated. Under this reading, wealth is a suspect classification because *Brown* explicitly rejects "Separate educational facilities [as] inherently unequal."[62]

Eschewing history and the persistence of structural inequality, the Court concludes that since every student receives some type of education that is adequate, then there is no injury (wealth is not a suspect class)[63] and the state's efforts are not discriminatory, but simply an attempt to provide an enhanced education (a benefit provided by the state, not a fundamental right) to all students through a tax system

---

[55] *Ibid.* at 30.

[56] *Ibid.*

[57] *Ibid.* at 47–55.

[58] *Ibid.* at 44.

[59] Derek W. Black, *The Fundamental Right to Education*, 94 Notre Dame L. Rev. 1059, 1085–112 (2019); Areto A. Imoukhuede, *The Fifth Freedom: The Constitutional Duty to Provide Public Education*, 22 U. Fla. J. Law and Pub. Pol'y 45 (2011).

[60] Peggy Cooper Davis, *Education for Sovereign People* in A Federal Right to Education: Fundamental Questions for our Democracy 175–81 (Kimberly Jenkins Robinson, ed. 2019) (connecting five explicit constitutional rights and normative principles – due process liberty; equal protection; privileges and immunities of citizenship, the Thirteenth Amendment freedom; and a republican form of government – to education and concluding that it is a fundamental right). If the democratic underpinnings of the First Amendment are added to these constitutional rights, there can be no question that education is a fundamental right).

[61] Charles R. Lawrence III, *If He Hollers Let Him Go: Regulating Racist Speech on Campus*, 1990 Duke L. J. 431, 462–66.

[62] *Brown v. Board of Ed.*, 347 U.S. 483, 495 (1954).

[63] *San Antonio v. Rodriguez*, 411 U.S at 24–25.

that favors the rich.[64] In other words, this is simply the way that the American taxing system works.[65]

Thus, the definitional myth rationalizes marketplace inequality as inherently neutral and as a result, the Court cannot identify any constitutionally cognizable injury. Moreover, the Court narrowly defines discrimination so that it fails to acknowledge the structural dynamics of oppression; specifically, the Court never analyzes the distinct difference between the discriminatory impact of a taxing system and structural inequality composed of segregated schools, segregated neighborhoods, and a skewed taxing system emanating from a state-mandated dual school system.

After revising history (or skillfully ignoring it) and defining discrimination so that there is nothing to remedy, the final step in the Burger Court's post-racial narrative is its articulation of the rhetorical myth, rationalizing the stark disparities of the San Antonio school system. Noting that the establishment of jurisdictional boundaries is "inevitably arbitrary"[66] to explain the massive inequities that it left undisturbed, the Court concludes that "it is equally inevitable that some localities are going to be blessed with more taxable assets than others."[67] But these "arbitrary" boundaries would become sacrosanct when an inter-district remedy was proposed in the Burger Court's next school integration decision, *Milliken v. Bradley.* This landmark decision stops desegregation efforts at the district line and locks in the "blessings"[68] that the Court referenced so that they are contained in the suburbs, not the segregated urban core of the city.

In tandem, *San Antonio v. Rodriguez* and *Milliken* erect impenetrable school district boundary lines that ultimately doom school integration efforts. *San Antonio v. Rodriguez* insulates an inequitable school financing tax structure from constitutional challenge, and *Milliken* finishes the job by demanding particularized proof of discriminatory state action thereby constitutionalizing formalistic equality. Neutrality is a normative principle of post-racialism.

Milliken v. Bradley: *Neutral Principles, and Post-Racial Constitutionalism*

Foregrounding the *de jure–de facto* distinction as a normative principle under the Fourteenth Amendment, *Milliken* anticipates the Roberts Court's absolute post-racial constitutionalism. Specifically, post-racial constitutionalism is driven by an outcome determinative approach to race-conscious remedial measures: in the absence of clearly identifiable discrimination by the state itself, race-based remedies

---

[64] *Ibid.* at 73–75 (Marshall, J., dissenting).

[65] *Ibid.* at 54–55.

[66] *Ibid.* at 54.

[67] *Ibid.*

[68] Daria Roithmayr, Reproducing Racism: How Everyday Choices Lock in White Advantage (2014).

are presumptively unconstitutional. Structural inequality and systemic racism persist because the decisions in race cases are outcome-determinative – post-racial determinism means that successful anti-racism claims are rare because any use of race is constitutionally suspect and presumptively unconstitutional.[69] Post-racial determinism ensures that the results in *Milliken* and *Parents Involved* are inevitable.

The inevitable result in *Milliken* is that school desegregation stops at the district line. Chief Justice Burger's 5–4 opinion for the Court recasts *Swan* as a nonstructural decision premised upon an exacting standard of discriminatory intent. By disaggregating the structural connection between the state of Michigan and the city of Detroit,[70] the Court significantly narrows the scope of the remedy because Detroit is the only place where discrimination can be specifically identified. There is no discrimination in the outlying suburbs – "the nature of the violation determines the scope of the remedy."[71] And since there was no evidence that the boundaries of the Detroit School District were intentionally drawn based on race, this presumed neutrality insulated the outlying suburban districts from the burden of school integration.[72]

Discounting the findings of the district court and court of appeals, presuming neutrality, and revising history so that there is no reference to systemic racism or structural inequality,[73] the Court holds that the districtwide relief was too broad and based on "an erroneous standard"[74] unsupported by the record "that acts of the outlying districts effected the discrimination found to exist in the schools of Detroit."[75] In the absence of an interdistrict violation, "there is no basis for an interdistrict remedy."[76] It is as if the segregated schools simply sprang into existence in Detroit, leaving the suburbs untainted by this localized scourge of *de jure* segregation. To the Court, segregation was simply cabined in Detroit without any connection to the nearly all-white suburbs which simply happened to be that way by "choice." This is obviously disingenuous, if not absurd. The sad thing is that these are not old arguments.[77]

The segregated schools in Detroit are emblematic of structural racism – there was a federal redlining policy that relegated Blacks to an urbanized ghetto in Detroit,

---

[69] Cedric Merlin Powell, Justice Thomas, *Brown and Post-Racial Determinism*, 53 WASHBURN L. J. 451, 452 (2014).

[70] *Milliken*, 418 U.S. at 748.

[71] *Ibid.* at 50.

[72] *Ibid.* at 750–52.

[73] *Ibid.* at 748–53.

[74] *Ibid.* at 752.

[75] *Ibid.*

[76] *Ibid.*

[77] Domenico Montanaro, *Trump Tries to Appeal to "Housewives" and White Suburbs, but His Views Seem Outdated*, NPR, July 26, 2020, www.npr.org/2020/07/26/895228366/ trumps-trying-to-appeal-to-real-housewives-and-white-suburbs-but-they-re-declini.

and this pernicious decision was reinforced by design at the state and local levels.[78] The Court's formalism obscured this systemic reality from it, and intensified hyper-segregation persists in the core city of Detroit.[79] *Milliken* is a post-racial decision, briefly mentioning *Brown* only to transform it into a school choice, marketplace decision. The Roberts Court will constitutionalize this ostensibly neutral proposition in *Parents Involved*.[80]

Except for *Green*, which is decided fourteen years after *Brown*, and is one of the last decisions of the Warren Court, all the Court's school integration jurisprudence is glaringly ahistorical. Most offer a passing reference to the constitutional significance of *Brown*, but there is no mention of the present-day effects of past discrimination or structural inequality. Post-racial constitutionalism and Rhetorical Neutrality explain the neutral and formalistic reasoning of *Milliken* – the Court avoids the question of race by erecting the *de jure–de facto* distinction, so that *Swann* is no longer about how broad remedies should be devised to dismantle dual school systems, but how they should be limited when there is no "intentional" discrimination by the state. The Court rationalizes this doctrinal avoidance through Rhetorical Neutrality.

After casually discarding *Brown*, the Court deploys a historical myth that obscures the significance of structural inequality. For example, while the Court acknowledges that a predominantly segregated school district, Carver, was allowed to operate, since the late 1950s, by "tacit or express approval" of the State Board of Education,[81] because of the refusal of the outlying white districts to accept Black students, the Court nevertheless concluded that the "segregative effect"[82] was limited only to the two school districts involved, not the other districts. To the Court, there must be a one-to-one correspondence to the segregative effect; discrimination had to be clearly identifiable.

Complementing the historical myth, the definitional myth defines discrimination so narrowly that it does not exist – discrimination clearly exists in *Milliken*, but the Court's definition narrowly confines discrimination at the district line in Detroit. "The constitutional right of the [African-American school students] residing in Detroit is to attend a unitary school system in that district."[83] The Court

---

[78] Mike Wilkinson, *Michigan's Segregated Past – and Present (Told in 9 Interactive Maps)*, BRIDGE, August 8, 2017, www.bridgemi.com/michigan-government/michigans-segregated-past-and-present-told-9-interactive-maps.; *See Milliken v. Bradley*, 418 U.S. at 790, 790–815 (Marshall, J., dissenting) ("… the record amply supports the District Court's findings that the State of Michigan, through state officers and state agencies, had engaged in purposeful acts which created or aggravated segregation in the Detroit schools").

[79] Cedric Merlin Powell, *Milliken*: "Neutral Principles and Post-Racial Determinism," 31 HARV. J. ON RACIAL & ETHNIC JUSTICE (Online) 1, 22 (2015).

[80] Powell, *supra* n. 6, at 168–70.

[81] *Milliken*, 4.18 U.S. at 750.

[82] *Ibid.*

[83] *Ibid.* at 746.

is clearly saying that a dual school system exists but stays in Detroit because it is exclusively *de jure* segregated, and the outlying white suburbs are off limits because, in the absence of identifiable state discrimination, school district lines and voluntary choice matter. Without particularized evidence of intentional discrimination by every one of the fifty-three outlying white suburban school districts, it is merely *de facto* segregation with no connection to the state.[84]

Finally, the neutral rhetorical rationale – the rhetorical myth – explains why segregation persists without any remedial intervention by the federal courts. *Milliken* introduces what will be the primary rationale in the Court's long retreat from the constitutional mandate of *Brown*, which is ultimately completed by the Roberts Court: local control must be preserved from the onslaught of limitless federal intervention and tutelage of school districts. Within this rationale, some segregation is constitutionally permissible because federal courts cannot be charged with making racial adjustments every school year.[85]

While *Milliken* is a school case, it has broader implications because it introduces the concept that while disproportionate impact is circumstantially relevant, there must be identifiable intentional discrimination by the state itself to establish a violation of the Fourteenth Amendment. In other words, segregated schools must be the result of intentional discrimination by the city of Detroit *and* the outlying suburbs to warrant relief under the Fourteenth Amendment. Without more, it is simply private discrimination. While this conception traces its doctrinal roots to the *Civil Rights Cases* discussed earlier, the Burger Court fashions the Court's modern-day race jurisprudence in such a manner that the Roberts Court's post-racial constitutionalism is doctrinally inevitable.

There is a direct doctrinal connection between the Burger Court's transitional equality – shifting dramatically from broad structural change to narrow incrementalism – and the Rehnquist Court's post-racial colorblindness and the Roberts Court's post-racial constitutionalism. The Burger Court constructs much of the malleable doctrinal edifice that will later be employed to completely neutralize race

---

[84] *Ibid.* at 750–52.

[85] A series of Rehnquist Court decisions built upon the post-racial district court lines erected by the Burger Court. *See, for example, Missouri v. Jenkins,* 515 U.S. 70, 100–103 (1995) (holding that interdistrict remedy of increased spending to bring whites into the school district was invalid in the absence of an interdistrict violation); *Freeman v. Pitts,* 503 U.S. 467, 490–91 (1992) (holding that federal courts should return supervisory control to local authorities as soon as possible; indeed, federal control may be withdrawn completely or partially based on good-faith compliance with the desegregation decree); *Bd. of Educ. v. Dowell,* 498 U.S. 237, 250 (1991) (explaining that based on a good-faith finding of compliance, a district court may dissolve a desegregation order where the vestiges of de jure segregation had been eradicated "to the extent practicable"). The Burger Court first articulated the terms of the Court's long retreat from school integration in *Pasadena City Bd. of Educ. v. Spangler,* 427 U.S. 424, 436–37 (1976) (stressing a temporal limit on federal court intervention, the Court concluded that once a court implemented a racially neutral attendance plan, in the absence of intentional racially discriminatory actions by the school board, the court could not adjust its desegregation order to address population shifts in the school district).

by the Rehnquist Court and for the Roberts Court to conclude that race is irrelevant and should be transcended considering the positive societal progress made by African Americans, so that race-conscious remedies are constitutionally invalid and anti-discrimination law itself is superfluous.

THE BURGER COURT: DISCRIMINATORY INTENT AND AFFIRMATIVE ACTION

Washington v. Davis: *Neutrality and Discriminatory Intent*

Just as the *Civil Rights Cases* before it, *Washington v. Davis*[86] is the modern Court's doctrinal denial of the existence of systemic racism and structural inequality. Coming just two years after *Milliken*, *Washington v. Davis* is a devastating opinion for anti-discrimination law as it constitutionalizes the state action requirement of the *Civil Rights Cases* into an evidentiary requirement of discriminatory intent, making it all but impossible to advance claims based on structural inequality.

The search for an illusory discriminatory perpetrator disconnects anti-subordination analysis under the Fourteenth Amendment[87] and shifts the focus to individuals rather than the systemic and structural factors buttressing discrimination. If the process producing disparate results appears neutral, then the Court will affirm its operation notwithstanding the structural inequality that produced the result.

African-American candidates for the D.C. Metropolitan Police Department failed the entrance examination for candidacy in disproportionate numbers. They sued, alleging that the promotion and examination policies of the Department were racially discriminatory. Reversing the Court of Appeals because it erroneously applied a disproportionate impact standard rather than discriminatory intent, the Court held that invidious discrimination must be "traced to a racially discriminatory purpose."[88] The fact that disproportionately higher numbers of African-American police officer candidates failed the entrance examination, Test 21, while not irrelevant, was not "the sole touchstone of an invidious discrimination forbidden by the Constitution."[89] Unless this disproportionality can be directly linked to intentional actions by the state, there is nothing to remedy. There must be discriminatory intent and disproportionate impact.[90]

This is a quintessential proposition of post-racial neutrality: unless intentional state action can be identified – disproportionate impact is circumstantially significant – the neutral process must be preserved because the impact, no matter how substantial

---

[86] 426 U.S. 229 (1976).
[87] Because D.C. is not a state, the analysis in *Washington v. Davis* proceeded under the Due Process Clause of the Fifth Amendment, which contains an equal protection component. The analysis is the same under the Fifth and Fourteenth Amendments. *Ibid.* at 239.
[88] *Ibid.* at 240.
[89] *Ibid.* at 242.
[90] *Ibid.* at 238–48.

and oppressive, is a rational outcome. The Burger Court's post-racialism is on full display in *Washington v. Davis*: since the cause of the subjugating impact cannot be identified with particularity, there is no discrimination. Because the Court interprets the Constitution as protecting equal opportunity, not equal results, access to the examination process is constitutionally sufficient. Thus, the fact that substantial numbers of African-American candidates fail the examination is not constitutionally suspect, as the Court concludes, "[w]e have difficulty understanding how a law establishing a racially neutral qualification for employment is nevertheless racially discriminatory and denies 'any person … equal protection of the laws' simply because a greater proportion of Negroes fail to qualify than members of other racial or ethnic groups."[91] There is no discrimination, only the failure of the Black candidates to compete effectively in the civil servant applicant marketplace.

Lacking a structuralist frame, the Burger Court accepts the neutrality of the testing process and presumes that the race-conscious claims of the unsuccessful Black applicants are invalid. The Court never asks: why are so many African-American applicants failing Test 21 if it is truly "neutral"? It is enough for that Court that Blacks and whites fail the examination; how many failed is of no constitutional significance because the test is "a racially neutral qualification for employment."[92] Indeed, the Court even lauded the D.C. Metropolitan Police Department for its recruitment efforts of Black officer candidates.[93] To the Court, this clearly proved that there was no discrimination by the state. But none of this explains the gross disparity in the officer candidate corps – the Court refuses to acknowledge structural inequality.

To reach its formalistically neutral conclusion, the Court disconnects Title VII's disproportionate impact standard, which requires no finding of discriminatory purpose, and the state action requirement of the Equal Protection Clause which requires discriminatory intent.[94] Concluding that the Court of Appeals misapplied the Title VII disparate impact standard in an equal protection case, the Court noted that while more "probing judicial review"[95] is warranted in Title VII cases, because hiring practices could be violated without reference to discriminatory intent, in *Washington v. Davis*, such analytical rigor was misplaced because "the special racial impact"[96] lacked a discriminatory purpose and should be subjected to deferential, rational basis review.[97]

---

[91] *Ibid.* at 245.
[92] *Ibid.*
[93] *Ibid.* at 246.
[94] There was a doctrinal debate as to whether Title VII and the Equal Protection Clause should be unified with a discriminatory intent requirement. *Ibid.* at 239. *See also* GIRARDEAU A. SPANN, THE LAW OF AFFIRMATIVE ACTION: TWENTY-FIVE YEARS OF SUPREME COURT DECISIONS ON RACE AND REMEDIES 31 (2000). This issue was resolved definitively in the Roberts Court's decision in *Ricci v. DeStefano*, which is fully discussed in Chapter 6.
[95] *Washington v. Davis*, 426 U.S. at 247.
[96] *Ibid.*
[97] *Ibid.* at 248–52.

But what is striking here is the Court's absolute fidelity to neutrality – *Washington v. Davis* is not about the present-day effects of past discrimination in the police department – the employment marketplace, according to the Court, is open and accessible, and to acknowledge disproportionate impact as a cognizable injury would invalidate "a whole range of tax, welfare, public service, regulatory, and licensing statutes that may be more burdensome to the poor and to the average black than to the more affluent white."[98]

Neutrality obscures the glaring effects of subjugation that are readily apparent in *Washington v. Davis*: the Court failed to reference an explosive history seared in the protests and riots of 1968 and an overwhelmingly white police force;[99] it focused only on recruitment efforts around the time of the litigation itself when the Department would have put on its most positive institutional face;[100] it accepted Test 21 as a neutral assessment tool without assessing the content of the questions and their slanted racial and cultural bias;[101] and it defined discrimination (disproportionate impact) so narrowly that it exists simply as a burden on the presumptive neutrality of the test, not a substantive constitutional claim for equality.[102] The Court rationalized this structural inequality by focusing on the recruitment efforts of the police force and the fact that 44 percent of the new police recruits had been Black, and this corresponded to the population in the fifty-mile recruiting radius targeted by the Department.[103]

The reason that the Department's recruitment outreach was so appealing to the Court is that it reinforces the doctrinal proposition that the Constitution protects equal opportunity and unfettered access to a neutral process; and, since the new recruits were afforded this process-based right, there was nothing constitutionally suspect about a disproportionate failure rate for African-American candidates. There was nothing discriminatory here because the process was neutral.[104]

Espousing neutrality as a defining feature of post-racial constitutionalism, the Burger Court constructs the modern edifice of the Court's race jurisprudence by establishing two principles – the discriminatory intent requirement, building upon the historical post-racialism of the *Civil Rights Cases*, and diversity. While the Rehnquist and Roberts Courts would further develop these tenets of post-racial constitutionalism, the only question would be how much positive race-conscious remedial efforts would be narrowed or discarded altogether. The Roberts Court has been actively engaged in diluting all anti-racist protections in the Constitution, and

---

[98] *Ibid.* at 248.
[99] Angela Onwuachi-Willig, *From Loving v. Virginia to Washington v. Davis: The Erosion of the Supreme Court's Equal Protection Intent Analysis*, 25 Va. J. Soc. Pol'y & L. 303, 315 (2018).
[100] *Ibid.*
[101] *Ibid.* at 313–16.
[102] *Ibid.* 308, n. 32.
[103] *Washington v. Davis*, 426 U.S. at 235.
[104] *Ibid.* at 245–52.

statutory law, because they are unnecessary considering all the progress that has been made by formerly oppressed minorities.

The Court has always been post-racial because it views any progress as an invitation to conclude that substantive equality has been achieved, and any acknowledgement of race, racism, and structural inequality would taint a neutral process and lead to political strife and balkanization. To avoid this undesirable conflict, the Court contrives analytical devices to ostensibly protect the rights of African Americans while limiting any burden or impact on the expectation interests of whites. The preservation of white privilege is a touchstone of post-racial constitutionalism. Neutrality is particularly appealing because it preserves the structural inequality of the status quo while rationalizing it as a natural outcome that must be accepted in the absence of a discriminatory state actor. Under this reasoning, race-conscious remedial approaches are presumptively unconstitutional, which means that reverse discrimination suits will be advanced by deploying this proposition. Indeed, the Burger Court supplies much of the doctrinal language for reverse discrimination suits, and such suits have a rhetorical appeal rooted in neutrality and post-racialism.

A reverse discrimination suit rests on the mythic premise that since racism has been formally eradicated, and all systemic processes are inherently neutral, then any race-conscious remedy is a presumptively unconstitutional windfall to African Americans and people of color. The neutral process must not be skewed with a racial result. The Burger Court is the primary purveyor of this concocted reality, which will be extended by the Rehnquist Court's post-racial colorblindness and the Roberts Court's post-racial constitutionalism. *Bakke* extends the formalism of *Washington v. Davis* and privileges reverse discrimination suits setting the stage for a series of distorted rulings on diversity, which perpetuate structural inequality.

Regents of the University of California v. Bakke: *Neutral Process Values*

After his application to the U.C. Davis Medical School was rejected twice, Alan Bakke, a white male, brought a reverse discrimination suit alleging that the special admissions program, which set aside 16 out of the 100 seats in the class for underrepresented minorities, violated the Equal Protection Clause of the Fourteenth Amendment and Title VI.[105] Justice Powell's opinion for a sharply divided Court held that the set-aside was an unconstitutional quota because Bakke was excluded from consideration for the 16 seats, but that race could be used, as one of many factors, in an admissions process that fully considered each individual applicant's credentials.[106] Race could be a "plus" factor in individualized admissions decisions, not the sole factor.[107]

---

[105] *Univ. of Ca. Regents v. Bakke*, 438 U.S. 265, 276–81 (1978).
[106] *Ibid.* at 317–20.
[107] *Ibid.* at 317.

Bakke is a 4–1–4 plurality opinion[108] without a definitive analytical principle that spawns twenty-five years of uncertainty until the Rehnquist and Roberts Courts reaffirm and "clarify" the doctrine only to make it even more opaque. The decision is based on a post-racial rhetorical move rooted in neutrality – Justice Powell's opinion rejects all the substantive rationales for addressing structural inequality in the medical profession, and he instead advances a malleable process based standard – diversity.

The substantive reasons underlying the special admission program: (i) addressing the present-day effects of the historic under-representation of African Americans in the medical profession; (ii) ameliorating the effects of societal discrimination; and (iii) increasing the proportion of African-American doctors who will serve excluded communities are all erased by the Rhetorical Neutrality underpinning the decision.

There is no discussion of the historical exclusion of Blacks from the medical profession. *Bakke* is completely devoid of a structuralist component – there is simply a neutral admissions marketplace with qualified and unqualified candidates, and a qualified white candidate's denial means that something must be wrong with that process.[109] The reverse discrimination suit becomes the touchstone of white innocence and victimization, and the Court actively engages, advances, and privileges this narrative.[110] As part of his post-racial narrative, Justice Powell neutralizes the historic oppression of African Americans and its present-day effects by noting that all majoritarian groups suffer some form of "disadvantage" because majorities shift over time.[111]

This historical myth lies at the core of post-racial constitutionalism – there is no structural inequality or systemic racism because the Constitution does not reach mere "societal discrimination."[112] The Constitution protects individuals, not racial groups.[113] This means that it is presumptively constitutionally invalid to use race to assure "some specified percentage"[114] of a racial group in a medical school class. Since there were no findings of intentional discrimination, race could not be used

---

[108] Concluding that Title VI and the Equal Protection Clause prohibit racial classifications, Justice Powell joins four justices (Chief Justice Burger and Justices Stewart, Rehnquist, and Stevens) to hold that the special admissions program was unconstitutional under Title VI, *Ibid.* at 271, 281–87; in holding that race may be used, as one of many factors, in admissions decisions, he joins another group of four justices (Brennan, White, Marshall, and Blackmun), but rejects their argument that intermediate scrutiny should be applied to positive, race-conscious remedial efforts to address systemic inequality. *Ibid.* at 295–306.

[109] Osamudia R. James, *Valuing Identity*, 102 Minn. L. Rev. 127, 170 (2017).

[110] Mario L. Barnes, *We Will Turn Back? On Why Regents of the University of California v. Bakke Makes the Case for Adopting More Radically Race-Conscious Admissions Policies*, 52 U.C. Davis L. Rev. 2265, 2276–82 (2019).

[111] 438 U.S. at 292.

[112] *Ibid.* at 307.

[113] *Ibid.* at 307–309.

[114] *Ibid.* at 307.

in fashioning a remedy.[115] Yet this is an interesting form of disaggregation that runs counter to the anti-subordination principle of the Fourteenth Amendment – the Constitution protects individuals, not racial groups – whites are a racial group composed of "various minority groups"[116] that need to be protected from the impermissible tainting of the neutral admission process with race. This suggests that the concept of liberal individualism shifts depending on who is burdened. Indeed, Justice Powell carelessly conflates the historical experiences of all minorities – Celtic Irishmen, Chinese, Austrian resident aliens, and Mexican Americans – in a creative immigration fantasy with no reference to systemic racism and its present-day effects.[117]

Definitionally, the Court embraces the myth that societal discrimination is "an amorphous concept of injury that may be ageless in its reach into the past."[118] This theme will be expanded and developed further by Justice Sandra Day O'Connor in her race opinions for the Rehnquist Court. Of course, societal discrimination is "amorphous" and ageless in its historical reach because the Court defines discrimination so narrowly – in its pursuit of a clearly identifiable discriminatory perpetrator – that, in the absence of particularized proof, discrimination does not exist. And it does not exist in *Bakke* because the Court privileges Allan Bakke's narrative over the clearly identifiable structural dynamics that led to the underrepresentation of doctors of color.

This result is rationalized because while increasing the number of Black physicians who will provide much needed healthcare to underserved communities is a laudable goal, there is no proof that doctors in the special admissions program will do so.[119] This is another theme that is deployed by the Rehnquist Court as well – it cannot be assumed that people of color will automatically practice in certain areas or trades because of their race. Of course, this is true, but it does not mean that the program is unconstitutional in light of this conclusion. The program is designed to foster and encourage those who are admitted to pursuing this career goal, and the Court could have just as easily presumed that this was a constitutionally permissible endeavor.

Instead, the Court focuses on the neutral process value of diversity. This minimalist approach is rooted in the First Amendment and does not critically assess structural inequality.[120] The marketplace of ideas paradigm, where students of diverse backgrounds learn through embracing their differences in an exchange of ideas, is a weak model for dealing with systemic racism. Essentially, while the white

---

[115] *Ibid.* at 309.
[116] *Ibid.* at 292.
[117] *Ibid.*
[118] *Ibid.* at 307.
[119] *Ibid.* at 311.
[120] Cedric Merlin Powell, *Rhetorical Neutrality: Colorblindness, Frederick Douglass, and Inverted Critical Race Theory*, 56 CLEVE. ST. L. REV. 823, 876–77 (2008).

"farm boy from Idaho"[121] and the Black student from Cleveland may share different experiences and engage in the classroom to enrich the educational experience, this is virtually meaningless in dismantling the barriers of exclusion. Diversity privileges the educational experience of white students because there will be so few students of color admitted.[122]

Bakke is a quintessential example of the Burger Court's transitional equality – it delivers a semblance of equality that ostensibly appears to be substantive, but equality is always defined secondarily by referencing whether achieving it burdens white interests. Therefore, Allan Bakke's reverse discrimination suit resonates with the Court – he was entitled to compete for all the seats in the class, not merely the remaining eighty-four seats, and he should have been admitted absent unqualified Black candidates being admitted to the sixteen special admissions seats. Admissions is not about numbered seats, but about individualized decisions reached in a wholistic process of evaluation and assessment.

There is a perverse one-to-one correspondence in reverse discrimination claims; it is as if there are numbered seats in the class, and those occupied by Blacks are the result of a tainted process, while all the other seats are pure because they are filled through a neutral process. This explains why Allan Bakke does not challenge the admission of white candidates, some of whom have lesser admission credentials than he possesses, in the remaining eighty-four seats.[123] Rather, his focus is exclusively on the sixteen seats of the special admissions program because the presumption, based solely on race, is that all of the Black candidates are unqualified; and, by their unearned presence based on a racial preference, they have displaced the entitlement interest of qualified white applicants to compete for every seat in the class.[124] This facile distortion is what drives the *Bakke* decision, affirmative action jurisprudence, and public discourse on race.

In the sense that the *Bakke* decision attempts to move beyond race by conflating the experiences of white immigrants and the descendants of chattel slavery and American apartheid, it is a post-racial decision. This explains why there is no agreement on the standard of review for race-conscious remedies: if there is no identifiable discrimination to remedy, then race is inherently suspect and the remedy is invalid; if there is, then race can be used, in narrow circumstances, but there must be a compelling interest to do so because there is no "two-class" theory under the Fourteenth Amendment;[125] or perhaps intermediate scrutiny is permissible because the use of race is positive and benign; or there should be complete deference for

[121] 438 U.S. at 323.
[122] Osamudia James, *White Like Me: The Negative Impact of the Diversity Rationale on White Identity Formation*, 89 N.Y.U. L. REV. 425, 450 (2014).
[123] Barnes, *supra* n. 110, at 2278–79.
[124] *Ibid.* at 2279, 2279 n. 47.
[125] 438 U.S. at 295.

the judgment of educational decisionmakers – if there is a rational basis for their decisions, they should be upheld. The Court would not reach analytical consensus on whether diversity was a compelling interest until twenty-five years later with the Rehnquist Court's decision in *Grutter*.[126]

After *Bakke*, the Burger Court continued to develop the diversity principle in its subsequent decisions in *Fullilove* and *Wygant*. *Fullilove* is a rare decision by the Court that acknowledges structural inequality in the marketplace, but it does so by deferring to Congress' institutional competence and without articulating a standard of review for race-conscious remedies. This is yet another example of the Burger Court's broad exposition of constitutional rights, which are transitory, and will later be narrowed.

Broad substantive advances by African Americans and people of color are consistently limited by the Court. There is a defining theme in post-racial constitutionalism that sufficient societal progress has been made, so consideration of race is an added burden. *Wygant* follows this post-racial pattern as well, ignoring structural inequality, to preserve a seniority system that favors the interests of whites over last hired, first fired Black schoolteachers.

Fullilove v. Klutznick: A *Structural Analysis or Undefined Standard of Review?*

Reviewing a federal Minority Business Enterprise ("MBE") program, enacted pursuant to the Public Works Employment Act ("PWEA") of 1977, which authorized that at least 10 percent of public work projects be expended for MBEs,[127] Chief Justice Burger's plurality opinion upheld the program as a valid exercise of an "amalgam" of Congress' enumerated powers.[128] *Fullilove* is a striking example of the Burger Court's transitional equality – the Court issues a deferential ruling embracing a broad conception of Congress' legislative powers to eradicate the present-day effects of past discrimination in the public contracts marketplace – it embraces a structural interpretation of inequality, but without a standard of review. Again, the failure to reach a judicial consensus on the standard of review, as in *Bakke*, leads to a holding that sounds substantive but really is not.[129] In overruling *Fullilove*, in *Adarand Constructors, Inc. v. Peña*, the Rehnquist Court unified all its race jurisprudence under the strict scrutiny standard. The broad mandate of *Fullilove* was only transitory, which is a recurring theme in the Court's post-racial jurisprudence.

Fullilove is a rare opinion in the Court's race jurisprudence that rejects neutrality and instead advances a structural view of inequality and systemic racism.

---

[126] Khiara M. Bridges, Critical Race Theory: A Primer 349 (2019).

[127] *Fullilove v. Klutznick*, 448 U.S. 448, 453 (1980) (Public Works Employment Act of 1977 § 103(f)(2), 42 U.S.C. § 6705 (1977).

[128] The PWEA was primarily an exercise of the Spending and Commerce Powers along with the section 5 enforcement power of the Fourteenth Amendment. *Ibid.* at 473–79.

[129] Drew S. Days, III, *Fullilove*, 96 Yale L. J. 453, 456 (1987).

Concluding that Congress acted well within its legislative powers because the MBE program was neither underinclusive (the program was not invalid because it disappointed the expectation interests of white firms)[130] nor overinclusive (the MBE program was not a race-based windfall because there were waivers and exemptions in the administrative process),[131] the Court gave special credence to the institutional competence and legislative primacy of Congress. Crediting substantial evidence from which Congress could draw the conclusion that minority businesses were systematically excluded from public contracting and that this was the result of "procurement practices that perpetuated the effects of prior discrimination,"[132] the Court specifically noted the present-day effects of past discrimination.

Indeed, what is particularly compelling about *Fullilove* is that the Court specifically references the broad remedial powers of Congress, while distinguishing decisions like *Swann* and *Milliken* as standing for the proposition that the scope of the remedy is determined by the scope of the violation, thereby underscoring the limited remedial powers of federal courts,[133] yet rejecting the formalism of a rigid discriminatory intent requirement and colorblindness. Congress had broad remedial powers to fashion race-conscious remedies.[134]

Acknowledging a history of disparities in the awarding of public contracts to minority business enterprises, the Court defines discrimination in structural terms – it is not some purported scarcity of qualified minority contractors that explains the disparity in the percentage of contracts awarded, but "the existence and maintenance of barriers to competitive access which had their roots in racial and ethnic discrimination, and which continue today, even absent any intentional discrimination or other unlawful conduct."[135]

Yet like most of the Burger Court's post-racial transitional equality jurisprudence, *Fullilove* promises a great deal but delivers little. It rejects colorblindness – noting that "[i]t is not a constitutional defect in this program that it may disappoint the expectations of nonminority firms"[136] – and acknowledges structural inequality but fails to articulate a fully developed anti-subordination rationale under the Fourteenth Amendment. Its post-racial conceptual move is to interpret Congress' power as an amalgam of neutral legislative powers unrelated to race.

Relying upon Congress' broad legislative power under the Spending and Commerce Clauses, the Court did not specifically address the exercise of the § 5 enforcement power of the Fourteenth Amendment.[137] This would have explicitly

---

[130] 448 U.S. at 482–86.
[131] *Ibid.* at 489.
[132] *Ibid.* at 477.
[133] *Ibid.* at 483.
[134] *Ibid.* at 482.
[135] *Ibid.* at 478.
[136] *Ibid.* at 484.
[137] *Ibid.* at 473–79.

linked Congress' enforcement power to the anti-subordination principle of the Fourteenth Amendment and to the eradication of racial discrimination in award-ing public contracts. *Fullilove*'s reasoning leaves it open to the critique that it is simply a marketplace decision based upon the racial spoils of a corrupt bidding process.[138]

Instead, this transitory moment of progress will be eclipsed when the Rehnquist Court offers doctrinal clarity and uniformity by declaring all race-conscious rem-edies inherently suspect. *Fullilove* is virtually gutted if not explicitly overruled by the advent of the Rehnquist Court's skepticism.[139]

Wygant v. Jackson Board of Education: *The Forward-Looking Approach and the Preservation of White Interests*

As one of the last decisions of the Burger Court, *Wygant* offers a doctrinal preview of the Rehnquist Court's post-racial colorblindness, a distinct type of neutrality that acknowledges race while simultaneously de-emphasizing its significance.

Analyzing a race-conscious layoff system agreed upon through the collective bargaining of the Jackson, Michigan, Board of Education and the teacher's union, the plurality opinion, by Justice Powell, held that the system was unconstitu-tional.[140] Notwithstanding the "serious racial discrimination in this country (and the fact that Black teachers were the last hired and first fired),"[141] there was no basis to burden innocent white schoolteachers in the absence of clearly identifiable discrimination.[142]

Rejecting the role model theory – that minority schoolteachers were essential as role models to minority students and should be retained during layoffs due to the present-day effects of past discrimination – the Court held that "[s]ocietal discrimi-nation, without more, is too amorphous a basis for imposing a racially classified remedy."[143] The role model theory was unconnected to any clearly identifiable harm (there are many neutral reasons for the "disparity between the percentage of minor-ity students and the percentage of minority faculty");[144] it could lead to the stereo-typical thinking and stigmatization rejected in *Brown*;[145] and the imposition of this burden on innocent whites could lead to "remedies that are ageless in their reach into the past, and timeless in their ability to affect the future."[146] While this neutral

---

[138] *Ibid.* at 542 (Stevens, J., dissenting).
[139] *Adarand Constructors v. Peña*, 515 U.S. 200 (1995).
[140] *Wygant v. Jackson Bd. of Educ.*, 476 U.S. 267, 278 (1986).
[141] *Ibid.* at 276.
[142] *Ibid.*
[143] *Ibid.*
[144] *Ibid.*
[145] *Ibid.*
[146] *Ibid.*

rhetoric sounds appealing and "fair," there is something disconcertingly post-racial about it. It is the great solicitude that the Court places on white expectation interests[147] while causally ignoring the structural inequalities that lead to the dearth of minority schoolteachers.

Wygant is ahistorical because it does not consider the fact that "there are no 'innocent whites' since all whites have reaped the benefits of racism for generations."[148] The Court's conception of societal discrimination harkens back to the formalism of the *Civil Rights Cases* – there is some undefined, amorphous discrimination that floats throughout society disconnected from the state. Private discrimination (and even structural inequality that cannot be specifically identified) is irremediable. This facile conception can always be deployed to dismiss substantive anti-racist claims against systemic racism and structural inequality.

Diversity's malleability is on full display in *Wygant*: it is ironic that Justice Powell, the author of the *Bakke* decision and its diversity rationale, rejects essentially the same proposition because of its impact on whites. There was no burden on white interests in *Bakke*, once the unconstitutional quota of sixteen seats was removed and all the seats were open, in a neutral admissions process where race was one of many factors that were considered in evaluating medical school candidates. Moreover, there was a broad educational benefit in diversity that would inure to whites and not displace their interests. Diversity was fully forward looking, and process driven, in *Bakke*.

By contrast, in *Wygant*, Justice Powell concludes that layoffs are more disruptive than general hiring goals;[149] and, applying strict scrutiny to the race-conscious layoff plan, holds that although there may be legitimate purposes to retaining minority teachers, the plan was not narrowly tailored because it placed "the entire burden of achieving racial equality on particular [white innocent] individuals."[150] The Court could see no injury to minority schoolteachers, and the remedial emphasis on the percentage of minority students, needing role models instead of the percentage of qualified minority teachers, led the Court to construe the layoff plan as akin to a quota plan of displacement of white interests: "There was no particularized injury with respect to minority teachers; the retention plan was, in effect, a race-based 'windfall' for minority school teachers with less seniority than white school teachers."[151]

This is an example of post-racial constitutionalism. Here, the neutral rhetorical move is to privilege the reverse discrimination claim of Wendy Wygant – the

---

[147] *Ibid.* at 277 ("Evidentiary support for the conclusion that remedial action is warranted becomes crucial when the remedial program is challenged in court by nonminority employees.").

[148] Goodwin Liu, *Affirmative Action in Higher Education: The Diversity Rationale and the Compelling Interest Test*, 33 HARV. CIV. RTS-CIV. LIB. L. REV. 381, 404 (1998).

[149] *Ibid.* at 423 n.194.

[150] *Wygant*, 476 U.S. at 283.

[151] Powell, *supra* n. 120, at 863.

claims of minority schoolteachers are ignored to preserve a layoff system that will inevitably undermine recruitment and retention efforts. Because the Court so eagerly protects the interests of white schoolteachers – who are nearly always the first hired – it is oblivious to the fact that the Black schoolteachers are virtually always the first fired.[152]

And scant attention is paid to the fact that this was a negotiated agreement, reached through collective bargaining, between the school board and the Jackson Education Association (the union).[153] Teachers with the most seniority would be retained, but in the event of layoffs, the percentage of minority teachers could not fall below the "current percentage of minority personnel employed at the time of the layoff."[154] This meant that tenured nonminority teachers would be laid off "while minority teachers on probationary status were retained."[155] Despite the collective bargaining agreement, the Board laid off the minority schoolteachers;[156] and after litigation in the state and federal courts,[157] the Court ultimately affirms the Board's decision to ignore its contractual obligations and preserve a seniority system that reifies the historical subordination of minority schoolteachers.

Joining the *Wygant* plurality, Justice O'Connor, who would emerge as the chief author of the Rehnquist Court's post-racial colorblindness, offered an illustrative preview of how Rhetorical Neutrality would ground the Court's race jurisprudence: the historical and structural implications of the lack of African-American teachers is obscured by an emphasis on harm to innocent whites; discrimination is defined so narrowly that societal discrimination is dismissed as natural and irremediable; and the lasting disparities in employment opportunities for African Americans is explained by a rigid adherence to the availability of qualified minorities "in the relevant labor pool."[158]

Essentially, the negotiated collective bargaining agreement, which was drafted to preserve the positive effects of a minority teacher recruitment plan, was transformed into a reverse discrimination claim.[159] This is a hallmark of post-racial constitutionalism and a unifying theme underlying the Burger Court's race jurisprudence – the protection of white interests. Nowhere is this more graphically illustrated than in the Court's Title VII jurisprudence, which starts out in the same manner as its Equal Protection jurisprudence with a broad structural proclamation only to be significantly limited to lessen the burden on white expectation interests.

---

[152] *Wygant*, 476 U.S., at 298, 306–307 (Marshall, J., dissenting).
[153] *Ibid.* at 296 (Marshall, J., dissenting).
[154] 476 U.S. at 270.
[155] *Ibid.*
[156] *Ibid.* at 271.
[157] *Ibid.* at 271–73.
[158] *Ibid.* at 294, 287–88 (O'Connor, J., concurring in part and concurring in the judgment).
[159] Powell, *supra* n. 120, at 863–65.

THE BURGER COURT: TITLE VII AND THE SETTLED EXPECTATIONS OF WHITE WORKERS

Griggs v. Duke Power: *Disparate Impact, Neutrality, and Structuralism*

Doctrinally, there is a clear jurisprudential pattern in the Burger Court's race jurisprudence – broad and powerful pronouncements of substantive equality, and accompanying remedial power, followed by an almost immediate retraction.[160] This is the essence of transitional equality; the Burger Court briefly recognizes structural inequality and race-conscious remedial approaches to eradicate it, only to abandon this approach when it comes too close to disrupting white expectations of uninterrupted privilege. This explains the marked shift from *Swann* to *Milliken*; the discriminatory intent requirement in *Washington v. Davis*; the weak diversity rationale in *Bakke*; and the protection of white teachers' seniority and employment interests in *Wygant*. *Griggs* continues this theme of transitional equality under Title VII – the Burger Court starts with a powerful affirmation of Title VII's power to reach ostensibly neutral processes which perpetuate subordination only to dilute this statutory mandate in the service of white expectation interests.

Writing for a unanimous Court, in *Griggs v. Duke Power*, Chief Justice Burger noted that the central purpose of Title VII was to provide equality of opportunity in employment, and to remove purportedly neutral tests, practices, or procedures which maintained the status quo of discrimination and exclusion of African-American workers.[161] *Griggs* was a class action brought by African-American employees of Duke Power alleging that high school education or standardized test requirements were unrelated to successful job performance and that such requirements disproportionately disqualified them in a longstanding employment system favoring whites. Construing Title VII as a statute that targeted structural inequality and dispensed with the formalistic discriminatory intent requirement, the Court focused on the business necessity of a high school diploma or a standardized general intelligence test as a prerequisite to employment or promotion.[162]

These neutral conditions – a diploma requirement and a standardized general intelligence test – served to disproportionally disqualify African Americans "at a substantially higher rate than white applicants,"[163] with the effect of preserving an institutionally based preference for white employees.[164] These were "practices that

---

[160] Graetz and Greenhouse, *supra* n. 3, at 286–87.
[161] *Griggs v. Duke Power*, 401 U.S. 424, 430–31 (1971).
[162] *Ibid.* at 426.
[163] *Ibid.* at 426.
[164] *Ibid.*

are fair in form, but discriminatory in operation"[165] because there was no business necessity for these requirements – they were unrelated to the jobs to be performed.[166] And the disproportionate result was that African-American employees were segregated in the Labor department, not the "operating" departments.[167]

While acknowledging the structural dimensions of inequality, *Griggs* nevertheless embraces neutrality as a guiding principle. This is yet another example of post-racial neutrality – the emphasis is on formalistic equality (symmetry between African-American employees who were disproportionately discriminated against and white workers who consistently advanced in the employment process); recasting structuralism by referencing the effects of segregated schools and not analyzing the impact on employment; and employing a fable to illustrate the absence of intent but actually underscoring its existence and revealing that systemic inequality is not an either–or proposition.

The Burger Court configures its race jurisprudence around an either-or premise – there is either discriminatory intent (*Washington v. Davis*) or no discrimination under the Equal Protection Clause; or, under Title VII, there is disproportionate impact, but it must be balanced against the burden on white employment interests. This leads the Court to reference systemic racism and structural inequality, but then diminish its overall impact. While noting that African Americans "have long received inferior education in segregated schools,"[168] and that this undermined the efficacy of standardized tests in measuring prospective job performance, the Court then goes on to note that Title VII "does not command that any person be hired simply because he was formerly the subject of discrimination, or because he is a member of a minority group."[169] This would be an impermissible racial preference, but why is this relevant if the Court is analyzing the subjugation of African-American workers who have been ghettoized in the Labor department for decades? Even here there is a pronounced concern for the prospective burden on white employees.

The Court has always been committed to formalistic equality: since overt discrimination has ceased, then any remedy must be rationalized so that it is not perceived as a racial employment windfall to African Americans.[170] It is striking that there is no examination of structural inequality especially since *Griggs* is decided just one month before *Swann* – the Court notes the inferior education that Blacks received with no analytical connection to their disproportionate exclusion in an ostensibly neutral employment promotion process. Rather than conceptualizing disparate impact as simply a *de facto* outcome of a flawed process, the

---

[165] *Ibid.* at 431.
[166] *Ibid.* at 431–35.
[167] *Ibid.* at 426–28.
[168] *Ibid.* at 430.
[169] *Ibid.* at 430–31.
[170] *See generally* Kimberly West-Faulcon, *Fairness Feuds: Competing Conceptions of Title VII Discriminatory Testing*, 46 WAKE FOREST L. REV. 1035 (2011).

Court should have adopted a structural analysis with a much broader conception of disproportionality.[171]

Finally, the Court fabulizes structural inequality with a parable – the offer of milk to the stork and the fox in a vessel that neither can access because of the way that it is constructed – to illustrate that business practices may be "fair in form (neutrality), but discriminatory in operation."[172] Discrimination is not simply purposeful or impactful, it is structural which means that there are manifestations of each in structural inequality. Indeed, the Court's own fable narrative emphasizes an aspect of intent – the choice of the vessel or employment requirements – and since there was no relationship between the requirements and effective job performance, there was a violation of Title VII.[173]

After *Griggs*, the Burger Court would consistently foreground the expectation interests of white workers in its Title VII jurisprudence. Ultimately, the Roberts Court would go even further by merging the Fourteenth Amendment's intent requirement with its Title VII jurisprudence. This is fully explored in Chapter 6. Post-racial constitutionalism actively seeks to preserve white interests while dismantling any transformative equality for African Americans and other people of color.

International Brotherhood of Teamsters v. United States: *Seniority, Neutrality, and the Preservation of White Employment Privilege*

Analyzing a pattern or practice lawsuit brought by the United States against a common carrier motor freight employer and a complicit union that agreed to "create and maintain a seniority system that perpetuated the effects of racial discrimination,"[174] the Court nevertheless upheld the seniority system. Both lower courts found that the employer engaged in a pattern and practice of discrimination against African Americans and Latino/as, and that the union collaborated with the employer to actualize a discriminatory seniority system that perpetually relegated Black and Brown employees to "lower paying, less desirable jobs as servicemen or local city drivers,"[175] rather than higher paying jobs as line drivers.

Yet the Court left this contractually agreed upon systemic inequality between the company and union in collective bargaining agreements intact. The seniority system actually routinized a "last hired, first fired, preference for white drivers because Black and Brown drivers, who transferred from lower paying positions as a city driver or serviceman to a higher paying line driver job, had to "forfeit all the competitive

---

[171] David Simson and Angela Onwuachi-Willig, *Griggs v. Duke Power* in Critical Race Judgments: Rewritten U.S. Court Opinions on Race and the Law 347–76, 361 (2022).

[172] *Griggs*, 401 U.S. at 431.

[173] *Ibid.*

[174] *Int'l Bro. Teamsters v. United States,* 431 U.S. 324, 328 (1977).

[175] *Ibid.* at 329.

seniority he ha[d] accumulated in his previous bargaining unit and start at the bottom of the line drivers' 'board.'"[176]

By distinguishing the type of remediable discrimination – post-Act discrimination as being remediable by direct remedy and pre-Act discrimination as being immune from remediation because, as enacted, Title VII would not affect seniority rights "even where the employer had discriminated prior to the Act" – the Court dilutes the power of Title VII's direct assault on ostensibly neutral processes that perpetuate caste. Interpreting § 703 (h) of Title VII as a legislative compromise that preserved "the routine application of a bona fide seniority system" as permissible, the Court protects the "vested seniority rights of [white] employees," and casually notes that employing the very artifices of discrimination that violate Title VII should not be outlawed. The circularity of the Court's counter-intuitive reasoning is highlighted in its holding: "… we hold that an otherwise neutral, legitimate seniority system does not become unlawful under Title VII simply because it may perpetuate pre-Act discrimination."[177]

This is an extraordinary holding. How is this seniority system "neutral" and "legitimate" if it permits and even reifies the present-day effects of past discrimination? The Court completely ignores how white employment privilege is locked into the very system that it chooses to preserve.[178]

This is yet another example of the Burger Court's transitional equality and post-racial constitutionalism: the rights of the African-American and Latino/a workers are dependent on whether, and to what extent, the seniority rights of white employees can be preserved. While *Griggs* is cited in *Teamsters*, the inevitable consequences of disparate impact caused by the skewed seniority system are not addressed by the Court; it reads § 703(h) as insulating the seniority system from review under *Griggs*.[179] Because formal employment discrimination has been "eliminated (in the company post-Act)," then race is insignificant, and the emphasis is on preserving the expectation interests of the white workers which fully flourished undisturbed before the enactment of Title VII (pre-Act discrimination and its continuing effects are left intact). The Court even notes that "the line drivers with the longest tenure are without exception white,"[180] and that all the advantages of the seniority system flowed directly to them and disproportionately excluded Black and Brown workers.[181]

Instead, the Court over-emphasizes the prospective impact on all employees without conceptualizing the scope of structural inequality. The bona fide seniority system "locks" all employees into non-line-driver jobs without regard to race so the

---

[176] *Ibid.* at 344.
[177] *Ibid.* at 353–54.
[178] ROITHMAYR, *supra* n. 68.
[179] *Teamsters*, 431 U.S. at 349–50.
[180] *Ibid.* at 350.
[181] *Ibid.*

fact that African-American and Latino/a drivers receive no retroactive seniority due to the continuing effects of pre-Act discrimination is of no statutory significance. This contrived symmetry obscures the structural inequality that the Court leaves undisturbed.

Justice Marshall's dissent, in *Teamsters*, rejects post-racial neutrality – the fact that all employees are entitled to equal employment opportunities after 1965 – and instead unpacks the locked in impact of structural inequality:

> The Court holds, in essence, that while after 1965 these incumbent employees are entitled to an equal opportunity to advance to more desirable jobs, to take advantage of that opportunity they must pay a price: they must surrender the seniority they have accumulated in their old jobs. For many, the price will be too high, and they will be locked into their previous positions. Even those willing to pay the price will have to reconcile themselves to being forever behind subsequently hired whites who were not discriminatorily assigned. Thus, equal opportunity will remain a distant dream for all incumbent employees.[182]

That equal opportunity remains a distant dream is directly attributable to the Burger Court's transitional equality – it recognizes that the government proved a pattern or practice of discrimination against Black and Brown incumbent employees and applicants for line driver jobs, but nevertheless affirms the very system that gave life to this ongoing structural inequality.

Apparently, what drives the reasoning in *Teamsters* is that there was a collective bargaining agreement that set up a series of expectations on the part of white workers and that Title VII was not intended to upset those settled expectations. It also appears that the Burger Court assesses the impact of such arrangements based upon the harm to white interests: although *Wygant* is decided under the Fourteenth Amendment, the Court rejected the collective bargaining agreement in that case because retaining Black teachers as role models was an insufficient remedial interest if it meant displacing white schoolteachers with more seniority. Likewise, in *Teamsters*, the seniority system is left intact, notwithstanding the explicit acknowledgement that there are present-day effects of past discrimination, so as not to disrupt the seniority interests of white workers.[183]

Just two years later, in *United Steelworkers v. Weber*, a case arising out of a collective bargaining agreement between the United Steel Workers union and Kaiser Aluminum, in Gramercy, Louisiana, the Court revisited these themes, but reached a conclusion that is ostensibly favorable to private, voluntary race-conscious affirmative action plans. Again, this decision must be viewed in the context of the

---

[182] *Ibid.* at 387–88 (Marshall, J., concurring in part and dissenting in part).
[183] Cheryl I. Harris, *Whiteness as Property*, 106 HARV. L. REV. 1709, 1768; 1777–91 (1993) (noting that "the parameters of appropriate remedies are not dictated by the scope of the injury to the subjugated, but by the extent of the infringement on settled expectations of whites.").

Burger Court's race jurisprudence, which is deceptively favorable, but uniformly consistent in privileging white expectation interests over the eradication of systemic racism.

Weber: *A Good Result? Voluntariness, Race, and Neutrality*

The Court analyzed another collectively bargained agreement between an employer and union in *Weber*, reserving 50 percent of the openings in an in-plant craft training program for African-Americans, and limiting the operation of the program "until the percentage of [African-American] craft-workers in the plant is commensurate with the percentage of [African Americans] on the local labor force."[184] In this classic reverse discrimination action, a white worker, Brian Weber, brought suit challenging the legality of the race-conscious affirmative action plan as violating Title VII because "[t]he most senior [B]lack selected into the program had less seniority than several white production workers whose bids for admission [into the craft-training program] were rejected."[185] Concluding that employers and unions, in the private sector, could voluntarily initiate and implement race-conscious remedial plans to eradicate "manifest racial imbalances in traditionally segregated job categories,"[186] the Court held that Title VII does not prohibit such plans.

Construing Title VII as a statutory catalyst for voluntary, private, race-conscious remedial efforts to eradicate systemic racism and underlying patterns of structural inequality, the Court held that the statute's prohibition against racial discrimination, under §§ 703 (a) and (d), does "not condemn all private, voluntary, race-conscious affirmative action plans."[187]

Writing for a 5–2 majority, Justice Brennan concluded that the race-conscious affirmative action plan was not an unconstitutional quota because: it was open to Black and white employees on a 50–50 basis ("half of those trained in the program will be white");[188] it was not an absolute bar to white employees' advancement; and the plan was temporary and not intended to maintain a perpetual racial balance, but "simply to eliminate a manifest racial imbalance."[189] As such, the "plan does not unnecessarily trammel the interests of white employees."[190] In breaking down the structural inequality and racial hierarchy inherent in the craft trades, the voluntary plan did not disrupt any white expectation interests because they were still able to advance without being replaced by new Black hires.

---

[184] *United Steelworkers of Amer. v. Weber*, 443 U.S. 193, 197 (1979).
[185] *Ibid.* at 199.
[186] *Ibid.* at 197.
[187] *Ibid.* at 208.
[188] *Ibid.*
[189] *Ibid.*
[190] *Ibid.*

But this "good" result belies the transitional nature of equality even within a decision that at least implicitly references structuralism. The Court goes to great pains to say that the race-conscious plan is only temporary, not intended to maintain racial balance, and "does not unnecessarily trammel the interests of the white employees."[191] This means that the possibility of retrogression is evident just as it was in the school decisions.

The *Weber* decision still speaks in the language of benefits and burdens premised on race – the "preferential selection of craft trainees ... will end as soon as the percentage of black skilled craftworkers ... approximates the percentage of blacks in the labor force."[192] So, there is an incremental benefit for African-American employees which is balanced against the burden on white employees' expectation interests – this is not a last hired, first fired scenario under the Fourteenth Amendment as in *Wygant*. Here there is no displacement of white workers and the race-conscious program is temporary. A key distinction is the voluntariness of the program by private actors.[193]

The voluntariness concept plays directly into a neutral marketplace rationale that essentially obscures the structural inequality at work in *Weber*. The majority and dissenting opinions miss the significance of the manifest imbalance in the craft workforce that the voluntary race-conscious remedy is designed to address: the majority emphasizes opening employment opportunities for African Americans,[194] and the dissent focuses on the impact on access to craft jobs for white employees.[195]

Dissenting Chief Justice Burger equates the Court's majority opinion to legislative decision-making as it revises Title VII to permit quotas and displace the interests and employment expectations of white workers.[196] Indeed, Chief Justice Burger notes that the Court has constitutionalized the very discrimination that is expressly prohibited by Title VII – "discrimination against some individuals to give preferential treatment to others."[197] This formalistic interpretation of Title VII ignores structural inequality and will eventually become the touchstone of the Burger Court's transitional equality.

The post-racial rhetoric of Chief Justice Burger's dissenting opinion underscores a literal interpretation that is perverse, given the fact that the employer's voluntary action sought to remedy a glaring disparity with 1.83 percent (5 out of 273 employees)

---

[191] Harris, *supra* n. 183, at 1782 ("Even when the Court has upheld affirmative action plans, it implicitly has accepted the notion that affirmative action burdens – that is, extracts compensation from – innocent whites.").

[192] *Weber* 443 U.S. at 208–209.

[193] *See Johnson v. Transportation Agency*, 480 U.S. 616 (1987) (the Rehnquist Court reaffirmed *Weber* and extended its reasoning to a public employer's gender-conscious plan upholding it on the principle that an employer could remedy segregated job categories where women had been generally excluded).

[194] *United Steel Workers v. Weber*, 443 U.S. at 208.

[195] *Ibid.* at 216–19 (Burger, C. J., dissenting).

[196] *Ibid.* at 216–18.

[197] *Ibid.* at 218.

of the skilled craftworkers being African-American while they comprised a total available workforce of 39 percent.[198] What is striking about Chief Justice Burger's dissent is that it is insufficient that 50 percent of the jobs are open and available to white workers because that percentage is limited by the 50 percent of the jobs that are available to Black workers.

While acknowledging the gross discrimination against African-Americans in the trade and craft unions as "one of the dark chapters in the otherwise great history of the American labor movement,"[199] the chief justice eschews the connection to structural inequality and instead posits liberal individualism as the animating force behind Title VII. Title VII simply prohibits discrimination against any individual, and "voluntary compliance" does not comport with the absolute statutory prohibition against discrimination.[200] None of the decisions in *Weber* analyze the dynamics of structural inequality in employment, which brings us back to seniority, neutrality, and the preservation of white employment privilege.

Teamsters and *Weber* reach different results – the former affirming the seniority structure that protects white expectation interests and the latter endorsing voluntary compliance initiatives to advance the anti-discrimination mandate of Title VII – but both assume that access to an ostensibly neutral employment process is conducive to substantive equality. This optimistic conclusion is belied by the fact that both decisions fail to unpack the significance of how "practices, procedures, or tests neutral on their face, even neutral in terms of intent, cannot be maintained if they operate to 'freeze' the status quo of prior discriminatory employment practices."[201]

Notwithstanding its "good result," *Weber* falls short because it relies upon the voluntary benevolence of private employers in the employment marketplace to do the right thing – temporary remedies do not eradicate systemic inequality. *Firefighters Local Union No. 1784 v. Stotts* continues the Burger Court's adherence to the settled expectations of white workers.

Firefighters Local Union No. 1784 v. Stotts: *Seniority, Layoffs, and Teamsters*

The settled pattern and practice claims against the Memphis Fire Department were consolidated in a consent decree which adopted remedies to address the continuing effects of past discrimination by mandating promotion, backpay, and hiring goals to approximate the proportion of African Americans in the labor force in Shelby County, Tennessee.[202]

---

[198] *United Steel Workers v. Weber*, 443 U.S. at 198–99.
[199] *Ibid.* at 218 (Burger, C. J., dissenting).
[200] *Ibid.*
[201] *Griggs v. Duke Power*, 401 U.S. at 430.
[202] *Firefighters Loc. Union No. 1784 v. Stotts*, 467 U.S. 561, 565 (1984).

A projected municipal budget deficit prompted city layoffs of firefighters, threatening the recently agreed upon remedial gains for the certified class of firefighters. Concluding that the layoffs would have a discriminatory impact on the African-American firefighters, the district court enjoined the layoffs, ordering the city to "not apply the seniority policy proposed insofar as it [would] decrease the percentage of black lieutenants, drivers, inspectors and privates that are presently employed."[203] Affirming the district court ruling, the Sixth Circuit Court of Appeals concluded that modifying the consent decree was appropriate in light of the "new and unforeseen circumstances that created a hardship"[204] for the African-American firefighters. In a 6–3 decision, the Court reversed.

From the outset, the Court's decision is premised, not on a critical assessment of structural inequality and systemic racism in the firefighting employment ranks but rather on whether there was a live case and controversy because of the impact on white firefighters with seniority. Concluding that the case was not moot because there was a continuing injury to white firefighters – they had lost a month's pay and unrestored seniority with some being "bumped down" – notwithstanding the fact that the city restored or offered to restore their former positions as the result of the layoffs.[205] It is as if the injunction hurt the white firefighters because the African-American firefighters were not, as is the usual custom, "last hired, first fired." Indeed, as Girardeau Spann notes, "[T]he majority did not discuss the fact that the layoffs were actually made in reverse alphabetical order because all affected black and white workers were hired on the same day and had accumulated the same seniority."[206] This suggests that the Court's analysis is incomplete and focuses predominantly on the impact on white expectation interests rather than the present-day effects of a discriminatory system that had been remedied, at least in part, by the agreed-upon settlement embodied in the consent decree.

Concluding that the consent decree did not permit overriding a bona fide seniority system, which is protected under Title VII, the Court stated that "it is inappropriate to deny an innocent [white] employee the benefit of his seniority in order to provide a remedy in a pattern-or-practice suit such as this."[207] Essentially, the district court lacked the authority to modify the consent decree, and the court of appeals erred in affirming its decision, because there was no intentional discrimination on the basis of race by the city.[208] Thus, the district court's injunction "conflicted with the seniority system,"[209] and this was error. This formalistic conception ignores structural inequality, elevates a nearly insurmountable burden of proof in

[203] *Ibid.* at 567.
[204] *Ibid.* at 568.
[205] *Ibid.* at 571.
[206] Spann, *supra* n. 94, at 34.
[207] *Stotts*, 467 U.S. at 575.
[208] *Ibid.* at 577.
[209] *Ibid.* at 578.

pattern-or-practice cases, and disaggregates the potency of class actions to promote broad systemic change in the employment marketplace.

Relying on *Teamsters*, the Court concluded that "mere membership in the disadvantaged class is insufficient to warrant a seniority award; each individual must prove that the discriminatory practice had an impact on him."[210] There must be an identifiable victim of discrimination, and the Black individuals to be protected from layoffs and loss of seniority had not been found to have been specifically discriminated against.[211] In some sense, the Court concluded, there was nothing to remedy in the absence of a particularized showing of discrimination by each alleged victim in the certified class. But this fundamentally misconstrues pattern-or-practice class action litigation, and instead the Court offers a novel balancing approach that seeks to insulate any impact on nonminority employees.[212] The Court would later distinguish *Stotts'* rigid actual victim requirement in two cases decided the same day: *Local Sheet Metal Workers International Association v. EEOC*[213] and *Local 93, International Association v. Firefighters v. Cleveland.*[214] The Burger Court's Title VII decisions left open many questions that were further complicated by its faelty to the expectation interests of incumbent employees.[215]

The Burger Court's decisions rest on a formalistic conception of equality premised on the protection of white employment and expectation interests; its race jurisprudence is discernibly post-racial. The unifying theme of post-racial constitutionalism underpins the Court's race jurisprudence from the *Civil Rights Cases* to the postracial transitional equality of the Burger Court to the Rehnquist Court's post-racial colorblindness to the Roberts Court's unyielding assault on anti-discrimination law through post-racial constitutionalism, which marks every reference to race as presumptively unconstitutional and noxious to a formally equal and open society. Race-conscious remedial efforts are beyond consideration – a race-neutral and post-racial society must move beyond race. Post-racialism is not aspirational, but a means of circumscribing any substantive progress for African Americans and people of color.[216]

---

[210] *Ibid.* at 579.

[211] *Ibid.*

[212] *Stotts* "had the effect of limiting race-conscious affirmative action remedies under Title VII to the *actual victims* of identifiable discrimination, rather than to members of *racial groups* who had historically been targets of discrimination." SPANN, *supra* n. 94, at 34 (emphasis in original).

[213] 478 U.S. 421, 474–75 (distinguishing *Stotts* and noting that individualized "make-whole" relief was not the exclusive remedy available, under Title VII, and that race-conscious remedial relief that benefitted non-victims was not prohibited as the purpose of affirmative action is to dismantle structural inequality).

[214] 478 U.S. 501, 525–26 (noting that voluntary adoption of race-conscious consent decree that may benefit nonvictims was permissible, and distinguishing *Stotts* by emphasizing that there was a conflict between the modified consent decree and the purpose of Title VII).

[215] Brian K. Landsberg, *Race and the Rehnquist Court*, 66 TUL. L. REV. 1267, 1281 (1992).

[216] Sumi Cho, *Post-Racialism*, 94 IOWA L. REV. 1589, 1645 (2008) ("… what is new and distinct about post-racialism (as compared to say, colorblindness) is that the state's retreat from race-based remedies is only possible in a society that is perceived as having made significant strides in racial equality, at least symbolically.").

The Burger Court constructs America's modern race jurisprudence with the Rehnquist and Roberts Courts, further refining the normative principles embodying post-racial constitutionalism. Each Court advances its post-racialism in distinct ways. Employing Rhetorical Neutrality, the Burger Court does not reference historical racism and its present-day effects or the structural inequality of the employment marketplace; it defines discrimination narrowly and formalistically either through a rigid discriminatory intent requirement under the Equal Protection Clause; or, under Title VII, though an actual victim requirement or a neutral voluntariness exception. And, it rationalizes inequality by emphasizing the burden on innocent whites, and privileging their expectation interests.

Next, the Rehnquist Court resolves lingering doctrinal questions such as whether heightened scrutiny applies to all race-conscious governmental action; whether diversity is a compelling interest; and, when, if ever, race may be used and for how long. In the most extreme incarnation of post-racial constitutionalism, the Roberts Court is actively engaged in eviscerating anti-discrimination law. Before the Roberts Court takes on this devastating constitutional enterprise, the Rehnquist Court conceptualizes post-racial colorblindness through the neutral rhetoric of Rhetorical Neutrality.

Advancing post-racial colorblind constitutionalism, the Rehnquist Court espouses a rhetorical and analytical approach that simultaneously acknowledges race to neutralize it (colorblindness) while endeavoring to transcend its existence (post-racialism). To the Rehnquist Court, race is irrelevant, and neutrality should be the touchstone of governmental decision-making; likewise, the Court shares the Burger Court's jurisprudential commitment to protecting white interests.

THE REHNQUIST COURT AND POST-RACIAL COLORBLINDNESS

Post-racial colorblindness references the Rehnquist Court's selective use of race, depending on whether there is an impact or burden on white interests.[217] The doctrinal and conceptual fabric that threads through the Burger Court's transitional equality, the Rehnquist Court's post-racial colorblindness, and the Robert Court's post-racial constitutionalism is an explicit jurisprudential concern for protecting white interests, or – at the very least – ensuring that there is no long-term burden on the privilege of being white. The Court actively protects this presumptive entitlement.[218]

---

[217] Bell, *supra* n. 39, at 149–51 (discussing Justice O'Connor's decisions advancing interest convergence – a commitment to protecting white interests and only permitting limited and narrow social change when there is no burden on, and it is beneficial to, those interests – and skepticism of race-conscious remedies as harming innocent whites as animating features of her opinions for the Rehnquist Court).

[218] Erwin Chemerinsky, *Making Sense of the Affirmative Action Debate*, 22 OHIO N. U. L. REV. 1159, 1173 (1996).

Three post-racial myths – historical, definitional, and rhetorical – serve to recast the Fourteenth Amendment so that the anti-subjugation and anti-caste principles are disconnected from its constitutional mandate. The race jurisprudence of the Rehnquist Court is anchored in Rhetorical Neutrality.

Eschewing any analysis of structural inequality and the present-day effects of systemic racism, the Court constructs a historical myth that emphasizes liberal individualism – the Constitution protects individuals, not groups – the historical oppression of African-Americans is irrelevant. The Fourteenth Amendment's anti-subordination principle is discarded for an anti-differentiation principle which foregrounds formalistic equality by focusing the analysis on whether the similarly situated have been treated similarly.[219]

Redefining discrimination so that formal equality is the touchstone, and any race-conscious remediation is inherently suspect, the Court's definitional myth defines discrimination so that it only exists in the rare instance that it can be proven with particularity. Just as the *Civil Rights Cases* required state action for discrimination to be remediable, the Rehnquist Court further expands the discriminatory intent requirement, under *Washington v. Davis*, so that intentional discrimination by the state must be established. In the absence of discriminatory intent, mere societal discrimination cannot be addressed. Under this inverted analysis, whites become discrete and insular minorities impermissibly burdened by race-conscious remedies. Reverse discrimination claims are favored due to this post-racial interpretation.

The Rehnquist Court deploys a rhetorical myth, which explains the persistence of structural inequality, by emphasizing liberal individualism which focuses on the availability of eligible workers rather than the structural exclusion of them from the marketplace itself;[220] the temporal limits of any significant advances by people

---

[219] CASS R. SUNSTEIN, The Partial Constitution 340 (1993).

[220] This is especially true in a series of Title VII decisions. *See, for example, United States v. Paradise*, 480 U.S. 149, 170 (relying on *Sheet Metal Workers* and upholding, under strict scrutiny review, a court ordered plan imposing a one-to-one promotion requirement for Black and white Alabama state troopers as an interim remedial measure for the continuing effects of identifiable past discrimination); *but see Ibid.* at 196–201 (O'Connor, J., dissenting) (concluding that the promotion requirement was an impermissible quota unrelated to the percentage of qualified and eligible African-American state troopers in the relevant work force). *Watson v. Fort Worth Bank & Trust*, 487 U.S. 977, 999 (1988) (concluding that disparate impact analysis applies to subjective and objective practices, and rejecting an African-American bank teller's Title VII claim because statistical evidence was not evaluated by the lower courts to determine whether a prima facie disparate impact case was made); *Wards Cove Packing Co., Inc. v. Antonio*, 490 U.S. 642, 657 (1989) (construing segregated workforce of unskilled predominantly nonwhite cannery line workers and predominantly white skilled workers, and holding that plaintiffs failed to establish a statistical case of disparate impact – there was no demonstration, beyond mere racial imbalance, that "the application of a specific or particular employment practice … has created the disparate impact under attack"). Advancing neutrality and heightened standards of proof for Title VII plaintiffs, the Rehnquist Court was actively engaged in significantly diluting, if not completely dismantling, the substantive mandate of *Griggs v. Duke*

of color must be referenced in terms of white interests (interest convergence); and colorblind neutrality must lead to outcomes that are truly post-racial – there is a designated time when race-conscious remedies will no longer be needed.

Apart from further diluting disparate impact analysis under Title VII and retreating from substantive remedial efforts to fully integrate schools, the Rehnquist Court's salience rests on its clarification of the standard of review in race cases. The Rehnquist Court's post-racial colorblindness is advanced thematically by several doctrinal propositions: colorblind neutrality is foregrounded as a normative principle so that race is neutralized or obscured to such an extent that it is transcended; there is a pronounced commitment to formalistic equality; there is a strict adherence to particularized findings of discriminatory intent; and there is a presumption in favor of reverse discrimination lawsuits by whites as a means to constitutionalize post-racialism and rationalize the continuing effects of past discrimination.

Post-racial colorblindness rejects the anti-subordination principle of the Fourteenth Amendment, and instead seeks to accommodate white interests and privilege through neutral rhetoric. Justice O'Connor's opinions for the Court use race selectively. This is the hallmark of the Rehnquist Court's post-racial colorblindness, which denotes a hybrid approach: at once, post-racial when it comes to any race-conscious remedial progress for African Americans which could conceivably "burden" whites, and colorblind when it is determined that a balance is needed because there is an identifiable benefit to white interests. This is interest convergence; it is no coincidence that most of the Court's race jurisprudence examines the legitimacy of substantive claims against anti-Black racism promoted by the reverse discrimination claims of whites.

Expanding upon her concurrence in the *Wygant* plurality opinion,[221] Justice O'Connor espouses several propositions that embody Rhetorical Neutrality: since there is no group history of oppression, her analysis consistently starts from the premise that any remedy must not unnecessarily trammel the rights of innocent whites; discrimination is defined narrowly so that societal discrimination is irrelevant in the absence of identifiable discrimination by the state; and remedies cannot be rationalized without clearly identifying qualified and eligible people of color who have been displaced by intentional discrimination. Each of these post-racial themes is posited in *City of Richmond v. Croson, Adarand Constructors v. Peña,* and *Grutter v. Bollinger*. All of these decisions, authored by Justice O'Connor, offer a distinct conception of the Court's post-racial colorblindness.

Power. Robert Belton, *Causation and Burden-Shifting Doctrines in Employment Discrimination Law Revisited: Some Thoughts on Hopkins and Wards Cove,* 64 TUL. L. REV. 1359, 1364 (1990). Moreover, the Court engrafts an intent requirement onto the disparate impact requirement so as to make disproportionality merely circumstantial proof in the absence of proof of intent. Robert Belton, *The Dismantling of the Griggs Disparate Impact Theory and the Future of Title VII: The Need for a Third Reconstruction,* 8 YALE L. & POL'Y 223, 240–43 (1990).

[221] 476 U.S. at 284–94 (O'Connor, J., concurring in part and concurring in the judgment).

Croson: *Post-Racial Colorblindness and Richmond Revisionism*

Framing the issue as one of liberal individualism – the right of individual citizens to equal treatment – and the legitimacy of race-conscious remedies in the absence of discriminatory intent, the Court invalidated the city of Richmond's Minority Business Enterprise (MBE) program.[222] Richmond's MBE program was patterned after the federal program upheld in *Fullilove*;[223] nevertheless, the Court held that it was constitutionally invalid which would seem counterintuitive in light of the Rehnquist Court's vaunted New Federalism.[224]

But the distinct doctrinal line between the two decisions is race. *Croson*, for the first time, holds that all state and local race-conscious remedial initiatives will be subject to strict scrutiny. *Fullilove* is not overruled but is distinguished by reframing the anti-subordination principle of the Fourteenth Amendment in terms of post-racial colorblindness. The plight of white contractors is privileged and that of the excluded African-American contractors is neutralized (discrimination essentially vanishes) because the opinion is an evaluation of an ostensibly open public contracting market that is simply devoid of eligible African-American contractors.

Revisiting the Burger Court's decision in *Fullilove*, Justice O'Connor offers a dramatically revised interpretation of sections 1 and 5 of the Fourteenth Amendment. Justice O'Connor reasons that Congress' § 5 power is a "specific constitutional mandate to enforce the dictates of the Fourteenth Amendment,"[225] which means that it has remedial and enforcement power that the states do not possess. "Section 1 of the Fourteenth Amendment is an explicit *constraint* on state power,"[226] so that any remedial efforts must be undertaken guided by the principle of equal protection (or equal treatment). Race-conscious remedies, when offered by state and local governments (as distinguished from the federal government), are illegitimate windfalls in the absence of particularized discrimination.

While how Congress exercised its remedial powers in enacting race-conscious remedies was viewed deferentially in *Fullilove*, Justice O'Connor's *Croson* opinion offers a

---

[222] *City of Richmond v. J.A. Croson Co.*, 488 U.S. 469, 510 (1989).

[223] The Richmond Plan required city prime contractors to subcontract at least 30 percent of the dollar amount of the contract to one or more MBEs, which were defined as "[a] business at least fifty-one (51) percent of which is owned and controlled .... by minority group members." "Minority groups members" were defined as '[c]itizens of the United States who are Blacks, Spanish-speaking, Orientals, Indians, Eskimos, or Aleuts." *Ibid.* at 477–78.

[224] Shirley S. Abrahamson, *State Constitutional Law, New Judicial Federalism, and the Rehnquist Court*, 51 CLEV. ST. L. REV. 339, 351 (2004) ("An underlying theme of the Rehnquist Court's federalism is to preserve the states as independent and autonomous political entitles. ... Yet ... while the Rehnquist Court's constitutional federalism has imposed new limits on Congress vis-a- vis the states, the Court has not really championed state autonomy."). The Roberts Court has championed a new brand of federalism, expanding state power to determine voting rights. *See* Chapter 8, *infra*.

[225] *Ibid.* at 490.

[226] *Ibid.*

clear and stark demarcation between federal and state power; Congress has remedial power to enforce the Fourteenth Amendment, and states cannot simply mimic this power because of the express limitation embodied in section 1. Moreover, to the Court, there is only one post-racial colorblind interpretation of the Fourteenth Amendment because the basic principles of federalism would be disrupted if fifty states were allowed to interpret its contents.[227] Congress was exercising its unique § 5 remedial powers in *Fullilove*, and the set-aside was flexible and could be rebutted or waived in specified circumstances. By contrast, the 30 percent set-aside in *Croson* was an inflexible quota unconnected to any clearly identifiable violation by the state.[228] The Court glosses over the point that the Richmond MBE had a waiver provision as well.[229]

The state can remedy discrimination, but only if it is particularized and clearly identifiable. This formalistic standard means that the state itself must openly acknowledge (or confess) its complacency in advancing structural inequality in the construction industry as a "passive participant."[230] Of course, this will virtually never happen – it would be extraordinarily rare for a state to implicate itself as a discriminatory actor – so discrimination becomes irremediable, invisible, and unmeasurable. This is reminiscent of the post-racial *Civil Rights Cases* where the Court concluded that discriminatory state action must be identifiable to be remediable under the Fourteenth Amendment.

Foregrounding the personal rights of white contractors not to be excluded from the public contract marketplace, the Court rejects the fixed contract percentage enacted by the Richmond City Council to eradicate the structural exclusion of Black contractors in the construction industry. Strict scrutiny applies to all state or local racial classifications, whether benign or invidious because the use of race is constitutionally noxious. To the Court, there is no way to clearly distinguish between "good" and "bad" discrimination because the Constitution is colorblind and should not accord advantages or disadvantages on the basis of race.[231] Certainly, this claim has literal appeal; yet, with a few exceptions, there is no recognition of the structural underpinnings of caste-based oppression.

Of course, the city of Richmond, in 1989, was dramatically different than it was from 1861 to 1865 when it was the capital of the Confederacy, but it is a glaring analytical omission to fail to critically assess the present-day effects of past discrimination in this context. If ever there was a place where the present-day effects of past discrimination are clearly discernible, it is the city of Richmond where Blacks represented 50 percent of the population but received only 0.67 percent of prime contracts.[232] This graphic marketplace disparity did not move the Court nor the white

[227] *Ibid.*
[228] *Ibid.* at 499.
[229] *Ibid.* at 479.
[230] *Ibid.* at 492.
[231] *Ibid.* at 493.
[232] *Ibid.* at 499.

contracting company that brought this reverse discrimination suit. This is Richmond Revisionism – the enduring legacy of slavery is erased and replaced with a neutral and open public construction marketplace which should not be tainted by race.[233]

Offering an inverted reading of the Process Theory – a pluralistic conception of a well-functioning polity where judicial review is exercised rarely and sparingly in the event of a system blockage against "discrete and insular" minorities – Justice O'Connor essentially prioritizes the interests of the white contractors as those who have been excluded by a majoritarian Black legislature.[234] The MBE program is dismissed by the Court as a racial spoils system displacing a neutral and legitimate contracting marketplace by using race as a remedy. Justice O'Connor's opinion summarily disregards all the supporting factual evidence that substantiates the program's constitutional validity.

The Rehnquist Court's post-racial colorblindness follows a consistent doctrinal pattern of historical denial or revisionism, formalistic definitions of discrimination and unrealistically heightened standards of proof, and a rationalizing narrative that ostensibly offers hope about the viability of future anti-discrimination claims while reinforcing systemic racism and structural inequality. Advancing the historical, definitional, and rhetorical myths that underpin Rhetorical Neutrality, the Court readily ignores the existence of structural inequality. The legislative findings of Congress and the Richmond City Council become constitutionally irrelevant given the Court's post-racial colorblindness.

Construing the Croson Company's reverse discrimination claim, the Court simply presumes the invalidity of the MBE program because, as the aggrieved white contractor, Croson did not receive a perceived benefit that the historically excluded Black contractor did. The Court disaggregates discrimination so that, under the Fourteenth Amendment, there are specific instances of state discrimination that must be identified. If not, mere societal discrimination cannot be remedied because this is a natural occurrence disconnected from any action by the state. This formulaic and stinted interpretation allows the Court to casually disregard the legislative findings of the Richmond City Council and reinterpret them as the result of racial politics, meaning that the majority Black City Council engaged in a racial spoils system notwithstanding its stated remedial purpose.[235] This is because there was no cognizable injury to remedy: "The 30 percent quota cannot in any realistic sense be tied to any injury suffered by anyone."[236] Through this analytical lens, the Court concludes that there was no strong evidentiary basis for the MBE program's remedial purpose. There was no compelling governmental interest for the program, and it was not narrowly tailored to achieve its stated purpose.

---

[233] Thomas Ross, *The Richmond Narratives*, 68 TEX. L. REV. 381, 405–409 (1989).
[234] 488 U.S. at 495–96.
[235] *Ibid.* at 496.
[236] *Ibid.* at 499.

Considering the evidence and the legislative findings, the Court's conclusion is demonstrably erroneous because its post-racial colorblindness presumes that the MBE program is constitutionally invalid. There was a pervasive history of systemic racism in Richmond that the Court chose to ignore – these "multifarious acts of discrimination"[237] included suppression of voting rights, massive resistance of school integration, and state legitimized housing discrimination. Within this context, it is no analytical leap to conclude that the miniscule proportion of public contracts obtained by Blacks, 0.67 percent, was a present-day manifestation of decades of structural exclusion in the construction industry. "There are roughly equal numbers of minorities and nonminorities in Richmond – yet minority-owned businesses receive *one-seventy-fifth* of the public contracting funds that other businesses receive."[238] Certainly, this belies Croson's reverse discrimination assertion of injury – there is no injury to remedy because the white contractor is not a discrete and insular minority in the construction marketplace.

The claim simply cannot be that white contractors dominate public construction contracts, and a 30 percent set-aside, which is the midway point between virtually zero Black contractors and the general population, is a threat to that dominance and should be held invalid. Indeed, Croson offered no direct evidence of an impermissible or discriminatory purpose by the majority Black City Council. It appears that the Court's proof requirements shift based upon the race of the burdened party. This is what makes the racial politics rationale especially disconcerting.

The Court's color-coded federalism is a throwback to the stereotypical characterizations of the First Reconstruction[239] and equally disturbing. A higher standard of proof is required of African-American lawmakers to ensure that whites are not burdened by their legislative decision-making.[240] This is post-racial colorblindness in full bloom.

Because the Court is consistently neutralizing race or obscuring its significance, post-racial colorblindness is a defining feature of its rationalizing narrative. The Court *explains* structural inequality by emphasizing neutral rationales. For example, the fact that there are so few Black contractors represented in trade association membership can be explained, not as an indicator of exclusion and disproportionate impact, but simply as the city's inability to fully ascertain the number of interested, qualified, and eligible Black contractors.[241] This underscores the lack of a structural analysis in the Court's race decisions, and the reason congressional findings with direct application to the local construction market are so important.

Congress, as national legislature, made a finding that was directly applicable to the city of Richmond. Pursuant to its § 5 remedial power, Congress identified a

---

[237] *Ibid.* at 544 (Marshall, J., dissenting).
[238] *Ibid.* at 542 (Marshall, J., dissenting) (emphasis in original).
[239] W. E. B. DuBois, Black Reconstruction in America, 1860–1880 711 (1935).
[240] 488 U.S. at 555 (Marshall, J., dissenting).
[241] *Ibid.* at 503–504.

nationwide pattern of systemic discrimination, of which cities and states were part and parcel; but such legislative action is illegitimate when advanced by the state in the absence of particularized discrimination in the construction industry itself that is directly traceable to the state. This turns federalism on its head because states are exercising power that is complementary to federal power to enforce the constitutional mandate of section 1 of the Fourteenth Amendment.

The Court's rejection of these substantive factual predicates for enacting the local MBE program exemplifies Rhetorical Neutrality: history is revised so that the systemic racism of the former capital of the Confederacy is ignored and the emphasis in on the availability of Black contractors, not their structural exclusion from a closed local and national marketplace; discrimination is defined so narrowly that there must be a specific instance of discrimination against a clearly identifiable group, and since there are no eligible Aleutian contractors residing in the city of Richmond, who have been discriminated against, there is no compelling interest to apportion public contracts on the basis of race;[242] and, finally, a rhetorical myth is deployed to explain that the only cognizable injury is the exclusion from competing for 30 percent of public contracts in much the same manner as white medical students were excluded from participating for 16 out of 100 medical school seats in *Bakke*.

The race-conscious remedies, in *Croson* and *Bakke*, are unconstitutional because they cast such a wide remedial net without a clear connection between injury and remedy. Quotas are constitutionally impermissible, and societal discrimination is too tenuous to remedy. In Croson, the 30 percent set-aside is invalid because it is unconnected to any discernible injury suffered by eligible and available Black contractors; in fact, the absence of Black contractors could be because of a myriad of race-neutral factors including interest in public contracting jobs.[243]

Next, the Rehnquist Court consolidates its analysis in *Croson* and makes it directly applicable to federally enacted race conscious remedies in *Adarand Constructors, Inc. v. Peña*. Ultimately, this sets the jurisprudential stage for the Roberts Court and post-racial constitutionalism.

Adarand: *Skepticism, Consistency, and Congruence*

Advancing a dramatically different analytical approach in reviewing a Disadvantaged Business Enterprise ("DBE") program upheld by the lower federal courts,[244] the Rehnquist Court, in an opinion authored by Justice O'Connor, concluded that strict

---

[242] *Ibid.* at 506.

[243] *Ibid.* at 503–508.

[244] *Adarand Constructors, Inc. Skinner*, 790 F. Supp. 240 (Dist. Colorado 1992) (granting government's summary judgment motion); *Adarand Constructors, Inc. v. Skinner*, 16 F.3d 1537 (1994) (applying intermediate scrutiny, per *Fullilove*, and upholding the DBE program).

scrutiny applied with equal force to federal race-conscious remedies, thereby federalizing its previous holding in *Croson*.[245] All local, state, and federal race-conscious remedies are subject to strict scrutiny, which means that such measures come with a strong presumption of invalidity. This is another example of the Rehnquist Court's post-racial colorblindness – the Court literally goes out of its way to ignore the economic status classification in the program to reach the racial classification and apply strict scrutiny to it.

Gonzales Construction Company, a certified DBE specializing in highway guardrails, was awarded a subcontract over the low bid of Adarand Constructors, which was not a certified DBE. The prime contractor "would receive additional compensation if it hired subcontractors certified as small businesses controlled by "socially and economically disadvantaged individuals.""[246] Under the provisions of the federal program, a DBE was defined as a small business that is "at least 51 percent owned and managed by disadvantaged individuals," and there was a presumption that "socially and economically disadvantaged individuals includes Black Americans, Hispanic Americans, Native Americans, Asian Pacific Americans, and other minorities ..."[247]

Advancing a challenge under the Fifth Amendment, Adarand asserted that the racial presumption violated "the federal government's Fifth Amendment obligation not to deny anyone equal protection of the laws."[248] The Court embraced Adarand's argument, and Justice O'Connor's opinion invokes three central tenets of post-racial colorblindness: skepticism (race is inherently suspect, it should be viewed skeptically, and any use of race is subject to strict scrutiny); consistency (race is irrelevant in determining a constitutional violation or injury because equal treatment is the touchstone of the Fourteenth Amendment); and congruence (analysis under the Fifth and Fourteenth Amendments is the same; thus, local, state, and federal race-conscious remedies must meet strict scrutiny).[249]

Overruling *MetroBroadcasting*,[250] which explicitly endorsed the broad remedial powers of Congress to eradicate structural inequality notwithstanding a particularized finding of discrimination, and gutting the doctrinal edifice of *Fullilove*,[251] *Adarand* narrowly circumscribes federal power to specific, identifiable discrimination. Any race-conscious remediation must be justified by a specified injury – affirmative action is little more than a racial windfall. Of course, this rationale only works if the present day effects of past discrimination – the core of structural inequality – are ignored.

[245] *Adarand Constructors, Inc. v. Peña*, 515 U.S. 200, 235 (1995).
[246] *Ibid.* at 205.
[247] *Ibid.* at 206.
[248] *Ibid.*
[249] *Ibid.* at 223–24.
[250] *Ibid.* at 227 (overruling *MetroBroadcasting v. FCC*, 497 U.S. 547 (1990)).
[251] *Ibid.* at 235.

The contrived tenets of skepticism, consistency, and congruence are paradigmatic examples of Rhetorical Neutrality and the Rehnquist Court's post-racial colorblindness. Skepticism advances the historical myth by ignoring the historically structural dimensions of racial subordination; consistency defines discrimination so narrowly that race is irrelevant unless the impact is on white interests (the definitional myth is malleable to preserve inequality under the guise of neutrality); and congruence posits a rationalizing narrative that serves to marginalize positive governmental efforts to eradicate structural inequality.[252]

(i) Skepticism and the Historical Myth

What is striking about *Croson* and *Adarand* is the Court's failure to acknowledge the systemic impact of historical discrimination – it does not matter that there is a clear legislative history detailing structural inequality in the construction industry because the Constitution protects individuals, not groups – there is no group history of race in the Court's race jurisprudence. Liberal individualism is the touchstone of the Court's equal protection analysis. The neutral underpinning of skepticism means that race is always suspect because there is no way to distinguish invidiousness from positive remediation by local, state, or federal governments.

But Justice O'Connor's invented proposition of skepticism misreads, misinterprets, and devalues the anti-subordination principle underlying the Fourteenth Amendment.[253] All of the Reconstruction Amendments are unified by the anti-subordination principle: racial subjugation is eradicated; there is no racial caste system in the United States; and all badges and incidents of slavery are dismantled in the name of full citizenship, especially the right to vote, for African Americans.

Skepticism does not resonate with the Fourteenth Amendment's constitutional legacy because it presumes that formalistic equality is the governing mandate. Since all forms of state-legitimized oppression have been removed in society, then any approach to race must be neutral. And it follows that any use of race should be viewed skeptically. The historical myth distorts the legislative and constitutional mandate of the Fourteenth Amendment so that strict scrutiny is misapplied to positive remedial efforts to eradicate structural inequality. There is a clear bright-line distinction between invidious discrimination and remedial action that embraces substantive equality.[254] Under the Equal Protection Clause, there is a fundamental difference between oppression and assistance.[255]

---

[252] Cedric Merlin Powell, *Blinded by Color: The New Equal Protection, the Second Deconstruction, and Affirmative Inaction*, 51 U. Miami L. Rev. 191, 261–64 (1997).
[253] Koteles Alexander, *Adarand: Brute Political Force Concealed as a Constitutional Colorblind Principle*, 39 How. L. J. 367, 378–88 (1995).
[254] *Ibid.* at 383.
[255] *Adarand*, 515 U.S. at 264 (Stevens, J., dissenting).

Race should not be viewed skeptically when the national legislature has made specific findings about structural exclusion from the public contracting market of small Black-owned businesses, and the presumption of economic disadvantage was not an unconstitutional racial proxy, but rather a reflection of the lingering effects of past discrimination.[256]

(ii) Consistency, Inconsistency, and the Definitional Myth

Paradoxically, *Adarand*'s tenet of consistency is anything but that. Ignoring the legislative history of the Fourteenth Amendment, consistency neutralizes the history of racial subordination that the Fourteenth Amendment was intended to eradicate and instead universalizes reverse discrimination claims by transforming whites, like Adarand Constructors, into discrete and insular minorities. Their "injury" was that a race-conscious factor was even considered – that is a threat to the status quo of white privilege. There was no quota, and economic status – not race – was the predominant determinative factor in awarding contracts. Thus, consistency fits within the Court's narrative framework of Rhetorical Neutrality because discrimination is defined so narrowly that it ceases to exist unless the burden is on white interests. This, again, is the definitional myth: discrimination is nearly impossible to prove if the plaintiff is advancing an anti-discrimination claim, but discrimination is presumed in *Croson* and *Adarand* because of the Court's skepticism of race and the belief that the Fourteenth Amendment should be whitewashed to protect white individuals, not subordinated racial groups.

A stark aspect of the definitional myth is that the Court is selective in how it uses race – it is simultaneously post-racial and race-conscious. In *Croson*, the Court found no identifiable discrimination because, in an ostensibly neutral contracting market, there was nothing to remedy (post-racial); but the majority Black racial composition of the Richmond City Council meant that the awarding of the contracts was likely the result of racial politics (race-conscious). This essentialism underscores the Court's post-racial colorblindness.[257] The Court does not scrutinize the racial composition of the 435 members of Congress; but it nevertheless advances a racial politics theory premised on what factors are considered in awarding contracts, and since race provided a presumption of economic disadvantage, race could serve as a proxy for a result that was not constitutionally colorblind.[258]

---

[256] *Ibid.* at 260 (Stevens, J., dissenting).
[257] Powell, *supra* n. 252, at 250–51 (*citing* Mary C. Daly, *Rebuilding the City of Richmond: Congress' Power to Authorize the States to Implement Race-Conscious Affirmative Action Plans*, 33 B.C. L. REV. 903, 904–905 (1992)).
[258] *Ibid.* at 261–62.

(iii) Incongruence and the Rhetorical Myth

The formalistically narrow definition of discrimination leads directly to the Court's distortion of remedial power under the Fifth and Fourteenth Amendments – congruence. Discarding *stare decisis* and the constitutional mandate of *MetroBroadcasting* and, by extension, *Fullilove*, the Court recasts section 1 of the Fourteenth Amendment as a strict prohibition against any consideration of race absent a compelling state interest, and Congress' section 5 enforcement power is significantly modified as a narrow remedial power which must meet strict scrutiny whenever race is used.

The fallacy of Justice O'Connor's judicially crafted conception of congruence, especially for the Rehnquist Court which inaugurated the New Federalism, is that it completely misconceives the scope of state and federal power. Section 1 is a prohibition on state action intended to perpetuate the badges and incidents of slavery so that the newly emancipated slaves would not become subordinated second-class citizens, Black citizens are entitled to equal protection of the laws. Section 5 of the Fourteenth Amendment ensures that federal legislative power will be deployed when the states intentionally perpetuate the present-day effects of systemic racism. The power to enforce, by appropriate legislation, means that Congress has the power to legislate to ensure that the historically oppressed African Americans are afforded equal protection of the laws.

All of the Reconstruction Amendments are race conscious[259] – slavery is eradicated by the Thirteenth Amendment; citizenship and due process are secured by the Fourteenth Amendment to the newly liberated citizens of the United States; and the Fifteenth Amendment establishes the core element of citizenship, the franchise to the former slaves who previously had no voice in their political destiny.

Congruence is a post-racial conception that ignores the significance of legislative remedial power to eradicate structural exclusion. The Court obscures the fundamental institutional and remedial distinction between a prohibition on state discrimination and the federal enforcement power to remedy such state-mandated inequality. As Justice Stevens pointedly notes in his dissent:

> The Fourteenth Amendment directly empowers Congress at the same time it expressly limits the States. This is no accident. It represents our Nation's consensus, achieved after hard experience throughout our sorry history of race relations, that the Federal Government must be the primary defender of racial minorities against the States, some of which may be inclined to oppress such minorities. A rule of "congruence" that ignores a purposeful "incongruity" so fundamental to our system of government is unacceptable.[260]

---

[259] Eric Schnapper, *Affirmative Action and the Legislative History of the Fourteenth Amendment*, 71 Va. L. Rev. 753, 754–84 (1985).

[260] *Adarand*, 515 U.S. at 255 (Stevens, J., dissenting).

Indeed, the post-racialism underlying *Croson* and *Adarand* is contrary to the Court's own precedents because when a state legislates to eradicate inequality, its efforts should be reviewed deferentially, as it is following the letter and spirit of the anti-subordination principle of the Fourteenth Amendment. Conversely, when the federal government exercises its power to advance the mandate of the Equal Protection Clause, by appropriate legislation, it should be accorded great deference. All positive remedial efforts to eradicate caste should have a constitutional presumption of validity rather than the scourge of skepticism.

The Fourteenth Amendment expands federal remedial power while expressly limiting such power for the states because of the legacy of state-mandated oppression after the Civil War – the "federal Government must be the primary defender of racial minorities against the states."[261] But even with these bright-line distinctions between federal and state remedial power, there is the proposition that the federal and state governments shall not stigmatize and subordinate on the basis of race, and that positive remedial measures to eradicate subordination should be upheld. *Bolling v. Sharpe*, the Fifth Amendment companion case to *Brown*, stands for this proposition – congruence means that the Fifth and Fourteenth Amendments prohibit race-based subordination by the federal and state governments,[262] but these prohibitions do not preclude the exercise of remedial power by the government.

The Court's "equal protection jurisprudence has identified a critical difference between state action that imposes burdens on a disfavored few and state action that benefits the few 'in spite of' its adverse effect on the many."[263] This is the classic majority–minority distinction, which presumptively favors the outcome of a decision where the majority imposes a burden on itself in order to advance substantive equality, but this leads to skewed results when African Americans attain a small semblance of power and exercise it in an attempt to eradicate the present-day effects of past discrimination.

This means that reverse discrimination claims will always be privileged by the Court,[264] and *Adarand* constitutionalizes this proposition through the post-racial concepts of skepticism, consistency, and congruence. Congruence rationalizes a virtually pre-determined outcome under either the Fifth or the Fourteenth Amendment – racial remedial efforts will be subject to strict scrutiny that is not "strict in theory but fatal in fact."[265] This rhetorical myth implies that there is a chance that a race-conscious remedial measure will be upheld, but this is an exceedingly rare occurrence in the Court's race jurisprudence.

---

[261] *Ibid.*
[262] *Bolling v. Sharpe*, 347 U.S. 497, 500 (1954).
[263] *Adarand*, 515 U.S. at 245–46 (Stevens, J., dissenting).
[264] *Croson*, 488 U.S. at 495–96.
[265] *Adarand*, 515 U.S. at 237.

It is possible to distinguish between invidious discrimination and positive remedial efforts by the government, particularly in a case like *Adarand*, where race was
not the sole determining factor in awarding contracts in the DBE program.[266] But
under the Court's post-racial colorblindness, there are only two instances where
race can be used and meet the nearly insurmountable standard of strict scrutiny –
where discrimination by the state can be identified with particularity and when
diversity is a compelling interest in post-secondary education.

Grutter v. Bollinger: *Diversity as a Post-Racial Process Value*

Reaffirming the ephemeral concept of diversity, introduced in *Bakke* twenty-five
years earlier, *Grutter* explicitly holds for the first time that diversity is a compelling
interest. Concluding that "strict scrutiny is not strict in theory, but fatal in fact" and
that context matters, the Court holds that the "[University of Michigan] Law School
has a compelling interest in attaining a diverse student body."[267] Race can be used
as one of many factors in a holistic review process that treats admissions candidates
as individuals, not members of racial groups.[268] The law school's program was narrowly tailored because there was a flexible review process that was not premised on a
quota, but on assembling a critical mass of students whose diverse viewpoints would
contribute to a classroom exchange of ideas.

This is a post-racial process view of equality under the Fourteenth Amendment.
The concern is not with the eradication of structural inequality, but simply access
to an ostensibly neutral process so that whites will receive the educational benefits
of diverse viewpoints from a critical mass of diverse students in a cross-cultural
exchange of understanding. *Grutter* is a First Amendment decision rather than one
rooted in the anti-subordination principle of the Fourteenth Amendment – all of
the principles espoused in the decision are post-racial and neutral: the marketplace
paradigm is the guiding principle, and the educational context is a "special niche"
in our society where post-secondary institutions must be given latitude to determine
their own destiny.[269]

There are serious doctrinal limitations to *Grutter* as an opinion because it makes
no reference to historical racial oppression, which is particularly glaring since it was
decided in the fiftieth anniversary year of *Brown v. Board of Education*. For example, it would have been instructive if the Court had referenced, or even acknowledged, the impact that *Milliken v. Bradley* had on African-American college and

---

[266] *Ibid.* at 260–62 (Stevens, J., dissenting).
[267] *Grutter v. Bollinger*, 539 U.S. 306, 328 (2003).
[268] In the undergraduate companion case, *Gratz v. Bollinger*, 539 U.S. 244, 271 (2003), the Court held
the college's race-conscious admissions program unconstitutional because it awarded fixed points
based on race, which was an inflexible approach akin to a quota that did not provide for holistic
individualized review like the law school admissions program.
[269] *Ibid.* at 328–33.

professional school students. Certainly, being relegated to the inadequate inner-city school system of Detroit would dramatically impact the educational paths of African-American students, and it would be reflected in the low numbers of college and professional school students.[270]

Grutter's exclusively forward-looking approach privileges neutrality by advancing paradigmatic post-racial themes like liberal individualism;[271] cross-racial understanding as a benefit to white majoritarian interests;[272] and deference to institutional autonomy based on the First Amendment.[273] None of these themes are structural – the present day effects of past discrimination and systemic racism are absent from the Court's analysis. This means that a historical myth is constructed about the openness of access. This access is severely limited because affirmative action, indeed diversity, must be rationalized so that white privilege remains intact; and, if it is burdened or impacted, the burden must be limited and incidental to white interests.

The most striking feature of *Grutter* is its twenty-five-year aspirational limitation on race-conscious remedies. Taking the law school at its word that it would prefer a race-neutral admissions program and that it intended to end it race-conscious program "as soon as practicable,"[274] Justice O'Connor concludes her last race opinion for the Court by stating that "We expect that 25 years from now, the use of racial preferences will no longer be necessary to further the interest approved today."[275]

This is a post-racial statement anchored in Rhetorical Neutrality: it is decidedly ahistorical because it ignores the history of school segregation and failed attempts at integration in Michigan – the historical myth reinterprets the present with no reference to the past; the definitional myth defines discrimination not as dismantling obstacles to entrance and achievement in elite post-secondary schools for African-Americans and other people of color, but in minimizing any harm to white students; and the rhetorical myth rationalizes the incremental outcome in *Grutter* as if it is a triumph for substantive equality when it simply opens a small space for students of color to perform the useful work of cross-cultural understanding and educating whites.[276]

The metaphorical time limit itself – twenty-five years since *Bakke* equals twenty-five more years until true equality is achieved and race-conscious remedies are a thing of the past – is a post-racial statement because it ignores centuries of oppression and places an arbitrary cap on the eradication of structural inequality.[277]

---

[270] Cedric Merlin Powell, *Milliken, "Neutral Principles," and Post-Racial Determinism*, 31 Harv. J. Racial & Ethnic Justice (Online) 1 (2015).

[271] *Grutter*, 539 U.S. at 326.

[272] *Ibid.* at 330.

[273] *Ibid.* at 329.

[274] *Ibid.* at 343.

[275] *Ibid.*

[276] Bryan K. Fair, *Re(Caste)ing Equality Theory: Will Grutter Survive Itself by 2028?*, 7 U. Pa. J. Const. L. 721, 761 (2005).

[277] *Grutter*, 539 U.S. at 344–46 (Ginsburg, J., concurring).

Ironically, *Grutter's* doctrinal validity in Michigan was scuttled, in *Schuette v. Coalition to Defend Affirmative Action*, when voters approved an initiative to amend the Michigan state constitution to prohibit the consideration of race in public employment, education, or contracting.

Schuette is the focus of Chapter 4, but it underscores the point developed here that *Grutter* is a process-based decision embracing post-racial neutrality and access rather than the eradication of structural inequality in post-secondary education. The Rehnquist Court's *Grutter* decision and the Roberts Court's decision in *Schuette* offer distinct illustrations of each Court's post-racial constitutionalism. Justice O'Connor's race decisions for the Rehnquist Court uniformly referenced race while trying to balance it in a way that advanced incremental progress premised on neutrality (post-racial colorblindness), and such progress had to be balanced against any burdens to whites and their settled expectations of privilege and power.[278]

When Justice O'Connor retired from the Court, Justice Kennedy became its center on race,[279] and with the ascendance of the Roberts Court, he offers an approach that focuses primarily on neutrality with the use of race as a last resort. But the doctrinal tenor of the Roberts Court is to move past race because formal equality is the touchstone. Chief Justice Roberts proclaims the Court's post-racial constitutionalism in *Parents Involved in Community Schools*, which is much more than a school integration decision – it is the doctrinal talisman of its post-racial jurisprudence.

Parents Involved begins with a post-racial edict that is the cornerstone of the Roberts Court's post-racial constitutionalism: race must be excised from the public sphere; thus, the Court conceptualizes a series of skewed rhetorical narratives that emphasize the end of formal discrimination and sufficient societal progress rendering race-conscious remedies superfluous.

---

[278] Joan Tarpley, *A Comment on Justice O'Connor's Quest for Power and Its Impact on African-American Wealth*, 53 S. C. L. Rev. 117, 120–49 (2001) (arguing that Justice O'Connor advances white privilege through shifting doctrinal contrivances).

[279] Stuart Chinn, *The Meaning of Judicial Impartiality*, 2019 Utah L. Rev. 915, 961.

3

The Roberts Court and Post-Racial Constitutionalism

The way to stop discrimination on the basis of race is to stop discriminating on the basis of race.

– Chief Justice Roberts, concluding his opinion in Parents Involved in Community Schools v. Seattle School District No. 1

The Roberts Court aggressively calibrates the parameters and vitality of white privilege – it rejects a voluntary attempt by the white majority to embrace substantive integration with the facile tautology "stop discriminating on the basis of race." This is a common analytical pattern within post-racial constitutionalism, the disruption of any remedial progress by invoking the distorted trope of racial politics. This is the same analytical device that Justice O'Connor used in overturning the City of Richmond's progressive remedial approach in *Croson*.

Applying strict scrutiny and striking down the voluntary school assignment programs in Louisville and Seattle because both school districts employed race as the predominant factor in school assignments, the Court held that the prospect of resegregation (or mere racial imbalance) was not a compelling interest.[1] Embracing liberal individualism as the touchstone of Fourteenth Amendment analysis, the Court espouses its post-racial mandate to ultimately eliminate race entirely from public decision-making.[2]

Parents Involved is much more than a decision in the long line of school cases where the Court retreats from the constitutional mandate of *Brown*; it is the post-racial constitutional edict of the Roberts Court. The Rehnquist Court drastically limited the equitable remedial powers of federal courts to adopt race-conscious remedies to dismantle segregated school systems – its colorblind mandate was to retreat altogether from school integration and rely instead on local school systems to

[1] *Parents Involved in Cmty. Schls. v. Seattle Sch. Dist. No. 1*, 551 U.S. 701, 730–33 (2007).
[2] *Ibid.* at 730.

complete the unfinished work of *Brown*. The result was resegregation and retrogression.[3] The Roberts Court's post-racial proclamation in *Parents Involved* effectively ends school desegregation – it invalidates voluntary integration remedial efforts by school boards. The clear post-racial signal to not only school boards, but any state actor, is that race should never be a consideration in governmental decision-making. This is the way to stop discrimination.

Chief Justice Roberts' tautology belies the outcome determinative reasoning of *Parents Involved* and indeed, all of the post-racial jurisprudence of the Court. With strict scrutiny, only two compelling interests, diversity and identifiable discrimination, are constitutionally cognizable, and these interests rarely validate the use of race-conscious remedies; thus, the results in the Roberts Court's race cases are virtually assured. This is post-racial determinism:

> Post-racial determinism describes the Court's formalistic adherence to a set analytical framework built upon three conceptual premises: (1) all claims for transformative racial justice are presumptively invalid, so reverse discrimination claims advanced by "injured" whites are virtually guaranteed success; (2) anti-discrimination law has largely achieved its purpose so an "expansive" view of constitutional protections must be rejected and replaced by a narrow view that ultimately leads to the reversal of these "unnecessary" race laws; and (3) the shift from colorblind to post-racial constitutionalism means that race should never be a factor in institutional decision-making—when it is, it is appropriate for the Court to intervene and "correct" the process notwithstanding the fact that the political community has chosen to pursue a race-conscious remedial approach.[4]

All of the Roberts Court's race jurisprudence advance these post-racial propositions, and they are unified by the narrative framework of Rhetorical Neutrality.

Advancing post-racialism as a normative constitutional principle, the Court deploys the three reinforcing doctrinal myths of Rhetorical Neutrality. First, the Court ignores history, and its present-day effects, and replaces it with a formalistic conception of equality. "This [post-racial] new equality emphasizes the non-existence of any invidious discrimination and instead advances the concept of formalistic equality."[5]

This doctrinal formalism runs through the entirety of the Roberts Court's race decisions. In *Parents Involved*, this means that the central meaning of *Brown* is radically reinterpreted so that the Fourteenth Amendment's anti-subordination principle is discarded and replaced with an anti-differentiation principle[6] premised on

3   DERRICK BELL, SILENT COVENANTS: BROWN V. BOARD OF EDUCATION AND THE UNFULFILLED HOPES FOR RACIAL REFORM 125–29 (2004); Boyce F. Martin, Jr., *Fifty Years Later, It's Time to Mend Brown's Broken Promise*, 2004 U. ILL. L. REV. 1023, 1210–11.

4   Cedric Merlin Powell, *Justice Thomas, Brown, and Post-Racial Determinism*, 53 WASHBURN L. J. 451, 452 (2014).

5   *Ibid.* at 453.

6   CASS R. SUNSTEIN, THE PARTIAL CONSTITUTION 340 (1993).

an individual right to choose a school in an ostensibly neutral school system. To the Roberts Court, *Brown* is a post-racial school choice decision. The Court is oblivious to the prospect of resegregation.[7] Racial balancing cannot be employed to maintain integrated schools because the ultimate goal of post-racialism is to completely eliminate any consideration of race in governmental decision-making.

Next, the Court redefines discrimination, in much the same manner as it did in the *Civil Rights Cases*, over a century earlier, as identifiable *de jure* discrimination by the state itself – societal discrimination is a natural and rational occurrence in the American polity because equality cannot be manufactured based on race. The definitional myth erases race with a formalistic standard of proof that is virtually insurmountable.

Finally, after history is obscured or dramatically revised (the historical myth) and discrimination is formalistically redefined (the definitional myth), a rhetorical myth is advanced so that structural inequality is denied, and inequality is rationalized as occurring as a natural compilation of neutral choices unconnected to any action by the state (the rhetorical myth). Since there are no *de jure* segregated schools in Seattle or Louisville, then the use of race is not remedial but an attempt to achieve "racial proportionality," which is constitutionally noxious because it is a race-based result.[8]

CHIEF JUSTICE ROBERTS' PLURALITY: THE POST-RACIAL EDICT AND RHETORICAL NEUTRALITY

Since there are only two compelling interests – diversity and identifiable discrimination – it is nearly impossible for a race-conscious remedial measure to pass constitutional muster. In most race cases, the result is already determined – this is post-racial determinism.

The Roberts Court's entire body of race jurisprudence is comprised of reverse discrimination suits brought either by aggrieved whites who argue that they have been burdened by a race-based process that undermines equal opportunity and focuses exclusively on racial windfalls to Blacks and other people of color[9] or by representatives of the state who argue that formal equality has been achieved and that further attention to race erodes the legitimacy of America's post-racial polity.

Chief Justice Roberts privileges the reverse discrimination claimant's contention by overstating the facts of the case to conclude that race was the sole factor in

7   Girardeau Spann, *Disintegration*, 46 U. Louisville L. Rev. 565, 607–608 (2008) (discussing how the Roberts Court rejected a voluntary decision by the political community itself to maintain integrated schools in order to preserve white privilege).

8   *Parents Involved in Cmty. Schls. v. Seattle Sch. Dist. No. 1*, 551 U.S. 701, 730–33 (2007).

9   Cedric Merlin Powell, *Harvesting New Conceptions of Equality: Opportunity, Results, and Neutrality*, XXXI St. Louis Univ. Pub. L. Rev. 255 (2012).

determining school assignments when race was one of several factors like parental choice, home address, and sibling's school.[10] "No student in *Parents Involved* was assigned solely because of race."[11] Thus, Chief Justice Roberts constitutionalizes the choice of white parents by refashioning *Brown* as a formalistic school choice case by "giv[ing] a seat in an oversubscribed school to a white student rather than a minority student, knowing that the likely result would be to promote segregation over integration."[12] This means that post-racial determinism guarantees that the white plaintiff's interest in her school choice will override any concerns about resegregation which is, after all, simply racial imbalance which must have a logical stopping point.[13]

There is no racially proportionate equality because racial balancing is impermissible – resegregation is a natural result of demographic choices. Professor Girardeau Spann aptly calls *Parents Involved* the Resegregation decision because it effectively overrules *Brown*; weaponizes the reverse discrimination suit of a white parent into a constitutional right of choice that dismisses the anti-subordination principle of the Fourteenth Amendment; and rationalizes resegregation as a natural occurrence because the goal of integration cannot be racialized by racial balancing.[14]

Post-racialism, then, is not neutral at all because it privileges whiteness as a normative baseline for any substantive remedy. That is, the Court's concern is not with the eradication of structural inequality but with insulating white privilege from any disruption that could be caused by the imposition of a race-conscious remedy or the result of so-called racial politics. "To stop discriminating on the basis of race" means that any perceived gain by people of color is viewed as an illegitimate racial windfall. The school assignment plan cannot burden the choice prerogatives of white parents. This component of post-racialism – the protection of white privilege – is the touchstone of the Roberts Court's race jurisprudence.[15]

Chief Justice Roberts' plurality opinion advances three mythological propositions (Rhetorical Neutrality) rooted in post-racial constitutionalism: (i) the historical myth posits that after the consent decree is lifted in Louisville in 2000, segregated schools are a thing of the past, and, since there was never any *de jure* discrimination in Seattle, there is no need for a race-conscious remedy; (ii) the definitional myth advances a literal *de jure–de facto* distinction so that discrimination is narrowly defined as identifiable state action to maintain a dual school system, and, since there is no evidence of such action, race-conscious remedial efforts, even if *voluntary*, are no more than impermissible racial balancing; and

---

[10] Wendy Parker, *Recognizing Discrimination: Lessons from White Plaintiffs*, 65 FLA. L. REV. 1871, 1877 (2013).

[11] *Ibid.*

[12] SPANN, *supra* n. 7, at 600.

[13] *Parents Involved*, 551 U.S. at 731–33.

[14] SPANN, *supra* n. 7, at 600–607.

[15] *Ibid.* at 607–608, 608 ("Therefore, the Supreme Court is now using the constitutional concept of equality to perpetuate racial discrimination").

(iii) the rhetorical myth rationalizes structural inequality as an exaggeration, and, while "societal discrimination" does exist, it is irremediable without a clear connection to state action. These are the underlying principles of the Court's post-racial edict.

The Historical Myth: School Segregation Ends in 2000

It is counterintuitive that the same democratic ideals underlying the compelling interest of diversity, acknowledged by the Court in *Grutter*, are inapplicable in the secondary school context. It appears that the First Amendment has a special application – a "special niche" – in the post-secondary school context, but not in elementary and high schools.[16] The only other compelling interest in the Court's race jurisprudence is "remedying the effects of past discrimination."[17] Where there is no identifiable *de jure* discrimination, the use of race-conscious remedies is constitutionally noxious. Without a compelling diversity interest or identifiable discrimination by the state itself, the voluntary school assignment plan designed to preserve an integrated school system is doomed to constitutional oblivion. This result is virtually predetermined.[18]

The Roberts Court adopts formalistic equality as the guiding principle of its race jurisprudence – since state-mandated segregation has been formally eliminated from the school systems by the constitutional mandate of *Brown*, there is no remedial basis for a race-conscious school integration plan in the absence of past intentional discrimination by the state itself. To the Court, neither the Seattle nor the Louisville public school system had a compelling interest justifying the use of race-conscious plans because Seattle public schools were never segregated by law; and, while Louisville public schools were *de jure* segregated, the desegregation decree ordering the schools to achieve unitary status was dissolved in 2000, twenty-five years after it was initially entered.[19]

The *de jure–de facto* distinction advances a historical fiction that because state-mandated discrimination was readily identifiable in the South, the discrimination in the North was somehow merely incidental and less invidious. This historical artifice has been thoroughly debunked.[20] By recasting history so that *Brown* is merely a neutral school choice decision, the Roberts Court ignores the inevitability of

---

[16] *Parents Involved*, 551 U.S. at 722–25.

[17] *Ibid.* at 720.

[18] Powell, *supra* n. 4, at 452, 454–55 (discussing the underlying normative principles of post-racialism, including post-racial determinism, which means that any use of race will be presumptively invalid even if the political community voluntarily chooses to employ race as a means to advance transformative social change).

[19] *Parents Involved*, 551 U.S. at 720–21.

[20] Brian Purnell and Jeanne Theoharis with Komozi Woodard, The Strange Careers of the Jim Crow North: Segregation and Struggle Outside of the South (2019).

resegregation[21] and simply focuses on incidental racial imbalance which is natural in a school system that is *de facto* segregated. To advance the historical myth, the Roberts Court ignores its own precedent to constitutionalize the *de jure–de facto* distinction as a constitutional prerequisite for a permissible integration plan.

The Court buries significant doctrinal precedent in a footnote[22] obscuring its authoritative resonance and applicability to *Parents Involved*. None of the Court's school decisions were initially conceptualized along a rigid and formalistic intent line; instead, the focus was on the eradication of dual school systems "root and branch."[23] It was not until 1974, twenty years after *Brown*, that the Court began to erect discriminatory intent as a nearly impenetrable proof barrier in school cases. *Parents Involved* completes this work – preserving white interests and discarding the anti-subordination principle of the Fourteenth Amendment. Applying the virtually fatal strict scrutiny test, the Court often notes that context matters, but it is rare for the Court to fully acknowledge the structural dynamics of context.[24] *Parents Involved* is historically acontextual.

Parents Involved is a dramatic departure from the legacy of *Brown*. It places a temporal limit on the existence of segregated schools – state-mandated segregation ended in 2000 in Louisville and it never existed in Seattle simply because it was never proclaimed by the state. This convenient historical distortion fuels the historical myth that the present-day effects of past discrimination are irrelevant, and that some inequality is to be expected as the natural result of neutral choices.

The Definitional Myth: The De Jure–De Facto Distinction and Racial Balancing

Advancing the Court's historical illusion that no remediable discrimination exists in the absence of intentional state action, the Court still must assess the good faith voluntary efforts of the political community to ensure that resegregation does not occur. It would seem that the Court would simply defer to the decision of the political community, especially given its endorsement in previous decisions. But post-racial constitutionalism necessarily means that all consideration of race must be eliminated from public decision-making because substantive progress cannot unduly burden white interests. This has been true since the First Reconstruction, and is no less different today.

---

[21] Jen Dev and Liz Brazile, In *Seattle, School Segregation Is Actually Getting Worse*, Crosscut, March 29, 2019 https://crosscut.com/2019/03/seattle-school-segregation-actually-getting-worse; John Eligon, *Busing Worked in Louisville. So Why Are Its Schools Becoming More Segregated?* New York Times, July 28, 2019, www.nytimes.com/2019/07/28/us/busing-louisville-student-segregation.html.

[22] *Parents Involved*, 551 U.S. at 721 n. 10.

[23] *Green v. Cnty School Bd*, 391 U.S. 430, 438 (1968).

[24] *Parents Involved*, 551 U.S. at 725 (noting that context matters but concluding that *Grutter* is inapplicable to *Parents Involved*).

Chief Justice Roberts' post-racial proclamation is a cornerstone of white privilege. "Stop discriminating on the basis of race" means stop thinking about race and it will cease to exist. Race is transparent and invisible to whites,[25] so systemic racism and structural inequality are virtually non-existent, which means that African Americans and other people of color must proffer definitive proof that discrimination exists while it is presumed that discrimination exists when the plaintiff is white and advancing a reverse discrimination suit.[26] This explains the inconsistent application of the discriminatory intent requirement and how the definitional myth – how discrimination is defined so narrowly or obscured so much that it ceases to exist – is advanced by the Court's post-racialism.

Another aspect of the *de jure–de facto* distinction's formalism is how it trivializes the significance of structural inequality and the stigmatizing effects of segregation. Chief Justice Roberts' opinion conflates diversity, racial proportionality, and integration as impermissible race-conscious outcomes which distort what should be the neutral school assignment choices of parents. Since there is no constitutional imperative on the part of school boards to constantly adjust school assignments to preserve integrated schools, then racial imbalance is a natural and neutral outcome unconnected to any discriminatory state action. This, of course, is a fundamental misreading of *Brown*.

The Roberts Court is willing to tolerate racial imbalance, which is really resegregation, in order to achieve the ultimate goal of post-racial constitutionalism: "eliminating entirely from governmental decision-making such irrelevant factors as a human being's race."[27] By invoking a new racial proportionality test, the Court discards the anti-subordination principle at the core of *Brown*, and instead advances the post-racial proposition that race-conscious remedial efforts must have a stopping point because, even if there is inequality, race should never have been used in public decision-making except in the pursuit of diversity, which is limited to the post-secondary school context, and clearly identifiable discrimination by the state, which is absent in Louisville and Seattle.

In *Parents Involved*, the definitional myth is deployed to transform *Brown* into a post-racial decision. That is, all the clearly defined interests in dismantling a caste-based dual school system are cast aside by conflating these substantive interests into little more than racial balancing in the pursuit of some undefined racial proportionality. Specifically, the Court concludes that there is no compelling interest

---

[25] STEPHANIE WILDMAN WITH MARGALYNNE ARMSTRONG, ADRIENNE D. DAVIS, AND TRINA GRILLO, PRIVILEGE REVEALED: HOW INVISIBLE PREFERENCE UNDERMINES AMERICA (1996).

[26] Parker, *supra* n. 10 at 1874, 1882–87 (discussing how the Roberts Court shifts discrimination analysis from substantive harm against African Americans and people of color to "process discrimination" protecting the interests of whites from being burdened with no showing of discriminatory intent – post-racialism presumes that any substantive gains for African Americans are tainted by race).

[27] *Parents Involved*, 551 U.S. at 730 (citations omitted).

to racial balancing. This deceptive analytical formulation is based on the notion that the entire school assignment process is based on race because the goal is some constitutionally flawed absolute racial proportionality in the school system. The Court is essentially saying that any voluntary attempts, by the political community, to preserve integrated schools is nothing more than an unconstitutional quota system designed with a particular racial result in mind.

The legacy of *Brown* is significantly diluted by the Roberts Court so that it becomes a decision about school choice – whether individual students are free to choose whatever school they wish to attend regardless of their race – and if the choice of a white student is burdened, in any way, the substantive mandate of *Brown* must be ignored to affirm the reverse discrimination claim of the aggrieved student. There is no diversity interest here, not only because *Grutter* is inapplicable, but because "[h]owever closely related race-based assignments may be to achieving racial balance, that itself cannot be the goal whether labeled 'racial diversity' or anything else."[28] In fact, "avoidance of racial isolation," "racial integration," and "school desegregation" are all semantic labels connected to impermissible racial balancing because there is no constitutional requirement that each and every school in a district must be desegregated.[29] The formalism of the *de jure–de facto* distinction provides the perfect cover for the Court to ignore the inevitability of resegregation. And this has certainly come to pass.[30]

Under the Roberts Court's post-racial edict, *Brown* becomes a decision about neutrality and equal access, and there is no reference to the continuing stigmatizing impact of the color-line, what message separate schools sends to students languishing in the duality of inferior schools,[31] and how school boards are empowered to eradicate segregated schools by transforming dual school systems into integrated unitary systems.[32] As recast by the Roberts Court, *Brown* is about the symmetrical

---

[28] *Ibid.* at 733.

[29] *Ibid.* at 732.

[30] Gary Orfield, Erica Frankenburg, Jongyeon Ee, and Jennifer B. Ayscue, *Harming Our Common Future: America's Segregated Schools 65 Years after Brown*, May 10, 2019, www.civilrightsproject.ucla.edu/research/k-12-education/integration-and-diversity/harming-our-common-future-americas-segregated-schools-65-years-after-brown.

[31] Laurence H. Tribe, American Constitutional Law § 12–6, at 821 (2d ed. 1988) (discussing *Brown* as communicating a message of Black inferiority); *accord* Charles R. Lawrence III, *If He Hollers Let Him Go: Regulating Racist Speech on Campus*, 1990 Duke L. J. 431, 439–40 (noting that segregation conveys the idea of Black inferiority and stigmatization). Rucker C. Johnson with Alexander Nazaryan, Children of the Dream: Why School Integration Works 218–21 (2019) (discussing the political backlash and anti-integration litigation efforts in Louisville, Kentucky). Today, there is a debate over a school choice plan with no reference to resegregation and structural inequality. Jess Clark, *As JCPS Moves Forward with Student Assignment Plan, Critics Worry about Resegregation*, WFPL (April 12, 2022), https://wfpl.org/as-jcps-moves-forward-with-student-assignment-plan-critics-worry-about-resegregation/.

[32] Powell, *supra* n. 4, at 457–61 (discussing how the Roberts Court advances neutrality through its re-interpretation of *Brown*).

right of white students not to be inconvenienced by the political community's desire to preserve integrated schools.

The "exclusion"[33] of the white student in *Parents Involved* sends no stigmatizing message of inferiority and stigmatization; indeed, the white student's claim is buttressed by white privilege – although there were several neutral factors considered in assigning students, race was presumed to have predominated the process because the white student did not get his first-choice school. The Court's own analysis belies this proposition.

When Chief Justice Roberts discusses racial imbalance and proportionality, he emphasizes how race should not be used in the pursuit of perpetual racial balancing to maintain integrated schools. Because the Seattle and Louisville school plans are connected to the demographics of their respective districts, Chief Justice Roberts concludes that Seattle, with its white (31 to 51 percent) – non-white (49 to 69 percent) binary, and Louisville, with its Black (15 to 50 percent) – white binary, are unconstitutional racial balancing plans with no educational or societal benefits.[34] Yet this analysis changes dramatically when he reviews the impact that the use of race has on school assignments.

By characterizing the demographic goals of the school districts as impermissible quotas adopted to preserve some inflated standard of racial proportionality, Chief Justice Roberts overemphasizes the impact of race in school assignments; paradoxically, this leads him to conclude that individual race classifications have a minimal impact on school assignments – a large number of students do not transfer to other schools so the demographic goals set by the districts are not substantially altered.[35] Ironically, the Court penalizes the school boards because race has a minimal impact in school assignments. It is odd that a post-racial Court would reason that since race had a minimal impact on school assignments, then the use of race in such a manner is unconstitutional. Perhaps recognizing this incongruity, Chief Justice Roberts adds a limitation to the Court's expansive post-racialism, stating that "[w]hile we do not suggest that *greater* use of race would be preferable, the minimal impact of the districts' racial classifications on school enrollment casts doubt on the necessity of using racial classifications."[36]

Rather it would seem that race's minimal effect on school assignments would suggest that race did not predominate in the decision-making process – there were other factors at work "in subtle and indirect ways."[37] So, the conclusion that the post-racial plurality opinion posits that the districts failed to consider race-neutral alternatives

---

[33] *Parents Involved*, 551 U.S. at 719 (noting that the student was allowed to transfer to the school that he was previously denied admission to).

[34] *Ibid.* at 726.

[35] *Ibid.* at 733–34.

[36] *Ibid.* at 734 (emphasis in original).

[37] *Ibid.* (*citing* Brief for Respondents).

seems contrafactual: if race had a minimal effect on school assignments, the assignment programs were working for the vast majority of students, and the political community had agreed that it would be committed to ensuring that resegregation did not occur, then there was no need to overturn the school assignment plans.

But the plans were overturned because the Court decided that they were unnecessary because segregation ended in 2000 in Louisville, with the lifting of the consent decree, and it never existed in Seattle because it was not explicitly mandated by the state. Post-racial constitutionalism is actively engaged in ignoring the structural dynamics of race – systemic racism and structural inequality are minimized as merely societal conventions, as in the early race decisions like the *Civil Rights Cases* and *Plessy* or conflated with irremediable societal discrimination. Chief Justice Roberts' plurality opinion fits squarely in this post-racial canon. The Rhetorical Myth rationalizes the denial of structural inequality by obscuring the present-day effects of past discrimination. The possibility of resegregation is a natural occurrence because formal discrimination has been eliminated from American society.

The Rhetorical Myth and the Denial of Structural Inequality

In his condescendingly cynical post-racial opinion, Chief Justice Roberts casually casts aside the substantive legacy of *Brown*, the anti-subordination principle of the Fourteenth Amendment, and the core values of education itself. The Rhetorical Myth constitutionalizes formal equality so that substantive equality is no longer the normative principle underlying the Fourteenth Amendment – the primary concern of the amendment now is to provide a post-racial rationale for any burden on innocent whites and the disruption of their expectation interest in privilege.[38]

Thus,

> The Court never adopts a substantive approach to race; the concern is not the eradication of caste under the Fourteenth Amendment. The unifying theme in *all* of its race decisions is either the accommodation of white interests through neutral [post-racial] rhetoric or the outright preservation of white privilege. Rhetorical Neutrality, with its underlying myths [historical, definitional, and rhetorical], serves to reinforce white privilege and to provide justifications (or some "legitimacy") when these interests are impacted by race-conscious remedies for African-Americans (or other people of color).[39]

---

[38] Helen Norton, *The Supreme Court's Post-racial Turn Towards A Zero-Sum Understanding of Equality*, 52 Wm. & Mary L. Rev. 197 (2010) (theorizing zero-sum understanding of equality where post-racial "success" means that any recognition of the continuing effects of structural inequality means "discrimination" against whites).

[39] Cedric Merlin Powell, *Rhetorical Neutrality: Colorblindness, Frederick Douglass, and Inverted Critical Race Theory*, 56 Clev. St. L. Rev. 823, 860 (2008).

The rhetorical tenor of post-racial constitutionalism is rooted in formalism – state-mandated oppression is always a thing of the past whether it is in 1883 (the *Civil Rights Cases*), 2007 (*Parents Involved*), or 2022. Race can no longer be a factor in public decision-making because to consider it would be a new form of racial discrimination. "The way to stop discrimination on the basis of race is to stop discriminating in the basis of race." There is a perverse symmetry between invidious state discrimination and positive race-conscious remedial approaches adopted voluntarily by the political community.

Formalistically, *Brown* is not about eradicating the colorline and its stigmatizing message of exclusion, but simply that race cannot be used by the state in school assignments for white or Black students. Of course, this make weight symmetry ignores the fact that whites have never received the message of inferiority as Blacks have through separate and inferior schools.[40] Reading Chief Justice Roberts' plurality opinion, one almost expects him to quote directly from *Plessy* that any stigma is in the minds of Black students,[41] it is not the product of state action because there is no *de jure* discrimination in Louisville or Seattle.

Taking this argument to its illogical conclusion, then the voluntary continuation of a school integration plan "stigmatizes" the white student whose choice is dishonored – race taints the process and the white student because it is impossible to distinguish benign from invidious discrimination by the state. In this manner, *Plessy* and *Parents Involved* are post-racial decisions, they deny the significance of race as a defining feature in American life and instead focus on superficial access. The disconcerting paradox is that the colorline is upheld in *Plessy*; and, although it is overturned in *Brown*, *Parents Involved* revives it by placing an individual white student's interest above the will of the political community to avoid resegregation.[42]

Discounting the existence of structural inequality, Chief Justice Roberts advances several neutral doctrinal propositions to refute Justice Breyer's comprehensive and powerful dissent which seeks to reclaim the substantive mandate of *Brown* and its progeny. These ostensibly neutral propositions serve to reify post-racialism by conceptualizing rationales for the permanence of structural inequality. So, the lasting legacy of segregation is equated with simple racial imbalance caused by "neutral" private choices unconnected to *de jure* segregation; *Brown* and the broad equitable remedial mandate of *Swann* are reinterpreted as non-binding precedent because they

---

[40] *Parents Involved*, 551 U.S. at 799 (Stevens, J., dissenting) ("The Chief Justice fails to note that it was only black schoolchildren who were so ordered; indeed, the history books do not tell stories of white children struggling to attend black schools").

[41] *Plessy v. Ferguson*,163 U.S. 537, 551 (1896).

[42] Spann, *supra* n. 7, at 615 ("The *Plessy* Supreme Court had an understanding of equality that permitted the maintenance of racial segregation, and the Roberts Supreme Court seems intent on reviving that understanding").

were decided before the Court applied strict scrutiny indiscriminately to all race conscious remedies; diversity is a compelling interest only when the Court chooses to recognize it outside of the elementary and secondary school context; and local control is meaningless unless it can be exercised neutrally to advance post-racialism.[43]

Post-racial constitutionalism exaggerates societal progress – there is a finite ending point for remediable discrimination – and understates the existence of structural inequality. Indeed, any reference to race is deemed irrelevant and illegitimate, and inequality is accepted as an inevitable outcome of a post-racial society. The substantial likelihood that resegregation will result from the Court's opinion is viewed as "greatly exaggerate[ed]," "unjustifiably alarmist," and hyperbolically "cataclysmic."[44] Chief Justice Roberts' visceral reaction to Justice Breyer's dissent is quite telling for it foreshadows the Roberts Court's active engagement with dismantling anti-discrimination law as unnecessarily race based. Chief Justice Roberts adopts the same blistering rhetorical tone in response to Justice Sotomayor's dissent in *Schuette*, which is discussed in Chapter 4. A major tenet of post-racial constitutionalism is its aggressive dismissal of valid claims premised on the effects of structural inequality; it is distinctly anti-structuralist in its analytical posture.

Perhaps the most graphic example of the Court's denial of the existence of structural inequality is how *Brown* is reconceptualized as a post-racial decision – it is simply a decision about neutral access to education for all students, not the eradication of caste-based oppression. Quoting the counsel for the *Brown* plaintiffs and later federal judge, Robert Carter, Chief Justice Roberts offers a particularly audacious reinterpretation of *Brown* characterizing it as a case about the *personal interest* of the plaintiffs to be assigned to schools on a *nonracial basis*.[45] The decision was not about "the inequality of the facilities but the fact of legally separating children on the basis of race on which the Court relied to find a constitutional violation in 1954 [and in 2007]."[46] Reading race out of the decision, *Brown* was a simple school choice case without reference to the separate and inferior school facilities where Black students attended schools.

This acontextual depiction of *Brown* is the embodiment of Rhetorical Neutrality: history is ignored; discrimination is defined so formalistically so that it does not exist; and there is a rationalizing narrative that ignores the white supremacy underpinning *Brown* and instead privileges the whiteness of individual choice. The pernicious shadow of *Plessy* is conveniently read out of this interpretation, it is as if *Plessy* were not overruled, and that the color-line was simply moved so that all students could attend schools together – there is no mention of the stigmatizing effects of segregation or of the resurgence of resegregation.[47]

---

[43] *Parents Involved*, 551 U.S. at 737–45.
[44] *Ibid.* at 745.
[45] *Ibid.* at 747.
[46] *Ibid.* at 746.
[47] Except to minimize its re-occurrence as unconnected to state action. *Ibid.* at 736.

Brown is simply about neutral school assignments, for whatever reason, and since race was used, the school districts in Louisville and Seattle violated the post-racial Constitution envisioned by Chief Justice Roberts:

> Before *Brown*, schoolchildren were told where they could and could not go to school based on the color of their skin. The school districts in these cases have not carried the heavy burden of demonstrating that we should allow this once again—even for very different reasons.[48]

White children were *not* told where to go, no colorline prohibited their movements anywhere in society, and it is no accident that Chief Justice Roberts simply ignores this fact of systemic racism and structural inequality. This is the essence of post-racial constitutionalism. The euphemistic, "very different reasons" equates systemic oppression with voluntary remedial efforts to avoid resegregation. The formalism underlying post-racial constitutionalism is absolute: "The way to stop discriminating on the basis of race is to stop discriminating on the basis of race."

By contrast to Chief Justice Roberts' absolute post-racial formalism,[49] Justice Kennedy offers a post-racial approach anchored in colorblind neutrality which is an even narrower version of the Rehnquist Court's post-racial colorblindness. *Parents Involved* represents Justice Kennedy's emergence as the center of the Court's race jurisprudence upon Justice O'Connor's retirement from the Court and the ascendence of the Roberts Court in 2005. But Justice Kennedy's approach is fundamentally distinct from Justice O'Connor's colorblind balancing approach.

JUSTICE KENNEDY'S CONCURRENCE: POST-RACIAL NEUTRALITY AND THE ILLUSION OF HOPE

Supplying the fifth and decisive vote to Chief Justice Roberts' post-racial plurality overturning the Louisville and Seattle school assignment plans, Justice Kennedy's concurrence harkens his arrival as the Roberts Court's doctrinal author of post-racial constitutionalism.[50] His opinions mediate between the absolute post-racialism

---

[48] *Ibid.* at 747.

[49] MARICA COYLE, THE ROBERTS COURT: THE STRUGGLE FOR THE CONSTITUTION 46 (2013) (*quoting* Michael Klarman describing conservative racial ideology as embracing a "narrow, formalist conception of what counts as race discrimination; abhor[ing] the use of racial preferences, whether benignly motivated or not; and deem[ing] this nation's ugly history of white supremacy as something more to be repudiated than remedied").

[50] Justice Kennedy writes the opinions in *Schuette v. Coalition to Defend Affirmative Action* discussed in Chapter 4; *Fisher v. University of Texas* discussed in Chapter 5; *Ricci v. DeStefano* discussed in Chapter 6; and *Texas Dep't of Housing v. Inclusive Communities* discussed in Chapter 7. Chief Justice Roberts authored the decision in *Shelby County v. Holder*, discussed in Chapter 8, gutting section 4 of the Voting Rights Act, and ushering in the advent of ostensibly neutral voting reform conceptualized as remedial attempts to eradicate fraud; but, in essence, they are bald attempts at voter suppression.

of Chief Justice Roberts' approach and the substantive anti-subordination principle advanced by Justices Breyer, Ginsburg, Sotomayor, and Stevens.

Ironically, Justice Kennedy embraces the same simplistic circularity of Chief Justice Roberts' post-racial postulate – "To make race matter so that it might not matter later may entrench the very prejudices we seek to overcome"[51] – simultaneously acknowledging the existence of systemic racism, only to diminish its existence in liberal individualistic terms. For example, he refers to *Plessy* as a "grievous error,"[52] to be sure, but he nevertheless defines state-mandated subjugation symmetrically as "official classification by race applicable to all persons who sought to use railway carriages."[53] This formalism rings true only if the colorline applies equally to "all persons" – the Blacks on the other side of the color-line in segregated carriages and schools certainly would not see the official classification this way, because whites were free to cross the colorline anytime and anywhere, and Blacks were imprisoned on the other side of it.

Post-racial constitutionalism privileges symmetry – invidious caste-based oppression is the same as positive voluntary race-conscious remedial efforts – over the reality of systemic oppression and structural racism. While Justice Kennedy embraces some of the formalism underlying post-racial constitutionalism, he rejects the notion that race can never be a factor in decision-making because while "race should not matter; the reality is that too often it does."[54] This means that there must be a critical distinction between the invidious use of race by the state and race-conscious remedial efforts that do not define individuals by race.

But remedial decision-making power is premised on the *de jure–de facto* distinction, and while Justice Kennedy notes that the "remedial rules are different"[55] when there is a *de facto* segregated school system, he nevertheless rejects a defining principle of post-racial constitutionalism that *de facto* segregation is an incidental occurrence that cannot be remedied. *De facto* segregation and racial isolation cannot be ignored, and Justice Kennedy reasons that "The plurality opinion is at least open to the interpretation that the Constitution requires school districts to ignore the problem of *de facto* resegregation in schooling. I cannot endorse that conclusion."[56] Thus, Justice Kennedy's analytical approach is not fully rooted in the absolute post-racial constitutionalism of Chief Justice Roberts, but it nevertheless produces the same result while being ostensibly more open to the use of race as a factor in remedying segregated schools.

By embracing most of the literalism of the *de jure–de facto* distinction, Justice Kennedy's concurrence essentially leads to the same result although it is relatively

---

[51] *Parents Involved*, 551 U.S. at 782 (Kennedy, J., concurring).
[52] *Ibid.* at 788.
[53] *Ibid.*
[54] *Ibid.* at 787.
[55] *Ibid.* at 796.
[56] *Ibid.* at 788.

less extreme than Chief Justice Roberts' post-racial edict. The only time that race can be considered, in the absence of identifiable discrimination or the compelling interest of diversity, is when race-neutral alternatives are fully considered and shown to be ineffective in avoiding resegregation.

Advancing post-racial neutrality as a normative principle, Justice Kennedy's concurrence holds that race-conscious remedies can still be used, and this is true superficially, but only after race-neutral alternatives have been fully explored. Race can be used, but only as a last resort.[57] To Justice Kennedy, factors such as "strategic site selection of new schools; drawing attendance zones with general recognition of the demographics of neighborhoods; allocating resources for special programs; recruiting students and faculty in a targeted fashion; and tracking enrollments, performance, and other statistics by race"[58] are factors that are subtly race-conscious but without defining individuals on the basis of race. These race-neutral proxies have proven unsuccessful because they focus on incremental factors that are not directly related to dismantling structural barriers that exclude students of color – this is why resegregation is a consequence of the plurality and concurring decisions.[59]

While acknowledging that there is a compelling interest in avoiding racial isolation, this seems to be a derivative approach to the Court's holding that diversity is a compelling interest in *Grutter*. The Kennedy concurrence offers no indication of what an acceptable race-neutral remedial approach is, specifically, how many race neutral alternatives should be considered, and when race can be considered as a last resort. Indeed, there is no articulation of what evidentiary support is needed to support a school district's assertion that the only way to avoid racial isolation is to consider race in school assignments. The hope offered in the concurrence is fleeting and illusory.

Post-racialism overstates neutrality, and Justice Kennedy's concurrence shares much of the same hyperbolic narrative tone as Chief Justice Roberts' plurality opinion. Envisioning the school assignment plans in Louisville and Seattle as a racial board game, Justice Kennedy characterizes students as "racial chits" traded along a racist school assignment cataloguing system.[60] This bears no resemblance to the voluntary school assignment plans under review in *Parents Involved*. Justice Kennedy's previous discussion of race and racism is rendered hollow and virtually meaningless because he presumes, as all post-racial constitutionalists do, the validity of the reverse discrimination claim advanced under a post-racial interpretation of *Brown*. Post-racial constitutionalism eschews any consideration of structural inequality in analyzing claims of discrimination, so formalistic equality is the guiding principle under Chief Justice Roberts' absolute post-racialism and under Justice Kennedy's

---

[57] *Ibid.* at 790.
[58] *Ibid.* at 789.
[59] *See supra* nn. 21 and 38.
[60] *Parents Involved*, 551 U.S. at 798 (Kennedy, J., concurring).

"race as a last resort" post-racialism – Chief Justice Roberts discounts the continuing effects of past discrimination; and, while Justice Kennedy acknowledges the present day effects of past discrimination (racial isolation), neutrality means that anti-discrimination claims are viewed individualistically, not structurally. Both the plurality and concurrence advance liberal individualism – the Constitution protects individuals, not racial groups. And while Justice Kennedy concedes that there is a "frustrating duality" in the Equal Protection Clause[61] – the prohibition against invidious state mandated race-based oppression and a corresponding prohibition of *any* consideration of race even if it is ameliorative – he offers a tautology revised slightly from that posited in the plurality: "The idea that if race is the problem, race is the instrument with which to solve it cannot be accepted as an analytical leap forward."[62] The hollow hope of Justice Kennedy's concurrence is that it "affirms" the legacy of *Brown* while simultaneously reinterpreting it as a post-racial decision. This is not the legacy of *Brown*, and Justice Breyer's sweeping and powerful dissent seeks to reclaim that legacy.

JUSTICE BREYER'S DISSENT: THE STRUCTURAL *BROWN*

Justice Breyer's wide-ranging dissent offers a searing critique of Chief Justice Roberts' absolute post-racialism and the neutral rhetoric underlying *Parents Involved*. His structuralist approach is a doctrinal counterpoint to the rhetorical myths employed by the Court. Identifying the structural dynamics of systemic school segregation in Louisville and Seattle, Justice Breyer's dissent unpacks the contrived formalism of the *de jure–de facto* distinction.[63] Both school systems were "highly segregated in fact."[64] This sobering reality was not an accident, but directly traceable to "state law separating the races"[65] in Louisville; and, in Seattle, by *"school board policies and actions that had helped to create, maintain, and aggravate racial segregation."*[66] And the possibility of resegregation was all but inevitable given this history.[67] Both school systems sought to avoid this by adopting assignment plans that progressively evolved, depending on specific developments in their systems, and diminished the explicit use of race.[68] Thus, under any of the Court's previous decisions extoling the value of local control and decision-making power for school systems, these plans should have been upheld.[69]

---

[61] *Ibid.* at 797.

[62] *Ibid.*

[63] *Ibid.* at 820–21 (Breyer, J., dissenting) (discussing the futility of relying upon a finding of *de jure* segregation as a remedial prerequisite). "No case of this Court has ever relied upon the *de jure/de facto* distinction in order to limit what a school district is voluntarily allowed to do." *Ibid.* at 844.

[64] *Ibid.* at 806.

[65] *Ibid.* at 806.

[66] *Ibid.* at 807 (emphasis in original).

[67] *Ibid.* at 807–23.

[68] *Ibid.* at 855.

[69] *Ibid.* at 823–37.

Justice Breyer reclaims the meaning of *Brown* – it means that the colorline is eradicated, society must be open and inclusive, and there is an affirmative duty to eradicate dual school systems. Separate is not equal, and for integration to be meaningful, school boards are empowered to address the inevitability of resegregation.[70]

This notion of remedial power is rooted in the structural conception of *Brown*. Justice Breyer illuminates the structural *Brown* by positing three defining elements that comprise the compelling interest of substantive integration – the elimination of racial isolation in the schools and the recurring systemic effects that could ultimately lead to resegregation – the historical and remedial element; the educational element; and the democratic element.

(i) *The Historical and Remedial Elements:*
The Anti-Subordination Principle

Locating the remedial mandate of *Brown* squarely within structuralism – the stupefying categorical labels of the plurality like the *de jure–de facto* distinction, racial balancing, proportionality, and imbalance, and societal discrimination are discarded – Justice Breyer underscores the structural factors that perpetuate structural inequality. He connects the present day effects of school isolation and resegregation to past discrimination explicitly mandated by the state and implicitly maintained by policies and practices intrinsic to a system of subordination.

Noting that hyper-segregated schools were the "result of legal or administrative policies that facilitated racial segregation in public schools,"[71] Justice Breyer defines the historical and remedial element of *Brown* as

> [A]n interest in continuing to combat remnants of segregation caused in whole or in part by these school-related policies, which have often affected not only schools, but also housing patterns, employment practices, economic conditions, and social attitudes. It is an interest in maintaining hard-won gains. And it has its roots in preventing what may become the *de facto* resegregation of America's public schools.[72]

Under this structural definition of *Brown*, the legislative history of the Fourteenth Amendment as an anti-caste and anti-subordination amendment is embraced, the present-day effects of past discrimination are the remedial threshold that activates local power to combat segregation, and school boards have broad powers to combat discrimination *in fact*,[73] which is the result of intentional state action and ostensibly

---

[70] *Ibid.* at 862–68.
[71] *Ibid.* at. 838.
[72] *Ibid.*
[73] Lani Guinier, *Foreword: Demosprudence Through Dissent*, 122 Harv. L. Rev. 4, 35–39 (2008) (discussing Justice Breyer's dissent as a rebuke to the Court's protection of white majoritarian interests and a call to school boards to fully exercise their powers to preserve *Brown*'s legacy).

neutral procedures designed to perpetuate the *status quo*, leading to resegregation (and this process has been anything but "gradual").

This is a clear break from the discriminatory perpetrator intent–driven jurisprudence of post-racial constitutionalism. And it also disrupts the historical myth's post-racial revisionism – the Fourteenth Amendment is a race-conscious amendment[74] that was enacted after the Civil War to *include* the newly emancipated slaves in the American polity. Any state action or societal condition that is a remnant of that oppressive legacy can be ameliorated by considering race and how it is used to subordinate. There is a bright-line distinction between invidious discrimination and positive remedial efforts to eradicate subordination.[75]

(ii) *The Educational Element: Substantive Integration*

It is counterintuitive that diversity is a compelling interest in the post-secondary school context, but not in the elementary and secondary school context where it is needed most. This is a direct result of the rigidity of the *de jure–de facto* distinction and is an instructive example of the definitional myth. Formalistic definitions of discrimination obscure the existence of structural inequality. To the post-racial plurality, there is nothing to remedy in the absence of *de jure* segregation or a post-secondary school diversity interest. But, again, this dramatically illustrates the lack of a structural perspective – Justice Breyer pinpoints "an interest in overcoming the adverse educational effects produced by and associated with highly segregated schools."[76]

Building upon the historical and remedial element, the educational element focuses on the present-day effects of segregated schools. The bedrock proposition underlying *Brown* is that separate is inherently unequal and that integrated schools provide full educational opportunity[77] to those who have been historically stigmatized by the colorline (the state-based message of Black inferiority) and oppressed by its lingering effects (the highly segregated schools). Educational opportunity is not about simple access; the opportunity must be meaningful. Specifically, substantive integration means closing the achievement gap and fostering academic gains in a racially diverse school with school boards that are empowered to maintain integrated schools amid all the systemic factors that lead to resegregation.

---

[74] Nathaniel R. Jones, *The Sisyphean Impact on Houstonian Jurisprudence*, 69 U. CINN. L. REV. 435, 438–51 (2001) (discussing the race-conscious Reconstruction era and enactment of the Fourteenth Amendment by a Congress that was race-conscious).

[75] *Parents Involved*, 551 U.S. at 862–63 (Breyer, J., dissenting) ("That is why the Equal Protection Clause outlaws invidious discrimination but does not similarly forbid all use of race-conscious criteria").

[76] *Ibid.*

[77] Kimberly Jenkins Robinson (ed.), A FEDERAL RIGHT TO EDUCATION: FUNDAMENTAL QUESTIONS FOR OUR DEMOCRACY 217–18 (2019) (discussing the significance of *Brown* in eradicating unequal and inferior education for Blacks; arguing for education as a fundamental right; and noting the intransigence of *de facto* segregation).

(iii) *The Democratic Element: Pluralism and the Political Community*

Obviously, the plurality's cramped conception of compelling interest is belied by Justice Breyer's structural interpretation of the core values underlying *Brown* and the third element, the democratic element, is rooted in substantive diversity, not simply a tolerance for difference so that whites receive an educational benefit but "an interest in producing an educational environment that reflects the 'pluralistic society' in which our children will live."[78] All of the elements combine to form the compelling interest of school integration. This is much more than simple "diversity," it is dismantling structural inequality in school systems by acknowledging the fundamental nature of education.

The democratic element means that schools should reflect the very values that they seek to educate about and instill in their students – schools are critical spaces for building reflective insights, a sense of community and civic identity, and a life's purpose. Indeed, the voluntary school assignment programs adopted by Louisville and Seattle are examples of the democratic element – the political community in both cities recognized that an inclusive education is the best education, and that resegregation must not be permitted to re-emerge under the guise of recurring racial imbalance or societal discrimination. Justice Breyer notes that there is much more at stake here:

> The compelling interest at issue here, then, includes an effort to eradicate the remnants, not of general "societal discrimination" … but of primary and secondary segregation … it includes an effort to create school environments that provide better educational opportunities for all children; it includes an effort to help create citizens better prepared to know, to understand, and to work with people of all races and backgrounds, thereby furthering the kind of democratic government our Constitution foresees. If an educational interest that combines these three elements is not "compelling," what is?[79]

There is indeed a compelling interest to eradicate systemic racism and structural inequality; moreover, post-racial constitutionalism's conflation of invidious racial subordination and any incidental burden on white privilege and expectation interests should be rejected:

> Indeed, it is a cruel distortion of history to compare Topeka, Kansas, in the 1950's to Louisville and Seattle in the modern day—to equate the plight of Linda Brown (who was ordered to attend a Jim Crow School) to the circumstances of Joshua McDonald (whose request to transfer to a school closer to home was initially declined).[80]

---

[78] *Parents Involved*, 551 U.S. at 840 (Breyer, J., dissenting).
[79] *Ibid.* at 843 (citations omitted).
[80] *Ibid.* at 867–68.

The harm to Joshua McDonald is a slight inconvenience because he did not get the assignment that he wanted initially, but he did ultimately receive a transfer to his first choice school.[81] The "injury," a burden on white privilege, "does not approach, in degree or in kind, the terrible harms of slavery, the resulting caste system, and 80 years of legal racial segregation."[82] But the Court nevertheless searches for an "injury" so that it can impose its post-racial stamp on the school assignment plans by declaring them constitutionally invalid. Post-racial constitutionalism's symmetrical universality[83] makes distinctions between inconvenient burdens on white privilege and invidious caste-based subjugation virtually impossible.

The Roberts Court's race jurisprudence is insidious, its corrosive effect undermines the edifice of the Fourteenth Amendment's anti-subordination principle, it guts the statutory framework enacted pursuant to the Reconstruction Amendments, and it cynically trumpets the moral righteousness of post-racialism while actively advancing the preservation of white privilege. This form of racism is a hallmark of the Roberts Court. As Professor Girardeau Spann writes, "This modern form of Roberts's racism … *constitutionalizes* the existing levels of discrimination in United States culture. It incorporates ongoing white privilege into a doctrinal baseline to which Chief Justice Roberts is willing to accord constitutional protection indefinitely into the future."[84]

The Roberts Court has also actively engaged and affirmed the political will of the white citizenry when it is aimed at pushing back any societal gains made through race-conscious remedial approaches in public decision-making; it constitutionalizes retrogression and retrenchment. *Schuette v. Coalition to Defend Affirmative Action* is a breathtaking example of how the Roberts Court's post-racial process discourse reifies structural inequality while ostensibly advancing democratic principles – this is the Democratic Myth.

---

[81] 551 U.S. at 719.

[82] *Ibid.* at 867 (Breyer, J., dissenting).

[83] Sumi Cho, *Post-Racialism*, 94 IOWA L. REV. 1589, 1602 and 1616–21 (2009) (discussing race-neutral universalism as a defining feature of post-racialism and the emergence of a post-racial Court).

[84] SPANN, *supra* n. 7, at 608 (emphasis in original); TERRY SMITH, WHITELASH: UNMASKING WHITE GRIEVANCE AT THE BALLOT BOX 112 (2020) ("We should, in other words, acknowledge that racial inequality and whitelash could not have flourished without the complicity of the judiciary").

4

Post-Racial Process Discourse

Schuette v. Coalition to Defend Affirmative Action

"Post-racial process discourse" is a term that encompasses all of the neutral themes proffered in the Roberts Court's race jurisprudence: that inequality is inevitable if it cannot be clearly identified as a product of state action; the most extreme instances of racism are merely aberrations in a society that has moved past its racism; valid claims of racial discrimination are inverted so that "neutral" reverse discrimination claims are privileged over anti-discrimination claims; and there is an ongoing exaggeration of racial progress and the fairness of a neutral process.

The Court itself has actively encouraged challenges to the validity of race-conscious remedies. In *Schuette v. Coalition to Defend Affirmative Action*, the Court's post-racial constitutionalism is on full display as it endorses the right of the citizenry to prohibit the consideration of race in all state decision-making. The Court, through its neutral rhetoric and institutional bias against race-conscious remedies, has actively diminished substantive equality for African Americans and other people of color by either severely narrowing rights in education, employment, the political system, and housing, or obliterating them as in its decision in *Shelby County v. Holder* where the Court rewrote the history of discrimination and dismantled the Voting Rights Act (Chapter 8). The Court, under the guise of process neutrality, has blocked these major societal entry points. The Court's race jurisprudence is premised on process values, liberal individualism, white victim-innocence narratives, and stringent proof requirements based upon the virtually illusive discriminatory intent requirement.[1]

SCHUETTE AND THE DEMOCRATIC MYTH

Under the Equal Protection Clause, all the Court's political process decisions represent, in varying forms, structural displacement. A central tenet of structural inequality is the displacement of discrete and insular minorities, those groups

---

[1] Darren Lenard Hutchinson, *"Unexplainable on Grounds Other Than Race": The Inversion of Privilege and Subordination in Equal Protection Jurisprudence*, 2003 U. ILL. L. REV. 615, 664–68.

that are targeted for exclusion based upon a history of oppression with present-day effects. These decisions illuminate how systemic exclusion is achieved explicitly or implicitly so that the neutral allure of "open" democratic decision-making becomes deceptively appealing. The Democratic Myth denotes the fact that while the rhetoric of direct democracy is inspiring because it embraces neutral concepts like access, organization, and even "change," the impact on the historically oppressed is devastating because it ratifies inequality by majority vote.[2]

The Court rejected this distorted democracy rationale in *Reitman, Hunter,* and *Washington v. Seattle,* but it then elevated the discriminatory intent requirement to a threshold standard that virtually precludes relief.[3] *Crawford* marks the beginning of this rigid analytical posture. *Schuette* is the doctrinal culmination of this conceptual shift.

Justice Kennedy's plurality opinion in *Schuette* advances the Court's post-racial constitutionalism by framing the analysis as not about the constitutionality of race-conscious remedies, but about whether "voters in the States may choose to prohibit consideration of racial preferences in governmental decisions, in particular with respect to school admissions."[4] The states as laboratories of democracy and experimentation[5] is a particularly appealing rhetorical tool in the Court's decision – the Court can exercise its judicial power cautiously in the name of the process and post-racial constitutionalism.

The real danger is that the voters may choose to "experiment" in a manner that harms discrete and insular minorities by targeting them for displacement from the process. This is why it is particularly telling that Justice Kennedy's opinion in *Romer v. Evans*[6] is never mentioned, analogized, or even distinguished in the *Schuette* plurality.[7] *Schuette* alters the doctrinal core of the political process decisions.

The Political Process Doctrine and Discrete and Insular Minorities

A central tension in constitutional jurisprudence is whether the Court should intervene in the legislative decision-making process, which is generally presumed to be functional, and render its opinion on the propriety of state action. This is

---

[2] Derrick A. Bell, Jr., *The Referendum: Democracy's Barrier to Racial Equality*, 54 WASH. L. REV. 1, 20–21 (1978).

[3] Mario L. Barnes and Erwin Chemerinsky, *The Once and Future Equal Protection Doctrine?* 43 CONN. L. REV. 1059, 1081 (2011) ("the combination of the tiers of scrutiny and the requirement for a discriminatory purpose combine to immunize from judicial review countless government actions which create great social inequalities.").

[4] *Schuette,* 572 U.S. 291 (2014) (plurality opinion).

[5] *Ibid.* at 310–14.

[6] 517 U.S. 620 (1996).

[7] *See generally Schuette,* 572 U.S. at 371–72 (Sotomayor, dissenting) (noting that Justice Kennedy's opinion does not contain any reference to *Romer v. Evans*).

the counter-majoritarian difficulty.[8] Analytically, the Court resolves this antidemocratic problem through its multitiered approach to judicial review under the Equal Protection Clause. In the famous footnote four of the *United States v. Carolene Products* decision, the Court sets the nascent tiers of equal protection review, explicitly noting that prejudice against discrete and insular minorities is subject to "a correspondingly more searching judicial inquiry."[9]

Starting from the pluralistic premise that the political process generally functions well, and that democracy truly means access, *Carolene Products* nevertheless identifies a narrow set of process malfunctions when judicial intervention is not only permissible, but mandated by our constitutional structure.[10] "[M]ore searching judicial inquiry"[11] is called for when structural animus targets the politically powerless, most notably, racial minorities or others who have been historically excluded from participating in the process.[12] It is clear that mere access is insufficient in such cases, because the process has been so fundamentally altered that it cannot be relied upon, certainly not by the excluded group, to correct itself.[13]

In *Democracy and Distrust*, Professor John Hart Ely posits the Process Theory, in which he conceptualizes footnote four of *Carolene Products* to offer a rationale for judicial review based upon a representation-reinforcement theory:[14] "The Process Theory, or representation-reinforcement rationale, does not address the present day effects of past discrimination – there is no substantive conception of equality because the Process Theory's primary focus is on those 'rare' process malfunctions

---

[8] Mark A. Graber, *The Countermajoritarian Difficulty: From Courts to Congress to Constitutional Order*, 4 ANN. REV. L. & SOC. SCI. 361, 363 (2008) (*citing* Alexander Bickel, THE LEAST DANGEROUS BRANCH: THE SUPREME COURT AT THE BAR OF POLITICS 16–17 (1962) as the originator of this term and discussing the literature).

[9] *United States v. Carolene Prods. Co.*, 304 U.S. 144, 152 n. 4 (1938).

[10] William N. Eskridge, Jr., *Pluralism and Distrust: How Courts Can Support Democracy by Lowering the Stakes of Politics*, 114 YALE L .J. 1279, 1281 (2005) (elaborating on the doctrinal contours of *Carolene Products* footnote four and identifying instances where there is no strong presumption of constitutionality, specifically, laws targeting discrete and insular minorities for exclusion and unequal treatment).

[11] *Carolene Prods.*, 304 U.S. at 152 n. 4.

[12] David A. Strauss, *Is Carolene Products Obsolete?* 2010 U. ILL. L. REV. 1251, 1257 (discrete and insular minorities are those "groups that are not able to play their proper role in democratic politics. They are 'discrete' in the sense that they are separate in some way, identifiable as distinct from the rest of society. They are 'insular' in the sense that other groups will not form coalitions with them – and, critically, not because of a lack of common interests but because of 'prejudice.'").

[13] *Ibid.* at 1257–58 ("But if a group has been silenced … or not allowed to play the game … then the process is not working as it should. Then the courts have a role to play, because the self-correcting properties of democratic politics will be nullified, and only the courts can make the democratic process work as it should.").

[14] John Hart Ely, DEMOCRACY AND DISTRUST: A THEORY OF JUDICIAL REVIEW 101–103, 146 (1980) (arguing that the Court should unblock any stoppages in the system, and should function as a referee to the process, not an evaluator of the substance of rights or issues).

that impede access to the political process."[15] This forward-looking approach obscures the complexity of structural inequality and the present-day effects of past discrimination. The same doctrinal and conceptual limitations are inherent in the Court's political process decisions.

The malleable factors of the political process doctrine allow it to be manipulated by the Court to reinforce post-racial process discourse as an explanation for the reversal of substantive race-conscious remedial approaches. This means that instead of interpreting and enforcing the mandate of the Fourteenth Amendment, some of that responsibility has now been given to the electorate to determine the efficacy of race-conscious affirmative action and the very substance of the anti-subordination principle. The post-racial process discourse outlined above is the rhetorical underpinning of voter initiatives, which seek to define equality by popular majority vote.[16]

All the political process decisions deal with structural animus aimed directly against one quintessential discrete and insular minority – African Americans. In *Reitman v. Mulkey*, the state stands behind a private right to discriminate in housing;[17] *Hunter v. Erickson* involves an explicit racial classification that treats housing matters differently based on race, thereby placing a "special burden" on African Americans;[18] the companion cases of *Washington v. Seattle*[19] and *Crawford v. Board of Education of Los Angeles*[20] raise analytical problems because the Court erects an intent requirement which dramatically transforms how harm is conceptualized when the political process is restructured;[21] and, finally, while *Romer v. Evans*[22] is generally not theorized as a political process decision, it is because it involves yet another discrete and insular minority (the LGBTQ+ community), and an attempt, by the state, through ostensibly neutral legislation, to exclude such a disfavored minority.[23]

---

[15] Cedric Merlin Powell, *Rhetorical Neutrality: Colorblindness, Frederick Douglass, and Inverted Critical Race Theory*, 56 CLEV. ST. L. REV. 823, 827 n. 15 (2008).

[16] Sylvia R. Lazos Vargas, *Judicial Review of Initiatives and Referendums in Which Majorities Vote on Minorities' Democratic Citizenship*, 60 OHIO ST. L. J. 399, 514–15 (1999) (critiquing the rhetorical allure of direct democracy–voter initiative movements, and discussing the heightened risks of exclusion from the process through (i) toxic rhetoric; (ii) "we-they" thinking; (iii) manipulation of issues through slanted framing ("special rights" or "preferences" that harm innocent whites); and (iv) "cultural-ideological initiatives set up a scenario where majorities cast votes on the minorities' very membership in the polity, and where the minorities almost always lose.").

[17] 387 U.S. 369, 381 (1967).

[18] 393 U.S. 385, 391 (1969).

[19] 458 U.S. 457, 485 (1982).

[20] 458 U.S. 527, 543 (1982).

[21] Crawford, 458 U.S. at 537–38 (upholding, as a mere repeal of race-related legislation, Proposition I, and stating that "when a neutral law has a disproportionately adverse effect on a racial minority, the Fourteenth Amendment is violated only if a discriminatory purpose can be shown.").

[22] 517 U.S. 620 (1996).

[23] *Ibid.* at 635–36.

This is structural animus. *Schuette* is the latest case in this line of decisions, and it erroneously expands the formalistic intent distinction that the Court creates to distinguish the results in *Seattle* and *Crawford*.

Reitman v. Mulkey: *Rejection of Neutrality*

California voters passed Proposition 14, a statewide initiative, which added Article I, Section 26 to the state constitution, and gave absolute discretion to any person to decline to sell real property.[24] Construing the "immediate objective,"[25] "ultimate effect,"[26] and "historical context"[27] underlying the enactment of section 26, the Court concluded, "Proposition 14 invalidly involved the State in racial discriminations in the housing market."[28] By giving individuals the "absolute discretion" to "decline to sell … to such persons as he … chooses,"[29] "the State had taken affirmative action designed to make private discriminations legally possible."[30]

What is striking here is that the Court rejects the neutral language of Proposition 14 and concludes that it nevertheless constitutes a violation of the Equal Protection Clause. Moreover, there is no formalistic discriminatory intent requirement.[31] To the Court, there was no other conceivable basis "for an application of Section 26 aside from authorizing the perpetration of a purported private discrimination."[32] Because Section 26 overturned "laws that bore on the right of private sellers and lessors to discriminate,"[33] and created a "constitutional right to privately discriminate"[34] the Court held that this was unconstitutional state action.[35]

In its analysis, the Court acknowledged that there was a "range of situations in which discriminatory state action has been identified."[36] In other words, there is an ultimate effect and impact to this deceptively neutral legislation.[37] Thus, *Reitman* establishes the important proposition that political process cases are fact specific, and the analytical inquiry should focus on the ultimate effect, impact, and context of the legislative action and process.[38]

---

[24] *Reitman v. Mulkey*, 387 U.S. 369, 371 (1967) (*quoting* ART. I, § 26 CA. CONST.).

[25] *Ibid.* at 373.

[26] *Ibid.*

[27] *Ibid.*

[28] *Ibid.* at 375.

[29] *Ibid.* at 388.

[30] *Ibid.* at 375.

[31] *Ibid.* (noting "a prohibited state involvement could be found 'even where the state can be charged with only encouraging' rather than commanding discrimination.").

[32] *Ibid.*

[33] *Ibid.* at 374.

[34] *Ibid.* (emphasis omitted)

[35] *Ibid.* at 380–81.

[36] *Ibid.* at 380.

[37] Stephanie L. Grauerholz, *Colorado's Amendment 2 Defeated: The Emergence of a Fundamental Right to Participate in the Political Process*, 44 DEPAUL L. REV. 841, 872 (1995).

[38] *Reitman*, 387 U.S. at 373, 378–80.

Hunter v. Erickson: *Explicit Racial Classification*

Unlike the purportedly race-neutral legislation in *Reitman*, here there was an explicit racial classification that treated housing matters differently based on race.[39] Specifically, the city of Akron, Ohio, amended the city charter "to prevent the city council from implementing any ordinance dealing with racial, religious, or ancestral discrimination in housing without the approval of the majority of the voters of Akron."[40] The effect of this amendment is even more damaging than that in *Reitman* because it "not only suspended the operation of the existing ordinance forbidding housing discrimination, but also required the approval of the [majority of] electors before any future ordinance could take effect."[41] This fundamental altering of the process was unconstitutional.[42]

This meant that the fair housing ordinance was unavailable to plaintiffs because of the amended city charter;[43] indeed, any future anti-discrimination ordinance had to "first be approved by a majority of electors."[44] Section 137, the amendment to Akron's City Charter, suspended the extant anti-discrimination housing ordinance and curtailed any subsequent remedial legislation in the absence of approval by the electors.[45] The fact that "implementation of this change"[46] occurred "through popular referendum"[47] did not "immunize it"[48] from strict scrutiny.[49]

Section 137 made enactment of anti-discrimination housing ordinances "substantially more difficult,"[50] and its ostensibly neutral tenor belies the fact that it explicitly targeted fair housing ordinances for suspension. Specifically, Section 137's purpose was to render anti-discrimination housing ordinances nugatory; its purported neutrality in application is undercut by the fact that the "law's impact falls on the minority. ... [Section]137 places special burdens on racial minorities within the governmental process. This is no more permissible than denying them the vote, on an equal basis with others."[51]

Here again, impact is significant. It is *how* the process is structured, designed, and implemented that impacts African Americans and places a "special burden" on them so that there is *no real chance* of effective redress because the law in place has been suspended, and any other legislation must be approved by a majority of a

---

39 Hunter v. Erickson, 393 U.S. 385, 389 (1969).
40 *Ibid.* at 386.
41 *Ibid.* at 389–90.
42 *Ibid.* at 393.
43 *Ibid.* at 387.
44 *Ibid.* at 397.
45 *Ibid.* at 389–90.
46 *Ibid.* at 392.
47 *Ibid.*
48 *Ibid.* at 392.
49 *Ibid.*
50 *Ibid.* at 390.
51 *Ibid.* at 390–91.

hostile electorate. To the Court, this is akin to the denial of the right to vote – the way the process is rigged ensures that anti-discrimination claims, like diluted or suppressed votes, will not be heard. "The *Hunter* case established the bedrock principle that a state may not restructure the procedures [or process] of the government for the purpose of targeting racial minorities, even if the manner is facially neutral."[52] Here, the law specifically targeted race, and it restructured the process in a manner that placed a special burden on African Americans (a discrete and insular minority).

Washington v. Seattle *and* Crawford v. Board of Education of
the City of Los Angeles: *Restructuring the Process?*

The doctrinal shift that sets the stage for *Schuette* and its underlying democratic myth is the Court's drawing of the rigid *de jure–de facto* distinction in *Washington v. Seattle* and *Crawford*. It should be noted that these cases were decided during the Court's wholesale retreat from school integration and its strict adherence to the discriminatory intent requirement in *Washington v. Davis*.[53] The analysis in the political process decisions changes from how the process impacts minorities to whether there is discriminatory intent to establish an equal protection claim. This explains the incongruent result in *Crawford*.[54]

Until the *Crawford* decision, all the political process decisions had held that targeting discrete and insular minorities for exclusion from the political process was unconstitutional. This structural animus is not tolerated under the Equal Protection Clause. Yet, *Crawford* erects the discriminatory intent requirement as the touchstone of constitutional analysis, raising the bar of proof and discounting the significance of structural impact, which unified all the pre-*Crawford* decisions.[55]

Recognizing the connection between segregated housing and racially isolated schools, the Seattle School District sought to advance integrated schools through transfer programs and magnet schools.[56] These efforts proved unsuccessful, and the District implemented the "Seattle Plan," which used busing and mandatory reassignments to dismantle segregated schools, and to prevent retrogression in the form of resegregation.[57] Citizens opposed to the desegregation plan formed a group called

---

[52] Laura McNeal, *Schuette Coalition to Defend Affirmative Action: The Majority's Tyranny Toward Unequal Educational Opportunity*, 59 ST. LOUIS L. J. 385, 390 (2015).

[53] 426 U.S. 229 (1976).

[54] Decided the same day, the Court holds the voter initiative unconstitutional in *Seattle*, and constitutional in *Crawford*. This is an example of the limits of the Court's doctrinal formalism.

[55] *See, for example*, Vicki C. Jackson, Constitutional Law *in an* Age of Proportionality, 124 YALE L. J. 3094, 3183 (2015) (noting that disparate impact on historically oppressed groups may be a signal of a process failure, and noting that "on an evidentiary theory," "such disparate impacts are likely to result from bias, whether conscious or not.").

[56] *Washington v. Seattle Sch. Dist.*, 458 U.S. 457, 460–61 (1982).

[57] *Ibid.*

Citizens for Voluntary Integration Committee ("CiVIC").[58] CiVIC "drafted a state-wide initiative designed to terminate the use of mandatory busing for purposes of racial integration."[59] Initiative 350 provided that "no school board ... shall directly or indirectly require any student to attend a school other than the school which is geographically nearest or next nearest the student's place of residence ... and which offers the course of study pursued by such student."[60]

The Seattle School District, along with the districts of Tacoma and Pasco, filed suit against Washington State, alleging that Initiative 350 violated the Equal Protection Clause of the Fourteenth Amendment.[61] Affirming the district court's holding that Initiative 350 violated the Equal Protection Clause and the principle set out in *Hunter*, the Court concluded that the initiative "uses the racial nature of an issue to define the governmental decision-making structure, thus imposing substantial and unique burdens on racial minorities."[62]

Thus, Initiative 350 was much more than a "simple repeal or modification of desegregation or antidiscrimination laws."[63] Here, the burden was on any and "all future attempts to integrate Washington schools in districts throughout the State, by lodging decision-making authority over the question at a new and remote level of government."[64] Authority over desegregation efforts was moved from the local board to the state level, and this fundamental structural reordering of the decision-making process "differentiat[ed] between the treatment of problems involving racial matters and that afforded other problems in the same area."[65] The restructuring is designed specifically to burden minority interests.[66]

Stating that the Court has "not insisted on a particularized inquiry into motivation in all equal protection cases,"[67] it held that Initiative 350 was the type of legislation that, like Section 137 in *Hunter*, falls within "an inherently suspect category."[68] This is significant because the Court noted that *Washington v. Davis* did not overturn *Hunter*.[69]

---

[58] *Ibid.* at 461–62. It is ironic that a group *opposed* to integration would call itself a "voluntary" integration committee.

[59] *Seattle*, 458 U.S. at 462.

[60] *Ibid.* (*quoting* WASH. REV. CODE § 28A.26.010 (1981)).

[61] *Ibid.* at 464.

[62] *Ibid.* at 470.

[63] *Ibid.* at 483. This is the proposition that the Court employed to distinguish the result in *Crawford*. See *Crawford*, 458 U.S. at 539; *accord Schuette v. Coalition to Defend Affirmative Action*, 572 U.S. 291, 311–12 (2014).

[64] *Seattle*, 458 U.S. at 483.

[65] *Ibid.* at 480.

[66] *Seattle*, 458 U.S. at 485 ("But when the political process ... used to *address* racially conscious legislation – and only such legislation – is singled out for peculiar and disadvantageous treatment, the government action plainly 'rests on distinctions based on race.'").

[67] *Ibid.*

[68] *Ibid.*

[69] *Ibid.* at 484–85.

Discriminatory intent, then, is not the touchstone, but how the process targets race-conscious anti-discrimination legislation and reallocates the structure of the process to burden minority interests. This is tantamount to rigging the process against discrete and insular minorities – the allocation of power "places unusual burdens on the ability of racial groups to enact legislation specifically designed to overcome the 'special condition' of prejudice."[70] Indeed, Initiative 350 all but guarantees continued isolation in the form of segregated neighborhood schools,[71] and it makes change within the process unusually difficult (and perhaps impossible) for minorities and desegregation advocates who want to pursue integrated schools. Participation, like the right to vote, must be meaningful.[72] There is no way that minorities can be successful under the reconfigured decision-making process. Thus, Initiative 350 is unconstitutional.

By contrast, although under similar facts and decided the same day, *Crawford* comes out with a completely different result. In *Crawford*, the issue, to the Court, was not how the process was structured but rather whether a state may recede in its remedial efforts after it chooses to do more than required under the Fourteenth Amendment.[73] The Court concluded that the state's "democratic processes" and ability to experiment with race-conscious policies allow it to do just that.[74] This is the democratic myth that will be the foundation of the *Schuette* decision thirty-two years later.

Voters ratified Proposition I, an amendment to the California Constitution, which confirmed "the power of state courts to order busing to that exercised by the federal courts under the Fourteenth Amendment."[75] Proposition I provided that no court-ordered remedy could be imposed "except to remedy a specific violation" under the Equal Protection Clause of the Fourteenth Amendment and unless a "federal court would be permitted under federal decisional law to impose that obligation" to remedy a specific Fourteenth Amendment violation.[76]

Concluding that Proposition I was constitutional because it was race neutral and simply "embrace[d] the requirements of the federal constitution with respect to mandatory school assignments and transportation,"[77] the Court then references the

---

[70] *Ibid.* at 486 (*quoting United States v. Carolene Prods. Co.*, 304 U.S. 144, 153 n. 4 (1938)).

[71] Sean Riley, *How Seattle Gave Up on Busing and Allowed Its Public Schools to Become Alarmingly Resegregated*, THE STRANGER (Apr. 13, 2016), www.thestranger.com/feature/2016/04/13/23945368/how-seattle-gave-up-on-busing-and-allowed-its-public-schools-to-become-alarmingly-resegregated [https://perma.cc/ZFB6-PJ2A]; *see* Nikole Hannah Jones, *Worlds Apart: How My Daughter's School Became a Battleground Over Which of New York's Children Benefit from a Separate and Unequal System*, N.Y. TIMES, June 12, 2016, at 34.

[72] *See Seattle*, 458 U.S. at 487.

[73] *Crawford v. Bd. of Ed. of City of Los Angeles*, 458 U.S. 527, 535 (1982).

[74] *Ibid.*

[75] *Ibid.* at 532.

[76] *Ibid.*

[77] *Ibid.* at 535.

discriminatory intent requirement as a constitutional prerequisite to a finding of a violation of the Equal Protection Clause.[78] In the absence of a constitutional violation (*de jure* segregation), state courts are forbidden to order pupil school assignment or pupil transportation.[79]

California's constitution places an affirmative constitutional obligation on the school board to eliminate segregation whether its origin is *de facto* or *de jure*.[80] This is more expansive than the federal Constitution's narrow prohibition of *de jure* segregation.[81] Proposition I, which addresses a racial matter in a neutral fashion, merely "repeals" the previously expansive interpretation of remediable segregation under the California Constitution;[82] and, the state "having gone beyond the requirements of the Federal Constitution, … return[s] in part to the standard prevailing generally throughout the United States."[83]

It is difficult to explain how the Court reaches two completely different conclusions in *Seattle* and *Crawford*. Both cases involve fundamental reorderings of the process: in *Seattle*, decision-making power was moved to the state level, adding a nearly insurmountable barrier to access for discrete and insular minorities;[84] in *Crawford*, the process was restructured to limit the equitable powers of courts to order remedies to dismantle segregated schools and prevent resegregation.[85] Notwithstanding their neutral rhetoric, both initiatives targeted race-conscious remedies, and sought to either prohibit (*Seattle*) or severely limit the scope of such remedies (*Crawford*).

To the Court, *Seattle* and *Crawford* are distinguishable based upon the formalistic *de jure–de facto* distinction. In *Seattle*, the restructuring of the political process is unconstitutionally overbroad because it removes mandatory busing as a remedy

---

[78] *Ibid.* at 537–38.

[79] *Ibid.* at 537.

[80] *Ibid.* at 530.

[81] *See, for example, Washington v. Davis*, 426 U.S. 229, 240 (1976); *Milliken v. Bradley*, 418 U.S. 717, 744–45 (1974); *Parents Involved in Cmty. Schls. v. Seattle Schl. Dist. No. 1*, 551 U.S. 701, 720–21 (2007) (noting the "compelling interest of remedying the effects of past intentional discrimination").

[82] *Crawford*, 458 U.S. at 538–39.

[83] *Ibid.* at 542.

[84] *Washington v. Seattle Schl. Dist. No. 1*, 458 U.S. 457, 474–75 (1982).

[85] *Crawford*, 458 U.S. at 548 (Marshall, J., dissenting). As Professor Laurence Tribe observes, *Seattle* and *Crawford* are essentially the same type of case, each restructuring the political process to harm minorities, but justifying the result in *Crawford* as a mere "repeal" of a state created right to desegregated education:

> [T]he change wrought by Proposition 1 [in *Crawford*] was strikingly analogous to that wrought by Initiative 350 [in *Seattle*] or by the *Hunter* charter amendment. In *Crawford* the shift in authority was from the courts to the state legislature or electorate; in *Seattle*, from the local school board to the state legislature or the electorate; in *Hunter*, from the city council to the city electorate. The majority and concurring opinions in *Crawford* misconstrued the impact of Proposition 1 because of confusion over just what "right" was at issue. What was at stake was not some sort of derivative "right to invoke a judicial busing remedy," but a state-guaranteed "right to be free from racial isolation in the public schools."

Laurence H. Tribe, American Constitutional Law 1487 (2d ed. 1988).

for even "school boards that had engaged in *de jure* segregation" in the absence of a court order.[86] Conversely, in *Crawford*, since there is merely *de facto* segregation (or no state-mandated discrimination), then the state is free to merely "repeal" a remedial policy that went beyond that mandated under the federal Constitution, which only prohibits *de jure* segregation.

Crawford, was wrongly decided. Under the political process doctrine, *Seattle* and *Crawford* are the same case: both restructure the process in a manner that perpetuates the subjugation of discrete and insular minorities, but their divergent results are premised on the outcome determinative *de jure–de facto* distinction. *Reitman*, *Hunter*, *Seattle*, and *Crawford* are all of a kind – they reallocate decision-making power unconstitutionally by codifying inequality and insulating it from judicial review.[87] That is, they leave any progressive social change to the electorate, which is against race-conscious remedial approaches to fulfill the anti-subordination principle of the Fourteenth Amendment. *Romer v. Evans*[88] fits squarely within this line of decisions as well. For while it is generally conceived as a case about legislative animus, there is nevertheless a structural dynamic to it that makes it particularly salient to the analysis here.

Romer v. Evans *and the Political Process Doctrine*

Amendment 2 to the Colorado Constitution was adopted in 1992 in a statewide referendum.[89]

This comprehensive amendment repealed anti-discrimination ordinances in Aspen, Boulder, and Denver; and, beyond the repeal, Amendment 2 prohibited "all legislative, executive or judicial action at any level of state or local government designed to protect" members of the LGBTQ community.[90]

The Court reaches two dramatically different results in *Crawford* and *Romer* on what is essentially the same type of structural exclusion. In *Crawford*, "Proposition I works an unconstitutional reallocation of state power by depriving California courts of the ability to grant meaningful relief to those seeking to vindicate the State's guarantee against *de facto* segregation in the public schools."[91] The reallocation of state power is even more pervasive and pernicious in *Romer*, as Amendment 2 "nullifies specific legal protections for this targeted class [LGBTQ] in all transactions in housing, sale of real estate, insurance, health and welfare services, private education, and employment."[92] Amendment 2's reach extends beyond the private sphere "to repeal

---

[86] *Seattle*, 458 U.S. at 466.
[87] *Crawford*, 458 U.S. at 558–61 (Marshall, J., dissenting).
[88] 517 U.S. 618 (1996).
[89] *Romer v. Evans*, 517 U.S. 620, 623 (1996).
[90] *Ibid.*
[91] *Crawford v. Bd. of Ed. of City of Los Angeles*, 458 U.S. 527, 554 (1982) (Marshall, J., dissenting).
[92] *Romer*, 517 U.S. at 629.

and forbid all laws or policies providing specific protections for gays or lesbians from discrimination by *every level of Colorado government.*"[93]

Nevertheless, the Court held Proposition I constitutional in *Crawford*, and Amendment 2 unconstitutional in *Romer*. Not only does this illustrate the elusiveness of the Court's political process doctrine, it also denotes the rigid formalism of the *de jure–de facto* distinction and the intent requirement. What is striking about *Romer* is that the Court, per Justice Kennedy's opinion, does not require a showing of discriminatory intent, but rather focuses on the impact and restructuring of the process through the Colorado constitutional amendment. The Court does not recognize LGBTQ as a suspect class,[94] so rationality of the process is the analytical focal point.[95] The animus is inherent in the process itself, but this analysis is qualitatively different when it comes to race. The shift is noticeably from impact (in *Romer*) to intent (in *Schuette*).

What the Court misses is that *Romer* is yet another form of political restructuring with direct implications to its analysis in *Schuette*. Rather, the Court disconnects *Romer* from its political process jurisprudence, elevates the intent requirement so that *Schuette* is more of a post-racial decision than a structural process decision, and creates a myth of democratic participation and experimentation that belies the complexity of race, racism, and retrogression. The Colorado amendment in *Romer* would be upheld as *constitutional* under the *Schuette* analysis.[96] This doctrinal disparity is even more disconcerting given that Justice Kennedy is the author of *Romer* and *Schuette*.

Perhaps the Court is more adept at recognizing "new" discrimination and less so when it comes to "old" discrimination – discrimination is presumed in *Romer*, and race is viewed skeptically in *Schuette*.[97] That is, the Court conceptualizes injury

---

[93] *Ibid.* (emphasis added).

[94] *See Romer*, 517 U.S. at 631.

[95] *Ibid.* at 632 (Amendment 2 fails rational basis review because it is a "broad and undifferentiated disability on a single group," and its enactment cannot be explained by anything except animus toward LGBTQ).

[96] Susanna W. Pollvogt, *Thought Experiment: What if Justice Kennedy Had Approached Romer v. Evans the Way He Approached Schuette v. BAMN?* (May 13, 2014), http://ssrn.com/abstract=2436616 [https://perma.cc/LG38-27NA] (noting that the divergent results in *Romer* and *Schuette* can be explained as the Court being adept at identifying "new" discrimination like sexual orientation discrimination, and less so with old, "second generation discrimination" like racial discrimination); *see generally* Susannah W. Pollvogt, *Unconstitutional Animus*, 81 FORDHAM L. REV. 887 (2012) (providing a detailed account of the Court's animus analysis in *Romer*).

[97] Darren Lenard Hutchinson, *Undignified: The Supreme Court, Racial Justice, and Dignity Claims*, 69 FLA. L. REV. 1, 44 (2017) (concluding that the Court is unlikely to alter its post-racial interpretation of the Fourteenth Amendment in the absence of a shift in public opinion about race, and stating that "while the Court decided the sexual-orientation dignity cases as public attitudes concerning LGBT rights shifted rapidly towards greater acceptance and tolerance, similar changes have not occurred with respect to public attitudes concerning substantive racial equality."). Indeed, this shift may never occur.

differently in the two cases: in *Romer*, the injury is borne out by the explicit language of exclusion in Amendment 2, and the underlying structural animus that it represents against the LGBTQ community; on the other hand, there is no injury in *Schuette* because the electorate chose to reorder the political process (and any exclusion or burden has been voted on and approved). The failure to reconcile these decisions underscores the Court's flawed reliance on post-racial process discourse.

The Court's political process jurisprudence foregrounds neutrality, post-racialism, and a mythological vision of democracy far removed from the devastating impact of exclusion. *Schuette* departs from firmly established precedent and the common doctrinal threads connecting *Reitman, Hunter, Seattle*, and *Romer*. Conflating the process values espoused in its equal opportunity/equal access decisions, the Court reinterprets the political process doctrine so that it now resembles all the Court's post-racial jurisprudence. That is, unless there is discriminatory intent manifested by the state itself, there is nothing to remedy.[98] The Court conceptualizes *Schuette* as simply about benefits and burdens.[99] Since African Americans have received a tainted racial benefit or "preference," the polity is free to take it back. Moreover, issues like diversity and race, although "sensitive" societal issues, are properly consigned to the ebb and flow of the democratic process.[100] After all, democracy is a great experiment. As *Schuette* demonstrates, this experiment will have grave consequences for historically oppressed minorities.

POST-RACIAL CONSTITUTIONALISM

The Fourteenth Amendment is inverted in *Schuette*, for it stands for the counterintuitive proposition that states, through their electorate, can amend their constitutions to limit the reach of the anti-subordination principle. The Court endorses voter initiatives to enact legislative amendments that preclude the consideration of race in any state decision-making process notwithstanding the Court's holding in *Grutter* and *Fisher*. Race is not inherently neutral, so it is appropriate for the citizenry to ban its use in the name of post-racialism.[101] This is the narrative core of the Roberts Court's race jurisprudence. In the absence of identifiable discrimination, race-conscious remedies are constitutionally prohibited; and race, as one of many factors in admissions, cannot be considered in Michigan.[102]

To bring doctrinal uniformity to its rigid formalism, the Court conceptualizes *Schuette* as a case about the democratic process, neutral results, and the virtues of

---

[98] *See Schuette v. Coalition to Defend Affirmative Action*, 572 U.S. at 316, 330 (2014) (Scalia, J., concurring).

[99] *See* Girardeau A. Spann, *Affirmative Action and Discrimination*, 39 How. L. J. 1, 68–69 (1995).

[100] *See Schuette*, 572 U.S. at 314–15.

[101] *See Schuette*, 572 U.S. at 310.

[102] *See Ibid.* at 314.

participating in direct democracy movements[103] rather than a case about race and the structure of the process itself. Of course, amid this comprehensive primer on democracy and the First Amendment, there is no mention of this new gloss on the Fourteenth Amendment. This is the New Equal Protection,[104] and it is advanced through the rhetorical allure of post-racial discourse and the Democratic Myth.

Justice Kennedy's Post-Racial Proceduralism

In 2006, Michigan voters adopted an amendment to the state constitution prohibiting consideration of race in government decision-making.[105] Ballot Proposal 2 passed by a vote of 58 to 42 percent, and became Article I, Section 26 of the Michigan Constitution when it was enacted.[106] The Sixth Circuit Court of Appeals, sitting en banc, concluded that, under the principles articulated in *Seattle*, the state constitutional amendment was unconstitutional.[107] Reversing the Court of Appeals, Justice Kennedy's *Schuette* plurality opinion advances a central tenet of post-racial constitutionalism – post-racial proceduralism, the notion that it is the process itself that shapes the substance of constitutional rights.

The *Schuette* plurality sets out three post-racial propositions: (i) neutrality is the guiding principle of the Court's analysis of race – so that the decision is not about race at all, but whether "racial preferences"[108] may be prohibited by Michigan voters through the political process; (ii) the political process decisions are unified by the requirement of discriminatory intent under the Fourteenth Amendment;[109] and (iii) citizen involvement in the democratic process means that voters have a unique opportunity to advance legislation that not only mirrors the post-racial discourse of the polity, but incorporates it into the text of the state constitution.

It is extraordinary that Justice Kennedy begins his analysis by proclaiming that this case "is not about the constitutionality, or the merits, of race-conscious admissions in higher education."[110] *Fisher*, of course, remains intact doctrinally in jurisdictions outside of Michigan,[111] and stands for the proposition that "consideration of race in admissions is permissible"[112] if race-neutral alternatives prove ineffective in

---

[103] *See Ibid.* at 1637–38.

[104] *See generally* Kenji Yoshino, *The New Equal Protection*, 124 HARV. L. REV. 747, 748 (2011) (discussing the shift from a group rights paradigm to a liberty-based conception as a means to alleviate balkanization and "pluralism anxiety").

[105] *Schuette*, 572 U.S. at 299.

[106] *Ibid.*

[107] *Schuette*, 572 U.S. at 300.

[108] *Ibid.*

[109] *Ibid.* at 303–306.

[110] *Ibid.* at 300.

[111] Meera E. Deo, *Faculty Insights on Educational Diversity*, 83 FORDHAM L. REV. 3115, 3122 (2015) (noting that *Schuette* left diversity in place while diluting affirmative action more broadly).

[112] *Schuette*, 572 U.S. at 300.

attaining diversity. *Schuette* is most certainly about race[113] – it is about whether the Michigan electorate can determine the scope and applicability of the Fourteenth Amendment in state decision-making, and thereby prohibit the use of race as a factor in such decisions. It seems odd that the Court would expand the interpretive powers of the citizenry in this manner, particularly since it is "the province and duty of [the Court] to say what the law is,"[114] in interpreting the Fourteenth Amendment as a limit on state power.[115]

Conflating the holdings of *Hunter, Reitman*, and *Seattle,* Justice Kennedy erects a discriminatory intent requirement where one did not previously exist. Before Justice Kennedy's reinterpretation of *Seattle,* all the political process doctrine decisions stood for the proposition that voter-initiated legislation that "places [a] special[] burden[] on racial minorities"[116] is constitutionally invalid. Concluding that this reading of the cases, particularly *Seattle,* was too broad, Justice Kennedy posits that *Seattle* must be understood as a case where the remedy – busing for integrated schools – was assumed so there was no focus on the *de jure–de facto* distinction.

To Justice Kennedy, *Seattle* is a doctrinal outlier, which must be rejected.[117] That is, because the Court assumed the legitimacy and constitutionality of busing as a remedy, there was no reference to the discriminatory intent requirement. This is too broad a reading of *Seattle.* Without a discriminatory intent requirement, *Seattle's* expansiveness would promote distribution of benefits based on race; standardless assessments of what is an "injury" to a racial minority's political interest in the process; and balkanization, as racial groups vie for a constitutionally guaranteed right to "win" in the process.[118] This is the classic racial politics rationale that the Court has employed to dismantle race-conscious affirmative action.[119]

Seattle, then, guarantees a racialized result premised on a stereotypical understanding of the political interests of minorities – this is contrary to neutrality and the

[113] TERRY SMITH, WHITELASH: UNMASKING WHITE GRIEVANCE AT THE BALLOT BOX 170 (2020).

[114] *Marbury v. Madison,* 5 U.S. 137, 177 (1803).

[115] This is an interesting strand of federalism, with state electorates determining the very parameters of a constitutional amendment intended to limit discrimination by the state. *See* Thomas D. Kimball, Schuette v. BAMN: *The Short-Lived Return of the Ghost of Federalism Past,* 61 LOY. L. REV. 365, 397 (2015) (discussing how *Schuette* promotes the flawed notion that voter initiatives that result in legislative enactments are insulated from review by federal courts).

[116] *Washington v. Seattle Schl. Dist. No. 1,* 458 U.S. 457, 470 (1982) (concluding that when "the State allocates governmental power *nonneutrally* by explicitly using the *racial* nature of a decision to determine the decision-making process," it places a *special* burden on racial minorities within the process) (emphasis added).

[117] *Schuette,* 572 U.S. at 306 (noting that the broad reading of *Seattle* that any state action, with a "racial focus," that makes it more difficult to achieve legislative success is subject to strict scrutiny, is contrary to the Court's equal protection jurisprudence).

[118] *Ibid.* at 306–11.

[119] Betrall L. Ross II, *Democracy and Renewed Distrust: Equal Protection and the Evolving Judicial Conception of Politics,* 101 CAL. L. REV. 1565, 1603–24 (2013) (discussing racial politics rationale and noting the process model that views any political gains by racial minorities skeptically).

post-racial constitutionalism espoused by the Court. *Schuette* purportedly rejects the race-consciousness of *Seattle*, but this is misleading.[120] All the political process decisions advance a structural view of polity premised on displacement, not a discriminatory intent requirement.

Distinguishing *Seattle* without explicitly overruling it, Justice Kennedy emphasizes the fact that there is no injury on the facts in *Schuette*.[121] Since there is no clearly identifiable discrimination to remedy, and diversity is not a compelling interest in the context of the Michigan voter initiative, the Court characterizes judicial review as overly intrusive and a burden on the right of voters to determine the state's course on issues of race.[122] Perhaps the most devastating aspect of *Schuette* is its universalist appeal[123] to voter empowerment, the First Amendment and underlying themes of participatory democracy, and states as laboratories of democracy where contentious "issues" like race can be resolved through public debate and experimentation.[124] The allure of this democratic myth is belied by its embrace of formalistic equality and cynical rejection of the anti-caste and anti-subordination principles of the Fourteenth Amendment.

The Court is more concerned with process (and how the status quo can be preserved) than with substantive constitutional rights. This means that most structural inequality is irremediable because the Court's post-racial constitutionalism requires definitive proof of purposeful discrimination by the state. Justice Kennedy's plurality decision is disingenuously neutral and moderate; it appeals to the higher democratic virtues of debate, participation, and experimentation, but there is an underlying tenor of what Professor Darren Lenard Hutchinson terms "Racial Exhaustion."[125] The voters of Michigan, after fifteen years of public "debate" on the issue of race in which their elected officials were "unresponsive," have chosen the "neutral" policy course of prohibiting consideration of race in all state policymaking.[126] Justice Kennedy even suggests that affirming the court of appeals would undermine the legitimacy of the process and the rights of the electorate to express their views through duly enacted legislation.[127]

---

[120] Under this conception, all race-conscious remedies are cast as unconstitutional windfalls to people of color, with whites as the "victims" of this racially tainted process. This rhetorical inversion has been thoroughly critiqued and rejected in the literature. *See* Girardeau A. Spann, *Good Faith Discrimination*, 23 Wm. & Mary Bill Rts. J. 585, 608 (2015) (noting how the Court is deferential to the political process when it rejects race-conscious affirmative action but will intervene and invalidate the will of the political community when it embraces race-conscious remedies to eradicate subordination and segregation).

[121] *Schuette*, 572 U.S. at 310.

[122] *Ibid.* at 310–14.

[123] Mario L. Barnes, *"The More Things Change …" New Moves for Legitimizing Discrimination in a "Post-Race" World*, 100 Minn. L. Rev. 2043, 2071–72 (2016).

[124] *Schuette*, 572 U.S. at 312–14.

[125] Darren Lenard Hutchinson, *Racial Exhaustion*, 86 Wash. U. L. Rev. 917, 922 (2009).

[126] *Schuette*, 572 U.S. at 311.

[127] *Ibid.* at 312.

While Justice Kennedy's analysis leaves a very small doctrinal space for consideration of race in state decision-making – for example, the voters may decide that diversity is a compelling interest in Michigan and should be pursued – there is little doubt that *Schuette* all but completes the Roberts Court's comprehensive assault on race-conscious remedies. What is particularly disconcerting is that Justices Scalia and Thomas would go even further by overruling *Hunter* and *Seattle*.[128]

Chief Justice Roberts' Concurrence: White Privilege as a Judicial Tenet

In Chief Justice Roberts' brief, dismissive and cynical concurrence, all the elements of post-racial constitutionalism are on full display – any reference to race, especially "preferences," has stigmatizing effects; race should be avoided in public discourse because it leads to racial politics and balkanization; and, since the voter initiative is presumptively legitimate, race has no place in a "good faith" dispute about policy. Chief Justice Roberts' tart retort to the dissent says it all: "People can disagree in good faith on this issue, but it similarly does more harm than good to question the openness and candor of those on either side of the debate."[129]

Chief Justice Roberts is noticeably irked at Justice Sotomayor's robust critique of his post-racial circularity that he carries over from *Parents Involved*. It is as if he is saying, "[W]e've already discussed this issue – "stop discriminating on the basis of race" – and any challenge to the will of the electorate is "reverse discrimination." White privilege means wilful blindness to structural inequality. The Court will determine when and how race will be discussed and addressed and this means almost never because any attempts to critically address race and racism will be met with post-racial constitutionalism's most potent weapon – white innocence and weaponized morality.[130]

Justice Sotomayor's Dissent: Race and Structural Inequality

By contrast, Justice Sotomayor's dissent envisions the representation reinforcement theory as embracing the anti-caste and anti-subordination principles underlying the Fourteenth Amendment.[131] Justice Sotomayor rejects the rhetorical allure of post-racial process discourse, and forcefully critiques the Democratic Myth relied upon by the plurality and concurring opinions.

Rejecting the plurality's distorted conception of democratic self-governance, Justice Sotomayor concludes that discrimination is not simply evinced by particularized

---

[128] *Ibid.* at 322–27 (Scalia, J., dissenting).
[129] *Ibid.* at 315–16 (Roberts, C. J., concurring).
[130] David Simon, *Whiteness as Innocence*, 96 DENV. L. REV. 635, 644–84 (2018) (discussing the "general white innocence presumption" and how it undermines the anti-subordination principle of the Fourteenth Amendment).
[131] *Schuette*, 572 U.S. at 341, 366–70 (Sotomayor, J., dissenting).

intent, it is *structural* in nature are well.[132] *Schuette* is a new form of voter dilution because the only manner in which proponents of race-conscious remedies can achieve "success" in Michigan's political process is to pass a *statewide* constitutional amendment.[133] Thus, there is a two-tiered – separate and unequal – system for racial minorities and advocates of race-conscious remedies and "a separate, less burdensome process for everyone else."[134] This is certainly a restructuring of the process that targets and excludes discrete and insular minorities, those without power to have meaningful participation in the purportedly neutral process. But the process is not neutral, colorblind, or post-racial because it specifically designates race-conscious remedies for invalidation.[135] Under the political process doctrine, this type of structural realignment calls for strict scrutiny.[136]

The plurality's attempt to neutralize this basic principle is unpersuasive. Since there is no compelling interest underlying Section 26, the reordering of the political system to place burdens on minorities is unconstitutional. Indeed, Section 26 disrupts the democratic process by essentially "overturning" the central holding of *Grutter*, which permits consideration of race in a holistic admissions process.

The Court has actively constitutionalized reverse discrimination suits through an insurmountable burden of proof of discriminatory intent, a rhetorical narrative that dismisses race and racism as components of structural inequality,[137] and a formalistic conception of equality that privileges white claims of entitlement over the claims of historically oppressed minorities under the myth that most discrimination has already been eliminated.

Justice Sotomayor critiques Justice Breyer's narrow conception of *Hunter* and *Seattle*, which leads him to concur with the plurality. While he would not overrule these decisions, as Justice Sotomayor concludes that the plurality did *sub silento*,[138] he nevertheless concludes that *Hunter* and *Seattle* are inapplicable. To Justice Sotomayor, Justice Breyer's central premise is inaccurate – this is *not* a case about simply moving decision-making authority from an unelected administrative body (faculty members and administrators who receive delegated authority from the elected board) to the voters. Because Justice Breyer views decision-making power symmetrically, he fails to acknowledge the asymmetrical impact on discrete and insular minorities. The elected Board "retain[ed] complete supervisory authority over university officials and over all admissions decisions,"[139] but Section 26

---

[132] *Ibid.* at 357–58 n.8.

[133] *Ibid.* at 354, 392.

[134] *Ibid.* at 341.

[135] *Ibid.* at 352 (noting that Section 26 has a racial focus and restructures the political process).

[136] *Ibid.* at 358.

[137] *See Ibid.* at 379–80 ("Race matters. Race matters in part because of the long history of racial minorities' being denied access to the political process.").

[138] *Ibid.* at 360.

[139] *Ibid.* at 364.

impermissibly reorders the process so that power is "removed ... from the elected boards and placed ... instead at a higher level of the political process in Michigan."[140] This is precisely what occurred in *Hunter* and *Seattle*.

There is a clear distinction between processual access and substantive participation in the political process unimpeded by legislative animosity camouflaged as neutral decision-making. Rejecting the plurality's approach as "'self-government' without limits,"[141] Justice Sotomayor identifies three essential features of the right to meaningful participation in the political process: (i) the right to vote;[142] (ii) the "majority may not make it more difficult for the minority to exercise the right to vote";[143] and (iii) "a majority may not reconfigure the existing political process in a manner that creates a two-tiered system of political change, subjecting laws designed to protect or benefit discrete and insular minorities to a more burdensome political process than all other laws."[144]

The plurality adopts a literal process view rooted in formalistic equality. Under this view, equal access and opportunity are sufficiently guaranteed once the Court removes formal barriers to access. Thus, the Court should not "interfere" in a neutral process because this would undermine state sovereignty. This view should be rejected because it is the constitutional duty of the Court to keep channels of political change open. It failed to do so in *Schuette*, and retrogression and retrenchment are almost certainly guaranteed.

Leveling a direct rebuke to the Court's post-racial constitutionalism and its contrived conception of participatory democracy, Justice Sotomayor concludes that the Court abdicated its role as interpreter of the Fourteenth Amendment's anti-subordination principle and guardian of the politically powerless, "permitting the majority to use its numerical advantage to change the rules mid-contest and forever stack the deck against racial minorities in Michigan."[145] The Court's race jurisprudence is rigged against racial minorities and the politically displaced.

DISMANTLING THE DEMOCRATIC MYTH

Advancing the appeal of post-racial democracy, the Court has created a new strand of its post-racial constitutionalism. The Court now gains "legitimacy" by constitutionalizing the post-racial discourse of a citizenry hostile to race-conscious remedies as a means of inclusion and transformative social change.

Applying the anti-subordination principle to the voter-approved Michigan constitutional amendment, the Court should have held it unconstitutional because it

---

[140] *Ibid.* at 364–65.
[141] *Ibid.* at 368.
[142] *Ibid.* at 368.
[143] *Ibid.*
[144] *Ibid.*
[145] *Ibid.* at 392.

"reenforce[s] systems of subordination that treat some people as second class citizens."[146] By restructuring the process so that proponents of race-conscious remedies can succeed in advancing their cause only through a statewide referendum to amend the Michigan Constitution, "[a] majority of the Michigan electorate changed the basic rules of the political process in that State in a manner that uniquely disadvantaged racial minorities."[147]

This is the essence of second-class citizenship and structural inequality. The anti-subordination principle rejects the formalistic intent requirement, rigid classification categories, and neutrality as a rationale for the present-day effects of past structural inequality.

The voter approved constitutional amendment is indicative of a legally reinforced system of subordination. African Americans, and other discrete and insular minorities, are targeted for displacement.[148] Thus, Section 26 of the Michigan Constitution is invalid. All the Court's political process decisions fit squarely within this canon, and explicitly reject such explicit or implicit exclusion from the political process.

The anti-subordination principle emanating in the Equal Protection Clause is concerned primarily with the eradication of caste and the advancement of substantive equality in the form of equal citizenship. This means that if the state targets an historically oppressed or disfavored group for exclusion, explicitly through identifiable state action or implicitly through neutral direct democracy initiatives, such action is a violation of the Fourteenth Amendment. In either case, the process is restructured so that "the state's allocation of power places unusual burdens on the ability of racial groups to enact legislation specifically designed to overcome the 'special condition' of prejudice," and the operation of the normal political process is "seriously curtailed" so that participation is meaningless.[149]

The Court should jettison its illusory equal opportunity rhetoric; acknowledge that structural inequality exists and that whites are not "victims" in the same sense that discrete and insular minorities are; reconceptualize anti-discrimination law so that disparate impact is as significant as discriminatory intent in establishing structural inequality and retrenchment;[150] and intervene, not to overturn race-conscious remedies adopted by the political community but to provide substantive access, inclusion, and a meaningful opportunity to participate and promote transformative social change. Of course, the Roberts Court is far from adopting any of these

---

[146] Tribe, *supra* n. 85, at 1515.

[147] 572 U.S. at 338 (Sotomayor, J., dissenting).

[148] *Ibid.* at 380–87 (chronicling the segregated history of Michigan schools and the precipitous decline in minority post-secondary school enrollments in Michigan and California as a direct result of "neutral" voter initiatives).

[149] *Ibid.* at 366–67 (quoting *United States v. Carolene Products*, 304 U.S. 144, 153 n. 4 (1938)).

[150] *Ibid.* at 366; *Yick Wo v. Hopkins*, 118 U.S. 356, 373–74 (1886) (concluding that ostensibly neutral laws may be applied with an "evil eye and an unequal hand" so as to violate the Equal Protection Clause).

doctrinal propositions, as it is enamored with the rhetorical allure of post-racial discourse and the Democratic Myth.

Under its own precedents, the history of the political process itself and how powerless groups have been excluded throughout time is an essential component of any analysis of the efficacy of voter initiatives. History played no part in the analysis of *Schuette*, so the value of democratic decision-making was exaggerated, and inequality was rationalized as the result of a neutral process, which gave voice to the demands of the citizenry.

The Roberts Court seeks to constitutionalize a mythic democracy that promises participation while implicitly endorsing structural exclusion. Voter initiatives should not determine the substantive core of the Fourteenth Amendment. *Schuette* marks the constitutionalization of post-racial process discourse and the Democratic Myth. The Roberts Court's post-racial constitutionalism is further advanced by process values – equal opportunity is the product of a neutral process untainted by race – and a post-racial interpretation of diversity.

5

Fisher II

Post-Racial Process Values and the Diversity Myth

Reaffirming the diversity interest in post-secondary education, *Fisher v. University of Texas* introduces a new process standard which undermines substantive equality. Without reference to history or context, the Court concluded that race could be used in a holistic admissions process when it is a "factor of a factor of a factor."[1] Diversity should be embraced, the Court reasons, but only when it does not conflict with neutrality, which means that diversity can be advanced only in a manner that is colorblind (race as merely one of many factors in a holistic review) or post-racial (as "a factor of a factor of a factor"). Diversity has been conceptualized as a threat to meritocracy and neutral values, and this has formed the basis of reverse discrimination lawsuits under the Fourteenth Amendment and anti-discrimination statutes as well.

Diversity has always been post-racial with race as a mere collateral add-on – devoid of substance and meaning because it is conflated with anything and everything that connotes difference – unconnected to structural change in institutions. Just as Justice O'Connor authored the Rehnquist Court's colorblind race jurisprudence, Justice Kennedy is the author of the Court's post-racial jurisprudence. He does not go as far as Chief Justice Roberts' absolute post-racial constitutionalism where race can never be considered,[2] but he nevertheless defaults to race-neutral alternatives as the starting point of analysis with the use of race as the last resort.

Fisher represents an analytical shift from *Grutter's* focus on diversity through race *as a factor*, in assembling a critical mass of students, to a post-racial process approach emphasizing neutrality with race three factors removed from any significant consideration. Process displaces race so that structural exclusion is still present

---

[1] *Fisher v. University of Texas at Austin*, 579 U.S. 365 (2016) ("*Fisher II*").

[2] *See, for example, Parents Involved*, 551 U.S. 701, 787–88 (2007) (Kennedy, J., concurring) (citation omitted) ("... parts of the opinion by the Chief Justice imply an all-too-unyielding insistence that race cannot be a factor in instances when, in my view, it may be taken into account." The plurality's postulate that "[t]he way to stop discrimination on the basis of race is to stop discriminating on the basis of race ... is not sufficient to decide these cases").

in institutions purportedly advancing diversity. But that has always been the diversity conundrum – it promises inclusion while erecting a process that, at best, offers limited access.[3]

When her application to the University of Texas (the "University" or "UT") was rejected, Abigail Fisher brought a reverse discrimination suit alleging that the University of Texas' holistic, full-file review process discriminated against her on the basis of race.[4] It is quite telling that standing was even granted in her case – Fisher "was not in the top 10 percent of her class,"[5] and there were forty-two white applicants who were offered provisional admission with lower test scores and grades, and another "168 black and Latino students with grades as good as or better than Fisher's who were denied"[6] admission – the only "injury" that Fisher could assert was "inability to tap into UT's alumni network and possibly missing out on a better first job."[7] These "injuries" are common to all rejected applicants yet standing was presumed because Fisher's reverse discrimination claim is a perfect vehicle for the Roberts Court's post-racial constitutionalism.[8]

Indeed, Fisher's argument is not so much that a person of color took her place, or that there was an impermissible quota that precluded her from consideration for all the admission seats; rather, her claim was that the process was tainted because race was even considered.[9] This is a post-racial argument that is especially appealing to the Roberts Court. Yet even the Court must concede that Texas' holistic review–percentage plan did not impact Fisher because of her race; rather, "the largest impact" on her application was the race-neutral Top Ten Percent Plan.[10] Ironically, the Court

---

[3] Charles R. Lawrence III, *Two Views of the River: A Critique of the Liberal Defense of Affirmative Action*, 101 COLUM. L. REV. 928, 941–42 (2001).

[4] *Fisher v. Univ. of Tex. at Austin*, 570 U.S. 297 (2013) ("*Fisher I*").

[5] *Fisher*, 579 U.S. 365, 374 (2016) ("*Fisher II*").

[6] Nikole Hannah-Jones, *What Abigail Fisher's Affirmative Action Case Was Really About*, PROPUBLICA (June 23, 2016), www.propublica.org/article/a-colorblind-constitution-what-abigail-fishers-affirmative-action-case-is-really-about.

[7] *Ibid.*; Mario Barnes, Erwin Chemerinsky, and Angela Onwuachi-Willig, *Judging Opportunity Lost: Assessing the Viability of Race-Based Affirmative Action*, 62 UCLA L. REV. 272, 286–88 (2015) (discussing Fisher's lack of standing to bring her claim and the Court's eagerness to ignore this procedural flaw to reach the merits of the case).

[8] Osamudia R. James, *White Like Me: The Negative Impact of the Diversity Rationale on White Identity Formation*, 89 N.Y.U. L. REV. 425, 499 (2014) (noting that the "increased focus on individual burdens for whites comes at the cost of minority interests and is only perpetuated by the diversity rationale").

[9] "The anti-affirmative action plaintiffs in these cases fail to acknowledge that the institutions to which they seek entry are already primarily white, further evincing the unacknowledged benchmark of whiteness." STEPHANIE WILDMAN, MARGALYNNE ARMSTRONG, ADRIENNE D. DAVIS, AND TRINA GRILLO, PRIVILEGE REVEALED: HOW INVISIBLE PREFERENCES UNDERMINES AMERICA xxv (2021).

[10] *Fisher II*, 579 U.S. at 378. Of course, there is a racial proxy element underlying the Top Ten Percent Plan where the "top ten percent" at a low-performing segregated school is relative in context to a stronger school with resources and predominantly white students. *Ibid.* at 387.

notes that Fisher may have fared better in a race-conscious holistic review process like that upheld in *Grutter*.[11]

The Court's analysis is further complicated by the fact that Fisher had "long since graduated from another college";[12] there was no challenge to the Top Ten Percent Plan;[13] and the percentage plan–holistic review had only been in operation for three years when Fisher's application was rejected, so there was scant evidence to evaluate; and, finally, the Court itself notes that "[t]he fact that this case has been litigated on a somewhat *artificial* basis, furthermore, may limit its value for prospective guidance."[14]

Applying *Grutter*, the district court and the Fifth Circuit Court of Appeals rejected Fisher's claim.[15] On certiorari to the Court, the judgment of the court of appeals was vacated and remanded.[16] Concluding that the appellate court failed to apply strict scrutiny to the University of Texas' admission program, the Court remanded for a proper determination under this heightened standard of review. The court of appeals, applying strict scrutiny, again held that the Texas admission plan passed constitutional muster.[17]

The Court granted certiorari a second time and upheld the Texas admission plan in a 4–3 decision.[18] *Fisher* was not a ringing reaffirmation of *Grutter*, nor was it a complete invalidation of affirmative action in post-secondary education – it did reset the deferential standard that the Court had previously adopted when reviewing diversity as a First Amendment consideration in admissions. And it further constitutionalizes post-racialism so that race and structural inequality are neutralized – the present-day effects of past discrimination are irrelevant because the ultimate goal is to eliminate race from all aspects of public decision-making.

Diversity is more of a justification than a theory of substantive equality – it seeks to mediate any burdens on the settled expectations of whiteness[19] by espousing the neutral and general process benefits to institutions and whites who get the pedagogical and experiential bonus of "difference" provided by people of color who constitute the "critical mass" of an otherwise homogenous class. Diversity is a myth in the same vein as the Democratic Myth examined in Chapter 4.

---

[11] *Ibid.* at 378.

[12] *Fisher II*, 136 S. Ct. at 378.

[13] *Ibid.*

[14] *Ibid.* (emphasis added).

[15] *Fisher*, 570 U.S. at 306–307 ("*Fisher I*").

[16] *Ibid.* at 315.

[17] *Fisher*, 579 U.S. at 376 ("*Fisher II*").

[18] *Ibid.* at 388. "Justice Scalia died after the oral argument and before the decision. Justice Kagan recused, likely because of her involvement with the case as solicitor general of the United States." ERWIN CHEMERINSKY, CONSTITUTIONAL LAW PRINCIPLES AND POLICIES 807 (6th ed. 2019).

[19] Cheryl I. Harris, Whiteness *as* Property, 106 HARV. L. REV. 1707, 1766 (1993) ("The assumption that whiteness is a property interest entitled to protection is an idea born of systematic white supremacy and nurtured over the years, not only by the law of slavery and 'Jim Crow' but also by the more recent decisions and rationales of the Supreme Court concerning affirmative action").

JUSTICE KENNEDY AND POST-RACIAL DIVERSITY

Emphasizing the three controlling principles of *Fisher I* – (i) race is inherently suspect and subject to strict scrutiny;[20] (ii) the pursuit of diversity is an academic judgment entitled to *some* deference;[21] and (iii) no deference should be given in determining whether a plan is narrowly-tailored if race is used in a holistic review process[22] – Justice Kennedy's post-racial decision is distinct from *Grutter's* conceptualization of diversity and its place in admissions decisions.

There is a more heightened and rigorous assessment of the legitimacy of diversity. While diversity is a compelling interest, its underlying racial component makes the Court less deferential. Some of the relatively expansive language of *Grutter* that "the Law School's educational judgment that diversity is essential to its educational mission is one to which we defer"[23] is qualified in *Fisher*. Now such educational assessments are accorded "some, but not complete, judicial deference"[24] to ensure that the admissions plan can be legitimized when the university "gives a reasoned, principled explanation"[25] for its decision to pursue diversity.

While context still matters,[26] admissions decisions to advance diversity are accorded some deference; and, when evaluating the narrowly tailored prong of strict scrutiny, "no deference is owed."[27] What is striking is that *Grutter's* robust First Amendment language is diluted in *Fisher*: while the decision notes the educational value of diversity, it does not reference the broad discretionary power of institutions in pursuing diversity as it did in *Grutter*.

Under *Grutter's* reasoning, good faith is presumed when the institution is advancing efforts to attain a diverse student body because "universities occupy a special niche in our constitutional tradition,"[28] and they have an inherent institutional freedom to make their own educational judgments, especially in assembling a class of engaged and diverse students from a myriad of backgrounds, life experiences, and perspectives. Now, under *Fisher*, the good faith diversity presumption is rejected because the Court concludes that it is too deferential.

Nevertheless, drawing all inferences in Fisher's favor, the Court concludes that the University's program was constitutional. Advancing four post-racial arguments, Fisher posits that: (i) the University's compelling state interest was not clearly defined ("critical mass" has no discernible meaning and can be deployed as a racial proxy

---

[20] *Fisher II*, 579 U.S. at 377.
[21] *Ibid.*
[22] *Ibid.*
[23] *Grutter*, 539 U.S. 306, 328 (2003).
[24] *Fisher II*, 579 U.S. at 377.
[25] *Ibid.*
[26] *Grutter*, 539 U.S. at 327.
[27] *Fisher II*, 579 U.S. at 377.
[28] *Grutter*, 539 U.S. at 329.

in the form of an impermissible quota);[29] (ii) consideration of race is unnecessary because the University has achieved a diverse critical mass of students;[30] (iii) since race has a "minimal impact" in the admissions process, it should not be considered;[31] and (iv) uncapping the Top Ten Percent program would admit more eligible students.[32] Tellingly, none of these arguments is accepted by the Court – Justice Kennedy's opinion applies strict scrutiny and upholds the admission program.

Rejecting Fisher's argument that the University's compelling interest was not clearly articulated because there was no specific indication of what level of enrollment constitutes a "critical mass" of diverse students, the Court notes that the benefits of diversity cannot be reduced to "pure numbers."[33] Embracing process-based values and utilitarian outcomes,[34] the Court emphasizes "the educational benefits that flow from"[35] a diverse student body – this institutional goal is not simply a function of student enrollment figures. Since quotas are constitutionally noxious, the University could not be held accountable for not specifically quantifying the level of enrollment necessary to attain the educational benefits of diversity.[36]

Relying on anecdotal and quantifiable data on diversity demographics, the Court rejected Fisher's contention that the University had attained a critical mass of diverse students. The enrollment numbers belied this contention as the University presented data establishing "consistent stagnation in terms of the percentage of minority students enrolling … from 1996 to 2002."[37] The Court was satisfied that the University consistently assessed and adjusted as to the need for race-conscious review and came to the reasonable conclusion that its goals had not been attained.[38]

Fisher's next post-racial argument was that the consideration of race in the admissions process was unnecessary because it had "only a minimal impact in advancing the [University's] compelling interest."[39] Again, Fisher's contention was belied by the facts showing that there were meaningful increases of African-American and Latino/a students from 2003 to 2007, and that consideration of race helped to produce a diverse freshman class. Moreover, the University met the narrowly tailored prong of strict scrutiny because "race consciousness play[ed] a role in only a small portion of admissions decisions."[40] Race did not predominate the decision-making

---

[29] *Fisher II*, 579 U.S. at 380.
[30] *Ibid.* at 382.
[31] *Ibid.* at 383.
[32] *Ibid.* at 385.
[33] *Ibid.* at 380.
[34] Ofra Bloch, Diversity Gone Wrong: A Historical Inquiry *into* the Evolving Meaning of Diversity, 20 U. Pa. J. Const. L. 1145 (2018) (analyzing the meaning of diversity in utilitarian and remedial terms).
[35] *Fisher II*, 579 U.S. at 381.
[36] *Ibid.*
[37] *Ibid.* at 383.
[38] *Ibid.* at 384.
[39] *Ibid.* at 384.
[40] *Ibid.* at 384.

process because race was simply a factor amongst numerous race-neutral factors. The University's efforts to diversify its entering class were comprehensive, including intensified outreach, new scholarship programs; over 1,000 organized recruitment events; and a substantial recruitment budget.[41] Also, pursuant to the mandate of the Fifth Circuit decision in *Hopwood v. Texas*,[42] the University spent seven years trying to implement race-neutral holistic review with no success.

Finally, Fisher fashions what she thinks is a completely race-neutral argument by proposing that the Top Ten Percent Plan should be uncapped so that all students are admitted through a percentage plan. Her argument highlights the complexity of race and the fallacy of neutrality. A major premise of the percentage plan was that racially segregated schools would be targeted so that promising students of color would be included in the entering class based upon their academic credentials. Shifting to an exclusive class rank paradigm would "sacrifice all other aspects of diversity in pursuit of enrolling a higher number of minority students."[43] Such an approach would "create[ ] perverse incentives for applicants to stay in low-performing segregated schools"[44] thereby perpetuating the very segregation that it seeks to dismantle.

Fisher is a post-racial diversity opinion: "race is a factor of a factor of a factor"; critical mass is unquantifiable but significantly relevant in the pursuit of diversity; relative progress does not mean that race can never be considered (after fully exploring the viability of race-neutral alternatives); and percentage plans are "blunt instruments"[45] with underlying racial underpinnings that should be employed very carefully, if not completely avoided. Justice Kennedy's post-racial conception of diversity does not go as far as Chief Justice Roberts' post-racialism – he would completely eliminate the consideration of race in all public decision-making – Justice Kennedy submerges race under a myriad of neutral factors along with the doctrinal prerequisite that race-neutral alternatives must be considered before race is used as a last resort. The University of Texas admissions program satisfied this test.

Concluding that the admissions program was narrowly tailored in its pursuit of the compelling interest of diversity, Justice Kennedy appears to return to the more broad and deferential view of the University's decision-making authority in defining diversity as part of its educational mission:

> Considerable deference is owed to a university in defining those intangible characteristics, like student body diversity, that are central to its identity and educational

---

[41] *Ibid.* at 385.
[42] 78 F.3d 932 (5th Cir. 1996). *Hopwood's* holding is abrogated by *Grutter. See generally* Cedric Merlin Powell, *Hopwood: Bakke II and Skeptical Scrutiny*, 9 SETON HALL CONST. L. J. 811 (1999) (discussing *Hopwood* and its doctrinal implications).
[43] *Fisher II*, 579 U.S. at 385.
[44] *Ibid.* at 387.
[45] *Ibid.*

mission. But still, it remains an enduring challenge to our Nation's education system to reconcile the pursuit of diversity with the constitutional promise of equal
treatment and dignity.

In striking this sensitive balance, public universities, like the States themselves,
can serve as "laboratories for experimentation."[46]

Justice Kennedy's pronouncement sounds very promising – it draws on principles
of representative democracy, policy innovation, and a vibrant exchange of inclusive
ideas and institutional ideals. Yet it rings hollow in light of the fact that *Schuette*
was decided just two years before *Fisher*, and it embraced the "democratic" concept
of voter-initiatives to overturn race-conscious affirmative action.[47] This ostensibly
neutral homage to states as sites of democratic invention and innovation is actually
a subtle invitation to overturn affirmative action.[48] What is particularly troubling is
that *Fisher* is the Roberts Court's most positive review of an affirmative action plan,
and it is limited because of the Court's strict adherence to post-racialism. The future
of affirmative action is uncertain, if not doomed.

JUSTICE ALITO'S DISSENT: STRICT SCRUTINY AND POST-RACIAL CONSTITUTIONALISM

With Justice Kennedy's retirement, and the appointment of Justices Gorsuch,
Kavanaugh and Coney Barrett, the Roberts Court has a formidable 6–3 conservative
majority that embraces post-racial constitutionalism – there is a pronounced doctrinal shift from Justice Kennedy's post-racial diversity to Chief Justice Roberts' formal
post-racial constitutionalism.[49] Justice Alito's dissent is the doctrinal harbinger of
this formalism. Invoking specificity akin to the discriminatory intent requirement of
Washington v. Davis, Justice Alito reasons that, in the absence of a clearly identifiable discriminatory practice by the state that excludes minority students, there is no
injury that would warrant a race-conscious remedy in the absence of a showing that
underrepresented enrollments correspond to race. Because the University failed to
clearly state its compelling interest in diversity by defining "critical mass," and there
was no specific fit between its race-based plan and the pursuit of diversity, the program was not narrowly tailored and was constitutionally invalid.[50]

---

[46] *Ibid.* at 387.
[47] *Schuette* is discussed in depth in Chapter 4.
[48] Dominique J. Baker, *Why Might States Ban Affirmative Action?* Brown Center Chalkboard,
      Brookings, April 12, 2019, www.brookings.edu/blog/brown-center-chalkboard/2019/04/12/
      why-might-states-ban-affirmative-action/.
[49] On January 24, 2022, the Court granted certiorari in *Students for Fair Admissions, Inc. v. Presidents
      & Fellows of Harvard College*, consolidated with an identical case against the University of North
      Carolina, in which Asian-American students alleged discrimination on the basis of race in violation
      of Title VI and the Fourteenth Amendment.
[50] 579 U.S. at 390 (Alito, J., dissenting).

Justice Alito's dissent brims with cynicism and insinuation that the University consistently changed its position during the litigation of the case, and he illustrates this by underscoring the racial underpinnings of the purportedly race-neutral Top Ten Percent program and the holistic review plan which employs race as one of many factors. The flaw in the University's admissions program was that there was no qualitative and quantifiable comparison between the two approaches and the respective effects each had on underrepresented minorities in the classroom:

> But UT has never shown that its race-conscious plan actually ameliorates this situation [underrepresentation of African-American, Hispanic, and Asian-American students in many classes]. The University presents no evidence that its admissions officers, in administering the "holistic" component of its plan, make any effort to determine whether an African-American, Hispanic, or Asian-American student is likely to enroll in classes in which minority students are underrepresented. And although UT's records should permit it to determine without much difficulty whether holistic admittees are any more likely than students admitted through the Top Ten Percent ... to enroll in the classes lacking racial or ethnic diversity, UT either has not crunched those numbers or has not revealed what they show. Nor has UT explained why the underrepresentation of Asian-American students in many classes justifies its plan, which discriminates *against* those students.[51]

This is a bold and disconcerting statement on many levels – Justice Alito presumes bad faith on the part of the University because of its use of race, in a limited and permissible manner, and this alters the equation on institutional decision-making on diversity; he seems eager to advance the raw stereotypes underlying race; and he constructs a post-racial rhetorical move deploying racial tropes, like the Model Minority,[52] while purportedly arguing for neutrality. Indeed, it is quite striking how Justice Alito's use of these stereotypes fall differently, depending on the racial group. Asian-Americans are discriminated against while African Americans receive a race-based windfall in a flawed system.

In essence, Justice Alito's dissent reads like a reverse discrimination suit for Asian-Americans and whites who have been "displaced" by the relative progress of African Americans and Latino/as in the admissions process. It is a small leap from

---

[51] *Ibid.* at 390 (emphasis in original).

[52] Frank H. Wu, *Neither Black Nor White: Asian Americans and Affirmative Action*, 15 B.C. THIRD WORLD L. J. 225, 226; 271–72(1995) (this myth is used to denigrate other minorities by constructing a hierarchy of oppression where Asian Americans have suffered discrimination, but overcome it by hard work, not race-based government handouts; "… the model minority myth may be expected to continue as an argument against affirmative action, and affirmative action may be expected as an explanation for mistreatment of Asian-Americans. They have become bound together, twin coded concepts: 'the model minority image' and 'reverse discrimination'"); Nancy Leong, *The Misuse of Asian Americans in the Affirmative Action Debate*, 64 UCLA L. REV. DISC. 90, 91–92 (2016) ("Asian Americans provide a convenient opportunity for affirmative action opponents to disguise their underlying motives. The true, unstated concern of such opponents is that affirmative action would disrupt the existing racial hierarchy – one that primarily benefits white people.").

Asian-Americans are being discriminated against, to progress has been made in advancing diversity,[53] to African Americans are receiving a racial windfall so race should not be considered.

While critical mass is undefined, it has been reached – there is a "more racially diverse environment at the University"[54] – so the use of race is strictly prohibited. This part of Justice Alito's argument seems counterintuitive: he critiques the decision for a lack of analytical precision in defining critical mass, but highlights it as evincing the success of the University's diversity efforts, and then concludes rather disparagingly that "[n]otwithstanding these lauded results, UT leapt at the opportunity to reinsert race into the process."[55]

To Justice Alito, post-racial diversity means that race should not be considered if the University can achieve nearly the same result without considering it.[56] Unlike Justice Kennedy's conception of post-racial diversity, race is not a default to a myriad of neutral factors after fully determining that they are unworkable; rather, race should not be considered because of its stigmatizing and divisive effects.

The most disturbing aspect of Justice Alito's post-racial dissent is its active engagement with stereotypical tropes to undermine the efficacy of race-conscious affirmative action. He focuses on the University's claim that holistic review, with race as one of many factors, was necessary because "the Top Ten Percent Plan admits *the wrong kind* of African-American and Hispanic students, namely, students from poor families who attend schools in which the student body is predominantly African-American or Hispanic."[57] Justice Alito critiques the assumption underlying the Fifth Circuit's opinion that race-neutral Top Ten Percent program admittees performed presumptively poorer academically because they did not compete academically against white and Asian-Americans in their segregated schools. He concludes that "this insulting stereotype is not supported by the record"[58] because students admitted under the Top Ten Percent program "receive higher college grades than African-American and Hispanic students admitted under the race-conscious program."[59]

So, a race-neutral approach (the Top Ten Percent program) leads to legitimate results that are tainted by racist stereotypes and race-based decision-making that privileges minorities with advantages over those minorities who are disadvantaged and need the support of affirmative action.[60]

---

[53] *Fisher II*, 579 U.S. 395 (Alito, J., dissenting).

[54] *Ibid.*

[55] *Ibid.*

[56] *Ibid.* at 427–28, 428 ("Where, as here, racial preferences have only a slight impact on minority enrollment, a race-neutral alternative likely could have reached the same result"); *Ibid.* at 425–27.

[57] *Ibid.* at 391 (emphasis in original).

[58] *Ibid.* at 392.

[59] *Ibid.*

[60] *Ibid.* at 419 (Justice Alito states, "This is affirmative action gone wild").

While it appears that Justice Alito is a stalwart proponent of substantive equality, his feigned indignation belies his true purpose – eliminating affirmative action. He concludes that "Because UT has failed to provide any evidence whatsoever that race-conscious holistic review will achieve its diversity objectives more effectively than race-blind holistic review, it cannot satisfy the heavy burden imposed by the strict scrutiny standard."[61]

Notwithstanding all of the standing and conceptual problems with Fisher's claim of injury, Justice Alito nevertheless concludes that "By all rights, judgment should be entered in favor of [Fisher]."[62] Indeed, he views the University's admissions program as a form of systemic racism – this is the heart of inversion and the reverse discrimination rationale[63] – because there is no adequate explanation as to why "discrimination is necessary to achieve the educational benefits of diversity."[64] Although acknowledging that diversity is a compelling interest, what is constitutionally fatal, in Justice Alito's view, is that the specific educational benefits of classroom diversity,[65] intraracial diversity ("diversity within diversity" referencing the distinction between advantaged and disadvantaged minorities),[66] and demographic parity (to avoid racial isolation)[67] are never explained by the University.

Race was not a "factor of a factor of a factor," but a determining feature of the admissions process.[68] Thus, the University failed to meet the demands of strict scrutiny. There was no constitutionally cognizable compelling interest, and the program was not narrowly tailored because "critical mass" is an "intentionally imprecise interest ... designed to insulate UT's program from meaningful judicial review."[69]

Neither Justice Kennedy's majority opinion nor Justice Alito's dissent are analytically satisfying because they operate on the edges of the substantive issue before the Court – the constitutional validity of race-conscious remedial measures to ensure meaningful inclusion in a manner that disrupts existing systems of structural exclusion – the majority opinion embraces neutrality and the implicit ambiguity of when the use of race is permissible, while the dissent rejects this indirectness and imprecision and posits specificity and rigorous strict scrutiny review whenever race is used.

Thus, there are two strands of post-racial constitutionalism: there is Justice Kennedy's implicit post-racial diversity that foregrounds neutrality before considering race as a last resort, and then as only one factor amongst many race-neutral factors;

---

[61] *Ibid.* at 427.
[62] *Ibid.* at 393.
[63] Cedric Merlin Powell, *Blinded by Color: The New Equal Protection, the Second Deconstruction, and Affirmative Inaction*, 51 U. Miami L. Rev. 191, 199–220 (1997).
[64] *Fisher II*, 579 U.S. at 437 (Alito, J., dissenting).
[65] *Ibid.* at 415.
[66] *Ibid.* at 415–22.
[67] *Ibid.* at 425–27.
[68] *Ibid.* at 398.
[69] *Ibid.* at 401.

and, by contrast, there is Justice Alito's (and Chief Justice Roberts') formal post-racialism which presumes that any and all uses of race are constitutionally suspect and ultimately invalid. Although differing significantly on the place of race in evaluating applicants, both the majority and dissenting opinions are committed to post-racial process values – the concern is with how the neutral process functions with either race submerged under several layers of factors, or no racial factors because there is no constitutionally acceptable reason for "discriminating" on the basis of race.

The Court's modern race jurisprudence is premised on legitimizing any incremental societal progress made by African-Americans, and other people of color, so that it is acceptable to whites and societal harmony is preserved. This is accomplished by circumscribing the scope of any remedy; neutralizing race, so that if it is a component of any evaluative process it is surrounded by a panoply of non-racial factors which minimize its significance; advancing post-racial process values like how much progress has been made (so race-conscious remedies are unnecessary); avoiding burdening innocent whites who should not be penalized for societal discrimination; and rejecting any reference to the present-day effects of past discrimination without discriminatory intent. Under this jurisprudential regime, progress will always be episodic and limited.[70] This is even more salient now that Justice Kennedy has retired,[71] and the Court's current composition is even more hostile toward race-conscious remedial approaches and affirmative action.

POST-RACIAL CONSTITUTIONALISM AND THE FUTURE OF AFFIRMATIVE ACTION

Analytically, *Fisher's* reliance on race as "a factor of a factor of a factor" is unconvincingly muddled – the proposition offers little doctrinal guidance to proponents or opponents of affirmative action. Depending on how race is conceptualized, the narrowly tailored prong of the strict scrutiny test is either met because race is invisible under so many neutral layers, or it is present but immeasurable as a quota or a preference thereby establishing constitutionally permissible "critical mass" for a diverse class. This is a dramatic example of what Yuvraj Joshi theorizes as racial indirection.[72]

---

[70] Elise C. Boddie, *Adaptive Discrimination*, 94 N. C. L. REV. 1235, 1247 (2016) (noting the structural and systemic underpinnings of racism, and stating that "racial progress is not inevitable but rather … it ebbs and flows through time").

[71] Justice Kennedy is the principal author of the Roberts Court's post-racial jurisprudence: his concurring opinion was controlling in *Parents Involved* discussed in Chapter 3; he authored *Schuette* discussed in Chapter 4; *Fisher I* and *II* (Chapter 5); *Ricci* (Chapter 6); and *Inclusive Communities* (Chapter 7). Chief Justice Roberts has taken an active role in authoring the Court's post-racial voting rights jurisprudence in *Shelby County* and *Rucho*. And Justice Alito adds an even starker strain of post-racialism in authoring *Husted* and *Brnovich*. All of these decisions are discussed at length in Chapter 8.

[72] Yuvraj Joshi, *Racial Indirection*, 52 U.C. DAVIS L. REV. 2495 (2019).

Race as "a factor of a factor of a factor," "critical mass," and the contextual consideration of race as a "plus" factor, amongst many other neutral factors, are ways of positing racial indirection.[73] In the Court's race jurisprudence, racial indirection is a permissible form of doctrinal avoidance – race is either conflated with so many other neutral factors that its significance is substantially muted, or it is re-conceptualized as a "plus" factor distinguished from a quota or set-aside, which would make race the determining factor in admissions plans.[74] This post-racial evasiveness is crafted rhetorically to de-emphasize the eradication of structural inequality and any potential progress by people of color, and to blunt white resentment while simultaneously pursuing diversity by obliquely referencing race.[75] Thus, Joshi concludes that "There is a basic constitutional principle that can be distilled from these [affirmative action] cases: *so long as the end is constitutionally permissible, the less direct the reliance on race to achieve that end, the less constitutionally problematic the means.*"[76]

Because the pursuit of diversity is a compelling interest and constitutionally permissible, the narrowly tailored prong of strict scrutiny is met by racial indirection. *Fisher* embodies the Court's post-racial constitutionalism – it foregrounds neutrality and signals the end of race-conscious remedial approaches unless they can be justified by indirection. Affirmative action's future is bleaker now given the fact that Justice Kennedy's post-racial diversity will no longer be the plurality position since he has retired from the Court. Indeed, *Fisher* was the only decision in which Justice Kennedy voted to uphold a race-conscious remedy.[77]

Justice Alito's *Fisher* dissent underscores the pronounced skepticism of the Roberts Court to race-conscious remedies, and the fact that racial indirection will soon prove inadequate to sustain affirmative action – "critical mass" diversity cannot be measured and the "intentionally imprecise interest is designed to insulate UT's program from meaningful judicial review."[78] This lack of precision means that strict scrutiny analysis is diluted because there can be no meaningful inquiry into whether a race-conscious remedial measure is narrowly tailored, as none of the goals associated with critical mass can be measured.[79] The Court will be much more rigorous in the future in requiring a justification for the consideration of race in admissions decisions.

All the Court's affirmative action jurisprudence is steeped in racial indirection – the consideration of race, and its potential impact on the settled expectations of white privilege, must be justified, legitimized, and ultimately sold to the white

---

73 *Ibid.* at 2497 (*quoting Fisher II*, 136 S. Ct. at 2207) ("Thus, race, in this indirect fashion, considered with all of the other factors … can make a difference to whether an application is accepted or rejected").

74 *Ibid.* at 2523.

75 *Ibid.* at 2538.

76 *Ibid.* at 2503 (emphasis in original).

77 Chemerinsky, *supra* n. 18, at 807.

78 *Fisher II*, 579 U.S. at 401 (Alito, J., dissenting).

79 *Ibid.* at 403–04.

majority so that there is no racial conflict or backlash.[80] Of course, this is impossible. Racial indirection is a doctrinal amalgamation of colorblindness, which is dichotomous because it acknowledges race while endeavoring to ignore it, and post-racialism which heralds the end of systemic racism while ostensibly transcending race by ignoring its structural impact.

Racial indirection has a structural element, too, where the Court actively embraces ostensibly neutral democratic action like states functioning as laboratories of democracy and innovation,[81] voting reform, and reverse discrimination suits to preserve the moral mandate of colorblindness,[82] all of which constitutionalize or codify structural inequality.[83] This is because the baseline concern in the Roberts Court's race jurisprudence is the preservation of white privilege so that any advance or progress must be weighed against the impact on white interests. This explains why "the end result of the *Fisher* majority opinion was the reinforcement and fortification of white privilege."[84]

It is ironic that most of the progress that African Americans and people of color have made is in the context of reverse discrimination lawsuits – *Bakke, Grutter,* and *Fisher* are all indicative of the leftover equality minorities receive after any gains are contextualized and counterbalanced through the norm of whiteness.[85] These decisions graphically illustrate Derrick Bell's conceptualization of interest convergence. Any progress that has been made coincides with a discernible benefit to whites, and any residual equality that is leftover goes to Blacks (and other communities of color – this is the essence of affirmative action).[86]

Process values like cross racial understanding, destruction of stereotypes, a diverse workforce and pluralistic society, and a legitimate pathway to leadership are

---

[80] Joshi, *supra* n. 72, at 2536–39, 2538.

[81] *Fisher II*, 579 U.S. at 387.

[82] *Ibid.* at 398–99 (Alito, J., dissenting).

[83] All of the Roberts Court's post-racial decisions share this doctrinal underpinning – the elevation of process values to supplant substantive equality: *Schuette* constitutionalizes voter-initiatives to abolish race-conscious remedies; *Fisher* approves doctrinal evasiveness to advance diversity but only on severely circumscribed terms; *Ricci v. DeStefano* (Chapter 6) codifies a strict intent requirement that privileges white plaintiffs' victimization while disregarding the disparate impact of structural inequality; and *Shelby County v. Holder* (Chapter 8) guts the substantive core of the Voting Rights Act premised on a contrived version of federalism which signals to the states that, in the absence of federal supervision of local affairs, it is open season on the voting rights of oppressed minorities.

[84] Barnes, Chemerinsky & Onwuachi-Willig, *supra* n. 7, at 288.

[85] *Ibid.* at 294 ("In essence, the Supreme Court's assumptions about race in *Fisher* only worked to reinforce white privilege by identifying the experiences of Whites as the normative standard by which all others are to be evaluated.").

[86] Melvin J. Kelley IV, *Retuning Bell: Searching for Freedom's Ring as Whiteness Resurges in Value,* 34 HARV. J. RACIAL & ETHNIC JUST. 131, 140 (2018) (merging Bell's interest convergence theory with Cheryl Harris' conception of whiteness as property and noting that "access to whiteness will only be provided when it yields political, economic, social or psychological benefits to owners of whiteness. As such, the license is revocable whenever the associated benefits are no longer sufficient to justify the permission to access whiteness.").

all process goals premised on access, to an existing system or institution, rather than the eradication of systemic subjugation. Affirmative action's future is tenuous; apart from a solid majority committed to post-racial constitutionalism, the acceptable means for justifying any consideration of race has significantly narrowed. There are only two constitutionally cognizable compelling interests – remedying identifiable discrimination and diversity – and now a permissible narrowly-tailored remedy means that race must be formally obscured. And if it is detected, beneath the underlying layers of neutrality and racial indirection, it must be rationalized with particularized clarity.

This exposes the doctrinal fallacy of diversity and the stunting effect that post-racial neutrality has on race-conscious remedial approaches designed to promote substantive equality and inclusion. *Fisher* illustrates the circularity of post-racial constitutional arguments: on the one hand, there is the promotion of Rhetorical Neutrality, as in Justice Kennedy's opinion, where history is ignored (there is no acknowledgement of the present-day effects of past discrimination); discrimination is defined formalistically so that the impact is on either whites or Asian-American interests both promoted by reverse discrimination rationales; and, a rhetorical myth is advanced by the Court purportedly preserving the discretionary power of educational institutions in employing race-conscious remedies while severely limiting any such flexibility. On the other hand, Justice Alito critiques racial indirection – "critical mass" and "race as a factor of a factor of a factor" – as amorphous and immeasurable so much so that such indirect racial approaches can never be fully reviewed under the strict scrutiny test.

While racial indirection describes the current state of affirmation action, it can only survive under the subterfuge of doctrinal misdirection, and this will ultimately spell its doom. A number of factors underscore this point: (i) racial indirection privileges neutrality, whiteness, and post-racialism so that race and racism are de-emphasized and diffuse process values are emphasized; (ii) it gives presumptive analytical power to decision-making that is ahistorical, acontextual, and formalistic so that the defining principle of the Court's race jurisprudence is lessening the burden on whites and explaining why any incremental progress by Blacks is permissible under a colorblind (and now post-racial) Constitution; (iii) it provides the basis for retrenchment and retrogression because any benefit to Blacks is limited and temporary, and based on the proposition that once formal equality is achieved, there is no need to consider race; (iv) it gives false hope that situational compromise is the best way to achieve structural change; and (v) racial indirection, while not always "invidious,"[87] is nevertheless a determining factor in the Roberts Court's post-racialism.

---

[87] This is meant to highlight the argument between Justice Kennedy, who advocates a race-neutral approach with race as a last resort default and Justice Alito's formal post-racialism, which views the University of Texas as engaging in unconstitutional racial balancing. *See Fisher II*, 579 U.S. at 407 (Alito, J., dissenting).

The ambiguous tenor of *Fisher* adds to the uncertainty about the doctrinal viability of diversity, but it nevertheless underscores the Court's institutional commitment to post-racial constitutionalism. The Roberts Court has even linked its conception of post-racialism under the Fourteenth Amendment to its Title VII jurisprudence – *Ricci v. DeStefano* is yet another canonical race opinion by Justice Kennedy that advances neutrality and foregrounds white victimization due to the impact of a process skewed by race.

The Roberts Court's solution is to infuse its post-racial constitutionalism into its interpretation of Title VII thereby significantly diluting the statute's recognition of structural inequality in the workplace – the analysis under the Fourteenth Amendment, and by extension, Title VII, shifts from anti-subordination to anti-differentiation, to anti-remediation. The Court has codified post-racialism under Title VII.

6

Ricci v. DeStefano

Post-Racial Neutrality, Opportunity, and Results

The common doctrinal proposition that connects the Court's post-racial jurisprudence under the Fourteenth Amendment and Title VII is that "the way to stop discrimination on the basis of race is to stop discriminating on the basis of race."[1] All of the underlying post-racial themes underpinning the *Parents Involved* decision are present in *Ricci*, a reverse discrimination case advanced by white firefighters: there is a marked skepticism toward any race-conscious remedial approach;[2] the rights of *individual* white test takers who passed the examination are presumptively valid so that a good faith effort by the City to avoid disparate impact liability is inverted into a disparate (reverse discrimination) treatment claim; Justice Alito's concurrence employs stereotypical rhetoric reminiscent of revisionist Reconstruction histories to "illustrate" how race skewed the "neutral" process;[3] and there is an even more pronounced concern here, under Title VII, that the innocent, hardworking white firefighters not be deprived of the awards for their meritorious achievement.[4]

It was well-settled precedent in the Second Circuit where the firefighters' reverse discrimination claim arose that disparate impact on minorities could be avoided without triggering a disparate treatment claim.[5] There was a bright line between

---

[1] *Parents Involved*, 515 U.S. at 748.

[2] *Ricci*, 557 U.S. 557, 579 (2009) ("… without some other justification … race-based decision-making violates Title VII[ ]."). Likewise, in *Parents Involved*, since race predominated in the school assignment process, the plans in Louisville and Seattle were held to be unconstitutional. 551 U.S. at 723.

[3] *Ricci*, 557 U.S. at 596–608, 607 (Alito, J., concurring) (arguing that the City's good faith, voluntary effort to avoid disparate impact liability was merely pretextual; the real reason for decertifying the test results was to "please a politically important racial constituency.").

[4] The Court itself privileges this narrative in *Ricci*. *See* 557 U.S. at 607–608 (Alito, J., concurring) (cataloguing the personal sacrifices of Frank Ricci and the only person of color to join the reverse discrimination suit, Latino firefighter Benjamin Vargas); A.G. Sulzberger, *For Hispanic Firefighter in Bias Suit, Awkward Position but Firm Resolve*, N.Y. TIMES, July 3, 2009, at A18.

[5] "It should be noted that civil rights statutes can, and often do, allow violations to be proved based on discriminatory impact without evidence of a discriminatory purpose. … For example, Title VII of the 1964 Civil Rights Acts allows employment discrimination to be established by proof of discriminatory impact. …" ERWIN CHEMERINSKY, CONSTITUTIONAL LAW: PRINCIPLES AND POLICIES 770 (6th ed. 2019) (*citing Griggs v. Duke Power Co.*, 401 U.S. 424 (1971)).

both types of discrimination. In *Ricci*, the Court merges both types of discrimination so that *intentional* racial discrimination is no different analytically than an attempt to avoid a disproportionately racial impact on a historically oppressed group. Just as there is no distinction between invidious and benign discrimination under the Court's Fourteenth Amendment jurisprudence, there is no distinction between intentional discrimination (disparate treatment) and good faith, race-conscious remedial attempts to avoid disparate impact liability under Title VII.[6] The Court's most glaring departure from precedent was its reinterpretation of *Griggs* and Title VII.

Ricci rejects the structural view of racial inequality, and instead offers a neutral rationale – the examination was fair and the high failure rate for African-American officer candidates was due to a lack of preparation – for the exclusion of African-American firefighters from the officer ranks; it inverts the disparate treatment and impact standards under Title VII so that intentional discrimination is the prerequisite for any actions under the statute; it crafts a novel evidentiary standard that presumes the validity of reverse discrimination claims; and, finally, employs racial politics to reach the conclusion that the process is flawed because race was the predominant factor in decision-making.

JUSTICE KENNEDY'S POST-RACIALISM: TITLE VII AND THE FOURTEENTH AMENDMENT

"In 2003, 118 New Haven [Connecticut] (the "City") firefighters took examinations to qualify for promotion to the rank of lieutenant or captain."[7] By City charter, a merit system was established that provided that vacancies in civil service jobs be filled by the most qualified individuals determined by the examinations.[8] The New Haven Civil Service Board ("CSB") "certifies a rank list of applicants who passed the test."[9] The charter's "rule of three" provided that "the relevant hiring authority must fill each vacancy by choosing one candidate from the top three scorers on the list."[10] Applicants for lieutenant and captain positions were screened through a written exam and an oral exam, which represented 60 and 40 percent of the total score, respectively.[11]

---

[6] *Ricci*, 557 U.S. at 585 ("… under Title VII, before an employer can engage in intentional discrimination for the asserted purpose of avoiding or remedying an unintentional disparate impact, the employer must have a strong basis in evidence to believe it will be subject to disparate-impact liability if it fails to take the race-conscious, discriminatory action."). The Court conflates discriminatory intent so that an attempt to avoid disparate impact liability is transformed into disparate treatment of displaced white employees of the fire department.

[7] *Ibid.* at 562.

[8] *Ibid.* at 564.

[9] *Ibid.*

[10] *Ibid.*

[11] The City hired Industrial/Organizational Solutions ("IOS") to develop the promotional exam. *Ibid.* at 564–65.

The passage rate for the lieutenant and captains' examinations showed stark racial disparities for African-American and Latino candidates:

> Seventy-seven candidates completed the lieutenant examination—43 whites, 19 blacks, and 15 Hispanics. Of those, 34 candidates passed—25 whites, 6 blacks, and 3 Hispanics. Eight lieutenant positions were vacant at the time of the examination. As the rule of three operated, this meant that the top 10 candidates were eligible for an immediate promotion to lieutenant. *All 10 were white.* Subsequent vacancies would have allowed at least 3 black candidates to be considered for promotion to lieutenant.
>
> Forty-one candidates completed the captain examination—25 whites, 8 blacks, and 8 Hispanics. Of those, 22 candidates passed—16 whites, 3 blacks, and 3 Hispanics. Seven captain positions were vacant at the time of the examination. Under the rule of three, 9 candidates were eligible for an immediate promotion to captain—7 *whites and 2 Hispanics.*[12]

This meant that while a very small number of African-American or Latino firefighters passed the examination, *no African-American* and only *two* Latino firefighters were eligible for promotion under the rules.[13]

Faced with this racially based adverse impact and the possibility of liability under Title VII; and, after conducting five hearings involving stakeholders from the designer of the test to the firefighters and community leaders, the CSB voted not to certify the results of the examinations and no one was promoted.[14] Seventeen white firefighters and one Latino who were eligible for promotion, upon passing the examination, sued the City in federal court. They alleged that the failure to certify the test results violated the Equal Protection Clause of the Constitution and the disparate treatment provision of Title VII.[15]

The district court granted the City's motion for summary judgment and the Second Circuit Court of Appeals affirmed.[16] Granting certiorari to re-examine the scope of race-conscious remedies under the Equal Protection Clause and Title VII, it is obvious from the very beginning of the Court's recitation of the underlying facts that the post-racial result is a foregone conclusion.

Several neutral rhetorical moves lead to the Court's holding: (i) the case is fashioned as a "contest" for goods with two competing parties: one with the presumption

---

[12] *Ibid.* at 566 (citations omitted) (emphasis added).

[13] "There were even greater disparities among those eligible under city policy for promotion based on these results: of the nineteen people who were eligible for promotion to lieutenant or captain, *seventeen were white, while only two were Hispanic and none were black, though blacks and Hispanics comprised more than 42* percent *of those who took the promotion test.*" Luke Appling, *Recent Development, Ricci v. DeStefano*, 45 Harv. C.R.-C.L. Rev. 147, 150 (2010) (emphasis added).

[14] *Ricci*, 557 U.S. at 567–74.

[15] *Ibid.* at 575 (*citing* 42 U.S.C. § 2000e-2(a)).

[16] 264 Fed. Appx. 106 (2nd Cir. 2008) (summary order), 530 F.3d 87 (2nd Cir. 2008) (summary order withdrawn), 530 F.3d 88 (2nd Cir. 2008) (motion for rehearing en banc denied).

of "merit" and entitlement because they passed the examination, and those who benefitted only because race was used to skew the process; (ii) *Griggs* is literally written out of the case as governing precedent; (iii) the Court begins with the premise that the City discriminated against the white firefighters because the failure to certify the examination results was based on race; and (iv) disparate impact liability is trivialized so that the racial disparities between white, Black, and Latino test takers are irrelevant in the absence of additional proof beyond the EEOC guidelines. Finally, the Court substantially alters Title VII jurisprudence by inverting the analytical principles underlying disparate impact liability and creating a Fourteenth Amendment–derived evidentiary standard ("strong basis in evidence") that will only serve to confuse employers and chill voluntary compliance efforts in the future.

Ricci is an acontextual and ahistorical decision: the Court's analysis does not acknowledge, in any way, the present-day effects of past discrimination. The Court goes through the facts of the five CSB meetings in great detail to emphasize how the process was flawed because it trammeled the *individual* interests of white firefighters who were entitled to promotions based on their test scores.[17] Liberal individualism is codified, and group-based statutory claims based on race take a backseat to Frank Ricci's reverse discrimination claim. Indeed, the Court privileges Mr. Ricci's narrative over the City's good faith efforts to avoid disparate impact liability.[18] Discrimination is "define[ed] … so narrowly that whites become the new 'discrete and insular minorit[y]' (systemic oppression against African-Americans and people of color is so amorphous that it cannot be specifically identified (or remedied), and *individualized* reverse discrimination claims are presumptively valid)."[19] The definitional myth, then, reifies notions of post-racialism – the white firefighters are perpetual victims notwithstanding the fact that many of them are legacies with direct access to all of the avenues of promotion compared to the overwhelming majority of Black applicants who were first generation firefighters.[20]

The Court constructs a neutral factual narrative of basic "fairness": the white firefighters, "at considerable personal and financial cost,"[21] simply outperformed the minority candidates; the process worked well until race infected it; and the City took the side of those who did not perform well based solely on complaints about a "statistical racial disparity"[22] that could be explained as the objective outcome of a

---

[17] *Ricci*, 557 U.S. at 561–76.
[18] *Ibid.* at 566; Cheryl I. Harris and Kimberly West-Faulcon, Reading Ricci: *Whitening Discrimination, Racing Test Fairness*, 58 UCLA L. Rev. 73, 74–77, 118–19 (2010) (discussing how the issue was framed as whites as racial victims notwithstanding the fact that there was no "injury" because no one was promoted).
[19] Cedric Merlin Powell, *Rhetorical Neutrality: Colorblindness, Frederick Douglas, and Inverted Critical Race Theory*, 56 Clev. St. L. Rev. 823, 858 (2008) (emphasis added).
[20] *Ricci*, 557 U.S. at 613–14 (Ginsburg, J., dissenting).
[21] *Ibid.* at 562.
[22] *Ibid.*

job-related examination. "In the end the City took the side of those who protested the test results. It threw out the examinations."[23] To the Court, the City chose the "wrong side" because its decision was not neutral.[24]

Similarly situated white firefighters were discriminated against on the basis of race. The process guarantees equal opportunity, not equal results[25] – this would certainly be true if the process were free from the lingering effects of past discrimination.

For example, despite some gains in entry-level firefighting positions, there were still significant disparities in the supervisory ranks – only 1 out of 21 department captains was African American – this is a clear remnant of past exclusionary practices with current disparate impact.

So, it is obvious that white firefighters and African-American firefighters did not start at the same place in the process. Next, the Court finds a neutral rationale to explain the cavernous disparity between white and African-American test takers. To do so, the Court offers a novel reinterpretation of *Griggs v. Duke Power*.

The Court inverts the central premise of *Griggs*: ostensibly neutral practices, procedures, or tests may nevertheless "operate to 'freeze' the status quo of prior discriminatory practices."[26] "Congress directed the thrust of the Act to the *consequences* of employment practices, not simply the motivation."[27] The Court shifts the analytical focus from the consequences of employment practices[28] to the "discriminatory" intent of the City – there must be a "lawful justification for its race-based action."[29] The Court takes this doctrinal leap by ignoring a long line of established Title VII precedent that permits voluntary compliance efforts to avoid disparate impact liability.[30] Once this core Title VII theme is dismantled by the Court, it goes on to construct a new presumption that radically modifies disparate impact liability.

Any use of race is presumptively a statutory violation unless there is a lawful justification for its use. The Court's analysis does not even begin from a point of

---

[23] *Ibid.*

[24] *Ibid.* at 563 ("We conclude that race-based action like the City's in this case is impermissible under Title VII unless the employer can demonstrate a strong basis in evidence that, had it not taken the action, it would have been liable under the disparate – impact statute. ... [T]he City's action in discarding the test was a violation of Title VII.").

[25] *Ibid.* at 580 ("... our decision must be consistent with the important purpose of Title VII – that the workplace be an environment free of discrimination, where race is not a barrier to opportunity").

[26] *Griggs*, 401 U.S. at 430.

[27] *Ibid.* at 432 (emphasis in original).

[28] Specifically, if the purportedly neutral testing system is left intact, "entrenched inequality" will continue to operate to exclude African-American firefighters from the officer ranks. *Ricci*, 557 U.S. at 610 (Ginsburg, J., dissenting); Harris and West-Faulcon, *supra* n. 18, at 133–57 (proving that the lieutenant and captain examinations violated the EEOC's 4/5ths rule and that the tests were unfair to people of color and whites).

[29] *Ricci*, 557 U.S. at 580.

[30] *Ibid.* at 628–29 (Ginsburg, J., dissenting).

deference to the City's good faith attempt to avoid disparate impact liability, the EEOC guidelines that clearly define the disparity here as a statutory violation, or Congress' legislative purpose of removing the present-day ("neutral") effects of past discrimination. Instead, the Court all but determines the result of this case by starting with the premise that "[t]he City's actions would violate the disparate-treatment prohibition of Title VII absent some valid defense."[31]

In much the same manner that the Court focuses on the discriminatory perpetrator through intent in its equal protection jurisprudence, *Ricci's* approach, under Title VII, emphasizes discriminatory intent so that the African-American firefighters' legitimate claim of disparate impact is subsumed under the premise that the only statutorily valid claim is that of the white firefighters. The white firefighters become "victims" of their own performance on the examination: "the City rejected the test results because 'too many whites and not enough minorities' would be promoted were the lists to be certified."[32] The City's voluntary attempt to comply with Title VII becomes intentional discrimination. Impact, whether under the Fourteenth Amendment or Title VII, is constitutionally or statutorily irrelevant in the absence of something more.

The Roberts Court's post-racial jurisprudence is based on the central theme that, even if there are significant disproportionalities between people of color and whites, actionable discrimination must be based on clearly identifiable intent. This narrow doctrinal rationale unifies the Court's affirmative action, school desegregation (integration) and, most recently, Title VII decisions. *Ricci* is an extraordinary decision because it acknowledges the existence of a "significant adverse impact"[33] which establishes "a prima facie case of disparate-impact liability,"[34] but nevertheless concludes that this "significant statistical disparity"[35] is meaningless (or natural) in the absence of some *additional* proof of liability. "The problem for respondents is that a prima facie case of disparate-impact liability – essentially a threshold showing of a significant statistical disparity ... *and nothing more* – is far from a strong basis in evidence that the City would have been liable under Title VII had it certified the results."[36] The Court reaches this conclusion by inverting disparate treatment and impact with a manufactured tension that distorts the meaning of Title VII, and by creating a new strong basis in evidence standard.

The Inversion of Disparate Treatment and Disparate Impact

Writing for the Court, Justice Kennedy attempts to chart a "middle" doctrinal course between what he views as the absolutist arguments advanced by the firefighter

---

[31] *Ibid.* at 578.
[32] *Ibid.* at 579 (citation omitted).
[33] *Ibid.* at 578.
[34] *Ibid.*
[35] *Ibid.*
[36] *Ibid.* (emphasis added).

petitioners and the City. He dismisses, as "overly simplistic and too restrictive of Title VII's purpose,"[37] the petitioners' argument that "an employer must be in violation of the disparate-impact provision before it can use compliance as a defense in a disparate-impact suit."[38] Referencing congressional intent that "voluntary compliance be the preferred means of achieving the objectives of Title VII,"[39] Justice Kennedy expresses concern that a requirement of certainty of a disparate impact violation "would bring compliance efforts to a near standstill."[40]

Justice Kennedy is equally adept at rejecting the City's argument that its good faith attempt to avoid disparate impact liability permits it to use race-conscious remedies. Concluding that the 1991 amendment to Title VII contained no good faith exception for race-based compliance efforts under the disparate impact provision,[41] Justice Kennedy posits that "[a]llowing employers to violate the disparate-treatment prohibition based on a mere good faith fear of disparate-impact liability would encourage race-based action at the slightest hint of disparate impact."[42] This would lead to an exclusive focus on statistics, with employers adopting a racial quota system designed to avoid even the "slightest hint of disparate impact." Essentially, any hint of the use of race will be rejected by the Court – post-racialism means that the results in race cases are virtually predetermined (this is post-racial determinism).

What is really telling about Justice Kennedy's discussion of the arguments advanced by the parties is that he embraces the core value of Title VII – voluntary compliance – while simultaneously rejecting such compliance as statutorily prohibited, race-based decision-making in violation of the disparate treatment provision. This is because the Court's analysis starts with the premise that the City violated the disparate treatment prohibition of Title VII: the white firefighters were discriminated against because of their race when the CSB failed to certify the results of the examinations due to the overwhelming disparate impact on the African-American firefighters. The Court itself acknowledges that this is a case where there is *prima facie* evidence of disparate-impact liability.[43] The pass rate for Black (31.6 percent) and Latino (20 percent) candidates "[fell] well below the 80-percent standard set by the EEOC to implement the disparate impact provision of Title VII."[44] Based on rankings and the "rule of three" (the employer must fill each vacancy with one candidate from the top three scorers),[45] if the examination had been certified, no African-American candidates could have been considered for promotion.[46] Finally, the disparity here is

37 *Ibid.* at 581.
38 *Ibid.* at 580–81.
39 *Ibid.* at 581 (citations omitted).
40 *Ibid.*
41 *Ibid.*
42 *Ibid.*
43 *Ibid.* at 586.
44 *Ibid.*
45 *Ibid.* at 564.
46 *Ibid.*

directly connected to an ostensibly neutral procedure which freezes the exclusionary practices of the past.[47] Yet, this was insufficient for the Court.

Discarding the EEOC's 80 percent standard, the Court constructed a new standard that shifts the focus from voluntary compliance to discriminatory intent. Employers will be presumed to have discriminated in violation of the disparate-treatment prohibition of Title VII "absent some valid defense."[48] It is insignificant whether the employer was trying to avoid disparate impact liability; if its decision was based on race, there must be a "strong basis in evidence" to support it.[49] This means that even a *prima facie* case of disparate impact is insufficient because this "*threshold* showing of a significant disparity"[50] does not meet the newly minted "strong basis in evidence" standard.

Justice Kennedy fabricates a "tension"[51] between the two Title VII provisions – disparate treatment and disparate impact – and then "resolves" it by transplanting Fourteenth Amendment colorblind principles into Title VII jurisprudence. But these colorblind principles take on an even narrower gloss. While the use of race is narrowly cabined to particularized discrimination or diversity under the Fourteenth Amendment, such use is presumptively forbidden here because disparate impact on the African-American firefighters is a neutral outcome of the process. Thus, an employer cannot "guarantee" race-based results through disparate treatment of the white firefighters. Eschewing the voluntary compliance mandate of Title VII, the Court viewed the city of New Haven's suspension of the test results to avoid disparate impact liability as disparate treatment in violation of Title VII. "Without some other justification, this express, race-based decision-making violates Title VII's command that employers cannot take adverse employment actions because of an individual's race."[52] The "other" justification is the strong basis in evidence standard.

---

[47] The Court itself in *Yick Wo v. Hopkins*, 118 U.S. 356 (1886); *Gomillion v. Lightfoot*, 364 U.S. 339 (1960); and *Village of Arlington Heights v. Metropolitan Housing Development Corp.*, 429 U.S. 252 (1977) held that there could be statistical disparities so stark that they could only be explained by reference to an invidious purpose based on race. *See, for example, The Vulcan Society, Inc. v. The City of New York*, 683 F.Supp.2d 225, 260–66, 260 (EDNY 2010) (citation omitted) (noting a 34-year history of discriminatory firefighter hiring policies with present-day disparate impact on African-American firefighters and stating, "Sometimes a clear pattern, unexplainable on grounds other than race, emerges from the effect of the state action even when the governing legislation appears neutral on its face."). There is no such analysis in *Ricci*.

[48] *Ricci*, 557 U.S. at 579.

[49] *Ibid.* at 582.

[50] *Ibid.* at 587 (emphasis added).

[51] *Ibid.* at 580 ("We consider, therefore, whether the purpose to avoid disparate-impact liability excuses what otherwise would be prohibited disparate-treatment discrimination. Courts often confront cases in which statutes and principles point in different directions."); *but see Ibid.* at 624 (Ginsburg, J., dissenting) ("Neither Congress' enactments nor this Court's Title VII precedents (including the now-discredited decision in *Wards Cove*) offer even a hint of 'conflict' between an employer's obligations under the statute's disparate-treatment and disparate-impact provisions.").

[52] *Ibid.* at 578.

The "Strong Basis in Evidence" Standard: A New Evidentiary Presumption?

By creating "intra-statutory discord,"[53] Justice Kennedy sets up an either–or choice between the presumption that the City has violated the disparate treatment prohibition of Title VII and the validity of disparate impact liability. To "reconcile" this conceived conflict, Justice Kennedy looks to the Court's Fourteenth Amendment jurisprudence.

Analytically, the Fourteenth Amendment decisions cited to support the newly transplanted "strong basis in evidence" standard are all reverse discrimination cases where the Court ignored the present-day effects of past discrimination to preserve the entitlement interests of non-minority plaintiffs. Obviously, this standard has a built-in evidentiary protection for the white firefighters – promotion tests will rarely, if ever, be deemed deficient and discarding test results based on race will be held to be disparate treatment discrimination.[54]

The Court's equal protection decisions are perfect conduits for the Court's post-racial jurisprudence: since it is "impossible" for the Court to distinguish between invidious racial discrimination and good faith efforts to eradicate caste-based discrimination, the strong basis in evidence standard is essential to "smoke out" impermissible employment decisions. "The Court has held that certain government actions to remedy past racial discrimination – actions that are themselves based on race – are constitutional only where there is a 'strong basis in evidence' that the remedial actions are necessary."[55]

The strong basis in evidence standard purportedly resolved the tension, under the Fourteenth Amendment, between invidious discrimination and race-based government decision-making – there must be evidentiary support for race-conscious remedies. This support is "crucial when the remedial program is challenged in court by non-minority employees."[56] The process must be open, and racial outcomes cannot be guaranteed.[57] Extrapolating this rationale into its Title VII jurisprudence, the Court concludes that the interests underlying disparate treatment and impact are the same, and that the unifying principle is the prohibition of any adverse employment action based on race.[58]

Thus, one form of "discrimination" (discarding the flawed test and starting over to avoid disparate impact liability) should not be excused in the name of voluntary compliance. Without a strong basis in evidence, the government's action is

---

[53] *Ibid.* at 626 (Ginsburg, J., dissenting).

[54] *See* James E. Fleming, "'There Is Only One Equal Protection Clause,'" 74 FORDHAM L. REV. 2301, 2308 (2006); Girardeau A. Spann, *Affirmative Action and Discrimination*, 39 HOWARD L. J. 1, 77 (1995).

[55] *Ricci*, 557 U.S. at 582 (*citing Richmond v. J.A. Croson*, 488 U.S. 469, 500 (1989) (*quoting Wygant v. Jackson Bd. of Ed.*, 476 U.S. 267, 277 (1986) (plurality opinion)).

[56] *Ibid.*

[57] *Ibid.* at 582–83.

[58] *Ibid.* at 583.

nothing more than disparate treatment discrimination.[59] Concluding that process values, equal opportunity, and access should be the touchstone of an employer's efforts in the employment marketplace, the Court concludes that the expectation interests of the white firefighters should not be disturbed on the basis of race;[60] racial preferences are prohibited; and "before an employer can engage in *intentional discrimination* for the asserted purpose of avoiding or remedying an *unintentional disparate impact*, the employer must have a strong basis in evidence to believe it will be subject to disparate-impact liability if it fails to take the *race-conscious, discriminatory action*."[61] This italicized passage illustrates the inversion of disparate impact and disparate treatment. Voluntary compliance to avoid disparate impact liability is transformed into intentional discrimination; the present-day effects of past discrimination evinced in the status quo of exclusion of African Americans from the firefighting officer ranks is "unintentional disparate impact" (there is no identifiable discriminatory perpetrator who is responsible for this neutral disparity); and the strong basis in evidence standard serves as an evidentiary device for the employer, who acts in good faith, to "convict" itself.[62]

Under the Fourteenth Amendment – and now under Title VII – *unintentional* discrimination is little more than circumstantial evidence. In a classic neutral rhetorical move of inversion, disparate impact must be established on the very terms that define disparate treatment liability. Essentially, an intent requirement now serves as an analytical bridge between the Equal Protection Clause and Title VII. While the Court notes that it did not address the constitutionality of the measures taken to comply with Title VII,[63] this issue is all but decided when the Court adopts the strong basis in evidence standard.

It is unclear how the strong basis in evidence standard will work. There are several concerns here: (i) when will it be appropriate to presume discriminatory intent on the part of an employer when it acts pursuant to the voluntary mandate of compliance under Title VII? (ii) how are burdens of proof assigned under the strong basis in evidence standard? and (iii) what quantum of proof is sufficient to establish "a strong basis in evidence to believe" that an employer will be subject to disparate impact liability? All these doctrinal queries point to the conceptual incompleteness of the Court's decision – there is no analytical framework for establishing when a

[59] *Ibid.* at 584 (emphasizing the neutral quality of employment tests and concluding that "the firefighters saw their efforts invalidated by the City in sole reliance upon race-based statistics.").
[60] *Ibid.* at 585 (emphasis added); *but see Ibid.* at 608 (Ginsburg, J., dissenting) (the white firefighters "had no vested right to promotion. Nor have other persons received promotions in preference to them.").
[61] *Ibid.* at 585 (emphasis added).
[62] *Ibid.* at 629 (Ginsburg, J., dissenting) (emphasis added) (citation omitted) (critiquing the strong basis in evidence standard and noting that "[i]t is hard to see how these requirements differ from demanding that an employer establish "a provable, actual violation" *against itself*.").
[63] *Ibid.* at 584.

disparity is transformed from a mere "threshold showing of significant statistical disparity"[64] to a remediable disparity under Title VII.

Moreover, the Court never defines what a "strong basis in evidence" is: an inference (a permissive fact that may be accepted or not as conclusive proof of an asserted proposition), a presumption (conclusive proof unless rebutted with counterproof),[65] or simply a reference to the *quality* of proof needed to establish a strong basis in evidence? Based on the outcome in *Ricci*, it appears that the latter definition is the most accurate denotation. The City is presumed to have engaged in intentional discrimination against the white firefighters, it must proffer a justification for such discrimination, and the justification must be supported by a strong basis in evidence that the City would be liable for disparate impact discrimination because "the examinations were not job related and consistent with business necessity."[66]

This leads to the most troubling aspect of the strong basis in evidence standard: in analyzing reverse discrimination claims, once it is presumed that an employer has intentionally discriminated, it will be difficult, if not impossible, for an employer to meet this test.[67] To make matters worse, the strong basis in evidence standard serves to reinforce the Court's initial analytical premise that "[t]he City's actions would violate the disparate treatment prohibition of Title VII absent some valid defense."[68] As *Ricci* graphically illustrates, a valid defense will be difficult to articulate as the Court discounts disparate impact and instead presumes that neutrality means that there is no statutorily cognizable discrimination. Rather, if there is any cognizable discrimination, it is the claims of the "displaced" white firefighters that will resonate. This is antithetical to *Griggs* and its doctrinal progeny, the 1991 amendment to Title VII, and the statutory goal of voluntary compliance.

(i) Job Relatedness and Business Necessity

The Court misconstrues the job relatedness and business necessity standard. In *Griggs*, the Court, deferring to the legislative intent of Congress, concludes that there are two distinct discriminatory practices proscribed by Title VII – overt discrimination and "practices that are fair in form, but discriminatory in operation. *The touchstone is business necessity. If an employment practice which operates to exclude Negroes cannot be shown to be related to job performance, the practice is prohibited.*"[69] Significantly, in 1971, when *Griggs* was decided, the concern was with the present-day effects of past discrimination – neutral systems should be viewed

---

[64] *Ibid.* at 587.
[65] CHRISTOPHER B. MUELLER AND LAIRD C. KIRKPATRICK, EVIDENCE § 3.4, at 115–18 (6th ed. 2018).
[66] *Ricci*, 557 U.S. at 587.
[67] *Ibid.* at 628–29 (Ginsburg, J., dissenting)
[68] *Ibid.* at 579.
[69] *Griggs*, 401 U.S. at 431 (emphasis added).

skeptically because they could replicate the effects of the recently dismantled for-malized system of discrimination.

The same is no less true today: when a "neutral" "employment practice which operates to exclude [African-American firefighters] cannot be shown to be related to job performance, the practice is prohibited."[70] Since the practice is statutorily prohib-ited, employers are free to avoid disparate impact liability by taking measures to vol-untarily comply with Title VII.[71] Voluntary compliance, where an employer throws out a flawed evaluative mechanism because it freezes the status quo of exclusion,[72] cannot be equated to disparate treatment discrimination. "Here, Title VII's dispa-rate-treatment and disparate impact proscriptions must be read as complementary."[73]

There is no doctrinal trace of *Griggs* in the Court's analysis of job-relatedness and business necessity. Instead, basing its conclusion on the anecdotal and subjective state-ments of three witnesses,[74] the Court concludes that "[t]here is no genuine dispute that the examinations were job-related and consistent with business necessity."[75] Without critically assessing the design and format of the examination, the Court summarily rejects the City's assertions that the examinations were not job related and consistent with business necessity. The Court's bare analysis consisted of crediting Chad Legel's – an Industrial/Organizational Solutions ("IOS") vice president – statements about the meticulous detail IOS used in developing and administering the examinations;[76] one outside witness, with firefighting experience, who had reviewed the examinations and concluded that the "questions were relevant for both exams";[77] and a competing test designer who "stated that the exams appea[r] to be … reasonably good."[78]

Legitimate claims that the examinations were not job related were categorically dismissed by the Court, relying on Legel's statement that IOS "reviewed those chal-lenges and provided feedback"[79] to the City. The Court's process-based analysis merely rubberstamps the reverse discrimination claim of the white firefighters. It is astonishing that the Court based its landmark holding on such a thin reed.[80] "In a characteristically arrogant tone, the Court proclaimed the test to be valid. … The Court boldly made this assertion even though no evidence regarding the test's

---

[70] *Ibid.*

[71] *Ricci*, 557 U.S. at 629 (Ginsburg, J., dissenting) (voluntary compliance is "the preferred means of achieving [Title VII's] objectives," *quoting Firefighters v. Cleveland*, 478 U.S. 501, 515 (1986)).

[72] *Griggs*, 401 U.S. at 430.

[73] *Ricci*, 557 U.S. at 625 (Ginsburg, J., dissenting).

[74] *Ibid.* at 588–89.

[75] *Ibid.* at 587.

[76] *Ibid.* at 588.

[77] *Ibid.*

[78] *Ibid.*

[79] *Ibid.*

[80] Harris and West-Faulcon, *supra* n. 18, at 143 (noting the racing of test fairness by presuming scientific validity simply because the test designer embraced facial fairness, not scientific and substantive standards).

validity had been submitted in the various proceedings. Not only was no evidence presented, but the Court was almost certainly wrong in finding it valid."[81]

Indeed, as many scholars have concluded, the design flaws alone in the promotion examinations are sufficient to support the conclusion that the examinations were *not* job related and consistent with business necessity. Several flaws have been identified: (i) the test did not evaluate the *practical aspects* of the job of lieutenant and captain in the fire department;[82] (ii) the sixty–forty, written (multiple choice) to oral weighting of the examination is arbitrary;[83] (iii) rank order promotions based on combined examination scores uniformly lead to the exclusion of candidates of color;[84] and (iv) "the arbitrary designation of the passing score as seventy."[85] These are core definitional and assessment flaws that belie the Court's faith in the neutrality of the promotion exam.[86]

The disparate impact in *Ricci* is directly traceable to the flawed tests used to evaluate the firefighters.[87]

(ii) Alternative Means

In equally cursory fashion, the Court concludes that there is no strong basis in evidence that the City refused to adopt "an equally valid, less discriminatory alternative" than the promotion examinations.[88] Noting that the sixty–forty written-oral weighting of the examination was required by the City's contract with the firefighters union, and that changing the weighting to thirty–seventy could violate Title VII's prohibition against racially altering test results, the Court held that a thirty–seventy weighting was *not* an equally valid alternative.[89]

The Court adopted the same rationale to reject the argument that "a different interpretation of the 'rule of three' … would have produced less discriminatory results."[90] Finally, the Court dismissed statements by Christopher Hornick, an organizational psychologist and competitor of IOS, that an assessment center process, which evaluates candidates' performance in specific job tasks, "would have demonstrated *less adverse impact.*"[91] To the Court, this was merely one of a few "stray (and contradictory)

---

[81] Michael Selmi, *Understanding Discrimination in a "Post-Racial" World*, 32 CARDOZO L. REV. 833, 850 (2011).
[82] Harris and West-Faulcon, *supra* n. 18, at 143.
[83] *Ibid.* at 134–35, 152 (noting that white firefighters have a claim for unfair testing as well).
[84] *Ibid.* at 141.
[85] *Ibid.* at 143.
[86] *Ibid.* at 126–27.
[87] Selmi, *supra* n. 81, at 846 (stating that the City purchased exactly the type of examination that "has historically had the greatest disparate impact").
[88] *Ricci*, 557 U.S. at 587, 588–92.
[89] *Ibid.* at 588; *but see Ibid.* at 632 n. 11 (Ginsburg, J., dissenting).
[90] *Ibid.* at 590.
[91] *Ibid.* at 591 (emphasis added).

statements" made by Hornick who was more interested in "marketing his services for the future"[92] than in critically analyzing the examination and any valid alternatives.

Again, it is the presumption of validity that guides the Court's analysis – there are no valid, less discriminatory alternatives because the test measured "merit," and the City cannot racially alter the results to ensure representation of African-American firefighters. To do so would create a racial *quota* in violation of Title VII (and the Equal Protection Clause). "Ironically, *Ricci*'s failure to apply Title VII's requirements regarding test validation actually enacts a presumption that *white over-representation is the natural product of merit selection*; Title VII's requirement that employers justify a racially skewed status quo, even in the pursuit of a fair test that actually measures job performance, is portrayed as making non-whites "the special favorite[s] of the law."[93] This is yet another example of the Court's post-racial historicism with the accompanying historical, definitional, and rhetorical myths comprehensively discussed in Chapter 1.

The Court's blind deference to the uncritical assessments cited in its opinion causes it to ignore a much broader context – promotion tests like the one at issue in *Ricci* have been uniformly criticized, and there is a move away from such tests as evaluative tools.[94] The true irony here is that the City chose the very type of examination that perpetuates systemic disparities – the same disparities it would seek to avoid by not certifying the disproportionate examination results.

The fact that there were a range of least discriminatory, viable alternatives underscores the fact that the City would be subject to disparate impact liability, not that it discriminated against the white firefighters. Indeed, if the Court is truly concerned about inequality, it should analyze whether the test is *unfair to all test takers*.[95] A reverse discrimination claim should not trump a city's good faith efforts to avoid disparate impact liability under Title VII. Therefore, voluntary compliance is central to the statutory purpose of Title VII – formal discriminatory barriers may have receded, but ostensibly neutral practices may preserve the enduring features of past discrimination.[96]

(iii) Rejection of Voluntary Compliance Efforts

Neutrality is central to the Court's formalistic conception of equality.[97] Thus, in *Parents Involved*, the Court construes the Fourteenth Amendment to prohibit "racial

[92] *Ibid.*

[93] Harris and West-Faulcon, *supra* n. 18, at 157 (emphasis added) (*quoting The Civil Rights Cases*, 109 U.S. 3, 25 (1883)).

[94] Selmi, *supra* n. 81, at 850–51; Harris and West-Faulcon, *supra* n. 18, at 144–57.

[95] Harris and West-Faulcon, *supra* n. 18, at 134–35.

[96] *Griggs*, 401 U.S. at 432–36 (stating that tests must be job-related to prevent the use of purportedly neutral tests that perpetuate systemic inequality).

[97] Mario L. Barnes and Erwin Chemerinsky, *The Once and Future Equal Protection Doctrine*, 43 CONN. L. REV. 1059, 1083–88 (2011) (arguing for rejection of the rigid, tiered approach to equal protection analysis, the intent requirement, and advancing a theory of substantive equality).

balancing" in the schools so that any resegregation is natural.[98] There is a bright-line distinction between *de jure* (state action) and *de facto* discrimination. Likewise, under Title VII, since there has been "no discrimination" against the African-American firefighters, their disproportionate failure rate on the examination is natural and any attempt to avoid this result is statutorily prohibited racial balancing (disparate treatment discrimination). Under both the Fourteenth Amendment and Title VII, the Court is acutely attuned to preserving an *individual* right to a racially neutral process – there is a personal interest to attend neighborhood schools and there is a personal interest to rely on the results of the firefighter's examination.[99] "Fear of litigation alone cannot justify reliance on race to the detriment of *individuals* who passed the examinations and qualified for promotions."[100]

It is difficult to discern where the Fourteenth Amendment ends, and Title VII begins – it is almost as if *Washington v. Davis* has crystallized in the strong basis in evidence standard. There can be no voluntary, race-conscious efforts to remedy the present-day effects of past discrimination in the absence of intent. Under Title VII, this means that there must be "a strong basis in evidence to believe that the [City] would face disparate-impact liability if it certified the examination results."[101] Of course, in the context of a reverse discrimination claim, it will be very difficult to proffer this strong basis in evidence. From the outset of the *Ricci* opinion, it is obvious that the City made the wrong choice.[102] The Court concludes that the City should have sided with the white firefighters. Specifically, an employer should resolve the manufactured doctrinal "conflict" between the disparate treatment and disparate impact provisions by rejecting the statutory objective of voluntary compliance.

Thus, an employer should certify disproportionate test results based on the "hope" that, with a reverse discrimination suit looming on the horizon, it made the right choice to avoid disparate treatment liability. This circularity is astounding because it privileges reverse discrimination (disparate treatment) claims over disparate impact claims. The structural dynamic of racism cannot be ignored; purportedly neutral policies with disparate impact tell us something about how processes function. In other words, disproportionality means something beyond presumed neutrality in the absence of discriminatory intent. The claims of the white firefighters are more important than those of the African-American firefighters because the Court concludes that the process is tainted by racial decision-making.[103]

---

[98] 551 U.S. at 736; see Anthony V. Alfieri, *Integrating into a Burning House: Race-and Identity-Conscious Visions in Brown's Inner City*, 84 S. CAL. L. REV. 541, 564–66, 573–81 (2011) (discussing the rhetoric of choice, liberal individualism, and the legacy of *Brown*).

[99] *Ricci*, 557 U.S. at 592.

[100] *Ibid.* (emphasis added).

[101] *Ibid.*

[102] *Ibid.* at 561, 578–85.

[103] Harris and West-Faulcon, *supra* n. 18, at 121.

Obviously, a strong basis in evidence is whatever the Court says it is. This is the only explanation for the result in *Ricci*: nearly every relevant conceptual or factual element of the case is distorted, neutralized, or ignored.[104] The Court's sole concern is the reverse discrimination claim and how such "intentional" discrimination by the City can be justified.[105] Of course, under the Court's post-racial analysis, any justification will be viewed skeptically and generally rejected. This is particularly true when the Court invokes the racial politics rationale.

JUSTICE ALITO'S CONCURRENCE: THE RACIAL POLITICS NARRATIVE

Purportedly to correct the dissent's factual "omissions,"[106] Justice Alito advances a racial narrative reminiscent of the stereotypical devices employed during the Reconstruction era.[107] There is an interesting rhetorical twist to Justice Alito's modern-day racial narrative: African Americans are not ignorant, lazy, dishonest, or extravagant, they are simply too powerful politically, and this led to racially skewed results in the process. Title VII and the Fourteenth Amendment protect an open and neutral process, not race-based results. Justice O'Connor employed an identical rhetorical device in *Croson*.[108]

Justice Alito cites very little case law in his concurrence; rather, he elicits stock characters in a racial narrative constructed on the premise that the City's attempt to avoid disparate impact liability was "pretextual."[109] Indeed, the "City's real reason for scrapping the test results was not a concern about violating the disparate-impact provision of Title VII but a simple desire to please a politically important *racial* constituency."[110] The most prominent member of this racial constituency was Reverend Boise Kimber who was described as a "powerful New Haven pastor and self-professed 'kingmaker'" who "call[ed] whites racist" and had previously "threatened a race riot during a murder trial."[111] Justice Alito portrays Kimber as a skilled practitioner of racial politics and powerful political player who was selected to chair the Board of Fire Commissioners "despite the fact that he had no experience" because he was an "invaluable political asset."[112]

---

[104] *Ricci*, 557 U.S. at 629–44 (Ginsburg, J., dissenting).
[105] Powell, *supra* n. 19, at 858–62; 865–68.
[106] *Ricci*, 557 U.S. at 596 (Alito, J., concurring).
[107] *See, for example,* Caleb A. Jaffe, *Obligations Impaired: Justice Jonathan Jasper Wright and the Failure of Reconstruction in South Carolina,* 8 MICH. J. RACE & L. 471, 473–48 (2003) (discussing historical stereotypes of African-American Reconstruction legislators as lazy, ignorant, and incompetent, and the progressive scholarship aimed at dismantling these bogus claims); *accord* W. E. B. DuBois, BLACK RECONSTRUCTION IN AMERICA, 1860–1880, 711–12 (1935); Eric Foner, RECONSTRUCTION: AMERICA'S UNFINISHED REVOLUTION, 1863–1877, xx–xxi (1988).
[108] Powell, *supra* n. 19, at 865–68.
[109] *Ricci*, 557 U.S. at 596–97 (Alito, J., concurring).
[110] *Ibid.* at 605 (emphasis added).
[111] *Ibid.* at 598.
[112] *Ibid.*

Justice Alito goes on to recount how Kimber dominated the process with his demands that the test be discarded because of its disparate impact on the African-American firefighters. The City, through the mayor, simply wanted to please Kimber and his constituents, so much so that Justice Alito reasoned that the process was tainted because the mayor had the ultimate authority to "overrule a CSB decision accepting the results."[113] The mayor did not exercise this power because the CSB concluded that the test results should not be certified. However, since the mayor *intentionally* chose not to exercise his corollary power to overrule the CSB's decision rejecting the test results, this proved "that the City's asserted justification [to avoid disparate impact liability] was pretextual."[114] Again, in resolving the "tension" between potential disparate impact and disparate treatment claims, the City made the wrong choice. It chose the racial claims of a historically subjugated group over the individualized claims of Frank Ricci and Benjamin Vargas. Liberal individualism has been codified in *Ricci*.

POST-RACIAL CONSTITUTIONALISM AND TITLE VII

Ricci fits squarely within the jurisprudential canon of Fourteenth Amendment Rhetorical Neutrality:[115] the history of racial discrimination in the firefighting ranks is ignored; disparate impact is redefined so that *any* impact on white interests (or privilege) is a violation of Title VII; and neutral rhetoric is employed to explain the present-day effects of past discrimination as natural (neutral), rational, and inevitable. The only reason that the African-American firefighters failed in disproportionate numbers is that they "did not study hard enough" – the white firefighters cannot be displaced by a race-conscious remedial approach designed to equalize results.[116]

Ricci reads like a Fourteenth Amendment decision rather than a Title VII decision. Discrimination has been redefined again in the Court's race jurisprudence. *Parents Involved* and *Ricci* rely exclusively on affirmative action decisions to erect a bedrock, post-racial principle: "The way to stop discrimination on the basis of race is to stop discriminating on the basis of race."[117]

The chart below illustrates how the Fourteenth Amendment and Title VII overlap doctrinally to form the Court's post-racial jurisprudence (Table 6.1).

Parents Involved and *Ricci* are the Roberts Court's explicit articulations of a post-racial theory. "The way to stop discrimination on the basis of race is to stop discriminating on the basis of race." Thus, anything that remotely benefits people of color

---

[113] *Ibid.* at 607.
[114] *Ibid.* at 608.
[115] Powell, *supra* n. 19, at 831–59.
[116] *Ricci*, 557 U.S. at 606 (Alito, J., concurring).
[117] *See* Steven V. Maze, *Up from Colorblindness: Equality, Race, and the Lessons of Ricci v. DeStefano*, 2 L. J. Soc. Just. 39, 53–54 (2011) (critiquing this formalistic tautology by noting the impact of systemic segregation).

TABLE 6.1 *Post-Racialism Conceptual Themes under the Fourteenth Amendment and Title VII*

Fourteenth Amendment	Title VII
Parents Involved	*Ricci*
1. The Fourteenth Amendment prohibits discriminatory state action.	1. Title VII prohibits discrimination in the workplace by public or private employers.
2. Discriminatory impact, in the absence of identifiable discriminatory intent, is insufficient to establish a claim under the Fourteenth Amendment.[118] There must be a strong basis in evidence to adopt a race-conscious remedy.	2. While there may be significant evidence of disparate impact, this is insufficient to prevail on a Title VII claim.[120] Where there is no strong basis in evidence to believe that the employer would be subject to disparate impact liability, an employer cannot engage in "intentional" discrimination to avoid "unintentional" disparate impact.
3. The *de jure–de facto* distinction in school cases sets the parameters of constitutionally cognizable violations: *intentional* discrimination is actionable, while *de facto* discrimination cannot be remedied by employing race-conscious remedies.	3. The "tension" between disparate treatment and disparate impact liability must be resolved so that a good faith attempt to avoid disparate impact liability does not result in disparate treatment discrimination against whites.
4. The mandate of *Brown* is a prohibition against race-based decision-making by the state. The Fourteenth Amendment protects neutral process (opportunity), not equal results. A school board cannot use race to maintain integration in the schools. The Constitution protects individuals, not racial groups.	4. *Griggs* stands for the proposition that race-based decision-making by an employer is prohibited because every *individual* is entitled to participate in an open and fair process.[121] Title VII protects equal opportunity, not race-based results: "[o]nce that process has been established and employers have made clear their selection criteria [even if that criteria has a disparate impact on Blacks], they may not invalidate the test results, thus upsetting an employee's legitimate expectation not to be judged on the basis of race."[122]
5. Voluntary remedial efforts will be overturned in the interest of *individual rights*. So, the fact that a school system needs to use race, as one of many factors, to achieve and maintain integration will be ignored to advance the interest of individual school choice.[119]	5. Disparate impact on people of color will be tolerated to avoid displacing the *individual* rights of whites.[123]

---

[118] Barnes and Chemerinsky, *supra* n. 97, at 1080–83.

[119] Girardeau A. Spann, *Disintegration*, U. LOUISVILLE L. REV. 565, 596–617 (2008).

[120] Charles J. Ogletree, Jr., *From Dred Scott to Barack Obama: The Ebb and Flow of Race Jurisprudence*, 25 HARV. BLACKLETTER L. J. 1, 37 (2009).

[121] *Ricci*, 557 U.S. at 585, 592.

[122] *Ibid.* at 585.

[123] Girardeau A. Spann, *Disparate Impact*, 98 GEO. L. J. 1133, 1147 (2010).

is viewed as presumptively invalid because the "neutral" process has been skewed to produce a racial result. Racial balancing, whether to preserve integrated schools, or to ensure inclusion in the historically segregated officer ranks of the fire department, is constitutionally infirm and statutorily prohibited.

Conversely, the claims of reverse discrimination claimants are presumptively valid because the Courts starts with the proposition, under either the Fourteenth Amendment or Title VII, that there is an actionable discrimination claim due to the burden on white interests. The inversion is complete under the Fourteenth Amendment and Title VII – the anti-caste principle is transformed into a literal anti-differentiation principle and disparate impact is redefined to include *intent* as an element of proof – and whites are now the injured party. Their individualized claims supersede the claims of subjugated racial groups. This approach should be rejected, and instead the Court should embrace the true substantive core of the Fourteenth Amendment and Title VII.

In *Ricci*, the Court is audacious in its exercise of unrestrained judicial power: it ignores the very EEOC guidelines that serve as a baseline for establishing potential disparate impact liability;[124] it causally discards its own precedent which acknowledged voluntary efforts by employers to avoid disparate impact liability;[125] and it substitutes its own judgment for that of Congress by "rewriting" the 1991 amendment to Title VII and "overruling," to some extent, *Griggs v. Duke Power* and resuscitating the discredited reasoning of *Wards Cove Packing Co. v. Atonio*.[126]

It is not an exaggeration to state that *Ricci* "overrules" Congress' 1991 amendment to Title VII;[127] or, at the very least, it substantially modifies how disparate impact discrimination will be defined. This is a doctrinal attack on Congress' § 5 power.[128] The Rehnquist Court ushered in the New Federalism,[129] and now the Roberts Court has gone even further in promoting post-racial federalism. Rather than attempting to limit the reach of congressional power under the doctrines of

---

[124] Harris and West-Faulcon, *supra* n. 18, at 136–42.

[125] *Ibid.* at 116–18.

[126] *Ibid.*

[127] Civil Rights Act of 1991, PL 102–66, November 21, 1991, 105 Stat. 1071: The purposes of this Act are – … (2) to codify the concepts of "business necessity" and "job related" enunciated by the Supreme Court in *Griggs v. Duke Power Co.*, 401 U.S. 424 (1971), and in other Supreme Court decisions prior to *Wards Cove Packing Co. v. Atonio*, 490 U.S. 692 (1989); (3) to confirm statutory authority and provide statutory guidelines for the adjudication of disparate impact suits under Title VII of the Civil Rights Act of 1964 (42 U.S.C. § 2000e *et. seq*); and (4) to respond to recent decisions of the Supreme Court by expanding the scope of relevant civil rights statutes in order to provide adequate protection to victims of discrimination.
Ricci directly undermines the legislative purpose of the 1991 Amendment: the "strong basis in evidence" standard supplants the concepts of "business necessity" and "job relatedness."

[128] "The Congress shall have power to enforce, by appropriate legislation, the provisions of this article." U.S. CONST. AMEND. XIV, § 5.

[129] Randy Lee, *Symposium: Is the Supreme Court Undoing the New Deal? The Impact of the Rehnquist Court's New Federalism*, 12 WIDENER L. J. 537, 539–43 (2003).

congruence and proportionality,[130] the Roberts Court reinterprets the boundaries of institutional power by radically altering its own precedent so that it directly contradicts the legislative purpose of Congress.

While the Court has never fully conceptualized how Title VII and the Fourteenth Amendment overlap doctrinally to permit race-conscious remedial efforts, the Court has noted previously that "Title VII and the Equal Protection Clause are the same for the purpose of analyzing voluntary race-conscious remedial measures implemented by public employers."[131] This meant that the Court subscribed to a narrow symmetry between Title VII and the Equal Protection Clause – there is an intent-based justification for disparate impact liability.[132] This justification should be rejected because it does not address, in any form or fashion, structural inequality.[133]

The same analysis applies to the Roberts Court's post-racial interpretation of the Fair Housing Act. Constitutional and statutory remedies are stripped of their anti-discrimination potency to reject any reference to race as discriminatory. "To stop discriminating on the basis of race" means ignoring racism and structural inequality everywhere it exists in society.

---

[130] Cedric Merlin Powell, *The Scope of National Power and the Centrality of Religion*, 38 Brandeis L. J. 643, 705–16, 711–12 (2000).

[131] Cedric Merlin Powell, *Hopwood: Bakke II and Skeptical Scrutiny*, 9 Seton Hall Const. L. J. 811, 930 (1999) (*quoting Johnson v. Trans. Agency, Santa Clara*, 480 U.S. 616, 649 (O'Connor, J., concurring) ("In my view, the proper initial inquiry in evaluating the legality of an affirmative action plan by a public employer under Title VII is no different from that required by the Equal Protection Clause.")).

[132] Rebecca Giltner, *Justifying the Disparate Impact Standard under a Theory of Equal Citizenship*, 10 Mich. J. Race & L. 427, 434–35 (2005).

[133] *Ibid.* at 437 (discussing how "a strict intentionality approach" privileges claims of those who have not been historically oppressed and impedes access to people of color); Llezlie Green Coleman, *Disrupting the Discrimination Narrative: An Argument for Wage and Hour Laws' Inclusion in Antisubordination Advocacy*, 14 Stan. J. C.R. & C.L. 49, 62–72 (2018) (discussing the limits of Title VII due to its formalism).

7

Texas Department of Housing Affairs v. The Inclusive Communities Project, Inc.

Disparate Impact and Post-Racialism

As the previous chapters demonstrate, there is a formalism that pervades the Court's post-racial jurisprudence – the Court exhibits a full-blown commitment to neutrality at the expense of substantive constitutional rights. Justice Kennedy develops this neutrality in his *Parents Involved* concurrence, where his fifth vote establishes that race can be used in very limited circumstances after race-neutral alternatives are explored first; he offers a misleadingly majestic view of democracy in action when he privileges voter initiatives that overturn race-conscious remedies in *Schuette*; in *Fisher*, he submerges the significance of race and the continuing effects of structural inequality in post-secondary education by stating that "race is a factor of a factor of a factor," and neutrality means that race must be evaded; and in *Ricci*, Justice Kennedy re-conceptualizes disparate impact liability by adding an explicit discriminatory intent gloss to Title VII. What is dramatic about all these post-racial decisions – and they are because they each seek to transcend race in particular ways – is that they are all compromises to substantive equality. So, even a "victory" for anti-discrimination advocates comes with a significant underlying cost – neutrality leaves structural inequality in place.

In *Texas Department of Housing Affairs v. The Inclusive Communities Project*,[1] Justice Kennedy yet again articulates the Court's post-racialism by concluding that disparate impact claims are properly cognizable under the Fair Housing Act (FHA), but the Act is interpreted to dilute such claims because they must be read against race-neutral reasons for housing disparities for low-income persons. While individuals are free to live wherever they wish in a pluralistic society, the structural factors that erase this possibility are ignored in favor of a free market where entrepreneurial decision-making power is privileged.

There is also a tension between *Ricci* and *Inclusive Communities*. Justice Kennedy's opinion in *Ricci*, where he identifies an intra-statutory tension between disparate treatment and impact and resolves it by crafting a new level of discriminatory intent, stands in contrast to his opinion in *Inclusive Communities* where he

---

[1]   576 U.S. 519 (2015).

acknowledges disparate impact claims as cognizable under the FHA. These seemingly discordant decisions say something about the complex doctrinal malleability of post-racialism.

Indeed, where the impact falls determines how it will be analyzed under Title VII and the FHA – under Title VII in *Ricci*, the dispute was between the *individualized* claims of Black and white firefighters for promotion under a contested examination system; in *Inclusive Communities*, there is no individualized dispute, the impact is on a regulated housing market and who has access to integrated communities. So, *Ricci* is more properly understood as a statutory incarnation of liberal individualism – Title VII protects the expectation interests of individual white workers not to be displaced by any race-conscious remedial efforts to disrupt structural exclusion in the workplace – and *Inclusive Communities* is a neutral marketplace decision which recognizes disparate impact while diminishing its significance.

While the disparate impact analysis is premised on the disproportionate effect on discrete and insular minorities, or historically disempowered groups, the Court's post-racial interpretation of it is directly influenced by the context in which it arises. In *Ricci*, the Court fashions its analysis on a job promotion competition between white and Black firefighters. As Chapter 6 illustrates, the outcome is assured in this context – the white firefighters' expectation interests must be protected notwithstanding a well-documented history of exclusion in the officer ranks for African Americans and a promotion test that was demonstrably flawed in its application. The protection of white employee expectation interests began with the Burger Court's Title VII jurisprudence discussed in Chapter 2.

Justice Kennedy's *Inclusive Communities* opinion advances the historical myth underlying Rhetorical Neutrality as he describes a linear and incremental history of progress premised on constitutional and statutory law; he espouses the definitional myth, by distilling the literal language of Title VII and the Age Discrimination Employment Act (ADEA), to locate disparate impact in the FHA only to neutralize it with an intent requirement; and he proffers the rhetorical myth to explain how some inequities are a natural part of a neutral marketplace where the government and entrepreneurs must make logical and practical business decisions even if those decisions perpetuate caste. So, just as in all the previous areas of law discussed in the preceding chapters, there is an explanation for the continuing effects of past discrimination that is a defining feature of post-racialism.

JUSTICE KENNEDY'S MAJORITY OPINION: POST-RACIAL HISTORICISM AND THE FHA

Inclusive Communities Project, Inc. ("ICP") brought suit against the Texas Department of Housing and Community Affairs (the "Department") alleging disparate impact discrimination because the Department's "disproportionate allocation of tax credits"² perpetuated segregated housing patterns by "granting too many credits for housing in predominantly inner-city areas and too few in predominantly white suburban neighborhoods."³ This contributed to a hyper-segregated inner city, with white suburbs in the outlying city being insulated from any policy based attempts at integration.

Concluding that ICP established a *prima facie* case of disparate impact⁴ due to the insufficiency of the Department's proof of "less discriminatory alternatives" to achieving affordable housing, the district court ordered new tax credit selection criteria.⁵ Pending the Department's appeal, "the Secretary of Housing and Urban Development ('HUD') issued a regulation interpreting the FHA to encompass disparate-impact liability."⁶

The HUD regulation included a burden-shifting framework for disparate impact claims which set out several steps for adjudicatory proof between the parties: (i) initially, the plaintiff carries the burden of establishing a discriminatory effect directly related to the defendant's policy; (ii) the burden then shifts to the defendant to "prov[e] that the challenged practice is necessary to achieve one or more substantial, legitimate, nondiscriminatory interests"⁷ (this is akin to job relatedness under Title VII); (iii) and, finally, after the defendant proffers a substantial nondiscriminatory interest(s), the plaintiff may still prevail upon proof that such "nondiscriminatory interests supporting the challenged practice could be served by another practice that has a less discriminatory effect."⁸

Concluding that disparate impact claims are properly cognizable under the FHA, the Fifth Circuit reversed and remanded holding that, based on the regulation, the district court erroneously placed the burden of proof on the Department – "to prove there were no less discriminatory alternatives for allocating low-income housing tax credits"⁹ – without fully considering whether ICP had made out a *prima facie* case of disparate impact. The Department filed a *writ of certiorari* on a question of first impression: "whether disparate-impact claims are cognizable under the FHA."¹⁰

Justice Kennedy's opinion for the Court held that disparate impact claims are properly cognizable under the FHA. The first prong of *Inclusive Communities* is its post-racial historicism – what is unique here is that this is a rare instance where the Court acknowledges the continuing effects of past discrimination; but it is

---

² *Ibid.* at 526.
³ *Ibid.*
⁴ A stark example of this disproportionality was that "92.29% of [low-income housing tax credit] units in the city of Dallas were located in census tracts with less than 50 percent Caucasian residents." *Ibid.*
⁵ *Ibid.*
⁶ *Ibid.* at 527.
⁷ *Ibid.*
⁸ *Ibid.*
⁹ *Ibid.* at 528.
¹⁰ *Ibid.*

nevertheless framed and discussed as a series of events, with structural and non-structural components, so that the significance of disparate impact is diminished. The historical myth functions differently here – there is a linear, neutral, and episodic depiction of history so that the present-day effects of past discrimination are implicitly acknowledged but structuralism is discounted.

For example, *Inclusive Communities* starts with this opening quote:

> *De jure* residential segregation by race was declared unconstitutional almost a century ago, *Buchanan v. Warley*, 245 U.S. 60 (1917), but its vestiges remain today, intertwined with the country's economic and social life. Some segregated housing patterns can be traced to conditions that arose in the mid-20th century. Rapid urbanization, concomitant with the rise of suburban developments accessible by car, led many white families to leave the inner cities. This often left minority families concentrated in the center of the Nation's cities.[11]

Beginning with the eradication of formal discrimination in *Buchanan v. Warley*,[12] the Court notes the unconstitutionality of *de jure* residential segregation without placing it into context. Specifically, *Buchanan* is a *Lochner*[13]–era decision, which means that liberty of contract was the animating concern in the Court's analysis of segregated neighborhoods in Louisville in 1917. There is a structural effect that is missing from the Court's analysis – while *Buchanan* certainly held that a Louisville ordinance mandating segregated neighborhoods was unconstitutional, it nevertheless left *Plessy v. Ferguson* intact so that separate but equal was still constitutionally permissible in all public spaces. The colorline remained in intact notwithstanding the fact that neighborhoods were now "open." *Buchanan* nevertheless left intact the perverse symmetrical "equality" that was the hallmark of American apartheid – Blacks were free to live wherever they wanted, if they could overcome the myriad of neutral schemes deployed to exclude them, but they had to observe the colorline on all public conveyances and accommodations. Resonating in substantive due process rather than equal protection, *Buchanan* essentially protects a "zone of private choice"[14] – where the government could not impose segregation or integration – rather than substantive equality.

This recounting of the origins of segregated housing is decidedly post-racial: whites exercise their choice to "leave the inner cities" for suburban enclaves in the face of "rapid urbanization" and the rise of accessible suburban communities, which are out of reach for Blacks who remain "concentrated" in the core of the Nation's cities. Whites have choice (to move away by car), Blacks have no agency, and this is underscored by how the conditions leading to segregated housing are described – there

---

[11] *Ibid.*
[12] 245 U.S. 60 (1917).
[13] *Lochner v. New York*, 198 U.S. 45 (1905) (invalidating New York maximum hours law as interfering with the freedom of contract and discounting the valid police purpose of the state in enacting such a law).
[14] Laurence H. Tribe, American Constitutional Law § 18–2, at 1696 (2d ed. 1987).

are neutral marketplace conditions that rationalize segregated housing. That is, the concentration of Blacks in the core cities is not so much explained as it is presumed.

But the Court nevertheless recognizes some of these factors as "various practices," sometimes augmented by government support, "to encourage and maintain the separation of the races," such as restrictive covenants, steering, discriminatory lending and mortgage practices and redlining. Yet these practices seem like individualized choices that taint a neutral marketplace rather than full-blown governmental policy designed to foster segregated neighborhoods. There is a tepidness to the Court's acknowledgement of structuralism. The Court notes that "By the 1960's, these policies, practices, and prejudices had created many black inner cities surrounded by mostly white suburbs."[15] The government's actual support of such policies is referenced in passing so that the narrative emphasis is on a series of individual decisions – ostensibly voluntary in nature – that lead to segregated neighborhoods. Yet the history of housing in the United States, and even the facts of *Inclusive Communities*, indicate that segregated neighborhoods are no mistake. As Princeton's Professor of African American Studies Keeanga-Yamahtta Taylor observes,

> The continued disinvestment and marginalization of the urban core helped to sustain suburbanization and all of the financial benefits for business that came along with it. The deterioration of urban neighborhoods are not simply a side effect of suburbanization or an "unintended consequence"; the two were dialectically connected. This connection meant that the proposition of a "dual market" was misleading. Duality suggested distinction and separation, as if the urban and suburban housing markets were not intimately related to each other. Instead, there was a single United States housing market that was defined by its racially discriminatory, tiered access – each tier reinforcing and legitimizing the other.[16]

Justice Kennedy's linear post-racial history obscures this structural impact so that the analysis of what disproportionality means in the housing market is neutralized, and history becomes a simple recitation of events connected by cause and effect. The first section of *Inclusive Communities* chronicles this in quick succession: the mid-1960's as a "period of considerable social unrest"[17]; the Kerner Commission Report and its famous admonition that the nation was "moving toward two societies, one black, one white – separate and unequal"[18]; and, finally, Dr. Martin Luther King, Jr.'s assassination which led to the passage of the FHA.[19] The opinion devotes one sentence to the amendment of the FHA in 1988.[20]

---

[15] *Inclusive Cmtys.*, 576 U.S. at 529.
[16] Keeanga-Yamahtta Taylor, Race for Profit: How Banks and the Real Estate Industry Undermined Black Homeownership 37 (2019).
[17] *Inclusive Communities*, 576 U.S. at 529.
[18] *Ibid.*
[19] *Ibid.* at 530.
[20] *Ibid.*

"History is decontextualized so that incremental progress is exaggerated, and structural inequality is largely ignored."[21] Indeed, it is particularly significant that the historical narrative of *Inclusive Communities* does not reference a landmark decision of the time period that explicitly noted the continuing effects of past discrimination and structural inequality – *Jones v. Alfred Mayer*.[22] Indeed, it is all the more important to reference *Jones v. Alfred Mayer* because *Buchanan* was decided on substantive economic due process grounds rather than under a statute enacted pursuant to the enforcement power of Congress under the Thirteenth Amendment.

By contrast to the post-racial, linear history of *Inclusive Communities*, *Jones v. Alfred Mayer* fully examines the First Reconstruction's anti-discrimination statutes and makes direction connections to modern-day oppression in 1968. *Inclusive Communities* should have done the same analysis for housing segregation in 2015, which would mean that disparate impact would not simply be the result of a series of disaggregated "conditions" and neutral market factors, but the direct result of structural inequality that exists to this day.

Indeed, both decisions reference the Civil Rights Act of 1968 but only to note the broad panoply and scope of anti-discrimination statutes enacted to combat public and private discrimination. This gives important context to how the housing market is regulated and how discrimination is defined. *Jones v. Alfred Mayer* and *Inclusive Communities* are linked, but the former explicitly acknowledges structural inequality while the latter superficially notes it to interpret whether "housing decisions with a disparate impact are prohibited" under the FHA.[23]

Instead, *Inclusive Communities*' historical discussion of the legislative purpose of the FHA moves from Dr. King's assassination to the amendment of the FHA in 1988 – it would have been a more complete history, and one which more fully explained the scope of Congress' power in identifying and eradicating the present-day effects of past discrimination, if it had acknowledged how systemic racism is advanced through policies and structures. There is a lot missing here, and this affects how the Court interprets disparate impact under the FHA.

Analytically, what distinguishes *Jones v. Alfred Mayer* from *Inclusive Communities* is that the former does not presume an open and accessible housing marketplace (or any other avenue of society); rather, it centers anti-discrimination law as an instrument in eradicating structural inequality. Concluding that "§ 1982[24] bars all racial

---

[21]   Cedric Merlin Powell, *Race Displaced: Buchannan v. Warley and the Neutral Rhetoric of Due Process*, in RACIAL JUSTICE IN AMERICAN LAND USE (Anthony Craig Arnold, Cate Fosl, Cedric Merlin Powell, and Laura Rothstein, eds., forthcoming).

[22]   392 U.S. 409 (1968).

[23]   *Texas Dep't. of Housing and Cmty. Affrs. v. Inclusive Cmtys. Project, Inc.*, 576 U.S. at 530.

[24]   42 U.S.C. § 1982 provides that:
    All citizens of the United States shall have the same right, in every State and Territory, as is enjoyed by white citizens thereof to inherit, purchase, lease, sell, hold, and convey real and person property. *Jones v. Alfred Mayer*, 392 U.S. at 412.

discrimination, private as well as public, in the sale or rental of property, and that the statute, thus construed, is a valid exercise of the power of Congress to enforce the Thirteenth Amendment."[25]

Jones v. Alfred Mayer is a rare decision that acknowledges the continuing effects of past discrimination, the badges and incidents of slavery, and the structural components of systemic racism. It is also the rare case that fully acknowledges the scope of congressional enforcement power to eradicate structural inequality through the Thirteenth Amendment – there is a direct link to present-day subjugation and chattel slavery.[26] Since the Court was construing the pre-FHA statutory and jurisprudential regime in its discussion of the historical legislative purpose of the FHA, it was imperative that the Court reference *Jones v. Alfred Mayer* in its analysis of legislative history. This is a significant omission because it ultimately shapes how the Court will conceptualize disparate impact under the FHA.

Context matters in interpreting the legislative history of a statute, and Justice Douglas' concurrence in *Jones v. Alfred Mayer* offers a compelling distillation of race and racism in American society that is directly applicable to *Inclusive Communities*. Tracing the Reconstruction era following the Civil War to the Second Reconstruction underway in America in 1968, just months after the assassination of Dr. King, Justice Douglas offers a catalogue of oppression with the accompanying legislation aimed at eradicating it:

> Some badges of slavery remain today. While the institution has been outlawed, it has remained in the minds and hearts of many white men. Cases which have come to this Court depict a spectacle of slavery unwilling to die. We have seen contrivances by States designed to thwart Negro voting … Negroes have been excluded over and again from juries solely on account of their race, … or have been forced to sit in segregated seats in courtrooms, … They have been made to attend segregated and inferior schools, … or denied entrance to colleges or graduate schools because of their color, … Negroes have been prosecuted for marrying whites, … They have been forced to live in segregated residential districts, … and residents of white neighborhoods have denied them entrance ….[27]

The badges and incidents of slavery – the present-day effects of past discrimination – the disparate impact that is part and parcel of structures that perpetuate caste are

---

[25] *Ibid.* at 413. Section 1982 was a Reconstruction-era statute used by plaintiffs prior to the passage of the comprehensive opening housing regulatory law – the FHA. "The 1968 [Fair Housing] Act was not intended to supersede [§ 1982]." T. A. Smedley, *A Comparative Analysis of Title VIII and Section 1982*, 22 VANDERBILT L. REV. 459, 462 (1969). By historical coincidence, "at the precise time the final debate on this statute was being conducted, in Congress, the Supreme Court was hearing arguments in the *Jones* case on the question [of] whether another federal statute, section 1982, enacted 102 years earlier, prohibits discrimination against Negroes in the sale of housing." *Ibid.* at 461.

[26] William M. Carter, Jr., *Race, Rights, and the Thirteenth Amendment: Defining the Badges and Incidents of Slavery*, 40 U.C. DAVIS L. REV. 1311 (2007); Douglas L. Colbert, Liberating the Thirteenth Amendment, 30 HARV. C.R.-C.L. L. REV. 1 (1995).

[27] *Jones v. Alfred Mayer*, 392 U.S. at 445 (Douglas, J., concurring).

endemic to the nation's history of abject subordination of Blacks and other people of color. Noting that formal oppression and discrimination have been eliminated, Justice Douglas acknowledges the limitations of anti-discrimination law: "Today the black is protected by a host of civil rights laws. But the forces of discrimination are still strong."[28]

Maybe even stronger. As Richard Rothstein vividly illustrates in *The Color of Law*, governmental policy incentivizes inequality and exclusion in a purportedly neutral marketplace. For example, the Low-Income Housing Tax Credit subsidizes developers to make housing available to low-income families in multi-unit projects, but there are provisions for community vetoes of such proposals, and developers build in segregated neighborhoods under the myth of revitalization and because the land is cheaper in low-income neighborhoods.[29] This perpetuates housing segregation.[30]

The Section 8 voucher program provides nominal amounts for rentals in middle-class areas so that low-income families are either stigmatized by landlords, who refuse to accept such vouchers, or do not have sufficient funds to move into an integrated, middle-class neighborhood but must stay within the segregated boundaries of high-poverty neighborhoods or segregated suburbs.[31]

Disparate impact is not happenstance; it is inherent in policies premised on the maintenance of white suburbs insulated from the perceived burdens of integration – this strain of post-racialism runs through the school cases, as in *Milliken v. Bradley*, as well because there is a direct connection between segregated schools and housing.[32] Both are remnants of the legacy of slavery. Segregation in housing is "not simply of history, but of current design."[33]

Because the historical context of the FHA is incomplete in Justice Kennedy's majority opinion, societal progress is seen as the function of a neutral housing marketplace because formal discrimination has been fully eradicated. This means that disparate impact, under the FHA, will be narrowly defined (the definitional myth) and its impact will be rationalized (the rhetorical myth) so that some inequality in terms of disproportionate impact will be rationalized as the natural and neutral functioning of a robust housing market.[34]

---

[28] *Ibid.* 447.
[29] RICHARD ROTHSTEIN, THE COLOR OF LAW: A FORGOTTEN HISTORY OF HOW OUR GOVERNMENT SEGREGATED AMERICA 190 (2017).
[30] Courtney Lauren Anders, *Affirmative Action for Affordable Housing*, 60 HOW. L. J. 105, 108 (2016).
[31] *Ibid.* at 190–91.
[32] STEPHANIE M. WILDMAN, MARGALYNNE ARMSTRONG, ADRIENNE D. DAVIS, AND TRINA GRILLO, PRIVILEGE REVEALED: HOW INVISIBLE PREFERENCES UNDERMINES AMERICA 53 (1996 and 2021 paperback ed.) ("Courts also reinforce popular notions of an extralegal 'right' to discriminate on the basis of race by recognizing residential segregation as a legal impediment to judicial intervention in school desegregation cases"). *See* Chapter 2, *supra*.
[33] Deborah N. Archer, The New Housing Segregation: The Jim Crow Effects of Crime-Free Housing Ordinances, 118 MICH. L. REV. 173, 178 (2019).
[34] Trina Jones, *Title VII at 50: Contemporary Challenges for U.S. Employment Law*, 6 ALA. C.R. & C.L. L. REV. 45, 68 (2014).

Justice Kennedy's comparison of Title VII and the ADEA draws upon the legislative history and language of these statutes in determining whether disparate impact is statutorily cognizable; and, after determining that it is, under the FHA, the opinion then adopts a neutral conception of the marketplace, complete with burdens of proof crafted to insulate decision-making that may have a disparate impact. In other words, there is no full structural conception of disparate impact under the FHA. This should come as no surprise, as this was the result under Title VII, too, as set out in Chapter 6's discussion of *Ricci*.[35]

ANTI-DISCRIMINATION STATUTES AND POST-RACIALISM: TITLE VII, THE ADEA, AND THE FHA

Interpreting § 703(a)(2) of Title VII through its analysis in *Griggs v. Duke Power*,[36] the Court noted that unlawful practices encompass "the discriminatory effect of a practice as well as the motivation behind the practice."[37] Section 703(a)(2) proscribes "not only overt discrimination but also practices that are fair in form, but discriminatory in operation."[38] Neutral practices, while "fair in form," may nevertheless be discriminatory in impact – the operation and function of the practice has an effect that is equivalent to intentional discrimination. The legislative purpose of Congress, in enacting § 703(a)(2), was to target "the consequences of employment practices, not simply the motivation."[39]

This is a structural interpretation of discrimination, focusing not on some identifiable discriminatory perpetrator, but on the systems, practices, and procedures that reify inequality in the labor market. Yet there must be some limit to the scope of disparate impact liability: "not all employment practices causing a disparate impact impose liability under §703(a)(2)."[40] For example, there may be a permissible disparate impact which is the result of "business necessity" where the hiring criteria has a "manifest relationship to job performance."[41] In *Griggs*, the business necessity defense was unavailing because no relationship could be established between high school diplomas, general intelligence tests, and manual labor.[42]

---

[35] Samuel R. Bagenstos, *Disparate Impact and the Role of Classification and Motivation in Equal Protection Law after Inclusive Communities*, 101 Cornell L. Rev. 1115, 1130 (2016) (arguing that Justice Kennedy's opinion in *Inclusive Communities* is informed by his concurrence in *Parents Involved* and an attempt to resolve the tension between equal protection jurisprudence and Title VII by embracing neutrality, but concluding that attempts to promote integration and overcome racial isolation do not raise the constitutional or statutory concerns associated with race-based decision-making).

[36] *See* Chapter 2, *supra*.

[37] *Texas Dep't. of Housing and Cmty Affrs. v. Inclusive Cmtys. Project, Inc.*, 576 U.S. at 530.

[38] *Ibid.* at 531.

[39] *Ibid.*

[40] *Ibid.*

[41] *Ibid.*

[42] *Ibid.* at 532.

Next, the Court construes the ADEA to locate disparate impact liability within the statute, which has similar language to Title VII, but with an emphasis on discrimination on the basis of age.[43] Interpreting the ADEA through its decision in *Smith v. City of Jackson*, the Court reviewed a challenge to proportionately greater raises to younger employees with "less than five years of experience,"[44] and concluded that the same reasoning it applied in its analysis of § 703(a)(2) of Title VII was applicable to its analysis of §4(a)(2) of the ADEA. Both Title VII's §703(a)(2) and the ADEA's §4(a)(2) "contain language "prohit[ing] such actions that 'deprive any individual of employment opportunities or *otherwise adversely affect* his status as an employee, because of such individual's' race or age."[45]

The *Smith* plurality highlighted the effects of the language of the provisions to conclude that the focus was not on intent or motivation, but on the effects of action on the employee – this is disparate-impact liability.[46] Taken together, *Griggs* and the *Smith* plurality stand for the proposition that disparate impact liability must be recognized when the statutory text references "consequences of actions and not just … the mindset of actors."[47] Moreover, these decisions establish the limits of disparate impact liability so that "employers and other regulated entities [like the Texas Department of Housing and Community Affairs] are able to make the practical business choices and profit-related decisions that sustain a vibrant and dynamic free-enterprise system."[48]

But what becomes clear in Justice Kennedy's interpretation of disparate impact is that these "business choices and profit-related decisions" will determine the scope and significance, if any, of disparate impact liability. Indeed, a plaintiff must show that "there is an available alternative … practice that has less disparate impact and serves the [entity's] legitimate needs."[49] So, a private employer's business justification, or the government's public interest, are broad, neutral defenses that will rationalize the existence of inequality, disproportionality, and structural inequality in the absence of proof. This is the same protection of white expectation interests advanced by the Burger Court and discussed in Chapter 2, and in the Roberts Court's expansion of this post-racial principle in *Ricci*[50] critiqued in Chapter 6.

---

43 *Ibid.*
44 *Ibid.*
45 *Ibid.* at 532–33 (emphasis in original).
46 *Ibid.* at 533.
47 *Ibid.*
48 *Ibid.*
49 *Ibid.*
50 Ronald Turner, *Title VII and the Roberts Court's Worldview Supremacy*, 65 LABOR L. J. 149, 154–55 (2014) ("… the Court saw the case through the eyes of white employees who, in the majority's view, were denied the fruits of their exam preparations and saw their legitimate expectations quashed by the city's conduct. Adding to the Court's accusation of anti-white discrimination by the city, Justice Alito's story-like concurrence harshly characterized the city's conduct as capitulation to the machinations of a racist black minister").

All of Justice Kennedy's post-racial decisions foreground neutrality as a defining and governing principle – race should only be considered after race-neutral alternatives are fully explored. In his interpretive analysis of the FHA, Justice Kennedy distills the language of Title VII and the ADEA to locate disparate impact liability under the FHA, and then he offers a comprehensive exposition about the post-racial limits of disparate impact liability. Indeed, his opinion reads like a guide to affirmative defenses to disparate impact lawsuits under the FHA.

This is the definitional myth – disparate impact is defined narrowly, and the business justification defense offers a formidable obstacle in establishing disparate impact liability. This is especially so in a context, like the housing market, which is fundamentally distinguishable from the job markets in *Griggs* (Title VII) and *Smith* (the ADEA). Here, disparate impact is defined in relation to economic interests[51] so that the rationale for continuing residential segregation is privileged over substantive integration. *Inclusive Communities* graphically illustrates this recurring tenet of post-racialism.

Applying the holdings of *Griggs* and *Smith*, in interpreting Title VII and the ADEA, the Court concludes that the FHA encompasses disparate impact claims. Justice Kennedy identifies several linguistic and structural[52] factors that support this conclusion: (i) Sections 804(a) and 805(a), of the FHA, both contain result-oriented language which focus on consequential impact rather than intent;[53] (ii) Title VII and the ADEA contain "otherwise adversely affect" language which is similar in function and kind to the FHA's "otherwise make unavailable" language so that all three statutes focus on results;[54] (iii) the 1988 amendments to the FHA support the conclusion that disparate impact is within its scope;[55] (iv) the central purpose of anti-discrimination statutes like Title VII, the ADEA, and the FHA is "to eradicate discriminatory practices within a sector of our Nation's economy";[56] and (v) the FHA's "clear national policy against discrimination in housing" targets practices that "reside at the heartland of disparate-impact liability."[57]

The unifying theme of the Roberts Court's post-racial constitutionalism is its adherence to formalistic conceptions of equality – in this vein, discrimination

---

[51] "The courts give economic status such primacy that considerations of wealth actually insulate otherwise prohibited housing discrimination from legal scrutiny. These general notions of wealth and earned privileges are replicated and prevail, even in the administration of our fair housing laws." STEPHANIE M. WILDMAN, MARGALYNNE ARMSTRONG, ADRIENNE D. DAVIS, AND TRINA GRILLO, PRIVILEGE REVEALED: HOW INVISIBLE PREFERENCE UNDERMINES AMERICA 53 (2021).

[52] *Inclusive Cmtys.*, 576 U.S. at 535 ("This similarity in text and structure is all the more compelling given that Congress passed the FHA in 1968 – only four years after passing Title VII and only four months after enacting the ADEA").

[53] *Ibid.* at 533–34.

[54] *Ibid.* at 534.

[55] *Ibid.* at 535–38.

[56] *Ibid.* at 539.

[57] *Ibid.*

is not systemic or structural, but clearly identifiable whatever its origin. And discrimination is rare and limited in scope. Thus, the "heartland of disparate-impact liability" includes "zoning laws and other housing restrictions that function unfairly to exclude minorities from certain neighborhoods without any sufficient justification."[58]

But these practices, residing in the heartland of disparate-impact liability, all sound *intentional* – there is a function with consequences (or impact) – without any permissible justification. Indeed, all of the decisions cited by Justice Kennedy in cataloguing these heartland examples are permutations of intentionality – an ordinance prohibiting construction of new multi-family dwellings (an ostensibly neutral measure crafted to exclude) and a restriction on rentals to "blood relative[es]" which maintained and reified segregation "in an area of the city that was 88.3 percent white and 7.6 percent black."[59] There is a discernible intent in these "neutral" actions which portend discrimination neutral in design, but discriminatory in effect.

Justice Kennedy's bright-line heartland conception of disparate impact liability is analogous to the *de jure–de facto* distinction discussed in reference to the school cases in Chapters 2 and 3. Formal, heartland (*de jure*) impact is remediable under the FHA, but bare statistical (*de facto*) disparities that are a natural part of the housing market are not. The rest of Justice Kennedy's post-racial decision is an exposition on how "[t]he availability of disparate-impact liability … has allowed private developers to vindicate the FHA's objectives and to protect their property right by stopping municipalities from enforcing arbitrary, and, in practice, discriminatory ordinances barring the construction of certain types of housing units."[60]

Disparate impact liability is defined narrowly, and the defense for private developers and the government is expanded. And from this point on in *Inclusive Communities*, disparate impact liability becomes a secondary consideration compared to the primacy of a defense under the FHA.

Rhetorically, the historical myth revises the legislative history of the FHA as a post-racial and linear progression of societal progress, with most formal housing segregation being eradicated; the definitional myth locates disparate impact liability, under the FHA, only to delineate it in formalistic terms – as identifiable "heartland" cases – and enhances the potency of defenses to rebut and neutralize such claims; and, finally, the rhetorical myth rationalizes the presumptive neutrality of the marketplace in the name of post-racialism. As with all the Roberts Court's post-racial jurisprudence, even an acknowledgment of discrimination comes at a great cost.

---

[58] *Ibid.*
[59] *Ibid.* at 540.
[60] *Ibid.*

THE FHA: NEUTRALITY, THE MARKETPLACE, AND POST-RACIALISM

In *Inclusive Communities*, the cost is a formalistic distinction between heartland discrimination and simple inequality that can be explained by a rationally functioning marketplace. So, after disparate impact is acknowledged, its significance is substantially diluted by the marketplace defense advanced by Justice Kennedy's opinion. The first step in diluting the substantive content of disparate impact liability is to characterize ICP's legitimate disparate-impact claim as a "novel theory of liability" which essentially seeks to "second guess" the housing authority's decision-making in choosing between "two reasonable approaches … in allocating tax credits for low-income housing."[61] Yet the reasonableness of the two approaches is attributable to Justice Kennedy's conception of business necessity and a free functioning marketplace.

To buttress his characterization of ICP's claim as "novel," Justice Kennedy cites a law review article and gives the erroneous impression that ICP's claim is "rare"[62] – it is outside of the mainstream of heartland disparate impact liability decisions. He does not offer the reason *why* such claims are rare, certainly not because of their validity, but because of a proof distinction between housing barrier discrimination cases and housing improvement regulation cases.[63] *Inclusive Communities* is essentially a housing improvement regulation case. As Professor Seicshnaydre notes: "Community and neighborhood revitalization plans will almost always be legitimate in the abstract but whether they are racially exclusionary will depend on the facts of a particular case."[64] It is clear that, under Justice Kennedy's analysis, the reasonableness of the government's choices will be framed by this proposition, and the only thing left to be explained will be the segregation that is left intact.

What is missing in the Court's analysis of the facts underlying *Inclusive Communities* is a structural conception of the housing marketplace, especially when the government is the regulator.[65] Justice Kennedy misses this essential distinction between private developer and governmental regulator in the very article that he cites to support the proposition that ICP is espousing a novel theory of liability.[66] By conflating these two distinct marketplace actors, the proof requirements are

---

[61] *Ibid.* at 541.

[62] *Ibid.* (*citing* Seicshnaydre, *Is Disparate Impact Having Any Impact? An Appellate Analysis of Forty Years of Disparate Impact Claims under the Fair Housing Act*, 63 AM. U.L. REV. 357, 360–63 (2013) (noting the rarity of this type of claim)).

[63] Stacy E. Seicshnaydre, *Is Disparate Impact Having Any Impact? An Appellate Analysis of Forty Years of Disparate Impact Claims under the Fair Housing Act*, 63 AM. U. L. REV. at 363–64.

[64] *Ibid.*

[65] Stacy E. Seicshnaydre, *Disparate Impact and the Limits of Local Discretion after Inclusive Communities*, 24 GEO. MASON L. REV. 663, 689–92 (2017).

[66] Yet another reason ICP's claim is "rare" and "novel" is that ostensibly neutral government action can perpetuate segregation under the guise of reasonableness:

skewed – the defense for private actors is the same for the state so that the analogy to Title VII's "business necessity" defense is distorted.

By merging the profit-making prerogatives of private developers with the public interest mandate of the government, the Court gives added potency to defense claims against disparate-impact plaintiffs like ICP.[67] Justice Kennedy impliedly concedes this when he notes that "the Title VII framework may not transfer exactly to the fair-housing context, but the comparison suffices for present purposes."[68] This is yet another example of how the rhetorical myth – the post-racial narrative that rationalizes subordination – advances process-based outcomes and pre-determines the Court's interpretation of the housing marketplace. Under this reading, the challenged practices will nearly always be consistent with business necessity because disparate impact is presumed to be a natural market outcome. In other words, private developers, and the government itself, should not be constrained by market choices simply because they could result in racial imbalance or persistent segregated housing.

The two reasonable approaches – between building "low-income housing in a blighted inner-city neighborhood instead of a suburb"[69] – are not discriminatory, although such a "neutral" decision will reify extant patterns of segregated housing. Notwithstanding its public obligation,[70] the Department is cast as a private entrepreneur with no institutional responsibility for eradicating segregated residential housing.

> A twenty-first century local government bureaucrat or elected official did not create racial segregation in housing, but he or she can virtually guarantee its perpetuation, with or without discriminatory purpose, by simply engaging in practices that help maintain the residential status quo. This could include not only adopting new rules but also enforcing longstanding zoning ordinances that "effectively foreclose the construction of any low-cost housing" in an all-white neighborhood. Officials also can take advantage of facially neutral rules that "bear no relation to discrimination upon passage but develop into powerful discriminatory mechanisms when applied." The most cursory examination of history undermines the proposition that the government can ever really be "neutral" on segregation. When local governments are not helping to undo segregation, they are almost always helping to keep it in place, with their actions serving as the functional equivalent of intentional discrimination. Seicshnaydre, *supra* n. 63, at 417–18 (citations omitted).

[67] Kristen Barnes, *The Pieces of Housing Integration*, CASE WESTERN RESERVE L. REV. 717, 727–30, 729 (2020) (discussing the inapplicability of the employment law model in the housing context and how the Court "elevated the business justifications it predicted government entities and developers would likely offer to defend their site and project selections for low-income housing").

[68] *Inclusive Cmtys.*, 576 U.S. at 541.

[69] *Ibid.* at 542.

[70] There is a provision of the FHA which requires administrative agencies to "affirmatively further fair housing" (AFFH) which means race can be a permissible component in decision-making. The AFFH provisions conflict with the Court's post-racial colorblindness, an attempt to conceal (or evade) race-conscious policy choices. *See* Blake Emerson, *Affirmatively Furthering Equal Protection: Constitutional Meaning in the Administration of Fair Housing*, 65 BUFF. L. REV. 163, 174–89 (2017) (conceptualizing "administrative equal protection" as a doctrinal means to resolve the tension between the post-racial equal protection clause and the AFFH provisions of the FHA).

After extoling the discretionary power of entrepreneurs to "consider market factors,"[71] Justice Kennedy offers a revisionist post-racial narrative that is jarring in its omission of historical facts and their present-day impact – urban development is simply a function of neutral choices, not policies buttressed by systemic racism and structural inequality·

> The FHA does not decree a particular vision of urban development; and it does not put housing authorities and private developers in a double bind of liability, subject to suit whether they choose to rejuvenate a city core or to promote new low-income housing in suburban communities. As HUD itself recognized in its recent rule-making, disparate-impact liability "does not mandate that affordable housing be located in neighborhoods with any particular characteristic."[72]

The casualness of Justice Kennedy's assertions and reasoning is disconcerting – promoting new low-income housing in suburban communities is more than a notion[73] and urban development (or renewal) is not nearly as clean and beneficial as he suggests.

It is astoundingly ahistorical to suggest that there was no "particular vision of urban development" – there was indeed a vision of urban renewal that devastated Black communities across the country. This "vision" included redlining, discriminatory mortgage practices, segregative zoning, and effective dismantling and displacement of Black communities by the interstate highway system.[74] This reasoning sets up an illusory choice between urban development in the segregated inner city or the white outlying suburbs – the Court's post-racial jurisprudence has already effectively isolated the suburbs from any substantive school integration efforts,[75] and now the Court's narrow definition of disparate impact liability, its presumption favoring neutral rationales for continuing segregation, and its guiding principle of post-racial neutrality in housing policy all but ensure that profit-based decisions leaving segregated housing intact will be affirmed.

The tenor of *Inclusive Communities* is quintessentially post-racial – structural inequality is virtually non-existent, so a decision to build low-income housing in a "blighted inner-city neighborhood instead of a suburb ... or vice versa"[76] is neutral

---

[71] *Inclusive Cmtys.*, 576 U.S. at 542.

[72] *Ibid.*

[73] Laura Sullivan, *Trump Stokes Fear in the Suburbs, but Few Low-Income Families Ever Make It There*, ALL THINGS CONSIDERED, October 28, 2020, www.npr.org/2020/10/28/926769415/trump-stokes-fear-in-the-suburbs-but-few-low-income-families-ever-make-it-there.

[74] Keeanga-Yamahtta Taylor, *supra* n. 16, at 40–42 (discussing the devastating impact of demolishing slum housing to promote economic revival but with minimal benefit to displaced Black communities); Scott Beyer, *How the U.S. Government Destroyed Black Neighborhoods Post-World War II Urban Renewal Replaced Thriving Black Hubs with Highways and Public Housing*, CATALYST, April 2, 2020, https://catalyst.independent.org/2020/04/02/how-the-u-s-government-destroyed-black-neighborhoods/.

[75] *See Milliken v. Bradley* discussed in Chapter 2.

[76] *Inclusive Cmtys.*, 576 U.S. at 542.

and non-discriminatory. It is simply a matter of "advantage or disadvantage to racial minorities,"[77] not fully integrating segregated residential communities. Indeed, this either–or approach to decisional choice underscores the analytical limitations of the decision: *Inclusive Communities* is a marketplace decision, with integration as only a secondary concern. And because race cannot be a determining factor in decision-making, any remedies should be "design[ed] … to eliminate racial dispari-ties through race-neutral means."[78]

This also means that while disparate impact liability is cognizable under the FHA, because of the presumption in favor of the housing marketplace[79] and its underlying profit motive, it will be difficult to prove disparate impact. While it is debatable whether the "robust causality requirement"[80] is an additional evidentiary proffer of implicit intent in establishing disparate impact liability, it is at least a com-ment on the higher quantum of evidence necessary to establish disparate impact liability. Mere statistical disparity in terms of impact is insufficient, a plaintiff must "point to a defendant's policy or policies causing that disparity."[81]

As in its school desegregation jurisprudence, the Court accepts racial imbalance as permissible when it is not intentional; and a robust causality requirement "pro-tects defendants from being held liable for racial disparities they did not create."[82] So, in the absence of discriminatory intent, there is no discrimination; moreover, disparate impact liability cannot be proven in the absence of an identifiable policy and impact. The Court offers no answers as to how this is qualitatively distinguish-able from a discriminatory intent requirement like that buttressing its equal protec-tion jurisprudence.

The Court is simply content to end on an empty post-racial sentiment that while "much progress remains to be made"[83] in eradicating the present-day effects of racial isolation, "we must remain wary of policies that reduce homeowners to noth-ing more than their race."[84] By impugning the validity of ICP's disparate impact claim as nothing more than impermissible racial balancing under a "novel theory," *Inclusive Communities*' acknowledgement of disparate impact liability is tepid. It is a claim without a solid statutory foundation. This is still insufficient to Justice Alito – in dissent, he concludes that the FHA does not encompass disparate impact.

Tellingly, there is not a huge doctrinal gulf between Justice Kennedy's post-racial conception of disparate impact and Justice Alito's – the key distinction is how they

---

[77] *Ibid.*

[78] *Ibid.* at 545.

[79] *Ibid.* at 544 ("The limitations on disparate-impact liability discussed here are also necessary to pro-tect potential defendants against abusive disparate-impact claims").

[80] *Ibid.* at 542.

[81] *Ibid.*

[82] *Ibid.*

[83] *Ibid.* at 546.

[84] *Ibid.*

conceptualize choice. For Justice Kennedy, disparate impact is statutorily cogni-zable, but it is limited by neutral market factors. Justice Alito's dissent advances the proposition that there is no disparate impact liability under the FHA, and recogniz-ing this form of liability makes the state and private actors liable for neutral choices that must be made, but which nevertheless have a disparate impact. In other words, private developers and the government should not be insurers of the inevitable impact of societal discrimination. In the absence of clearly identifiable discrimina-tion, landlords should not be punished for a myriad of societal ills not of their own making.

JUSTICE ALITO'S POST-RACIAL DISSENT: A RAT'S NEST AND THREE POST-RACIAL HYPOTHETICALS

Opening his dissent with "No one wants to live in a rat's nest,"[85] Justice Alito offers a comprehensive critique of Justice Kennedy's majority opinion and concludes that the FHA does not encompass disparate impact claims. Drawing upon the text and content of the FHA, Justice Alito concludes that it is a disparate treatment (intent) statute rather than a disparate impact statute.[86] As he did in his *Ricci* dissent, Justice Alito propagates racial tropes and stereotypes to advance post-racialism. He disin-genuously alters the meaning of disparate impact so that it means any societal impact that falls on subordinated people so that the benevolent (and innocent) landlords are subject to race-based claims that thwart their ability to provide decent housing. The spectra of disparate impact liability, under a statute that does not provide for it, has a chilling effect[87] on the availability of "minimally acceptable housing for its poorest residents."[88] That's relatively better than a rat's nest.

To equate the "because of" statutory language of §§ 804(a) and 805(a) with intent, Justice Alito crafts three post-racial hypotheticals emphasizing discrete, individualized factors rather than structural ones. To illuminate the text and con-tent of the FHA, Justice Alito posits three scenarios where discriminatory intent is absent and thus not covered by the statute: (i) a minimum wage increase that impacts Black workers so that jobs are unavailable to those who are unskilled;[89] (ii) a National Football League (NFL) first round draft "with an overwhelming major-ity" of racial minorities so that most of the draft slots are available to Black and Brown players, not white players;[90] and (iii) the Solicitor General's Office where argument opportunities before the Court are filled by 76 percent of attorneys

---

[85] *Ibid.* at 557 (Alito, J., dissenting).
[86] *Ibid.* at 558–63.
[87] *Ibid.* at 558 ("Something has gone badly awry when a city can't even make slumlords kill rats without fear of a lawsuit").
[88] *Ibid.*
[89] *Ibid.* at 555–56.
[90] *Ibid.* at 565.

under the age of 45.[91] In each of these instances, Justice Alito asks whether "unavailability" is the result of discrimination – is the impact "because of" some discriminatory action?

(i) *The Minimum Wage Increase*

Noting that African-Americans and Latinos would be impacted by a minimum wage increase which would displace unskilled workers, Justice Alito queries: "would it be fair to say that Congress made jobs unavailable to African-Americans or Latinos 'because of' their race or ethnicity?"[92] Of course, the answer to this rhetorical question is "no." But it would be fair to say that there are structural factors that disproportionately impact African Americans and Latinos in the employment marketplace because of their race.

A finding of discriminatory intent is not a prerequisite to establishing why jobs were disproportionately unavailable to employees of color. There are numerous factors as to why unskilled workers are displaced, and some could be deemed as comporting with a reasonable business necessity. But the point here is that disparate impact is about the consequences of governmental, or private actions which, while ostensibly neutral, mask arbitrary and discriminatory practices that perpetually subordinate people of color. The analysis should not focus on Congress as a singular institutional discriminatory perpetrator – it did, after all, raise the minimum wage in this fanciful hypothetical – the focus should be on the structural factors that made jobs unavailable to African Americans and Latinos. This structural component is absent in Justice Alito's postulate of statutory interpretation.

(ii) *The 2015 NFL Draft*

Since the "overwhelming majority [of first round draft picks] were members of racial minorities," Justice Alito asks, "Would anyone say the NFL teams made draft slots unavailable to white players 'because of' their race'?"[93] This second post-racial hypothetical is even less convincing than the first because Justice Alito deploys the reverse discrimination analogy to the NFL draft. There is no discriminatory intent or impact here – this is the rare instance where "meritocracy" works, as players are chosen strictly by their physical performance at the NFL combine.

Justice Alito's selection of this purportedly neutral example is quite telling because he posits a reverse discrimination trope – where slots are unavailable to white players – to make the point that the FHA requires intentionality and disparate impact is not reached by the statute. But what is missing again is the structural underpinning of this example, Justice Alito's analysis does not envision the unavailability of

[91] *Ibid.*
[92] *Ibid.*
[93] *Ibid.*

coaching jobs to African-American coaches in the NFL, and this is because he fails to fully conceptualize structural disproportionality. This is a more apt example than simply focusing on players because the draft is certainly more open and accessible than the coaching and senior management ranks.

(iii) *The Solicitor General's Office and Attorney Age*

As to Justice Alito's third example, the fact that "of the 21 attorneys from the Solicitor General's Office who argued [before the Court]," "all but 5 (76%) were under the age of 45," is unintentional as well and does not warrant the conclusion that "argument opportunities [were made] unavailable to older attorneys 'because of' their age."[94]

All of Justice Alito's examples are inapposite; they illustrate unintentional results with no connection to the structures that produced them. There is no fundamental distinction between neutral disproportionality (a rational impact without any discriminatory underpinning) and structural disproportionality (an impact resulting from systemic and structural factors designed to be neutral but with real discriminatory impact) emanating from past discrimination. Justice Alito's examples are all rooted in neutral disproportionality – none of the discriminatory impact is "because of" race, reverse discrimination (a fraught term), or age discrimination. But this says nothing as to why discriminatory intent is Justice Alito's touchstone for analyzing the FHA.

Moreover, the examples are from the employment market, not the housing market, which is distinctly different. Indeed, this says nothing about the scope of disparate impact liability. Specifically, none of these hypotheticals answer the majority's conclusion that the FHA encompasses discriminatory impact.

The interpretive statutory question is much more nuanced than literally whether the FHA encompasses either discriminatory intent or impact – most systemic discrimination can be explicit and implicit with variants in between; the question is how we eradicate the present-day effects of past discrimination.[95] *Inclusive Communities* fails to answer this question because both Justices Kennedy and Alito embrace post-racialism and a presumption in favor of a profit-making housing market.

THE FINAL HOUSING AND URBAN DEVELOPMENT ("HUD") RULE: "ROBUST CAUSALITY" AND DISCRIMINATORY INTENT

In codifying the Court's decision in *Inclusive Communities*, the Trump administration went even further to make the burden of proof for disparate impact claims virtually insurmountable and to provide potent affirmative defenses for defendants:

---

[94] *Ibid.* at 565.
[95] *See generally* Girardeau A. Spann, *Disparate Impact*, 98 Geo. L. J. 1133, 1162 (2010) (discussing post-racial discrimination and how it evolves from intentional to "neutral" with the same result – the perpetuation of caste-based oppression).

The proposed rule … grafts a discriminatory intent requirement on to disparate impact liability by (i) de-emphasizing the structural dimensions of racial discrimination and its impact, and instead focusing on particularity and specificity in identifying disparate impact; (ii) requiring a showing by the plaintiff of a "robust causal link" between the challenged policy and its impact on members of a protected class; this is an undefined evidentiary standard reminiscent of the Court's novel "strong basis in evidence" standard [in *Ricci*]; (iii) adding yet another layer of intent by requiring a plaintiff to explain how the challenged policy produces an adverse impact on the protected class; (iv) establishing [an additional] pleading requirement that the disparity caused by the policy or practice is significant, which would mean any statistical disparity identified must be "material;" and, finally, (v) adding an additional causal requirement that the challenged policy or practice "directly caused" the alleged injury.[96]

The Trump administration also eviscerated the FHA's affirmative obligation to HUD to "affirmatively further fair housing" (AFFH).[97]

The Biden administration reversed this rule by issuing a memorandum to the HUD Secretary to redress systemic housing discrimination.[98] Pursuant to this memorandum, HUD reinstated the AFFH definition, and reinstated the 2013 Disparate Impact Rule restoring it to the statutory regime in effect before *Inclusive Communities*.[99] It remains to be seen what this statutory restoration will mean in light of eradicating deeply rooted systems of segregated housing throughout the United States.[100]

The Roberts Court's post-racial constitutionalism serves as a signpost – it signals to society that it is in accord with its societal, cultural, and political aspirations. Within the context of the Third Reconstruction, the Racial Reckoning, and attacks on the validity of Critical Race Theory in illuminating systemic racism and structural inequality, the Court's post-racial neutrality (its blind insistence that race should be eliminated from society and all decision-making) actualizes and emboldens efforts to subordinate African-Americans and other discrete and insular minorities.[101]

---

[96] Powell, *supra* n. 21.

[97] *See supra* n. 70.

[98] The White House, *Memorandum on Redressing Our Nation's and the Federal Government's History of Discriminatory Housing Practices and Policies*, January 26, 2021, Presidential Actions www.whitehouse.gov/briefing-room/presidential-actions/2021/01/26/memorandum-on-redressing-our-nations-and-the-federal-governments-history-of-discriminatory-housing-practices-and-policies/.

[99] National Low Income Housing Coalition, *HUD Disparate Impact Proposed Rule Clears Review*, June 1, 2021nlihc.org/resource/hud-disparate-impact-proposed-rule-clears-review.

[100] David D. Troutt, *Inclusion Imagined: Fair Housing as Metropolitan Equity*, 65 Buff. L. Rev. 5, 60–91, 108 (2017) (arguing for recognition of structural inequality and robust enforcement policy to advance AFFH through a theory of equity as a legal norm).

[101] Terry Smith, Whitelash: Unmasking White Grievance at the Ballot Box 112 ("We should … acknowledge that racial inequality and whitelash could not have flourished without the complicity of the judiciary").

Certainly, the Court is not a protector of subordinated minorities – the Court advances its own view of a post-racial society where racism and discrimination does not exist because it has been eliminated (or is in the past), or will not exist if we simply "stop discriminating on the basis of race." This formalism ignores the reality of structural inequality and the permanence of racism. As the Court's post-racial voting rights jurisprudence devastatingly illustrates, the Court is actively engaged in empowering the forces that would undermine substantive equality, especially voting rights.

8

Voting Rights

Contrived Federalism and the Problem of Second-Generation Discrimination

Under the Roberts Court's conception of formalistic equality, the Voting Rights Act ("VRA") is superfluous because lynching and the poll tax have been eradicated, and there is no proof of anything other than racial progress. This is the hallmark of all Reconstruction periods – great progress has been made, so any further remedial efforts are unnecessarily disruptive to the settled expectations of whites that have been unduly burdened by race-conscious remedies.[1]

The U.S. Supreme Court sustains its legitimacy by mirroring post-racial public sentiment, and the Roberts Court's post-racial constitutionalism reflects the backlash against any progressive efforts to eradicate structural inequality. Nowhere is this more graphically illustrated than in the Court's recent voting rights decisions. In *Shelby County v. Holder*, the Court, in a 5–4 opinion, gutted Section 4 of the VRA, concluding that "decades-old data" of voting suppression was irrelevant considering all the progress made by Blacks in the political process, and any burdens on the states had to be justified by some showing of current discrimination.[2]

The Court perpetuates racial inequality by actively protecting white majoritarian interests, even if this means that previously covered jurisdictions will regress to their original state of suppressing the Black vote. The Court's novel conception of federalism sent a signal to states to pursue deceptively neutral ways to dilute the voting rights of people of color.[3] The feigned crisis of voting fraud is an example of this; this ugly side of federalism is apparent in the Court's recent decision, *Husted v. A. Philip Randolph Institute*, holding that an Ohio law permitted the state to remove nearly 1 million voters from its rolls.[4] While this decision reads like a neutral interpretation of a statute, its language, and the purportedly neutral process underlying it, this

---

[1] *See, for example,* Michael D. Shear, Stacy Cowley, and Alan Rappeport, *Biden's Push for Racial Equity Hits Legal and Political Snags,* N.Y. TIMES, June 27, 2021.

[2] 570 U.S. 529, 553 (2013).

[3] Brennan Center for Justice, *Voting Laws Roundup: December 2021 This Year's Tidal Wave of Restrictive Voting Legislation Will Continue in 2022,* December 21, 2021, www.brennancenter.org/our-work/research-reports/voting-laws-roundup-december-2021.

[4] 138 S. Ct. 1833, 1844–46 (2018).

chapter argues that this is an example of the Court's post-racial proceduralism. An ostensibly neutral law, crafted to prevent voter fraud, is instead transformed into an instrument of voter suppression, and the Court presumes its fairness because race is never mentioned – the voting process is fair. There is a direct connection between voter suppression and the Court's cynical manipulation of democratic ideals, which exclude rather than include oppressed communities of color.[5]

In *Rucho v. Common Cause*, the U.S. Supreme Court held that partisan gerrymandering was a political question beyond the decision-making authority of the Court.[6] This is the most recent example of the Court's post-racial constitutionalism under the guise of neutrality. The Court readily ignores the present-day effects of structural inequality – partisan gerrymandering is a proxy for racial gerrymandering. The issue isn't political identity, commonality of political cause, or partisan voting strength; rather, it is the dilution of voting strength for people of color.

With Justice Kennedy's retirement from the Court in 2018, there is a profoundly hard right shift toward post-racial constitutionalism. Chief Justice Roberts authors 5–4 decisions in *Shelby County* and *Rucho*, and Justice Alito authors the 5–4 decision in *Husted* (Justice Kennedy signed on to the majority opinion in one of his last opinions for the Court) and the 6–3 decision in *Brnovich*, signaling the emergence of a new entrenched conservative majority. Not only are these decisions landmark voting rights decisions, but they are also bellwethers for the new strain of the Roberts Court's post-racial constitutionalism – the new enterprise is not only to excise race from all decision-making, it is to deny the existence of structural inequality so the Court rewrites history to conform with popular conceptions of post-racialism.

Through ostensibly neutral decisional rhetoric advancing federalism (*Shelby County*), the elimination of voting "fraud" and the preservation of American democracy (*Husted*), and empowering political parties to determine their own destiny (*Rucho*), the Court has rationalized the subordination of oppressed minorities. Most recently, in an opinion by Justice Alito, the Court continued its work in hollowing out the VRA by rejecting a claim of disparate impact vote dilution of minorities in *Brnovich v. Democratic National Committee*.[7] Advancing a perverse conception of federalism, the Roberts Court has insulated the states from any meaningful scrutiny under the VRA and has diminished congressional power as it aggrandizes state power in enacting voter suppression legislation.

---

5 *Compare City of Cuyahoga Falls v. Buckeye Community Hope Foundation*, 538 U.S. 188, 197 (2003) (affirming white majority community's referendum – a "basic instrument of democratic government" – to repeal an ordinance approving construction of low-income housing despite abundant evidence of racist sentiments) *with Husted*, 138 S. Ct. at 1844–46 (purporting to eliminate voter fraud while perpetuating inequality by ignoring the disproportionate impact of voter purges on communities of color). Both decisions advance ostensibly neutral democratic goals but reify structural political exclusion by privileging white interests and the maintenance of entrenched power).

6 139 S. Ct. 2484, 2506–07 (2019).

7 *Brnovich v. Democratic National Committee*, 141 S. Ct. 2321 (2021).

These doctrinal developments are not coincidental; they stretch all the way back
to the First Reconstruction, the *Civil Rights Cases*, and *Plessy v. Ferguson*.[8] Terry
Smith makes this point powerfully, when he observes:

> In short, the Supreme Court in 1883 was as fed up with attempts to secure equality
> for blacks as the Supreme Court was in 2013. And just as the *Civil Rights Cases* set
> the stage for 75 years of Jim Crow, *Shelby County* unleashed America's racist poten-
> tial like no other modern decision of the Court. The decision forecasted the age of
> Trump and has made more imperative than at any time since Jim Crow the need
> for structural reforms to protect people of color against voter whitelash.[9]

While demographics is not destiny, it nevertheless can be said, particularly after the
ubiquitous racism of the Trump era,[10] that there is a concerted effort, at every level of
society, to preserve the status quo power arrangements rooted in white supremacy.[11]
Yet another avenue of obstruction, retrenchment, and retrogression is through voter
suppression under the guise of combatting fabricated voter fraud.

The Roberts Court has been actively engaged in giving voice to this whitelash.[12]
Of course, the Court espouses neutral principles like federalism, the end of formal
discrimination, and a robust political process open to all; but decisions like *Shelby
County, Husted, Rucho*, and *Brnovich* send a signal to those who would undermine
the power, validity, and primacy of the VRA. The more things change, the more
they stay the same[13] – voter suppression has morphed into a new form of discrimination masquerading as a campaign to invigorate American democracy.

A cavalcade of "fraudits" – fraudulent voting audits commissioned to find fraud
where none exists – have cropped up across the country to recount votes in a quixotic

---

[8] *See* Chapter 1; Adam Serwer, *Opinion: The Cruel Logic of the G.O.P.*, N.Y. TIMES, June 27, 2021, at 8.
[9] TERRY SMITH, WHITELASH: UNMASKING WHITE GRIEVANCE AT THE BALLOT BOX 159 (2020).
[10] *Ibid.* ("Republicans have responded with zeal, even in the aftermath of [Trump's] loss, with
     Republican-controlled legislatures targeting constituencies they identify either with Democrats or
     with the rapid cultural change that conservatives hope to arrest. The most significant for democracy,
     however, are the election laws designed to insulate Republican power from a diverse American
     majority that Republicans fear no longer supports them").
[11] Jamelle Bouie, *American Democracy Has Never Shed an Undemocratic Assumption Present at
     Its Founding: That Some People Are Inherently Entitled to More Power Than Others*, N.Y. TIMES
     MAGAZINE, THE 1619 PROJECT, August 18, 2019, at 50, 54 ("There is a homegrown ideology of reac-
     tion in the United States, inextricably tied to our system of slavery. And while the racial content of
     that ideology has attenuated over time, the basic framework remains: fear of rival political majorities;
     of demographic 'replacement'; of a government that threatens privilege and hierarchy").
[12] Smith, supra n. 9, at 8 ("A salient feature of whitelash is the construction of equality as zero-sum: the
     advancement of minorities must necessarily come at the expense of whites").
[13] Mario Barnes, *"The More Things Change …": New Moves for Legitimizing Racial Discrimination in
     a "Post-Race" World*, 100 MINN. L. REV. 2043, 2080 (2016) (noting that Chief Justice Roberts, while
     acknowledging race, nevertheless, concludes that race "no longer matters enough to upset states'
     rights"; and, that Justice Scalia outrageously characterized the VRA as the perpetuation of "racial
     entitlement").

attempt to substantiate the Big Lie.[14] The legislative response has been enactments to reconfigure voting strength so that Republicans can reclaim lost seats, expand their base in state and federal elections, and ensure impenetrable partisan electoral support.[15] *Shelby County* is the doctrinal signpost to the states to begin their work of subjugation – targeting discrete and insular minorities for limited participation (or exclusion) from the political marketplace through voter suppression. This subjugation is endemic to American democracy – African Americans have been targeted for second-class citizenship by concerted efforts to devalue the representative power of their vote.[16]

SHELBY COUNTY v. HOLDER: CHIEF JUSTICE ROBERTS' POST-RACIAL FORMALISM, THE SECOND POST-RACIAL EDICT, AND RHETORICAL NEUTRALITY

Chief Justice Roberts offers another post-racial edict in *Shelby County* – formal oppression by the state in voting has been eliminated at least since 1965, "so the way to stop discriminating on the basis of race" is to limit the reach of any anti-discrimination statute or remedy to clearly identifiable current discrimination. And the federal government cannot unconstitutionally intervene in the affairs of the states where there is no current discrimination. The relative progress of formerly oppressed minorities underscores the fact that anti-discrimination laws, like the VRA, are unnecessary.

Underlying the Roberts Court's post-racialism is Rhetorical Neutrality: rhetorically, Chief Roberts advances a post-racial history (the historical myth) extoling the progress of Blacks in electoral politics and downplaying the existence of voter discrimination so that federal supervision is an anti-democratic intrusion on state power; he defines discrimination narrowly (the definitional myth) so that voter discrimination is only a collateral concern and the focus is on the disruption of state power; and the evisceration of the VRA is rationalized as prudent (the rhetorical myth) because basic principles of federalism have been undermined by imposing perpetual supervision of formerly discriminatory states by the federal government and judiciary.

The Historical Myth: Voting Discrimination Ends in 1965 and Post-Racial Progress Begins

Espousing a fabricated federalism and equal state sovereignty rationale, the Court holds that § 4 (b) of the VRA, the coverage formula applying to states with a

---

[14] Laura Clawson, *It's a Failure. It's a Joke,*" *Republican Operative Says of Arizona Fraudit,* DAILY KOS, June 29, 2021, www.dailykos.com/stories/2021/6/29/2037605/-New-poll-finds-Arizona-independent-voters-are-opposed-to-Republican-fraudit.

[15] Brennan Center for Justice, *Voting Law Roundup: May 2021,* www.brennancenter.org/our-work/research-reports/voting-laws-roundup-may-2021.

[16] CAROL ANDERSON, ONE PERSON, NO VOTE: HOW VOTER SUPPRESSION IS DESTROYING OUR DEMOCRACY (2018).

documented history of voter suppression and discrimination, was unconstitutional.[17] Section 5, the preclearance requirement for states with discriminatory histories, was rendered nugatory by this holding as well.[18]

Chief Justice Robert's recitation of the history of voting rights is linear, revisionist, and post-racial. But the most striking aspect of this history is that it begins with the presumption that, at least on some level, the Fifteenth Amendment of 1870, the VRA of 1965, and all the subsequent reauthorizations of the Act were either extraordinary remedial measures, limited to a specific time and duration, or unduly disruptive of state power.

It is as if the VRA is presumptively invalid, an unwarranted intrusion on the validity and primacy of state power. From the beginning of the opinion, Chief Justice Roberts casts the VRA as an "extraordinary measure [] to address an extraordinary problem," "a drastic departure from basic principles of federalism," and discriminatory against the state principle of "equal sovereignty" because § 4 targeted some states but not others – all of this is "strong medicine."[19] The Chief Justice's disdain for the VRA and its remedial purpose is palpable.[20]

Under Chief Justice Roberts' post-racial reading of the VRA, voting discrimination is limited in time; its existence and relevancy is determined by the life of the statute enacted to eradicate it. So, the historical persistence of present-day voting rights discrimination is obscured by a temporal limit set by the Court itself – these extraordinarily unprecedented measures, prescribed by the VRA, were so disruptive that they were intended to be "temporary" and "scheduled to expire after five years."[21] The Court revises history to conform to its own conception of federalism.

After a cursory reference to the caste-based oppression that followed the Fifteenth Amendment, Chief Justice Roberts glosses over the 100-year period of the Black Codes and Jim Crow before the passage of the VRA, and simply notes that the civil rights movement "inspired"[22] Congress to pass voting rights legislation in 1965. It's as if the right to vote was a gift to African Americans that had to be carefully balanced against the "burden" imposed on the states to ensure that all citizens had full and equal access to the franchise. Under this reasoning, it is not surprising that, to Chief Justice Roberts, substantive equality has a five-year temporal limit.

---

[17] *Shelby County,* 570 U.S. at 557.
[18] *Ibid.* While the Court rendered no opinion on §5, it invited Congress to come up with a new coverage formula which would determine the applicability of §5.
[19] *Ibid.* at 534–35.
[20] Eric Levitz, *Man Who Gutted Voting Rights Act Says Americans "Take Democracy for Granted,"* NEW YORK MAGAZINE, January 2, 2020, https://nymag.com/intelligencer/2020/01/john-roberts-americans-take-democracy-for-granted.html; Ari Berman, *Inside John Roberts' Decades-Long Crusade against the Voting Rights Act,* POLITICO MAGAZINE, August 10, 2015, www.politico.com/magazine/story/2015/08/john-roberts-voting-rights-act-121222/.
[21] *Ibid.* at 538.
[22] *Ibid.* at 536.

While noting that covered jurisdictions, under § 4, were those states or counties that "maintained a test or device [like literacy and knowledge tests, good moral character requirements, and vouchers] as a prerequisite to voting," Chief Justice Roberts nevertheless highlights how these "covered" jurisdictions were targeted with the anti-federalism imposition of obtaining preclearance to change voting procedures under § 5. While §§ 4 and 5 were to expire after five years, Chief Justice Roberts notes that "[n]early 50 years later, they are still in effect; indeed, they have been made more stringent, and are now scheduled to last until 2031."[23] After cataloguing all of the previous reauthorizations of the VRA through 2006,[24] Chief Justice Roberts essentially says that the unaltered coverage formula, based on "old" discrimination from 1965, is unwarranted and unconstitutional. He does so by redefining voting rights discrimination: while discrimination may exist, it must be proven by current data; and, because so much progress has been made by minorities in our democracy, there is no injury to remedy.

The Definitional Myth: Current Discrimination?

Shelby County's exclusive focus on its concocted federalism (the equal sovereignty of the states) transforms the intended five-year expiration date for the VRA into an end date for any remediable voting discrimination. The states cannot be targeted after this date, and the burdens imposed by §§ 4 and 5 must be lifted because there may be societal discrimination, but no identifiable current voting discrimination. This is analogous to the Court's retreat from school integration discussed in Chapter 2; both the school cases and the voting rights cases emphasize limited impact on established systems that perpetuate structural inequality.

Yet in its post-racial voting rights jurisprudence, the Court makes an inverted argument that positions African-Americans as politically powerful, so much so that the states must be protected from Congress' unjustified intrusion into them in the absence of current discrimination:

> But history did not end in 1965. By the time the Act was reauthorized in 2006, there had been 40 more years of it. In assessing the "current need []" for a preclearance system that treats States differently from one another today, that history cannot be ignored. During that time, largely because of the Voting Rights Act, voting tests were abolished, disparities in voter registration and turnout due to race were erased, and African-Americans attained political office in record numbers. And yet the coverage formula that Congress reauthorized in 2006 ignores these developments, keeping the focus on decades-old data relevant to decades-old problems, rather than current data reflecting current needs.[25]

---

[23] *Ibid.* at 535.
[24] *Ibid.* at 538–39.
[25] *Ibid.* at 552–53.

History did not end in 1965, but neither did voter suppression and other forms of race-based disenfranchisement – the continuing effects of past discrimination in voting is precisely why reauthorizations of the VRA are necessary. These reauthorizations are not intrusions on the sovereignty of the states, nor do they disrupt basic principles of federalism; rather, they reaffirm the federal government's role in dismantling structural inequality in the states. Ironically, the Court's decision actualizes the very oppressive voting regime that the VRA seeks to eradicate.[26] This is because the Court is presumptively skeptical of laws that "burden" whites and disrupt their political power and privilege – the VRA is a likely target for this insidious skepticism.[27]

The Court defines discrimination as a series of episodic events that are directly linked to the intended expiration date of the VRA: since the Act was extraordinary legislation set to expire after five years; discriminatory voting practices have been eradicated "for over 40 years";[28] and there is no racial disparity in voter registration and turnout in the covered states, so there is no current discrimination necessitating division between equal states based on "decades-old data."[29] To the Court, the VRA is a disproportionate response to discrimination that does not exist[30] – the "current burdens" of the statute on state sovereignty are unjustified by the "current needs" because there is no current discrimination,[31] only "old" discrimination extrapolated from 2006 and projected forward to 2013 (and even further today). As will be illustrated later in this chapter, there is a disconcerting symmetry between the Court's dismantling of the VRA (in the absence of "current discrimination") and its expansion of state power with the fictionalized fraud narrative readily advanced by Justice Alito in *Brnovich*. How discrimination is defined is based on whether it fits within the Court's conception of post-racial constitutionalism – any relative progress for African Americans is viewed as a threat to the neutral (and natural) order of the American polity.

---

[26] Ari Berman, *Eight Years Ago, The Supreme Court Gutted the Voting Rights Act. Widespread Voter Suppression Resulted*, MOTHER JONES, June 25, 2021, www.motherjones.com/politics/2021/06/eight-years-ago-the-supreme-court-gutted-the-voting-rights-act-widespread-voter-suppression-resulted/.

[27] Khiara M. Bridges, *Class-Based Affirmative Action, or the Lies That We Tell about the Insignificance of Race*, 96 B.U. L. REV. 55, 73–74 (2016) (noting that, to the Roberts Court, "any benefit given to racial minorities is an illicit one that unjustly burdens non-minorities," and concluding that *Shelby County* illustrates the Court's skepticism: "the increased skepticism of law took the form of the Court being as suspicious of a law that was designed to protect racial minorities' voting rights as it would have been suspicious of a law that was designed to burden racial minorities' voting rights").

[28] *Shelby County*, 570 U.S. at 551.

[29] *Ibid.*

[30] *Ibid.* at 554 ("Congress did not use the record it compiled to shape a coverage formula grounded in current conditions. It instead reenacted a formula based on 40-year-old facts having no logical relation to the present day").

[31] Bridges, *supra* n. 27, at 77 (commenting that the Court "is comfortable declaring the elimination of a particular, historically specific type of discrimination as the elimination of discrimination in its entirety").

Definitionally, the appropriate starting date for determining the statutory viability and currency of the VRA is 2006, the last reauthorization date, to assess whether the "current burdens" [on the covered states] is justified by "current needs" [present-day voter suppression].[32] It is particularly audacious for the Court to reference the Fifteenth Amendment's command that "the right to vote shall not be denied or abridged on account of race," and Congress' accompanying enforcement power, only to conclude that "The Amendment is not designed to punish for the past; its purpose is to ensure a better future."[33] This post-racial proclamation means that formal discrimination has ended, states should not be "discriminated" against or punished for this historical discrimination, and all states have equal sovereignty to govern their voting processes.[34]

This is a cramped and fundamentally flawed reading of the Fifteenth Amendment and Congress' enforcement power – the Fifteenth Amendment's command went unenforced for 100 years,[35] and *Shelby* is a paradigmatic example of how caste-based denial of the franchise continues, in new forms,[36] to this day. The "past" has reinvented itself, so there is no better future for the voting rights of minorities. And there is little hope for this future because the Court rationalizes the persistence of voting rights discrimination against minorities as a natural consequence of state autonomy in voting rights policy and legislation.

The Rhetorical Myth: Post-Racial Separation of Powers

What drives Chief Justice Roberts' improvised notion of separation of powers is the post-racial proposition that racism is a thing of the distant past or, at the very least, a "unique circumstance"[37] that compelled Congress to act forty years ago. The VRA and the Equal Protection Clause are turned inside out – it is discrimination against covered jurisdictions that warrants scrutiny not the obstacles to access, vote dilution schemes, and other devious state stratagems crafted to exclude African Americans.

Congress has overstepped its bounds because it failed to "start [] from scratch in 2006,"[38] as if systemic racism and discrimination ebbs and flows based on specific

---

[32] *Shelby County*, 570 U.S. at 551.

[33] *Ibid.* at 553.

[34] *Bridges, supra* n. 27, at 77 (noting that the Court has no capacity to conceptualize structural inequality, but "Instead, in the vanquishing of antiquated forms of racism, the Court sees society's entrance into a post-racial future").

[35] *Shelby County*, 570 U.S. at 560–62 (Ginsburg, J., dissenting).

[36] *Ibid.* at 563–64 (discussing second-generation barriers in voting); *see also* Attiba Ellis, *The Cost of the Vote: Poll Taxes, Voter Identification Laws, and the Price of Democracy*, 86 DEN. U. L. REV. 1023 (2009) (discussing access barriers to voting as structural disenfranchisement); Ryan Partelow, *The Twenty-First Century Poll Tax*, HASTINGS CONST. L. Q. 425 (2020) (discussing felony disenfranchisement based on unpaid financial obligations).

[37] *Shelby County*, 570 U.S. at 546.

[38] *Ibid.* at 556.

calendar years or statutory expiration dates, and it singled out, for discriminatory treatment, covered states without chronicling specific instances of current discrimination. Dismissing "second-generation barriers" to voting as mere "electoral arrangements that affect the weight of minority votes" (this is discriminatory vote dilution),[39] Chief Justice Roberts insists on a literal formalism to cognizable discrimination: the coverage formula must be based on current conditions, not "40-year-old facts having no logical relation to the present day."[40] Section 4 must be supported by current evidence of discrimination "based on voting tests and access to the ballot, not vote dilution."[41]

Certainly, the Court cannot be suggesting that vote dilution is permissible in covered jurisdictions because this simply affects the weight of minority votes, not because it is a barrier to the casting of ballots. Access to the ballot is a mere formalism if the value of the vote cast is diluted or meaningless. But this is the Roberts Court's brand of post-racial democracy – the protection of states' federalism "rights" at the expense of the voting rights of discrete and insular minorities.

Acknowledging that "voting discrimination exists; no one doubts that"[42] Chief Justice Roberts nevertheless fashions an inquiry that foregrounds "disparate treatment of the States" rather than voting discrimination in jurisdictions with well-documented histories of Black voter oppression. This requires a dramatic revisioning of federalism principles – state power is aggrandized by diminishing the enforcement power of Congress under the Fifteenth Amendment. Four years earlier, *Northwest Austin Municipal Utility District v. Holder* was a doctrinal preamble to *Shelby County*. While not addressing the constitutionality of the coverage formula and preclearance requirement, the Court emphasized the progress made by African-Americans in the democratic process; the equal sovereignty of the states; and the bailout provisions designed to preserve state autonomy, and stated that the "Act's preclearance requirements and its coverage formula raise serious constitutional questions."[43] The Court completed the demolition of § 4 and, by implication, § 5 by striking down the coverage formula of § 4(b) but noting that "[o]ur decision in no way affects the permanent, nationwide ban on racial discrimination in voting found in §2." As with all the Roberts Court's post-racial jurisprudence this assurance rings hollow, as § 2 would be gutted only eight years later in *Brnovich v. Democratic National Committee*.

To rationalize its obliteration of the principle of separation of powers, the Court feigns caution by offering the rhetorical myth (a rationalizing narrative on inequality and disproportionate state power) of respect for a co-equal branch of government,

---

[39] *Ibid.* at 554.
[40] *Ibid.*
[41] *Ibid.*
[42] *Ibid.* at 536.
[43] *Northwest Austin Mun. Util. Dist.*, 557 U.S. 193, 203 (2009); *accord Shelby County*, 570 U.S. at 550.

concluding that [s]triking down an Act of Congress "is the gravest and most delicate duty that this Court is called on to perform."[44] The Court observes no such delicacy in declaring § 4(b) unconstitutional – it views the VRA as an "extraordinary departure from the traditional course of relations between the States and Federal Government."[45]

What is indeed extraordinary is the Court's departure from bedrock principles of federalism through its inversion of state and federal power[46] – states are free to chart their own course of voter disempowerment of feared minorities free from federal or judicial oversight. The explosion of voter restriction and suppression legislation across this nation illustrates this, as does the Court's own post-racial voting rights decisions in *Husted, Rucho,* and now *Brnovich.*

Federalism has never meant that state power expands as federal power contracts, and that the Court should intervene and place its hand on the scale to insulate states from scrutiny, especially where the states have perpetually exercised their raw power to subjugate, exclude, and stigmatize African Americans.[47] Justice Ginsburg makes this point eloquently and forcefully in one of her most famous dissents.

JUSTICE GINSBURG'S *SHELBY COUNTY* DISSENT: STRUCTURALISM IN A RAINSTORM

Throwing out preclearance when it has worked and is continuing to work to stop discriminatory changes is like throwing away your umbrella in a rainstorm because you are not getting wet.[48]

Not only does *Shelby County* throw away the umbrella – the protective shield of § 4 against the steady downpour of voter discrimination – it sends torrential rains of oppression down on unprotected minority voters who will be the inevitable victims of

---

44 *Shelby County,* 570 U.S. at 556 (citation omitted).

45 *Ibid.* at 557 (citation omitted).

46 Steven A. Ramirez and Neil G. Williams, *Deracialization and Democracy,* 70 CASE W. RES. L. REV. 81, 109 (2019) (noting that in *Shelby County* "precedent matters little and that the very concept of constitutionality is politically pliable").

47 Aderson Bellegarde Francois, *To Make Freedom Happen: Shelby County v. Holder, the Supreme Court, and the Creation Myth of American Voting Rights,* 34 N. ILL. U. L. REV. 529, 537 (2014) (discussing the creation myth of voting rights – a linear progression of relative progress highlighted by a cramped view of federal power – and stating that "[v]iewed from that perspective and contrary to the Supreme Court's voting rights foundation mythology, the need for federal protection against voter suppression is neither a temporary nor extraordinary departure from federalist principles, but is instead a necessary and permanent corrective to the ever present tendency of 'political factions' to exclude real or perceived 'minorities' from our national political family"); Jack Balkin, *The Reconstruction Power,* 85 N.Y.U. L. REV. 1801, 1805 (2010) ("Modern doctrine has not been faithful to the text, history, and structure of the Thirteenth, Fourteenth, and Fifteenth Amendments. These amendments were designed to give Congress broad powers to protect civil rights and civil liberties: Together they form Congress's Reconstruction Power.").

48 *Shelby County,* 570 U.S. at 590 (Ginsburg, J., dissenting).

state created devices to maintain power through subordination.[49] Justice Ginsburg's metaphoric retort captures the essence of the Roberts Court's post-racialism: *any* advance by minorities is perceived as an existential threat to white supremacy and must be neutralized[50] by seemingly impartial laws "applied and administered … with an evil eye and unequal hand."[51] As discussed in Chapter 1, this has always been the posture of the post-racial Court since the end of the first Reconstruction.

Rejecting Chief Justice Roberts' post-racial history and his illusory federalism, Justice Ginsburg's dissent offers a structural analysis of voting discrimination by (i) tracing the legislative history of the Reconstruction Amendments and how racial discrimination persisted and reified for 100 years after the Civil War;[52] (ii) rejecting the formalistically narrow definition of voter discrimination (the definitional myth) and emphasizing the present-day effects of past discrimination in the form of "second-generation barriers" to minority voting;[53] and (iii) restoring the primacy of Congress' enforcement power under the Reconstruction Amendments, so that state power is properly circumscribed, Congress' legislation is accorded deference,[54] and "equal sovereignty" does not displace federal power.[55] "In summary, the Constitution vests broad power in Congress to protect the right to vote, and in particular to combat racial discrimination in voting."[56]

Context matters because racial discrimination evolves and retrogression to the status quo of voter discrimination must be avoided.[57] The legislative history underlying the 2016 reauthorization clearly illustrates this. Indeed, voting discrimination in covered jurisdictions took on many forms and variations during the period reviewed by Congress in evaluating the need for reauthorization. History did not end in 1965, and neither did the oppression of minority voters. Justice Ginsburg's dissent catalogues numerous instances of intentional discrimination in covered districts that were blocked because of §§ 4 and 5.[58] "The record supporting the 2006 reauthorization of the VRA is … extraordinary."[59]

---

[49] *Ibid.* at 578 ("… places where there is greater racial polarization in voting have a greater need for prophylactic measures to prevent purposeful race discrimination").

[50] Serwer, *supra* n. 8; ADAM SERWER, THE CRUELTY IS THE POINT: THE PAST, PRESENT, AND FUTURE OF TRUMP'S AMERICA (2021).

[51] *Yick Wo v. Hopkins*, 118 U.S. 356, 373–74 (1886).

[52] *Shelby County*, 570 U.S. at 560–70 (Ginsburg, J., dissenting).

[53] *Ibid.* at 563–66. While not direct attempts at blocking access to the franchise such as the poll tax, literacy tests, and intimidation; these "second-generation barriers" – racial gerrymandering; at-large voting; discriminatory annexation; and other vote dilution devices – are just as discriminatory in excluding minority voters. Either access to the ballot is blocked directly, or the vote cast is so diluted that it is meaningless – the voter is not heard whether she votes or not.

[54] *Ibid.* at 566–69.

[55] *Ibid.* at 587–94.

[56] *Ibid.* at 570.

[57] *Ibid.* at 575–76.

[58] *Ibid.* at 573–75.

[59] *Ibid.* at 593.

What Justice Ginsburg's dissent reveals is how brazen the Court is in advancing its post-racial view of democracy: an extensive legislative history and record supporting the 2006 reauthorization is simply ignored to invent a new theory of federalism that does not balance power, but displaces it, so that Congress must "defer" to the states' interpretation of what the Fifteenth Amendment means and how the franchise will be exercised by minority voters.

Shelby County announces the Court's post-racial federalism where the enforcement power of Congress is turned inside out – states should be protected from "targeting" under the VRA, so any intervention to protect the interests of Blacks and other people of color is viewed as presumptively unconstitutional because sufficient progress has been made on issues of race, especially as to voting rights and representation in the political process. Justice Alito takes this proposition to its limit in *Husted* and *Brnovich*, and Chief Justice Roberts embraces the same post-racial outlook in *Rucho*.

Today, Justice Alito, along with Chief Justice Roberts, is the Court's primary doctrinal purveyor of post-racialism. *Shelby County's* progeny – *Husted, Rucho,* and *Brnovich* – all expand state power to control voting and elections in ways that threaten to undermine American democracy. After *Shelby County* aggrandizes state power and insulates it from any meaningful scrutiny under the VRA, the Court then expands on its post-racial political process discourse[60] by advancing the false regulatory machinery of voter purges premised on illusory fraud (*Husted*); ignoring partisan gerrymandering, as a proxy for racial gerrymandering, to dilute minority voting strength (*Rucho*); and trivializing disparate impact so that mere burdens on voting are insufficient to raise any constitutional concern (*Brnovich*).

An animating feature of the Roberts Court's post-racial constitutionalism is its appeal to ostensibly positive process values so alluring that they seem to advance core democratic principles like access and political progress, substantive representation, neutral values, and the protection of the process from anti-democratic influences. Yet these alluring democratic features have been weaponized by the Court. *Husted* is a paradigmatic example of the Court's post-racial process values and the Democratic Myth explored in Chapter 4. Here, instead of encouraging repressive voter initiatives to overturn the gains made by affirmative action, the Court signals to the states that it is open season on minority voting rights.

HUSTED v. A. PHILIP RANDOLPH INSTITUTE:
THE VOTING FRAUD ILLUSION

To increase voter registration and remove ineligible voters from the registration rolls, the National Voter Registration Act (NVRA) "erect[s] a complex superstructure of

---

[60] Recall the discussion of the political process theory in Chapter 4.

federal regulation atop state registration systems."[61] Pursuant to the NVRA, and its accompanying amendment, the Help America Vote Act (HAVA), Ohio is required to: (i) make a "reasonable effort to remove the names" of ineligible voters;[62] (ii) provide prior notification before a registrant is removed from the rolls – the state may not remove a registrant's name unless either the "registrant confirms in writing that he or she has moved," or the "registrant fails to return a preaddressed, postage prepaid "return card" containing statutorily prescribed content";[63] (iii) conduct a state removal program that is "uniform, nondiscriminatory, and in compliance with the Voting Rights Act of 1965";[64] and, under the Failure-to-Vote Clause, the program "shall not result in the removal of the name of any person … by reason of the person's failure to vote";[65] and (iv) to fulfill these statutory obligations, Ohio uses change-of-address information from the Postal Service to send notices to registrants identified as having moved and it uses a Supplemental Process to identify and send notice to "registrants who have not engage[d] in any voter activity for a period of two consecutive years."[66] "Voter activity" includes "casting a ballot" in any election" and broader acts of franchise such as "signing a petition."[67]

Ohio removes registrants from the rolls "if they fai[l] to respond" and "continu[e] to be inactive for an additional period of four consecutive years, including two federal elections."[68] Challenging Ohio's voter roll purging process, A. Philip Randolph Institute, and a voter whose name had been stricken from the rolls, alleged that Ohio purged the rolls of eligible voters "who [had] not actually moved,"[69] and the Failure-to-Vote Clause was violated because the "failure to vote for two years triggers the sending of a return card, and if the card is not returned, failure to vote for four more years results in removal."[70] This meant that eligible voters were removed solely for the failure to vote.

The Supplemental Process is based on a single event of non-voting for two years which triggers the purging of registered voters: the prepaid return card provides "notice" that the voter will be removed from the rolls if the card is not returned with verifiable address information; if the card is unreturned and the person does not vote in any election for four years, then it is *presumed* that the voter moved and the person's name is removed. The failure to vote triggers the notice and removal.[71]

---

[61]   *Husted v. A. Philip Randolph Institute*, 138 S. Ct. 1833, 1838 (2018).
[62]   *Ibid.* at 1838 (*quoting* § 20507 (a)(4)).
[63]   *Ibid.* (*quoting* § 20507 (d)(1)).
[64]   *Ibid.* at 1840 (*quoting* § 20507 (b)(1)).
[65]   *Ibid.* (quoting § 20507 (b)(2)).
[66]   *Ibid.*
[67]   *Ibid.* at 1840–41.
[68]   *Ibid.* at 1841.
[69]   *Ibid.* at 1841.
[70]   *Ibid.*
[71]   *Ibid.* at 1853–54 (Breyer, J., dissenting).

Writing for a 5–4 majority, Justice Alito concludes that Ohio's program is constitutional because non-voting is only a factor for removal along with an unreturned notice card.[72] Yet Justice Alito's opinion never references *why* the prepaid notice card was sent – failure to vote for two years – and why the voter's name was removed (failure to vote for four years). Interpreting the NVRA, Justice Alito holds that removing a voter from the rolls was not based on a single factor of non-voting, but on non-voting and failure to respond to a notice of removal from the voting rolls.[73] While formalistically and textually correct,[74] the impact of this ruling on minority voters is singularly devastating, especially considering *Shelby County*. It is as if voting is a procedural right, which can be discarded or preserved based on the arbitrary literalism of the NVRA and how it is applied, not a fundamental right. While *Husted* reads like a neutral interpretation of the statute, its language, and the purportedly neutral process underlying it, is an example of the Roberts Court's post-racial proceduralism – an ostensibly neutral procedural law, crafted to prevent voter fraud where none demonstrably exists, is transformed into an instrument of oppression.

Husted advances the historical myth of democratic access to all voters without any reference to context; it ignores intentional voter suppression and instead focuses on newly imagined fraud, so voter discrimination is not referenced because it does not exist to the Court; and removal of voters from the rolls is rationalized by a hyper-technical procedural framework. Within the Court's post-racial constitutionalism, Justice Alito offers two narrative approaches: one, discussed in Chapter 6, is to deploy stock racial stereotypes to highlight the divisiveness of racial politics (*Ricci*); the other is to advance a post-racial narrative rooted in formalism that ignores systemic racism and its underlying effects on minority voting (*Husted*). Both post-racial narratives are grounded in the protection of white innocence[75] – a strain of white resentment that dismisses claims of systemic racism as unsubstantiated attacks on a presumptively neutral and equal society.[76]

Justice Alito accepts, as a defining principle, the inherent fairness of the American polity and his statutory interpretation of the NVRA reflects this post-racial process bias – "States can use whatever plan they think best."[77] Concluding that Ohio fully complied with federal law because it "simply treats the failure to return a notice and the failure to vote as evidence that a registrant has moved, not as a [sole] ground for

---

[72] *Ibid.* at 1842 (emphasis in original) (the Failure-to-Vote Clause, originally and as amended by HAVA, "simply forbids the use of nonvoting as *the sole criterion* for removing a registrant, and Ohio does not use it that way" – removal is only after a registrant has "failed to vote *and* [has] failed to respond to a notice").

[73] *Ibid.* at 1843, 1843–46.

[74] Anthony J. Gaughan, *Notice, Due Process, and Voter Purges*, 67 CLEVE. ST. L. REV. 485, 502 (2019).

[75] Ian Millhiser, *Justice Alito's Jurisprudence of White Racial Innocence*, VOX, August 13, 2020, www.vox.com/2020/4/23/21228636/alito-racism-ramos-louisiana-unanimous-jury.

[76] *Husted*, 138 S. Ct. at 1848 (dismissing as "misconceived" the dissent's "accusation" that the majority ignores the history of voter suppression – the issue is the statutory text and the absence of discriminatory intent).

[77] *Ibid.* at 1847.

removal,"[78] the Court holds that there is no violation of the Failure-to-Vote Clause. But this conclusion is belied by the fact that the only reason that a registrant receives a notice is because of a failure to vote – the fundamental right to vote serves as the trigger for its removal.[79]

Justice Alito states that, in the absence of discriminatory intent by Ohio, this simple notice provision "warns recipients that unless they take the simple and easy step of mailing back the preaddressed postage prepaid card … their names may be removed from the voting rolls if they do not vote during the next four years."[80] This boils down to if the statute says it's non-discriminatory, it's non-discriminatory. The way to stop discriminating on the basis of race is to stop discriminating on the basis of race. This jurisprudential formalism underscores the Roberts Court's inherent cynicism against the very minorities it is obligated to protect from a process rigged against them.[81] All of this occurs under the cover of the voting fraud illusion, yet the "threat of widespread, relevant voter fraud remains a fantasy."[82]

Essentially, the majority and dissenters part company on two pivotal contextual and statutory issues – the continuing significance and effect of systemic racism on minority voting rights and whether non-voting is a single causal event triggering the NVRA's Failure-to-Vote Clause. To the majority, non-voting equates to change of residence,[83] while the dissenters point out that there must be more than this skewed presumption of ineligibility through non-voting buttressed by illusory fraud prevention. Whenever the Court must resolve the conflict between discriminatory intent and disparate impact, it does so by emphasizing the absence of intent and engrafting an implicit intent requirement onto disparate impact. The Court's equal protection, Title VII, and voting rights decisions follow this pattern discussed in the previous chapters.

JUSTICE BREYER'S *HUSTED* DISSENT: THE UNREASONABLENESS OF PURGING ELIGIBLE VOTERS

Justice Breyer offers a comprehensive textual critique of the formalism in Justice Alito's decision,[84] concluding that the supplemental process removed voters "from

---

[78] *Ibid.* at 1846.

[79] Myrna Pérez, Brennan Center for Justice at New York University School of Law, Voter Purges 27 (2008) ("States should ensure that registrants are sent address confirmation notices only in response to an indication that the registrant has moved – not when a registrant has not voted for some time").

[80] *Husted*, 138 S. Ct. at 1848.

[81] Betrall L. Ross II, *Democracy and Renewed District: Equal Protection and the Evolving Judicial Concept of Politics*, 101 Cal. L. Rev. 1565, 1570 (2013) (concluding that the jurisprudence of the Rehnquist and Roberts Courts is suspicious of discrete and insular minorities rather than protective of them).

[82] Lisa Marshall Manheim and Elizabeth G. Porter, *The Elephant in the Room: Intentional Voter Suppression*, 2018 Sup. Ct. Rev. 213, 233.

[83] *Ibid.* at 222.

[84] Justice Breyer does not adopt a structuralist approach to the holding in *Husted*, his dissent focuses on statutory interpretation so there is a deferential posture in his analysis much like his concurrence

the federal voter roll by reason of the person's failure to vote,"[85] thus violating the NVRA because the failure to vote was the sole basis for initiating a registered voter's removal from the rolls. Noting that only a small number of registrants actually move, and many fail to vote, Justice Breyer pointedly notes that *"there were more than 1,000,000 notices ... to which Ohio received back no return card at all."*[86]

There is no other reason than their failure to vote that could be the reason for their removal from the voting rolls.[87] Potentially, 1 million voters are the casualties of Justice Alito's post-racial textualism – there is no mention of them in his opinion. And this staggering number of purged voters is meaningless to the Court because the system is functioning the way it should be.[88] And the history of voter suppression from the first Reconstruction to the present day illustrates the adaptability of subordinating practices by the states.[89]

Both Justices Breyer and Sotomayor point to how voting purges are antidemocratic, are disruptive of our polity, and diminish voting as a fundamental constitutional right. All of this is missing in Justice Alito's opinion which reads like a hyper-technical procedural primer on voter eligibility. Perhaps the most glaring flaw in Justice Alito's opinion is that it places the literal meaning of the statute over the practical effect of how it operates on the ground – it presumes regularity, consistency, and uniformity which are not readily identifiable in the supplemental process. There have been significant errors in the Ohio purging process since the *Husted* decision.[90] Justice Sotomayor's dissent offers a compelling account of structural inequality in voting: "Concerted state efforts to prevent minorities from voting and to undermine the efficacy of their votes are an unfortunate feature of our country's history."[91]

---

in *Schuette*, 572 U.S. 291, 332–37 (Breyer, J., concurring), discussed in Chapter 4. This explains the distinct analytical approaches adopted by Justices Breyer and Sotomayor in dissent. Justice Breyer's focus is on the textual reasonableness of Ohio's program.

[85]　*Husted*, 138 S. Ct. 1850 (Breyer, J., dissenting).

[86]　*Ibid.* at 1856 (emphasis in original).

[87]　*Ibid.* at 1856–59, 1859 ("... our precedent strongly suggests that, given the importance of voting in a democracy, a State's effort (because of failure to vote) to remove from a federal election roll those it considers otherwise qualified is unreasonable").

[88]　Manheim and Porter, *supra* n. 82, at 219–25 (discussing how the Court advances the rollback of fundamental voting rights).

[89]　Carol Anderson, One Person, No Vote: How Voter Suppression Is Destroying Our Democracy (2018).

[90]　*Ohio Nearly Purged 10,000 Voters Who Ended Up Casting 2020 Ballots*, The Guardian, January 27, 2021, www.theguardian.com/us-news/2021/jan/27/us-voting-rights-voter-registration-ohio-purge (stating that voting inactivity is a poor measure for identifying ineligible voters and pointing out that Ohio has a flawed system that on at least two occasions has "nearly purged scores of eligible voters from its rolls").

[91]　*Husted*, 138 S. Ct. at 1863 (Sotomayor, J., dissenting).

JUSTICE SOTOMAYOR'S *HUSTED* DISSENT: STRUCTURAL INEQUALITY AND VOTING AS A FUNDAMENTAL RIGHT

By contrast to Justice Breyer's textual reasonableness analysis, Justice Sotomayor offers a structural critique which unpacks the neutrality and formalism that is at the core of *Husted* – her analysis obliterates Rhetorical Neutrality by disrupting the historical, definitional, and rhetorical myths. Justice Sotomayor centers history and the present-day effects of past discrimination to interpret not simply the meaning of the NVRA but how it functions to displace eligible voters.

Rejecting the majority's formalistic post-racial history, which only references race to say that any mention of the history of voter suppression is "misconceived," Justice Sotomayor emphasizes the permanence and adaptability of systemic racism with states enacting restrictive laws and discriminatory artifices – like poll taxes, literacy tests, residency requirements and selective purges and recurring registration requirements[92] – designed to depress, dilute, and cast aside the votes of minorities.

What is striking about Justice Alito's opinion is that it does not reference voting as a fundamental right, nor does it even acknowledge the impact of voting purges on the historically oppressed. This is of no moment to the Court because the only relevant issue is the language of the NVRA. And there is a good faith presumption that state power is exercised in the best interest of the voting registration system and that all citizens' voting rights are protected. But Justice Sotomayor pinpoints how the supplemental process undermines voting rights and erects barriers to voting even if a voter clears the hurdle of "reregistering":

> Ohio's Supplemental Process reflects precisely the type of purge system that the NVRA was designed to prevent. Under the Supplemental Process, Ohio will purge a registrant from the rolls after six years of not voting, *e.g.*, sitting out one Presidential election and two midterm elections, and after failing to send back one piece of mail, even though there is no reasonable basis to believe the individual moved. … This purge program burdens the rights of eligible voters. At best, purged voters are forced to "needlessly reregister" if they decide to vote in a subsequent election; at worst, they are prevented from voting at all because they never receive information about when and where elections are taking place.[93]

There are significant numbers of voters who are ineligible at home – they are where they should be but presumed to be where they are not for failure to return "one piece of mail." This explains the disproportionate impact in the facts of *Husted*: "African-American-majority neighborhoods in downtown Cincinnati had 10 percent of their votes removed due to inactivity since 2012, as compared to 4 percent of voters in a suburban, majority-white neighborhood."[94]

92 *Ibid.* at 1863.
93 *Ibid.* at 1864.
94 *Ibid.*

This disparate impact is unexplainable on any other grounds except targeting discrete and insular minorities for exclusion.[95] Ostensibly, being purged from the voting rolls is a "minor" inconvenience of life (simply mail the card back and there is no barrier to voting) – Justice Alito enthusiastically embraces this rationale in *Brnovich* – but this and other substantive barriers to the franchise are exacerbated by the Court's obliviousness to structural inequality. The structural impact of voter purges – the possibility that hundreds of thousands, if not millions of eligible voters, will have their fundamental right to vote marked off the voting rolls – should mean that the state losses the presumption of good faith and must justify its sweeping conduct with a legitimate reason.[96] And this reason must be more than the formalisms proffered by Justice Alito.

The Roberts Court's post-racial voting jurisprudence makes clear that states should be free from federal scrutiny to determine who gets to vote, how votes are valued, and what access means in a representative democracy. The history of voter suppression cannot be ignored, as Justice Sotomayor concludes in dissent: "Communities that are disproportionately affected by unnecessarily harsh registration laws should not tolerate efforts to marginalize their influence in the political process, nor should allies who recognize blatant unfairness stand idly by."[97]

Justice Sotomayor's clarion call to progressive action is especially compelling given the ever-expanding power of the state to determine the political destiny of discrete and insular minorities like Blacks, other people of color, and the poor. The post-racial constitutionalism of the Roberts Court is inherently political; since race is irrelevant, states should determine how political power is distributed and who gets to retain power. As all the preceding chapters illustrate, and especially this chapter on voting rights, this determination has already been made – whites will retain power under the guise of a neutral polity (process) open to all without reference to race.

RUCHO v. COMMON CAUSE: POLITICAL GERRYMANDERING AND THE POLITICAL PROCESS MYTH

In *Rucho v. Common Cause*, the U.S. Supreme Court held in a 5–4 decision authored by Chief Justice Roberts, that partisan gerrymandering was a political question beyond the decision-making authority of the Court. Chief Justice Roberts'

---

[95] *See* Terry Smith, *Autonomy versus Equality: Voting Rights Rediscovered*, 57 ALA. L. REV. 261, 264 (2005) ("… courts have treated race as a proxy for partisanship when doing so has facilitated curtailing minority political autonomy … the Supreme Court engages in racially correlative doctrinal shifts in defining the nature of the right to vote … finding voting to be a fundamental right when the interests of whites are at stake, but insisting on a showing of discriminatory intent when the plaintiffs are people of color"); *see generally* Darren Lenard Hutchinson, *"Unexplainable on Grounds Other Than Race": The Inversion of Privilege and Subordination in Equal Protection Jurisprudence*, 2003 U. ILL. L. REV. 615. This explains Justice Alito's retort to Justice Sotomayor when she references the history of voter suppression. *See Husted*, 138 S. Ct. at 1848.

[96] Manheim and Porter, *supra* n. 82, at 239–49.

[97] *Husted*, 138 S. Ct. at 1865 (Sotomayor, J., dissenting).

opinion is premised on the fact that there is no discernable standard that the Court could use to evaluate the fairness of a partisan gerrymander, and if courts were to intervene in such matters, they would be impermissibly reallocating power between political parties. The Court readily ignores the present-day effects of structural inequality. The Court again affirms process values that perpetuate structural inequality by insulating partisan gerrymandering from judicial review. Concluding that "fairness" in apportioning political power is not a "judicially manageable standard," the Court stated that "partisan gerrymandering claims present political questions beyond the reach of the federal courts."[98]

With *Husted* and *Rucho*, the Court left it to the states to define the protections that will be appropriate under the VRA. In effect, the Court has gutted the VRA and left it to the states to shape applicable remedies for vote suppression. This neutral approach, based on the Court's equal sovereignty federalism, will ultimately lead to the dilution and further suppression of the votes of historically disempowered groups.

But this neutrality is belied by a pronounced interpretive and ideological shift. During his confirmation hearing, then Judge Roberts extoled the virtues of neutral decision-making with his invocation of calling "balls" and "strikes," and endorsed the Court's institutional obligation to clear blockages in the political process[99] by applying "more exacting scrutiny" when "those political processes ordinarily to be relied upon to protect minorities" malfunction,[100] resulting in exclusion and intractable obstacles to political success through organizing around common political interests. Yet *Rucho* represents a completely opposite analytical posture and outcome.[101]

In *Rucho*, Chief Justice Roberts offers a wide-ranging account of politics, political power, and the rationale for political gerrymandering without acknowledging the significance of race. Of course, this is yet another example of the Roberts Court's post-racial constitutionalism but what is particularly jarring here is that the disproportionate impact on discrete and insular minorities – Blacks, people of color, and the poor – is ignored based on the Court's institutional reluctance to intervene in political conflicts.[102] This expansion of the Court's New States' Rights Federalism – a means to expand state power based on equal sovereignty – serves to insulate the

---

[98] *Rucho v. Common Cause*, 139 S. Ct. 2484, 2506–07 (2019).
[99] Joan Biskupic, The Chief: The Life and Turbulent Times of Chief Justice John Roberts 163 (2019).
[100] *United States v. Carolene Products*, 304 U.S. 144, 152 n. 4 (1938).
[101] Nicholas O. Stephanopoulos, *The Anti-Carolene Court*, 2019 Sup. Ct. Rev. 111, 180–81 (discussing how the Roberts Court consistently undermines *Carolene Products* footnote 4 by failing to protect discrete and insular minorities: "By holding its fire when *Carolene* says to shoot [*Rucho*], and by stepping in when *Carolene* advises stepping back [*Shelby County*], the Court improves Republican electoral prospects at every turn").
[102] Lynn Adelman, *The Roberts Court's Assault on Democracy*, 14 Harv. L. & Pol'y Rev. 131, 140–58 (2019).

exercise of the raw political power of exclusion by the state from judicial review.[103] *Shelby County* leads directly to this result.

As discussed in Chapter 4, the Court is actively engaged in promoting post-racial process discourse. The concern is not the protection of fundamental rights, like voting, but the protection and expansion of state power and the elimination of any consideration of race in decision-making. This is a vivid illustration of the Roberts Court's post-racialism: "The Roberts Court ... is the anti-*Carolene* Court. It has a near perfect record of doing nothing when it should have done something, doing all too much when it should have sat still, and promoting the same party's interests through it maneuvers."[104] *Rucho* is a "doing nothing" opinion.

The result in *Rucho* is all but assured because Chief Justice Roberts frames the issue as an unconstitutional intrusion on the power of the states to resolve their own political disputes. The congressional redistricting plans enacted by the Republican-controlled North Carolina Assembly and the Democratic-controlled Maryland legislature (*Lamone v. Benisek*) were challenged as unconstitutional partisan gerrymanders.[105] Vacating the lower courts in this consolidated appeal, the Court held that partisan gerrymandering claims are non-justiciable.[106] Purportedly exercising judicial restraint, respect for separation of powers, and wariness of the counter-majoritarian difficulty,[107] the Court expands state power even more radically than it did in *Shelby County*. Partisan gerrymandering claims are not claims of legal right, but merely "political questions that must find their resolution elsewhere."[108]

Chief Justice Roberts posits the issue expansively from the beginning of the decision – the issue is not whether voters have lost their voice in a representative democracy through redistricting that targets voters because of their party affiliation (with its predictable impacts on people of color and the poor), but "determining when *political* gerrymandering has gone too far."[109] There is no clear attempt to distinguish "partisan" (impermissible) from "political" (permissible) gerrymandering, which is ironic given the Court's emphasis on the lack of judicially manageable standards throughout the decision.[110] But what is the essence of this distinction? It complements the Court's conception of equal sovereignty and attaches a new state right to engage in partisan gerrymandering.[111] The only limit is what is permissible in politics, and the Court concludes that there is no way to measure that.

[103] Cynthia Boyer, *The Supreme Court and Politics in the Trump Era*, 12 Elon L. Rev. 215, 230 (2020).
[104] Stephanopoulos, *supra* n. 101, at 182.
[105] *Rucho*, 138 S. Ct. at 2491–93.
[106] *Ibid.* at 2506–08.
[107] *Ibid.* at 2507.
[108] *Ibid.* at 2494.
[109] *Ibid.* at 2497 (emphasis added).
[110] *Ibid.* at 2497–500.
[111] Richard L. Hasen, *The Supreme Court's Pro-Partisanship Turn*, 109 Geo. L. J. Online 50, 61 (2020).

Rhetorically, Chief Justice Roberts performs a doctrinal "sleight of hand" when he inverts constitutional political gerrymandering – in cases where the state defended itself by asserting that its redistricting was for *political* reasons rather than racial ones – and constitutional partisan gerrymandering.[112] This redefines discrimination and advances the political process myth – extreme partisanship is permissible because both political parties compete in an electoral process with political consequences (there are winners and losers).[113] This also completely disaggregates race from the analysis because the issue is the limits and scope of the political gerrymander (with its presumption of legislative good faith and legitimacy), not whether the state has evidence that race did not predominate in its drawing of voting districts.[114]

The Roberts Court's post-racialism means that it will do nothing when discrete and insular minorities are marginalized in the political process, and this racial indifference to the plight of historically subjugated minorities is not neutral. It exhibits the Court's complicity "in efforts by Republican state actors to allow white voters to hold onto power even if the party's political fortunes decline."[115] It is no coincidence that the onslaught of voter suppression legislation came after record numbers of African Americans and other under-represented groups came out to vote.[116] The Roberts Court has even embraced the Big Lie circulating ubiquitously in the public sphere.[117]

Just as he did in *Shelby County*, Chief Justice Roberts expands state power but here he does so not by diminishing Congress' enforcement powers, but by centering the role of the Court in the federal system.[118] *Rucho* is advanced by several propositions: (i) the Court has no institutional expertise in determining political questions – the legitimacy of judicial review rests in determining case and controversies under Article III of the Constitution;[119] (ii) there is a lack of judicially manageable standards to determine political disputes;[120] (iii) the facts here are distinguishable because this case is a pure political case so the one person, one vote and racial gerrymandering standards in voting cases are inapposite;[121] (iv) there is no right to proportional representation (and

---

[112] *Ibid.*

[113] *Rucho*, 139 S. Ct. at 2502–03 (stating that "securing partisan advantage" can predominate in districting decisions); *see generally* Hasen, *supra* n. 111, at 60 n. 58.

[114] Hasen, *supra* n. 111, at 71–73.

[115] *Ibid.* at 78.

[116] Lisa Hagen and Susan Milligan, *How Voting Laws Suppress the "New South,"* U.S. NEWS & WORLD REPORT, April 9, 2021, www.usnews.com/news/the-report/articles/2021-04-09/how-voting-laws-suppress-the-new-south.

[117] *Brnovich v. Democratic National Committee*, 141 S. Ct. 2321, 2340 (2021) (without identifying any in the case noting that fraud is a valid concern).

[118] *Rucho*, 139 S. Ct. at 2494; *see* Boyer, *supra* n. 103, at 230 (discussing the Court's desire to reduce federal constraints on the states by rarely intervening in state matters).

[119] *Rucho*, 139 S. Ct. at 2494.

[120] *Ibid.* at 2496.

[121] *Ibid.* at 2496–98.

no right to win because elections have consequences), and it is impossible to define what "fairness" is in electoral politics;[122] and (v) judicial power cannot be expanded in such a manner as to undermine the legitimacy of the federal system.[123]

Concluding that it is impossible to determine whether there was a predominant partisan intent in the redistricting plan because securing partisan advantage is an inevitable feature of electoral politics, Chief Justice Roberts rejected any doctrinal connection between the racial gerrymandering cases.[124] Next, as to vote dilution, in the context of a partisan gerrymandering case, he noted that such a determination would require "[j]udges not only [to] have to pick the winner – they have to beat the point spread"[125] to decide whether a party has lost its relevance to its constituents. Voters have many preferences as to policies and candidates, and courts lack the institutional expertise to determine "how a particular districting map will perform."[126] Indeed, the Court should not be in the business of allocating power between political rivals.[127]

In the area of voting rights, the Court has decided to do nothing – the states will determine the plight of African Americans and every discrete and insular minority in the polity – federal interventionalism has no place in a post-racial world. Each decision discussed thus far leads to this conclusion: *Shelby County* discards the statutory apparatus that provided essential protections against voter discrimination in jurisdictions with past histories and present-day inclinations to continue the subordination of oppressed communities; *Husted* affirms state power to strip eligible citizens from the voting rolls and the added substantial burden of regaining eligibility; and *Rucho* unleashes an expanse of state power with virtually no limit in determining who wins, for how long, and at what cost to those who inevitably lose for decades to come. All these decisions appear neutral – *Shelby County* focuses on the need for current discrimination; *Husted* on the precise statutory language of the NVRA and its effect; and *Rucho* on justiciability and standing – but they are not. They are inherently outcome-determinative statements of state power.

Rucho is all about state power and whatever voting strength is leftover to citizens who may not be able to select their own representatives because the system does that for them. What is extraordinary is that the Roberts Court recognizes this – "Excessive partisanship in districting leads to results that reasonably seem unjust. But the fact that such gerrymandering is 'incompatible with democratic principles' …does not mean that the solution lies with the federal judiciary" – and does not care. Where does the solution lie? Certainly not with a flawed polity skewed toward the preservation of minority power.

---

[122] *Ibid.* at 2499–502.
[123] *Ibid.* at 2506–07.
[124] *Ibid.* at 2502–03.
[125] *Ibid.* at 2503.
[126] *Ibid.*
[127] *Ibid.* at 2508.

JUSTICE KAGAN'S *RUCHO* DISSENT: VOTE DILUTION

Unpacking the intricacies of structural inequality in voting, specifically how politicians "entrench themselves in office against voter's preferences,"[128] Justice Kagan's dissent offers a wide-ranging, compelling, and eloquent argument as to how partisan gerrymandering is anti-democratic and the Court undermines its legitimacy by failing to act.[129] There is a fundamental right here that must be preserved and vindicated.

Concluding that partisan gerrymandering is a form of vote dilution and a violation of the First Amendment as well because a citizen's vote is devalued and the content of what the vote expressed is diminished because political views are selectively disfavored,[130] Justice Kagan rejects the literal concept of proportional fairness employed by the majority. It is not whether federal courts should determine "fairness" between rival parties, but rather whether "the extreme manipulation of district lines for partisan gain"[131] could be eliminated as an anti-democratic practice. Thus, Chief Justice Roberts' extended foray into the questions underlying a fairness analysis is revealed as a contrivance – there are judicially manageable standards to resolve this unconstitutional practice of targeted vote dilution and the Court should have applied them.[132]

Justice Kagan's dissent disrupts the majority opinion's overly deferential posture toward state power and analyzes how partisan gerrymandering, insulated from judicial review, "harms our political system" and "create[s] the polarized political system so many Americans loathe."[133] And the Court clearly recognizes this, but hides behind its reluctance to allocate power without any discernible judicial standards. It is truly ironic that the Court references racial gerrymandering cases as easier to decide because they have standards, but in a partisan gerrymander case – where power shifts but the impact on people of color is always the same – the Court has no answer.

The Court's voting rights jurisprudence reveals something eerily distinct about the Roberts Court's post-racial constitutionalism – the fundamental rights of minorities will be sacrificed to maintain white supremacy in every area of the law, as we have seen in each of the chapters in this book, but the most discordant component of the Court's jurisprudence is its active engagement in dismantling the edifice of anti-discrimination law and voting rights.

BRNOVICH v. DEMOCRATIC NATIONAL COMMITTEE: POST-RACIAL DISPARATE IMPACT

When the Roberts Court gutted the VRA in *Shelby County*, scholars, activists, and jurists took uneasy solace in the fact that § 2 was left intact, believing that there was a

---

[128] *Ibid.* at 2509 (Kagan, J., dissenting).
[129] *Ibid.* at 2515.
[130] *Ibid.* at 2513–15.
[131] *Ibid.* at 2523.
[132] *Ibid.* at 2519–23.
[133] *Ibid.* at 2525.

narrow sliver of statutory hope that voting rights could still be protected in a limited manner[134] – this transitory hope was obliterated in *Brnovich v. Democratic National Committee.* Chief Justice Roberts and Justice Alito have succeeded in dismantling the VRA. There is nothing left except the hollow acknowledgement that voting discrimination still exists, but it is up to the states to define it and determine how it should be eliminated.[135] "Supreme Court decisions are influenced by the political environment,"[136] and by the public discourse underpinning it. The Roberts Court has taken the next rhetorical and doctrinal step of adopting Republican rhetoric to preserve white power.[137]

Affirming Arizona's out-of-precinct rule and ballot collection regulations, the Court, in an opinion by Justice Alito and marking the consolidation of a new 6–3 majority, held that neither law violated § 2 of the VRA. In yet another expansive reading of state power, the Court essentially gave states unlimited power to exercise how the franchise is to be exercised. Citizens can vote, but how, when, where, and what votes are counted will be determined by the state. This is vote dilution disguised as state electoral autonomy.

The Court's non-interventionist, states' rights jurisprudence means that voting rights discrimination may exist, but addressing it must never burden the post-racial prerogatives of the state. This is the New States' Rights Federalism – state power is expanded so that the scope of fundamental rights, like voting, is determined by the states. This is in vivid contrast to the Rehnquist Court's New Federalism which set the boundaries between state and federal power by advancing state autonomy in the federal system;[138] the Robert Court's jurisprudential agenda is to expand state power in the service of erasing race-conscious decision-making.

Justice Alito's opinion starts with how "Arizona law generally makes it very easy to vote."[139] Readers of the opinion know that minority voting rights are in peril here, given Justice Altio's casual disregard of how systems impact politically powerless minorities (*Husted*) and his absolute disdain for any discussion of racial discrimination.[140] So, just as he did in *Husted*, Justice Alito offers a textual reading of § 2 rooted in

---

[134] *Brnovich v. Democratic National Committee*, 141 S. Ct. 2330, 2356 (2021) (Kagan, J., dissenting).

[135] *Ibid.* At 2343, 2343–44 (critiquing the dissent's "attempt to bring about a wholesale transfer of the authority to set voting rules from the States to the federal courts").

[136] DERRICK BELL, AND WE ARE NOT SAVED: THE ELUSIVE QUEST FOR RACIAL JUSTICE 92 (1987).

[137] *Ibid.* (noting that the hard-fought campaign for voting rights and the passage of the VRA of 1965 "did little more than put whites to the task of designing newer, more subtle, but no less effective means of barring blacks from the polls or ensuring that their votes, once cast, would not alter outcomes favoring the maintenance of white power in the political structure").

[138] And even this boundary setting has an impact on rights that can undermine them. *See, for example,* Mitchell F. Crusto, *The Supreme Court's "New" Federalism: An Anti-Rights Agenda?* 16 GA. ST. U. L. REV. 517, 562 (2000) (noting how the Court invalidates any plan that seeks to address unequal voting representation through race-conscious remedial measures in districting). The situation is even worse under the Roberts Court – it does not simply invalidate districting plans, it severely circumscribes the Reconstruction Amendments and nullifies anti-discrimination statutes like the VRA.

[139] *Brnovich*, 141 S. Ct. at 2330.

[140] *Ibid.* at 2342 (noting how the dissent spends twenty pages discussing historical background "that all Americans should remember").

literal formalism that ultimately leads to the conclusion that if a voter can functionally "vote," then any obstacles that may be placed in her way are merely incidental (or the "usual burdens of voting")[141] in the absence of intentional discrimination by the state.

Enacted pursuant to the Fifteenth Amendment, § 2 "addressed the denial or abridgment of the right to vote in any part of the country,"[142] by prohibiting voting qualifications, prerequisites, standards, or procedures imposed by the state "which [result] in a denial or abridgement of the right … to vote on account of race or color."[143] In order to prove a § 2 violation, "consideration of the 'totality of the circumstances' … demands proof that the political processes leading to nomination or election in the State or political subdivision are not *equally open* to participation" by members of a protected class "*in that its members have less opportunity* than other members of the electorate to participate in the political process and to elect representatives of their choice."[144] Section 2 focuses on the structural aspects of voting discrimination in that "a certain electoral law, practice, or structure interacts with social and historical conditions to cause an inequality of opportunities" of "minority and non-minority voters to elect their preferred representatives."[145] Section 2 is broad in its focus on structural impact, not discriminatory intent.

In Arizona, on election day, in-person voters must cast their vote in their own precinct or their vote will not be counted (out-of-precinct policy); and early mail-in ballots cannot be collected by anyone other than "a postal worker, an elections official, or a voter's caregiver, family member, or household member."[146] Concluding that an *en banc* panel of the Ninth Circuit "misunderstood and misapplied §2"[147] by relying upon these rules' small disparate impacts on minority groups and past discrimination, the Court reversed and held that Arizona's out-of-precinct policy and HB 2023 were constitutional because there was no racially discriminatory intent in these voting regulations.[148]

Justice Alito's post-racial history of the VRA simply catalogues previous voter suppression methods by the states, briefly mentions sections 4 and 5, which were eviscerated in *Shelby County*, and then turns to a discussion of the statutory language of § 2 and what he skeptically references as "a steady stream of §2 vote-dilution cases." He frames the issue as whether "§2 applies to generally applicable time, place, or manner voting rules."[149] Disparate impact here becomes a non-factor[150] – if there is

---

[141] *Ibid.* at 2344.
[142] *Ibid.* at 2331.
[143] *Ibid.* at 2337 (emphasis in original).
[144] *Ibid.* at 2332 (emphasis in original).
[145] *Ibid.* at 2333 (*citing Thornburg v. Gingles*, 478 U.S. 30, 47 (1986) construing § 2 as amended).
[146] *Ibid.* at 2334 (*quoting* House Bill 2023 ("HB 2023")).
[147] *Ibid.* at 2330, 2346–50.
[148] *Ibid.* at 2350.
[149] *Ibid.* at 2333.
[150] *Ibid.* at 2361 (Kagan, J., dissenting) (noting that the majority "only grudgingly accepts – and then apparently forgets – that [Section 2] applies to facially neutral laws with discriminatory consequences").

disparate impact, it is negligible because every voter has access to a political process that is equally open to all (there are slight administrative burdens to be borne by all). Of course, this depends on equality of access, and Justice Alito defines this in a way that dramatically expands the scope of state power while ignoring the fundamental right to vote. Whether voting is "equally open" depends on five newly minted factors[151] that privilege state power over voting rights. All the factors serve to diminish the significance of disparate impact, trivialize structural inequality in the political process, and expand the power of the state.

JUSTICE ALITO'S POST-RACIAL VRA: THE FIVE-FACTOR ARTIFICE

The boldness of Justice Alito's transformation of § 2's totality of circumstances test – from the local factors within a district that foreclosed an equally open process – to "*any* circumstance that has a logical bearing on whether voting is 'equally open' and affords equal 'opportunity'"[152] is indicative of post-racial determinism. The result here is predetermined because the impact on minorities is barely referenced in the analysis, and a purportedly neutral process with "incidental" burdens on voting is affirmed[153] to devastating effect. Justice Alito ignores the fact that Arizona is the epicenter of the Big Lie and repressive voting laws,[154] and instead focuses on the presumptive openness of a system with a generally applicable regulatory framework.

The first factor, "the size of the burden imposed by a challenged voting rule,"[155] is discussed routinely, as Justice Alito notes that "every voting rule imposes a burden of some sort"[156] – there are universal burdens that everyone experiences like time, travel, and compliance with rules, so an "equally open" voting system with an "equal opportunity" to vote "must tolerate the "usual burdens of voting" – "mere inconvenience"[157] is insufficient to violate § 2.

A defining feature of post-racialism is universalism,[158] which focuses on the general applicability of a rule or policy by displacing race – if everyone is subject to the same voting regulations, there is no disparate impact. But § 2 does not permit such ad-hoc qualitative assessments by the Court. Because the first factor does not contextualize the significance of race and the impact of numerous inconveniences and race-based abridgments of voting, it fails to note that entrenched systemic

---

[151] *Ibid.* at 2361 (Kagan, J., dissenting) ("The majority's opinion mostly inhabits a law-free zone").
[152] *Ibid.* at 2338 (Alito, J.).
[153] *Ibid.* at 2346, 2346–47 ("Even if plaintiffs had shown a disparate burden caused by HB 2023, the State's justifications would suffice to avoid § 2 liability").
[154] *Ibid.* at 2366–73 (Kagan, J., dissenting).
[155] *Ibid.* at 2338 (Alito, J.).
[156] *Ibid.*
[157] *Ibid.*
[158] Sumi Cho, *Post-Racialism*, 94 IOWA L. REV. 1589, 1601–02 (2009) (discussing the fallacy of universalism as whiteness is the governing principle so that Blacks and other people of color are displaced).

inconveniences can "deter minority votes."[159] By embracing such a skewed political process, Justice Kagan, in dissent, concludes that the Court chooses "equality-lite."[160]

This watered-down version of substantive equality explains the Court's narrow post-racial framing of whether, under Justice Alito's second factor, "a voting rule departs from what was standard practice when § 2 was amended in 1982."[161] It is interesting that the focus is on 1982, when in *Shelby County*, the Court insisted on current conditions of discrimination. By freezing time in 1982, Justice Alito can catalogue narrow and limited state voting rules from that period and then reaffirm the general nature of these practices as normal in 2021 – the practices are "facially neutral time, place and manner regulations that have a long pedigree or [are] in widespread use in the United States."[162] Of course, this cannot be the standard; there are many things that have a long pedigree and are widespread that systemically oppress and subjugate minority voters, and that is what §2 was enacted to eradicate – those neutral, subtle, and widespread systems that suppress the right to vote under the auspices of the democratic myth or mystical searches for fraud.[163] Employing a long string cite of in-person and limited-excuse absentee voting laws in various states,[164] Justice Alito's analysis completely misses the disparate impact of Arizona's voting practices on the ground. Section 2 "calls for an 'intensely local appraisal,' not a count-up-the States exercise."[165]

Third, "the size of any disparities in a rule's impact on members of different racial or ethnic groups" is a consideration in determining if the political process is equally open. This is essentially a restatement of the first factor but with a specific reference to disparate impact as a burden rather than the usual burdens of voting. Here, Justice Alito acknowledges disparate impact (just as the Court does with societal discrimination), only to dismiss it: "the mere fact there is some disparity in impact does not necessarily mean that a system is not equally open or that it does not give everyone an equal opportunity to vote. The size of any disparity matters."[166] What this really means is that there will be numerous "small" disparities that will not be constitutionally cognizable, but how small is too small when the fundamental right to vote is at risk? Justice Alito's arbitrary test offers no answer.

The Court's callous formalism is truly on display in Justice Alito's fourth factor – "the opportunities provided by a State's entire system of voting,"[167] which means if there are multiple ways to vote provided by the State, then any burden must be assessed in relation to the available options. This would seem to mean that a

---

[159] *Brnovich*, 141 S. Ct. 2362 (Kagan, J., dissenting).
[160] *Ibid.*
[161] *Ibid.* (Alito, J.).
[162] *Ibid.* at 2339.
[163] *Ibid.* at 2364–65 (Kagan, J., dissenting) ("Section 2 was meant to disrupt the status quo, not to preserve it – to eradicate then-current discriminatory practices, not to set them in amber").
[164] *Ibid.* at 2339 (Alito, J.).
[165] *Ibid.* at 2364 (Kagan, J., dissenting).
[166] *Ibid.* at 2339 (Alito, J.).
[167] *Ibid.*

permissible voting process could close off many opportunities so long as there were other "opportunities" (or maybe only one) to formally vote. Constitutionally, how many voting options should be available to voters? An electoral process is not equally open if minority citizens have less of an opportunity to participate in the process – the availability of opportunities will have a disparate impact on minority voters.[168]

Finally, the fifth factor is the embodiment of the Court's New States' Rights Federalism: "the strength of the state interests served by the challenged rule"[169] with the Court embracing the fraud trope and the Big Lie that has permeated public discourse on voting. Without identifying any fraud in Arizona, the Court simply concludes that the prevention of fraud is a "strong and entirely legitimate state interest."[170] As a feature of the Court's state empowerment federalism, the detection and prevent of "fraud" can be used to expand state power exponentially, maintain the status quo of white political domination, and perpetually suppress minority votes so that there is exclusion in violation of § 2.[171] "Throughout American history, election officials have asserted anti-fraud interests in using voter suppression laws."[172]

In yet another expansion of state power, Justice Alito concludes that the Title VII and the FHA's disparate impact provisions are inapplicable to §2 because employment, housing, and voting are distinct contexts; and, imposing "a strict 'necessity requirement' forcing states 'to demonstrate that their legitimate interests can be accomplished only by means of the voting regulations in question'"[173] would invalidate "many neutral voting regulations with long pedigrees …"[174] The presumption that neutral processes advance equality is a core normative principle of the Court's post-racial constitutionalism, but as demonstrated previously neutrality preserves structural inequality. Justice Alito's opinion does not even mention the disparate impact on voters in Arizona – the out-of-precinct policy "results in Hispanic and African American voters' ballots being thrown out at a statistically higher rate than those of whites" and the ballot-collection ban "makes voting meaningfully more difficult for Native American citizens than for others."[175]

The table below illustrates the Court' post-racial interpretation of the VRA, which is an extension of the Court's post-racial interpretations of the Fourteenth Amendment, Title VII, and the FHA (Table 8.1).[176]

---

[168] *Ibid.* at 2363 (Kagan, J., dissenting).

[169] *Ibid.* at 2339 (Alito, J.).

[170] *Ibid.* at 2340.

[171] Carl Hulse, *For Voting Protections, It May Be Democrats vs. The Roberts Court*, N.Y. Times, August 22, 2021, at 19.

[172] *Brnovich*, 141 S. Ct. at 2365 (Kagan, J., dissenting).

[173] *Ibid.* at 2341 (Alito, J.) (*citing* Stephanopoulos, *Disparate Impact, Unified Law*, 128 Yale L.J. 1566, 1617–19 (2019)).

[174] *Ibid.*

[175] *Brnovich*, 141 S. Ct. at 2366 (Kagan, J., dissenting). Arizona is the epicenter of the fraudits, and it discards ballots at an alarming rate: eleven times the rate of the second-place state in discarded votes in 2012. *Ibid.* at 2367.

[176] *See* Chapters 6 and 7.

TABLE 8.1 *Post-Racialism and the Voting Rights Act (VRA): Equal Sovereignty, the New States' Rights Federalism and Formalistic Equality*

Shelby County v. Holder (2013) (Roberts, C.J.)	Husted v. A. Philip Randolph Coalition (2018) (Alito, J.)	Rucho v. Common Cause (2019) (Roberts, C.J.)	Brnovich v. DNC (2021) (Alito, J.)
1. Equal sovereignty of the state means that federal intrusion disrupts federalism.	1. Formalistic textualism is the guiding principle in interpreting state regulation of voting procedures and processes.	1. Partisan gerrymandering claims are non-justiciable because there is no discernible test for determining fairness between political parties.	1. Construing § 2 of the VRA to determine if the political process is equally open and not an abridgment of the right to vote on the basis of race, the Court creates a five-part totality of the circumstances test to further expand state power.
2. "History did not end in 1965" – there must be current discrimination for current remedial legislation. Section 4 of the VRA is unconstitutional.[177]	2. The disproportionate impact of voter purges on minority voters is constitutionally irrelevant.	2. Eschewing the structural dimensions of race, vote dilution, and systemic political power, the Court reasons that the exercise of judicial power should be limited.	2. The out-of-precinct ballot rule and ballot-collection laws do not violate §2 because any burdens on voting are "unremarkable" and there is no discriminatory purpose to deny the right to vote.[182]
3. Black political progress and voting strength means that continuous amendment of the VRA is unnecessary.[178]	3. In the absence of discriminatory intent, "states can use whatever plan they think best" to ensure eligible voters are registered and accounted for.[180]	3. Discrete and insular minorities are left vulnerable and politically powerless by the Court's acquiescence to state power.[181]	3. Disparate impact is statutorily irrelevant because the state provides "multiple ways to vote."[183]
4. Congress breached federalism principles by imposing federal oversight of covered states without evidence of current discrimination.[179]	4. Systemic racism and voter suppression are ignored because post-racial proceduralism is the touchstone for expanding state power.	4. Insulating partisan gerrymandering claims from judicial review permits parties to entrench political power diluting the voice and interests of voters.	4. The prevention of "fraud" is a legitimate state interest.[184]

[177] 570 U.S. at 552, 552–54.
[178] *Ibid.* at 553.
[179] *Ibid.* at 556–57.
[180] 138 S. Ct. at 842–46.
[181] 139 S. Ct. at 2513–16 (Kagan, J., dissenting).
[182] 141 S. Ct. at 2344.
[183] *Ibid.* at 2339, 2345–47.
[184] *Ibid.* at 2343.

The most disconcerting aspect of the Roberts Court's post-racial voting rights jurisprudence is its nearly limitless expansion of state power[185] over the electoral process – the New States' Rights Federalism – where Congress' enforcement power under the Reconstruction Amendments is eviscerated and repressive state action is insulated. Disparate impact, which was previously statutorily cognizable, is of no moment – the formal right to cast a ballot is all that is protected notwithstanding the myriad of state-sponsored barriers[186] erected to block, thwart, or diminish this bedrock right of citizenship.

And the Court has gone even further recently intervening and casting aside federal injunctive relief for Black voters in Alabama. Granting a stay for injunctive relief and ostensibly not ruling on the merits, the Court, 5–4, endorsed Alabama's redistricting plan which concentrated (or packed) Black Alabamians in one district, thereby diluting their voting strength and electoral power. Invoking the *Purcell* principle[187] to conclude that any injunctive relief would be too disruptive only seven weeks away from the election, the Court stayed the district court's injunction which found that "Alabama's congressional districting plan likely violates [Section 2 of the VRA] federal voting rights law" (as an unconstitutional racial gerrymander resulting in vote dilution).[188] In dissent, Justice Kagan captures the essence of the Roberts Court's post-racial distortion of democratic principles: "Today's decision is one more in a disconcertingly long line of cases in which this Court uses its shadow docket to signal or make changes in the law, without anything approaching full briefing and argument."[189]

Evoking neutral process rationales, like the *Purcell* principle, The Roberts Court bestows legitimacy on a process rigged against Black Alabamians.[190] It is time for a New Reconstruction.

---

[185] *Schuette v. Coalition to Defend Affirmative Action*, 572 U.S. 291, 327 (2014) (Scalia, concurring) (referencing the "near limitless sovereignty of each state to design its governing structure as it sees fit").

[186] *Brnovich*, 141 S. Ct. at 2355–56; 2366–72 (Kagan, J., dissenting); Atiba R. Ellis, *The Dignity Problem of American Election Integrity*, 62 HOWARD L. J. 739, 739–43, 773 (2019).

[187] *Purcell v. Gonzalez*, 549 U.S. 1, 4–5 (2006) (*per curiam*).

[188] *Merrill v. Caster*, 142 S. Ct. 879 (2022).

[189] *Ibid.* at 889 (Kagan, J., dissenting).

[190] *Ibid.* at 886 (Kagan, J., dissenting) ("... less than one-third of Alabama's Black population resides in a majority-Black district, while 92 percent of Alabama's non-Hispanic white population resides in a majority-white district").

Conclusion

The Third (New) Reconstruction in a Post-Racial Age

When a man has emerged from slavery, and by the aid of beneficent legislation has shaken off the inseparable concomitants of that state, there must be some stage in the progress of his elevation when he takes the rank of a mere citizen and ceases to be the special favorite of the laws.

– The Civil Rights Cases[1]

I think it [the reenactments of the VRA] is attributable … to a phenomenon that is called perpetuation of racial entitlement. … Whenever a society adopts racial entitlements, it is very difficult to get out of them through normal political processes.

– Justice Scalia during oral arguments in Shelby County v. Holder[2]

Beginning in 1883 with the *Civil Rights Cases* and the end of the first Reconstruction, this book ends with the Third Reconstruction – a period when whites finally began to acknowledge the structural inequality, systemic racism, and present-day effects of past discrimination because an existential pandemic and racial reckoning has laid everything bare. There is also the rise (or, more accurately, resurgence) of white supremacy camouflaged as populism, patriotism, and libertarianism.[3] Post-racial constitutionalism's neutrality ultimately leads to retrogression after brief periods of progress. The Court lends its legitimacy to the subjugation of oppressed peoples; it provides the rationalizing rhetoric of oppression. Both epigrams above, 130 years apart, one a mere 18 years after the Civil War and the other at the beginning of the second term of President Obama, endorse the limited nature of racial progress – they are post-racial in the sense that Blacks (and other people of color) should not receive any illegitimate race-based entitlements because everyone is formalistically equal. Racial entitlements such as the Reconstruction Amendments, Title VII, the

---

[1] 109 U.S. 3, 31 (1883).

[2] Nicole Flatow and Ian Millhiser, *Scalia: Voting Rights Act Is "Perpetuation of Racial Entitlement*, February 27, 2013, https://archive.thinkprogress.org/scalia-voting-rights-act-is-perpetuation-of-racial-entitlement-d64c9a4be44b/.

[3] Simon Clark, *How White Supremacy Returned to Mainstream Politics*, July 1, 2020, www.americanprogress .org/issues/security/reports/2020/07/01/482414/white-supremacy-returned-mainstream-politics/.

Fair Housing Act, and the Voting Rights Act must be circumscribed by the Roberts Court since, and Justice Scalia notes, the political process cannot readily do it without difficulty.

The Burger, Rehnquist, and Roberts Courts are all post-racial when analyzing the constitutional or statutory rights of oppressed minorities; each tried to transcend race in distinct ways – each Court diminished the significance of race as an organizing feature of American society because whiteness is the normative baseline of analysis. Compared to the Courts preceding it, the Roberts Court's post-racial constitutionalism is striking – where the Burger Court attempted to limit the scope of race-conscious remedial measures and protect whites' expectation interests, and the Rehnquist Court worked to limit the scope of race-conscious remedies through colorblind constitutionalism and temporal limits, the Roberts Court seeks to eliminate race from *all* decision-making by formalizing post-racial equality, dismantling the constitutional and statutory edifice of anti-discrimination law, and rationalizing the persistence of structural inequality by privileging reverse discrimination claims.

Social change for people of color is viewed as a threat to the post-racial order, and the Roberts Court is committed to disrupting any such progress from school integration to voting rights. This is an outcome determinative value judgment made by the Court – post-racial determinism, as discussed in Chapter 3, means that any race-conscious remedy (or perceived advantage) will be deemed unconstitutional or statutorily invalid because of the Court's strict adherence to post-racialism.

By now, it should be obvious that Chief Justice Roberts' baseball metaphor of judges simply calling "balls and strikes" in a neutral system is a fallacy[4] – even baseball umpires inject their subjective reading of the plate and strike zone. The Roberts Court has chosen to do so in a manner that preserves structural inequality – the strikes are predetermined due to the Court's formalistic post-racialism. Chapters 1 through 8 illustrate that the Court has always been post-racial – its central enterprise has been to reflect society's views on white supremacy and to constitutionalize, codify, and normalize those views through ostensibly neutral principles.

THE ROBERTS COURT AND POST-RACIAL CONSTITUTIONALISM: PROPOSITIONS

The institutional mission of the Court has been to explain racial progress in a manner that is palpable to whites. By constructing the narrative of racial progress, the Court determines when such progress should end because it threatens white supremacy and is antithetical to post-racialism. The Roberts Court has decided that

---

4   ERWIN CHEMERINSKY, THE CASE AGAINST THE SUPREME COURT 337–42 (2014).

all societal racial progress must end – it has constitutionalized retrogression. This is the permanence of racism.[5]

The Roberts Court's post-racial constitutionalism is advanced on numerous levels: (i) formalistic equality – the "way to stop discriminating on the basis of race is to stop discriminating on the basis of race" – as a post-racial theme denoting that race-conscious remedies are obsolete and unfair to whites in a neutral process; (ii) Rhetorical Neutrality as a set of post-racial myths – historical, definitional and rhetorical – that obscure the racially oppressive history of the United States, redefine discrimination so narrowly that proof of it is nearly impossible, and rationalize structural inequality as a neutral result of an open process; (iii) post-racial process discourse and proceduralism serving to advance the democratic myth that the political process is accessible to previously subjugated groups; (iv) post-racial diversity as a process value where race is subsumed as a "factor of a factor of a factor"; (v) the re-conceptualization of disparate impact in Title VII, the FHA, and the VRA so that structural inequality is excised from the analysis and the focus is on the burden on white expectation interests in employment, the housing marketplace and political power; and (vi) the New States' Rights Federalism expanding the concept of "equal sovereignty" so that Congress' enforcement power under the Reconstruction Amendments is significantly undermined, and enforcement power over the political process is shifted to the states.

All these propositions are central to the Roberts Court's post-racial constitutionalism, and each positions the law in a manner that reinforces the preservation of white privilege and political power and structural inequality.

(i) *Formalistic Equality*

The Roberts Court's post-racial jurisprudence does not contemplate structural inequality.[6] And even when it comes close to doing so, as in evaluating disparate impact claims, it adds an implicit intent requirement: this is true under Title VII (Ricci, Chapter 6), the FHA (*Inclusive Communities*, Chapter 7), and now the VRA (*Brnovich*, Chapter 8). Disparate impact has been de-contextualized so that any burden or impact is merely circumstantial evidence, and the Court never offers any guidance as to what a sufficient impact is to establish the validity of a disparate impact claim.

What is judicially cognizable disparate impact depends on where the impact falls, and if it falls on white interests, the Court will uniformly protect them. Formalism

---

5   Derrick Bell, *Racism as Ultimate Deception*, 86 N.C. L. Rev. 621, 631–33 (2008); Anthony C. Thompson, *Stepping Up to the Challenge of Leadership on Race*, Hofstra L. Rev. 735, 736 (2020) ("As a nation, we have never been willing to address racism, its history, or the fact that it is still part of our DNA").

6   Doron Samuel-Siegel, Kenneth S. Anderson, and Emily Lopynski, *Reckoning with Structural Racism: A Restorative Jurisprudence of Equal Protection*, 23 Rich. Pub. Int. L. Rev. 137 (2020).

serves to rationalize inequality. The Court advances this formalism through its neutral rhetoric and reinforcing myths.

(ii) *Rhetorical Neutrality and Post-Racial Constitutionalism*

The Court derives its legitimacy not only from the power of judicial review; "saying what the law is"[7] often means reflecting public discourse within the polity where the Court issues its holdings – the Court's post-racialism is directly related to the citizenry's sentiments on race. The Court has turned away from the Racial Reckoning (and the Third Reconstruction) and has tried to neutralize it. "White supremacy keeps its power because it is neutral, traditional, and never truly acknowledged."[8]

All the Roberts Court's race decisions fit within Rhetorical Neutrality: history is either ignored, with events historized so that there is a formal end date for inequality[9] or presented as a linear progression of uninterrupted racial progress;[10] or, most recently, it is simply referenced in the context of a textualist reading of an anti-discrimination statute like the VRA.

There is a new strand to the definitional myth underlying Rhetorical Neutrality. The Court, in addition to defining discrimination narrowly, now considers whether state power will be impacted by how discrimination is defined.[11] While the notion of slippery slope invalidation of neutral laws has always been a primary concern of the Court,[12] now the focus is on expanding state power to determine whether discrimination exists. The Roberts Court has done this by endorsing voter initiatives to overturn race-conscious remedies in *Schuette* and by affirming the power of the state to regulate its own electoral process free from federal interference. Through its rationalizing rhetoric, the Court advances the democratic myth of openness and inclusion with an emphasis on process discourse and proceduralism.

(iii) *Post-Racial Process Discourse, Proceduralism, and the Democratic Myth*

As explained in Chapter 4, the Roberts Court has redefined the political process doctrine in post-racial terms. Purporting to embrace an active and engaged

---

7   *Marbury v. Madison*, 5 U.S. 137, 177 (1803).

8   Kathryn Stanchi, *The Rhetoric of Racism in the United States Supreme Court*, 62 B.C. L. Rev. 1251, 1256 (2021).

9   *Parents Involved*, 501 U.S. 701, 722 (2007) ("Once Jefferson County achieved unitary status, it had remedied the constitutional wrong that allowed race-based assignments").

10   *Shelby County*, 570 U.S. at 552 ("But history did not end in 1965. … voting tests were abolished, disparities in voter registration and turnout due to race were erased, and African-Americans attained political office in record numbers").

11   *Brnovich*, 141 S. Ct. at 2340–41 (noting that Title VII and the FHA are inapposite to the VRA and expressing concern that requiring states to demonstrate the legitimacy of their voting regulations would impermissibly transfer power from the states to the federal courts).

12   *Washington v. Davis*, 426 U.S. 229, 248 (1976).

citizenry, with states as democratic laboratories, the Court ignores the restructuring of the political process to target discrete and insular minorities for exclusion, and then offers direct democracy process values like open access and opportunity, interest group organization, and voter choice to explain a reconfigured process where it is significantly more difficult to successfully achieve policy goals.[13] Post-racial proceduralism – a positive process view of polity – serves as a neutral rationale for structural inequality. All the rules, processes, and procedures of the political system are presumptively favored as operating inclusively and neutrally without reference to the significance of race. This is the Democratic Myth.[14]

The disconcerting result is that the electorate, through voter initiatives, is now given the democratic right and imperative to define the scope of equality under the Fourteenth Amendment. This is yet another example of the Court reflecting the public's post-racial sentiments.

(iv) *Post-Racial Diversity*

The Roberts Court continues the Court's tenuous and ambiguous relationship with race as a positive factor for diversity in post-secondary education. Interestingly, diversity is not a compelling interest for elementary and secondary schools, even with the legacy of *Brown*, because somehow the First Amendment underpinnings inherent in higher education are non-transferable to elementary and high school students because colleges and universities occupy a "special niche" in terms of the First Amendment and diversity in higher education.[15] So, a broader interpretation of diversity is appropriate in the post-secondary education context, but not for elementary and secondary schools – there must be clearly identifiable discrimination by the state for a race-conscious remedy to be constitutionally permissible. The discriminatory intent requirement is the touchstone of the Court's race jurisprudence.

Post-racial diversity describes the Court's active narrative enterprise of diminishing the significance of race – a kind of racial avoidance – so that diversity can be defined in post-racial terms. Indeed, diversity is a process value espoused by the Court, it is not rooted in a theory of substantive equality, and its unifying premise is the cross-racial educational benefit (under the First Amendment) of an inclusive learning environment for white students.[16]

As discussed in Chapter 5, the Roberts Court goes even further in neutralizing diversity, affirming it as a compelling interest but making race "a factor of a factor of a factor" which means that race is one of many factors that may be considered

---

[13] Cedric Merlin Powell, *The Rhetorical Allure of Post-racial Process Discourse and the Democratic Myth*, 2018 UTAH L. REV. 523, 563–64 (2018).

[14] Cedric Merlin Powell, *From Louisville to Liddell: Schools, Rhetorical Neutrality, and the Post-Racial Equal Protection Clause*, 40 WASH. U. J. L. & POL'Y 153, 168 (2012).

[15] *Parents Involved*, 501 U.S. at 724–25.

[16] Meera E. Deo, *Affirmative Action Assumptions*, 52 U.C. DAVIS L. REV. 2407, 2421 n. 75 (2019).

in admissions decisions. The Court offered no guidance on what this statement (or test) meant, and there will be a new reverse discrimination (or model minority)[17] case where a challenge will be advanced to determine the significance of race in a presumptively neutral process.

(v) *The Demise of Disparate Impact*: Ricci, Inclusive Communities, *and* Brnovich

Statutorily, disparate impact liability covers persistent disproportionalities that fall on Blacks, and other discrete and insular minorities, through the "normal" functioning of ostensibly neutral processes and procedures – absent discriminatory intent. This systemic inequality underscores the subordinating force of structures.

A doctrinal hallmark of the Roberts Court is how it neutralizes race, preserves extant systems of inequality, and then rationalizes it as normal. While Title VII, the FHA, and the VRA all incorporate disparate impact liability, the Court's post-racialism renders any structuralism in these statutes merely referential to be balanced against the neutral rationales justifying the challenged disproportionality. Chapter 6 discusses *Ricci* and the "strong basis in evidence" standard which adds a layer of intent to disparate impact analysis; Chapter 7 deconstructs the Court's acknowledgement of disparate impact liability under the FHA, only to add a profit-necessity-marketplace defense that significantly cramps such claims; and, finally, Chapter 8 critiques the Court's decision in *Brnovich* disrupting the potency of § 2 of the VRA by rewriting the totality of circumstances test to focus not on the impact of voting procedures on voters' right and opportunity to vote, but on a series of make-weight "burdens" that expand the power of the state to determine the structure of the electoral process.[18] And this, of course, will diminish Congress' enforcement power because the Roberts Court is all too eager to invalidate anti-discrimination statutes that do not specifically identify current discrimination.

(vi) *The New States' Rights Federalism*

As Congress' enforcement power under the Reconstruction Amendments contracts, the power of states to set the boundaries of political power expands – there is a state right to be free from federal intervention in the absence of intentional discrimination. The New States' Rights Federalism advances the concept of equal

---

[17] Jonathan P. Feingold, *SFFA v. Harvard: How Affirmative Action Myths Mask White Bonus*, 107 CAL. L. REV. 707 (2019); Oi Yan A. Poon, Liliana M. Garces, Janelle Wong, Megan Segoshi, David Silver, and Sarah Harrington, *Confronting Misinformation through Social Science Research: SFFA v. Harvard*, 26 ASIAN AM. L. J. 4 (2019).

[18] *Brnovich*, 141 S. Ct. at 2343 (While no one suggests that discrimination in voting has ended, "§ 2 does not deprive States of their authority to establish non-discriminatory voting rules").

state sovereignty to expand state power and insulate it from judicial review – an unwarranted judicial intrusion into a state's electoral process would undermine democratic ideals and expose the counter-majoritarian difficulty undercutting the Court's legitimacy.[19] Voting is collateral in this novel conception of federalism; it is akin to a procedural privilege (or benefit) rather than a fundamental right. And this novel conception of federalism serves to preserve white minority political power.

It is historically inaccurate to refer to the "rise" of white supremacy because it is a founding principle of American society and its polity[20] – the propositions of post-racial constitutionalism advance neutral rationalizations of white supremacy. White supremacy is resurgent whenever there is significant progress made by Blacks[21] and people of color, or when there are demographic shifts that threaten white homogeneity. The question is, and always has been, who will be included in the political community, and what will be the extent of their engagement in shaping American democracy? The Roberts Court's post-racial constitutionalism forecloses any meaningful consideration of race-conscious remedies and constitutionalizes retrogression.

THE THIRD (NEW) RECONSTRUCTION IN A POST-RACIAL AGE

The permanence of racism means that a Third (New) Reconstruction is not only needed, but inevitable.[22] The First and Second Reconstructions, 100 years apart, empowered former slaves as free citizens with the passage of the Reconstruction Amendments; and it would take the enactment, pursuant to Congress' enforcement powers, of the Civil Rights Act of 1964 and VRA of 1965 to complete the unfinished work of the First Reconstruction. There is still much to be completed.[23] The First and Second Reconstructions were squarely focused on the *rights* of equal citizenship,

---

[19] *Ibid.* ("… there is nothing democratic … about a wholesale transfer of the authority to set voting rules from the States to the federal courts").

[20] Ursula Moffitt, *White Supremacists Who Stormed U.S. Capitol Are Only the Most Visible Product of Racism*, THE CONVERSATION, January 15, 2021, https://theconversation.com/white-supremacists-who-stormed-us-capitol-are-only-the-most-visible-product-of-racism-152295.

[21] TERRY SMITH, WHITELASH: UNMASKING WHITE GRIEVANCE AT THE BALLOT BOX 146 ("Just as the building of Confederate monuments spiked after the ruling in *Brown v. Board of Education*, voter ID laws became a Republican fixation only after the election of the first black president Barack Obama").

[22] Wilfred Codrington, III, *The United States Needs a Third Reconstruction*, THE ATLANTIC, July 20, 2020, www.theatlantic.com/ideas/archive/2020/07/united-states-needs-third-reconstruction/614293/; *Do We Need a Third Reconstruction?* LIVE AT THE NATIONAL CONSTITUTION CENTER PODCAST (May 4, 2021), https://constitutioncenter.org/interactive-constitution/podcast/do-we-need-a-third-reconstruction.

[23] Yuvraj Joshi, *Racial Transition*, 98 WASH. U. L. REV. 1181, 1195–96 (2021) (discussing how the Roberts Court consistently practices a rhetorical distancing move to recast America's racist history and concluding that "In short, racism did not end with the abolition of slavery and Jim Crow – it endured and evolved. Nor was racial transition completed with the First and Second Reconstructions – it was postponed and prolonged").

due process, and voting, essential prerequisites to membership in the political community, but the Third (New) Reconstruction, in this post-racial era, must emphasize
the centrality of race, the eradication of structural inequality, and the rejection of
neutrality which preserves white supremacy and ultimately leads to cyclical retrogression. The Third (New) Reconstruction would move the emphasis from simply
maintaining constitutional rights to upending oppressive structures. The parentheti-
cal "new" highlights this doctrinal, discursive, and democratizing shift.

A Third (New) Reconstruction would focus on dismantling structural inequality on a rhetorical level by disrupting post-racial narratives of neutrality; reconcep-
tualizing equality as a move away from formalism toward substantive equality by
rejecting the rigidity of the discriminatory intent requirement and acknowledging that disparate impact has structural meaning; pursuing legislative remedies to
restore voting rights, such as the For the People Act,[24] the John Lewis Voting Rights
Restoration Act,[25] and the Right to Vote Act,[26] and ensuring that these measures
provide meaningful opportunities to vote in a free and fair electoral process where
each vote is cast and counted; considering the political reality of a third party movement so that progressive claims and candidates are given representational voice in
the process; and, finally, a truth, reckoning, and reconciliation framework so that
the nation can move beyond mere ceremonial commemorations, such as a national
Juneteenth holiday, to identifying, acknowledging, and remedying the generational
damage done by centuries of violent repressions such as the Tulsa, Oklahoma Black
Wall Street bombing and massacre as well as hundreds of others.[27]

The Third (New) Reconstruction would reaffirm the Thirteenth, Fourteenth,
and Fifteenth Amendments as race-conscious constitutional amendments enacted
to eradicate slavery and its badges and incidents; include Blacks in the American
polity through equal protection, due process, and the fundamental right to vote;
and give Congress the enforcement power to ensure that states did not replicate
the oppression that was abolished by the Reconstruction Amendments.[28] The New
States' Rights Federalism would be rejected as a violation of this structural constitutional principle.

---

[24] For the People Act, H.R. 1 (2021), www.congress.gov/bill/117th-congress/house-bill/1/text?format=xml
(providing for expanded voting access through internet registration, automatic voter registration,
early voting, same-day registration, and other open access measures).

[25] John Lewis Voting Rights Advancement Act (formerly H.R. 4; S. 4263) (2020), www.congress.gov/116/
bills/s4263/BILLS-116s4263is.xml (re-establishing the preclearance process, which was overturned
by the Roberts Court in *Shelby County*).

[26] Right to Vote Act (2021–2022) (Senator Ossoff introduced legislation on August 4, 2021, providing citizens with a statutory right to sue where access to voting is restricted by the state), www.ossoff.senate
.gov/press-releases/sen-ossoff-introduces-bill-establishing-first-ever-statutory-federal-right-to-vote/.

[27] Channon Hodge *et. al.*, Burned *from the Land: How 60 Years of Racial Violence Shaped America*,
CNN, May 30, 2021, www.cnn.com/interactive/2021/05/us/whitewashing-of-america-racism/.

[28] Michael A. Lawrence, *Racial Justice Demands Truth & Reconciliation*, 80 U. Pitt. L. Rev. 69, 83
(2018).

Indeed, the Thirteenth Amendment serves as the foundational amendment to eradicate structural inequality, in all forms directly traceable to slavery, and the enforcement clause power of Congress integrates this mandate in the Fourteenth and Fifteenth Amendments. Whenever Congress exercises this power, either through legislation or re-authorization, the Court must defer. This is an acknowledgement of Congress' power to eradicate caste-based oppression.

Centering the Reconstruction Amendments as anti-subordination amendments means that history is acknowledged because the present-day effects of past discrimination are constitutionally cognizable; discrimination is not defined formalistically as particularized intent, but rather in terms of how systemic racism subjugates historically oppressed groups. And there is no rationalization of inequality as neutral and natural – the myths of Rhetorical Neutrality are rejected. Given the Roberts Court's strict adherence to post-racial constitutionalism, doctrinal change – or evolution – here is unlikely. The Third (New) Reconstruction advances a broad approach embracing legislative and political change.

Given our history, political heritage, and uncritical acceptance of the two-party system, it is political blasphemy to suggest the formation of a viable, progressive, and strategically radical political party. Moderation, incrementalism, and compromise are heralded as the guiding principles of our polity, without much reflection on where these neutral principles leave the historically oppressed. Where was "compromise" when Senator Mitch McConnell commandeered the judicial confirmation process? The result is three judicial appointments for the forty-fifth president based on a fictious election year exception for Supreme Court nominations and a Biden presidential commission exploring whether to add more seats to the Court in search of some illusory party parity.[29] The system is broken, and compromise is a fallacy when the minority party does not respect the majority's will to win by advancing its first principles.

Theorizing the Racial Reckoning into substantive action would mean an expansive view of the remedies designed to eradicate structural inequality. Other lawyer-scholars have suggested this referencing a national discussion about racism with the goal of a broad structural remedy,[30] but here the proposal is to harness all the current events evincing centuries of structural inequality and use them to begin a discussion on structural responses to systemic racism, not simply a process of discussion and reconciliation, but structural remedies beyond payment of reparations – an acknowledgement that structural inequality exists and must be dismantled.[31]

It is no coincidence that, through cynicism, willful ignorance, and political calculation, there is a movement to excise fundamental aspects of American history

---

[29] *See generally* Smith, *supra* n. 21, at 178.
[30] ALFRED L. BROPHY, REPARATIONS PRO & CON 167–79 (2006) (discussing various aspects of reparations and conceptualizing a realistic approach to defining and quantifying harm).
[31] Lawrence, *supra* n. 28, at 104–33 (discussing awareness, acknowledgement, and substantive structural remedies such as criminal justice reform, reparations, and truth and reconciliation processes).

through "banning" Critical Race Theory (CRT)[32] and books chronicling the experience of oppressed peoples. CRT cannot be banned because it explains the racial state of our nation: past, present, and future. And it also locates the far-reaching implications of white supremacy, domination, and oppression in all sectors of American society.

In *On the Court-House Lawn*, the path-breaking book on lynchings in the public square and how a conspiracy of silence and complicity of whites served to obscure or substantially revise this horrifying history as simply a societal aberration, law professor and former director-counsel of the NAACP-LDF Sherrilyn A. Ifill advances a broad conceptualization of reparations:

> Reparations, like reconciliation, must be regarded as a process, not an event. ... Where criminal trials or reparations litigation is pursued, community members must emphasize that these measures do not in and of themselves constitute reparation. They are, at best, a gesture, not a substantive solution.[33]

Ifill offers a powerful point about the limitations of litigation that is directly related to how most legal scholars conceptualize the doctrinal underpinnings of the Court's jurisprudence. Our approach to combatting society's post-racialism and the Roberts Court's post-racial constitutionalism must be multi-faceted, and it must begin by shaping the narrative framework of the discussion – post-racial neutrality must be rejected.

To the Court, the relative progress made since the two previous Reconstructions is sufficient – "the way to stop discriminating on the basis of race is to stop discriminating on the basis of race." This facile circularity belies the profound systemic racism confronting us in the Third Reconstruction.

What is even more troubling is the emergence of Justice Alito as the chief protagonist of the Court's post-racial constitutionalism – his concurring views in *Ricci*, dissents in *Fisher II* and *Inclusive Communities*, and his majority opinions in *Husted* and *Brnovich* portend a more extreme form of post-racialism rooted in historical denial, cynical outrage at those who would dare mention systemic racism, and doctrinal artifice crafted to transcend race and constitutionalize subordination as the neutral result of a legitimate process.

The Roberts Court reflects the post-racial tenor of a minority political party dedicated to this subordination.[34] The first step toward dismantling this edifice of

---

32 Terry Gross, *Uncovering Who Is Driving the Fight against Critical Race Theory*, NPR, June 24, 2021, www.npr.org/2021/06/24/1009839021/uncovering-who-is-driving-the-fight-against-critical-race-theory-in-schools.

33 SHERRILYN A. IFILL, ON THE COURT-HOUSE LAWN: CONFRONTING THE LEGACY OF LYNCHING IN THE TWENTY-FIRST CENTURY 131 (2007).

34 Joshi, *supra* n. 23, at 1250–51 ("... the Roberts Court seems ready to abandon racial reckoning in favor of an illusory distancing. By casting civil rights measures aside as obsolete and even detrimental, such a jurisprudence would help to maintain America's legacies of racism as well as Americans' misperceptions regarding racial equality, impeding possibilities for transition").

oppression will be to disrupt the enduring influence of neutrality in our constitutional canon. The Third (New) Reconstruction will advance the unfinished work of the previous two, but this time there will be a direct confrontation with post-racial constitutionalism by illuminating the present-day effects of past discrimination, emphasizing the centrality of race in American society, and conceptualizing structural remedies to eradicate systemic racism. And one day, this will mean the end of the Roberts Court's post-racial constitutionalism and a new Reconstruction of America.

Index

Printed in the USA
CPSIA information can be obtained
at www.ICGtesting.com
LVHW011959070224
771230LV00004B/65